CADOGAN

Michael Haag

Alistair Mathers

Cairo Luxor
Aswan

D0676422

Cadogan Guides
West End House, 11 Hills Place,
London W1R 1AG, UK
becky.kendall@morrispub.co.uk

Distributed in North America by
The Globe Pequot Press
246 Goose Lane, PO Box 480, Guilford
Connecticut 06437–0480

Copyright © Michael Haag 1993, 1998, 1999, 2000

Book and cover design by Animage
Cover photographs by Ian Lazarus
Maps © Cadogan Guides,
drawn by Map Creation Ltd and Adrian McLaughlin

Editorial Director: Vicki Ingle
Series Editor: Linda McQueen

Editor: Kate Paice
Indexing: Isobel McLean
Production: Rupert Wheeler Book Production Services

A catalogue record for this book is available from the British Library
ISBN 1–86011–964–6

Printed and bound in England by Cambridge University Press

All rights reserved. No part of this publication may be reproduced, stored in a retrieval system, or transmitted, in any form or by any means, electronic or mechanical, including photocopying and recording, or by any information storage and retrieval system except as may be expressly permitted by the UK 1988 Copyright Design & Patents Act and the USA 1976 Copyright Act or in writing from the publisher. Requests for permission should be addressed to Cadogan Guides, West End House, 11 Hills Place, London W1R 1AG.

To Anton and Isis

About the Author

Michael Haag has written, photographed and published several books on Egypt and other countries of the Middle East and the Mediterranean, and his journalism has appeared in major newspapers and magazines in Britain, America and Egypt. He has also broadcast for the BBC. In addition to this guide, he is the author of the *Cadogan Guide to Egypt* and the *Cadogan Guide to Syria and Lebanon*. He lives in London but spends part of each year in Egypt and Greece.

Please help us to keep this guide up to date

We have done our best to ensure that the information in this guide is correct at the time of going to press. But places and facilities are constantly changing, and standards and prices in hotels and restaurants fluctuate. We would be delighted to receive any comments concerning existing entries or omissions, as well as suggestions for new features. Authors of the best letters will be offered a copy of the Cadogan Guide of their choice.

Please Note

The author and publishers have made every effort to ensure the accuracy of the information in the book at the time of going to press. However, they cannot accept any responsibility for any loss, injury or inconvenience resulting from the use of information contained in this guide.

Contents

Egypt is a land of spectacle, a country vast in time, but, far from being a daunting experience for the traveller, its story is there for anyone to comprehend and enjoy. That is the purpose of this book, a guide and narrative spanning five thousand years, in which the exuberance of Cairo, the splendour of Luxor and the beauty of Aswan form the principal chapters. There will be your experience too of the Egyptian people, whose vitality, warmth and friendliness will help make your journey a pleasure.

Cairo is an exploding modern metropolis which nevertheless preserves within its

Introduction

heart the finest medieval city in the world, its mosques and caravanserais the setting for the Arabian Nights, whose atmosphere is palpable still for the visitor wandering through its bazaars. There are remarkable museums in Cairo too, storehouses for Egypt's Islamic, Christian and pharaonic periods, and these are covered in detail, while on the horizon to the west loom the mysterious Great Pyramids of Giza.

As it happens, the sites of ancient Egypt most visited by travellers are strung along the Nile from north to south in roughly the order in which they were built. Therefore the pyramids and tombs at Giza and neighbouring Saqqara, the funerary districts of Egypt's first capital at Memphis, are not only among the greatest monuments of all time but also mark the earliest phase of Egyptian history, the Old Kingdom.

At Luxor, upriver to the south, you move forward a thousand years to the New Kingdom, a period of opulence and power, when Egypt ruled an empire stretching from the Sudan to Syria, and pharaohs built magnificent temples and housed themselves for eternity in immense and elaborately painted tombs dug deep into the Valley of the Kings.

Further upstream, between Luxor and Aswan, you enter another age, that of the Greeks and Romans, who in their turn built Egyptian-style temples along the Nile. A chapter covers this river journey which, though it can be travelled overland, becomes magical when you follow this stretch on a cruise.

At Aswan, where travel up the Nile was interrupted in antiquity by the granite boulders of the river's First Cataract, is the loveliest of the Graeco-Roman temple complexes, on the island of Philae. But perhaps the greatest appeal of Aswan is its tropical mood of restfulness, a place simply to hire a felucca for the day and to drift with the current and the breeze.

Beyond lies Nubia, which since the construction of the High Dam at Aswan has been drowned beneath the waters of Lake Nasser. A number of the old monuments have been salvaged, Roman, Greek and New Kingdom, and raised to higher ground. The most famous of these are the rock-cut temples of Ramses II at Abu Simbel, which can be visited as a cruise on the lake or an excursion by air.

A Guide to the Guide

However you choose to combine Cairo, Luxor and Aswan, and use them as bases for further excursions, this guide provides you with all the necessary practical information. It begins with a **Travel** chapter, which covers how to get to Egypt and how to travel around when there, followed by a **Practical A–Z** dealing with communications, health, food, drink, accommodation, shopping and so on. A **History** follows, then a selection of **Egyptian Essays**, which cover such topics as Security, Grand Hotels, Islam and the Coptic people.

The gazetteer comes next, covering **Cairo**, **Luxor** and **Aswan**, and also excursions from each city: the **Pyramids, Memphis** and **Saqqara**; the **River Journey** between Luxor and Aswan; and **Nubia**, including Abu Simbel. Each chapter is accompanied by further on-the-spot practical details. At the back of the guide there is a **Glossary**, a note on **Language**, a **Further Reading** list and a general **index**.

Finally, apart from the maps and plans throughout the guide, there is a full-colour **map of Cairo** on the inside front cover and a full-colour **map of Egypt** from Cairo to Luxor and Aswan on the inside back cover.

Travel

By Air

There are scheduled and charter flights to the international airports at **Cairo** and **Luxor**. You can save a great deal on the normal fare by purchasing an APEX or other discounted fare ticket. Direct scheduled flights from **Britain** are operated by Egyptair and British Airways (London–Cairo 5 hours), and from the **United States** by Egyptair and TWA (New York–Cairo 11 hours). Egyptair offers an excellent service; the one drag is that it does not serve alcohol on its flights, though it does permit you to bring your own.

discount and student fares

UK

Europe Student Travel, 6 Campden St, London W8, ✆ (020) 7727 7647, catering to non-students as well.

STA Travel, 6 Wright's Lane, London W8 6TA, or 85 Shaftesbury Ave, London W1V 7AD, ✆ (020) 7361 6161/6262; Bristol, ✆ (0117) 929 4399; Leeds, ✆ (0113) 244 9212; Manchester, ✆ (0161) 834 0668; Oxford, ✆ (01865) 792800; Cambridge, ✆ (01223) 366966 and many other branches in the UK.

Trailfinders, 194 Kensington High St, London W8 7RG, ✆ (020) 7938 3939.

Travel Cuts, 295a Regent St, London W1R 7YA, ✆ (020) 7255 1944.

USIT Campus Travel, 52 Grosvenor Gardens, SW1W 0AG, or 174 Kensington High St, London W8 7RG, ✆ (020) 7730 3402 with branches at most UK universities, including Bristol, ✆ (0117) 929 2494; Manchester, ✆ (0161) 833 2046; Edinburgh, ✆ (0131) 668 3303; Birmingham, ✆ (0121) 414 1848; Oxford, ✆ (01865) 242 067; Cambridge, ✆ (01223) 324283, *www.usitcampus.co.uk.*

Ireland

Budget Travel, 134 Lower Baggot St, Dublin 2, ✆ (01) 661 1866.

United Travel, Stillorgan Bowl, Stillorgan, County Dublin, ✆ (01) 288 4346/7.

USIT, Aston Quay, Dublin 2, ✆ (01) 679 8833; Cork, ✆ (021) 270 900; Belfast, ✆ (01232) 324 073; Galway, ✆ (091) 565 177; Limerick ✆ (061) 415 064; Waterford ✆ (051) 72601. Ireland's biggest student travel agents.

USA and Canada

It's worth sifting through the small ads in newspaper travel pages (e.g. the *New York Times, Chicago Tribune, Toronto Globe & Mail*) before contacting travel clubs and agencies, some of whom may require an annual membership fee.

Airhitch, 2472 Broadway Suite 200, New York, NY 10025, ✆ (212) 864 2000.

Council Travel, 205 E 42nd St, New York, NY 10017, ✆ (800) 743 1823.

Last Minute Travel Club, 132 Brookline Avenue, Boston, MA 02215, ✆ (800) 527 8646.

STA Travel, 10 Downing St, New York, NY 10014, ✆ (212) 627 3111 or (800) 777 0112; 51 Grant Ave, San Francisco, CA 94108, ✆ (415) 391 8407.

Travel Cuts, 49 Front St East, Toronto, ON M5E 1B3, ✆ (416) 365 0545.

On the **Internet**, you can often get good cheap deals at sites like *www.lastminute.com*, *www.travelocity.com*, *www.cheapflights.com*.

Even if you are an independent traveller, you should also see what **tour operators** (pp.4–6) have to offer; they can have some very attractive deals. Tour operators sometimes offer flights only, or flights with a package at such a competitive price that you can afford to take as much or little of the package as you like and still come out ahead. Almost all travellers staying at five- and four-star hotels are on packages and probably paying no more, maybe less, than the independent traveller at three-star hotels.

By Sea

Car ferry services from Italy and Greece to Egypt no longer operate, and even passenger services from Europe, Turkey and Lebanon have been suspended.

Entry Formalities

Passports and Visas

Note that the following information on passports, visas, customs and currency is subject to change (there has recently been a rapid trend towards greater liberalization) and should be checked in advance.

Almost all visitors to Egypt (most Arab nationals excepted) require a **visa**. To obtain a visa, your passport must be valid for at least six months following the date of your proposed arrival in Egypt; you will need to fill in an application form, provide a photograph and pay the fee. Visas (valid for one or three visits) can be obtained at Egyptian embassies and consulates abroad in person (usually within 24 hours) or by post (allow at least 2 weeks)—often your tour company will take this on for you. Both types of visa are valid for a month; in the case of a multiple entry visa this means valid for one month from the date of your first arrival.

Most foreigners (EU, US, Canadian, Australian, New Zealand and Japanese passport holders, but check as the list is subject to change) can obtain a visa **on arrival** at Cairo or Luxor for $15. This often works out cheaper and is definitely less of a nuisance than obtaining one beforehand; no photograph is required and these visas too are valid for a month.

Whether obtained before or on arrival in Egypt, visas can be **extended** for an additional month at the Mugamaa in Cairo (*see* p.74) or at passport offices in Luxor and Aswan.

However, if arriving in **Sinai** you must obtain a full Egyptian visa in advance; a visa obtained on arrival in Sinai is not valid for the rest of Egypt. Most Arab countries except Egypt and Jordan will deny entry to anyone whose passport shows evidence of a visit to Israel. Though the Israelis are willing to give you an entry stamp on a separate piece of paper, the Egyptians always insist on stamping your passport, with the consequence that an entry stamp for the Sinai border towns of Rafah or Taba will give you away. Therefore if your Middle Eastern itinerary also includes Lebanon, Syria, etc., be sure to leave your visit to Israel till last.

Customs

Adults may bring in their luggage **without payment of duty** one litre of alcohol and 400 cigarettes (two cartons) or 250g of tobacco or 50 cigars, but if you bring in greater quantities you will be liable to customs duty and/or confiscation. However, in addition you may also purchase a further four litres of alcohol and four cartons of cigarettes at the duty-free shops at Cairo and Luxor airports. These purchases are normally noted in your passport. If you do not take advantage of this (or even if you have, but airport customs have neglected to note the fact in your passport—usually next to your visa or on the inside back cover of your passport), you can go with your passport within 30 days of your arrival to one of the duty-free shops in Cairo and purchase four cartons of cigarettes but only three litres of alcohol. A carton of imported beer can be substituted for a litre of alcohol.

You may also bring into Egypt, exempt from duty and other taxes, all **personal effects**, used or new, including camera equipment, radios, word processors, jewellery, diving equipment. It is not mandatory but is probably a good idea to list these on the customs declaration form.

Genuine **antiquities**, including items from the Islamic period (indeed usually anything over 100 years old), cannot be exported without the approval of the Department of Antiquities, 4d Sharia Fakhry Abd el Nour, Abbassia, Cairo, ℗ (02) 839637. The law also forbids the removal of coral from the sea and its export.

Currency

You may bring into and out of Egypt **unlimited amounts** of foreign and Egyptian currency, though you might be asked to declare the import of any very large sum. It makes little sense to buy Egyptian pounds abroad as you will get a better rate of exchange for your currency within Egypt; also you should change out of Egyptian currency before leaving the country, as you are unlikely to find anyone interested in exchanging outside the country.

As large numbers of American $100 bills have been counterfeited in recent years (mostly in Lebanon), these will be closely examined when you try to exchange them.

Tour Operators and Specialist Holidays

Tour and Cruise Operators

A variety of package tours are offered to Cairo, Luxor and Aswan, allowing you to combine any or all of these destinations with a cruise on the Nile, a voyage on Lake Nasser or a flight to Abu Simbel. Some leave you to your own devices, others include guided tours and may also be accompanied by a guest lecturer. Prices vary accordingly and depend also on the quality of accommodation you require and your length of stay.

Cox & Kings Travel, Gordon House, 10 Greencoat Place, London SW1P 1PH, ℗ (020) 7873 5000, ✆ (020) 7630 6038; and in the US, 25 Davis Boulevard, Tampa, Florida 33606, toll-free ℗ (800) 999 1758, ✆ (813) 258 3852. Their mouthwatering portfolio of tours covers everything in this guide: Cairo and the Pyramids, Luxor and Aswan, flights to Abu Simbel and cruises on Lake Nasser and the Nile, for anything from 9 to 13 days, with options of additional tours and extended stays. The premium is on quality and character: for example, among their choice of Nile cruisers is the elegant Edwardian-style MS *Oberoi Philae*, while on Lake Nasser they use the sophisticated art deco MS *Kasr Ibrim*, two of the finest boats afloat, while stays in Luxor are at the Old Winter Palace and in Aswan at the Old Cataract, two of the most atmospheric and luxurious hotels in Egypt.

Explore Worldwide, 1 Fredrick St, Aldershot, Hampshire GU11 1LQ, ✆ (01252) 760 000, ✆ (01252) 760 001. Inexpensive and adventurous tours and Nile cruises. One popular offering involves clearing litter from the banks of the Nile. It seems Egyptian cruise boat crews simply throw rubbish overboard, including non-biodegradable plastic mineral water bottles and suncream tubes. 'They don't appreciate that our rubbish isn't like theirs and won't just rot away. It's not that they are lazy, it's just that they need re-educating.' Meanwhile, the British pay £250 a head to spend a week on a sailing boat with only the most basic facilities, huddling together on deck in sleeping bags by night, and donning rubber gloves and overalls to fill up black plastic bags with the detritus of Western civilization by day. 'It was not a pleasant job, but there was a great group spirit and we all felt a real sense of achievement.'

The Imaginative Traveller, 14 Barley Mow Passage, London W4 4PH, ✆ (020) 8742 3049, ✆ (020) 8742 3045. Offers a considerable variety of journeys, first class to camping, including Nile and Lake Nasser cruises, usually with small, youthful groups.

Kuoni, Kuoni House, Dorking, Surrey RH5 4AZ, ✆ (01306) 743000, ✆ (01306) 744222. The emphasis is on pick and mix: starting from a basic price for a one-, two- or three-centre stay, you can then pretty much tailor-make your holiday by adding on tours and cruises, choosing your level of hotel and upgrading the service you receive, meaning that you can keep your costs down, though it is easy to let them rip.

Maupintour, PO Box 807, Lawrence, Kansas 66047, toll-free ✆ (800) 255 4266. An established upmarket operator offering a wide range of escorted tours and cruises.

Misr Travel, in Britain, Rooms 201–4, Langham House, 308 Regent St, London W1R 5AL, ✆ (020) 7255 1087, ✆ (020) 7255 1089; in the US, 630 Fifth Ave, New York, NY 10011, ✆ (212) 582 9210, or toll-free ✆ 1 800 22 EGYPT, ✆ (212) 247 8142; head office 1 Sharia Talaat Harb, PO Box 1000, Cairo, ✆ (02) 3930010, ✆ (02) 3924440. Egypt's national travel operator (Misr means Egypt); much of their business is wholesaling to operators worldwide, so that their New York office tends to shun individual enquiries, but their Cairo office is much more helpful, and their London office is staffed with angels. Apart from offering standard tours, their insider knowledge ensures that they can expertly tailor-make your arrangements for getting to and travelling around the country, and can fix up accommodation, often at a good price.

Thomas Cook Holidays, PO Box 36, Peterborough PE3 6SB, ✆ (01733) 332255. The inventors of the package holiday: Cook himself conducted his first tour of Egypt in 1869. Has a strong presence in the country, offering many tours and cruises.

Voyages Jules Verne, 21 Dorset Square, London NW1 6QG, ✆ (020) 7616 1000, ✆ (020) 7723 8629. Though an upmarket company, it has a tendency to dump holidays on the market using charter flights, so that often you can pick up a good and fairly cheap package such as Cairo or Luxor combined with a Nile or a Lake Nasser cruise.

tours booked in Egypt

You can always package yourself by taking a tour on the spot. **American Express** offers a number of tours from Cairo to Luxor, Aswan and Abu Simbel. **Thomas Cook** does the same sort of thing, but also offers more personalized tours for a few people at a time. **Misr Travel** offers the most varied and flexible packages of all: apart from the head office at 1 Sharia Talat Harb, ℂ (02) 3930010, Cairo, they have offices at both Cairo's airport terminals, several Cairo hotels (Sheraton, Nile Hilton, Ramses Hilton, Inter-Continental, Marriott Meridien, Mena House), and at Luxor's Old Winter Palace Hotel and on the corniche at Aswan.

Nile Cruises

Ideally you should arrange a cruise before coming to Egypt, whether as part of a package or to fit with your independent travel plans. Space permitting, you may also be able to book yourself onto a cruise once in Egypt. Agencies like **Misr Travel**, **Thomas Cook** and **American Express** can make the arrangements, either in Egypt or abroad. Also the **Oberoi**, **Hilton**, **Mövenpick**, **Sheraton** and other hotels operate Nile cruises, which similarly can be booked through their hotels or reservations centres either in Egypt or abroad.

Prices are highest from October through May, falling by about 40% in summer, and include meals, sightseeing ashore, taxes and service charges. **Local operators** offer cruises at rates substantially lower than those of the international hotels (*see* under Cairo, p.65). The hotel boats, 'floating hotels' as they are called, and others like them, are the behemoths of the Nile. Equipped with boutiques, bars, hairdressers and discos, you are not certain that you have ever left dry land. They can provide luxury, though much of it may seem to you extraneous, and because of their size you may feel lost in the crowd. The **Sheraton** boats are the largest, with 80 cabins, and are utterly lacking in style. The **Hilton** boats have only 48 cabins, and are trim, well-run vessels. In size the **Oberoi** boats fall in between, with 69 cabins and two suites; they are the most luxurious, the best-run and have the best cuisine.

There are now about 200 cruise boats on the river, plying between Aswan and Luxor and calling on Esna, Edfu and Kom Ombo along the way. Some of these loop a bit further north to allow visits to Dendera and Abydos. Generally you spend 4–8 days on the boat, though for about half this time you will be tied up at Luxor and Aswan while you go off touring their sights. When sailing along this upper part of the river, there is something to be said for heading south to Aswan for the sense of threading one's way more narrowly through the encroaching desert, but in whichever direction you sail, the Luxor–Aswan run covers the greatest concentration of spectacular ancient sites. Unfortunately the longer cruises between Aswan and Cairo, lasting 11–13 days, have been suspended for security reasons. But should the situation ease and you get your chance to enjoy this most wonderful of voyages, there is no equal to the special cumulative impression that the Nile makes upon you.

felucca journeys

For the adventurous, sailing the Nile in a traditional small sailing boat, the **felucca**, is the thing. These trips have been **suspended for security reasons**, except for local hirings in the immediate vicinity of Aswan, Luxor and Cairo. If the situation changes, the following advice applies. Sleeping bags may be necessary, though often blankets will be provided. Meals are usually included in the cost, which varies with the number of people aboard and your bargaining powers. Make arrangements with boatmen at Luxor or (better) Aswan.

Lake Nasser cruises

Particularly now that cruises along the Nile between Cairo and Upper Egypt have been suspended, the Lake Nasser cruise has come into its own. Several tour operators offer cruises on the lake (*see* p.321), some of them aboard the MS *Eugénie* and the MS *Kasr Ibrim*, which are by far the finest boats plying between the High Dam at Aswan and Abu Simbel. Bookings for these can be made direct with the operator, Belle Époque Travel, 17 Sharia Tunis, New Maadi, Cairo, ✆ (02) 3528754, ✉ (02) 3536114, or through a travel agent abroad.

Getting Around

Travel in Egypt has been affected by **security restrictions**, *see* pp.15 and 50–51.

By Air

The principal carrier within the country is **Egyptair**, which operates flights between Cairo, Luxor, Aswan and Abu Simbel, as well as other destinations in the country.

		one-way fare (return is double)	
Cairo to Luxor	LE420	Luxor to Aswan	LE190
Cairo to Aswan	LE580	Luxor to Abu Simbel	LE340
Cairo to Abu Simbel	LE820	Aswan to Abu Simbel	LE150

Always try to make **advance reservations**. In winter it is advisable to make reservations as far in advance as possible for Upper Egypt, especially to Abu Simbel.

By Rail

Air-conditioned rail travel is comfortable but not as cheap as it was: in 1997 fares for non-Egyptians were made double the price applying to Egyptians. Students in possession of an ISIC card get discounts of 30–50% (but not on sleepers or Wagons-lits). By way of example, from Cairo the **one-way fare for non-Egyptians** to Luxor (671km, 11 hours) is LE80 first class, LE50 second class; to Aswan (879km, 15 hours) LE100 first class, LE69 second class. **Snacks** and **meals** are served at your seat in first and second class for a few pounds.

All first-class and combined first- and second-class trains are air-conditioned; others are not. **Local trains** serving smaller stations are likely to be slow, crowded and uncomfortable, and will not be air-conditioned—the experience can be interesting if it does not go on for too long. Travelling aboard a non-air-conditioned train can be like sharing a room in a tenth-rate Arab hotel with scores of guests, the only difference between second and third class being the number of Egyptians per cubic metre. In third class especially, it is to suffer an intimacy one would prefer to do without. No matter what class of train you take, bring **toilet paper**.

Almost all air-conditioned trains require **reservations** and you should book at least a day in advance; in winter try to book several days in advance for Upper Egypt. You can try getting on a train at the last moment to see if there is any space (a bit of baksheesh to the carriage attendant would not go amiss). When queuing for tickets, men approach the ticket window from the right, women from the left, taking turns. The women's queue is shorter and quicker.

There is a **Wagons-lits** sleeper service between Cairo and Luxor/Aswan using modern if dull German rolling stock. Each compartment has a washbasin and two berths and is taken either as a single or a double. Meals are served in the compartments, and there is a club car for drinks and socializing—this can be a lot of fun when a party atmosphere is got going by the exceptionally agile Nubian staff who dance across tables with drinks balanced on their heads. The one-way **fare**, either to Luxor or Aswan, is LE288 per person on a double-berth basis (this is called second class); if one person takes the entire cabin (this is called first class), the cost is LE443. **Reservations** are essential and should be made at least a week in advance if possible. There are daily departures, leaving in the early evening. Book through a good agent abroad or in Egypt, or go direct to the wagons-lits office at Ramses Station, Cairo.

On all services, **children** under four travel free; those aged from four to 10 obtain a 50% reduction and on sleepers are expected to share a berth with an adult.

By Car and Taxi

Car hire is not expensive, and petrol is very cheap (around 25PT a litre). To hire a car you should be between 21 and 70; you will need an **International Driving Licence**. Local and international companies are represented in Cairo, but there is no car hire in Luxor or Aswan.

Cairo is a madhouse on wheels, while country roads are often busy with trucks, donkeys and camels; at night oncoming car and truck lights are either beamed in the wrong direction or not on at all, and Egyptians are in any case very odd drivers. With little appreciation of the virtue of keeping to a lane or even to the right side of the road (they drive on the right), they meander about as though negotiating mudbanks in the Nile. To survive, you must wander with them, which requires eyes on the sides and back of your head—or no eyes at all. But do not be put off: you soon get the hang of it. A word of **warning**: if you run somebody over outside Cairo, immediately get into your car and either await the police or drive to find them. Do not hang about on a lonely country or desert road on your own, certainly not at night. The families of victims have been known to exact instant justice, especially if they are Bedouin.

You can still have the advantage of a car without any of the problems if you hire one with a **driver** from Misr Travel for example (not very expensive) or hire a taxi (*see* 'By Service Taxi', below)—among several people it can be quite reasonable to hire a taxi to explore, say, the line of ancient sites and pyramids from Giza south to Meidum.

By Bus

Long-distance buses can be fast, cheap and comfortable. From Cairo there are regular runs to Upper Egypt; there are frequent services between Luxor and Aswan. You should buy your ticket a day, preferably two days, in advance. Fares are significantly less than those by rail.

By Service Taxi

Service taxis run just about everywhere. They are like buses in that they follow regular routes and you pay a **fixed fare** for your seat. They are fast and cheap, and are good both for long-distance travel and for hopping from town to town or site to site. They operate on a first come first served basis and can usually carry seven passengers, setting off the moment they are full. You can buy the seat next to you for greater comfort (women often do this to minimize groping; it is also advisable for women not to sit next to the driver). You can also hire the entire taxi for private use. Fares are a bit higher than most bus fares.

By Thumb

Hitchhiking is possible but uncommon and can be difficult; a payment will be expected.

Practical A–Z

Baksheesh

Tipping is expected for all services, and often for no service at all. Too often tourists are absurdly ignorant or generous, which has led some Egyptians to believe, often rightly, that if they pull a sour face, even vociferously complain, they can milk you for more. The Egyptian term for a tip is baksheesh, which means literally 'share the wealth', and helps explain why sometimes an Egyptian is not at all abashed at wanting something for nothing: you have it, he does not but feels you should pass it round. Baksheesh can be a plague, and you may find yourself pestered for it in the streets. The rule is obvious: offer baksheesh only in return for a service, do not pay until the service has been performed, and do not pay too much.

Tip 10% on restaurant bills, LE1 to the porter who carries your bag to your hotel room (though LE2–5 at top hotels); if you are staying at a hotel for a while, LE10 per week or pro-rata is appropriate for the person who cleans your room and also to others, such as concierges and doormen, who have been of regular service to you.

To put matters in perspective (and so to justify either not paying too much or your desire to be generous), consider the following monthly incomes: a full-time housemaid earns LE125–300; a sales assistant at a middle-range shop, LE250; a government teacher or mid-ranking public servant, LE400; a recently graduated accountant at a large international firm, LE500; a labourer with a private company, LE750; a university professor with twenty years' experience, LE900. The average per capita income in Egypt is LE200 per month.

Business Facilities

Five-star hotels in Cairo and elsewhere have business centres, usually available to non-residents, which will photocopy, send and receive faxes and e-mail, and provide secretarial and translation services. Many other hotels can at least provide you with a fax service.

Calendar of Events

National Holidays and Festivals

There are five secular holidays during the year, when banks, government offices, businesses and schools are closed.

25 April	Liberation of Sinai Day
1 May	Labour Day
23 July	Anniversary of the 1952 Revolution
6 October	Armed Forces Day
Monday after Coptic and	
Greek Orthodox Easter	Sham el Nessim, an ancient spring festival

Of more importance, however, are the various Muslim and Coptic holy days, and to understand these, something must be said about the Egyptian calendars.

Egyptian Calendars

Egypt uses three calendars: the Islamic, the Coptic and the Western. The Western calendar takes the birth of Christ as its starting point; the Coptic starts at AD 284, the accession of

Diocletian, during whose reign the most ferocious Roman persecutions of the Christians, particularly in Egypt, occurred; the Islamic calendar starts at the flight (hegira) of Mohammed from Mecca in AD 622. Both the Western and Coptic calendars are solar; the Islamic calendar is based on 12 lunar months and therefore rotates in relation to the other two, each Islamic year beginning 11 days sooner than the last.

To calculate the equivalent Western date for an AH year (AH standing for Anno Hegirae, the number of years since Mohammed's flight from Mecca), use this simple formula:

1. Divide the Islamic year by 33 (the Islamic year is 11 days, or one thirty-third, shorter than a Western year).
2. Subtract the result of (1) from the Islamic year.
3. Add 622 to the result of (2) and this will give you the Western year.

For example:

1. AH 1421 divided by 33 = 43.
2. 1421 less 43 = 1378.
3. 1378 plus 622 = AD 2000.

In fact, AH 1419 began on 6 April 2000.

Another point worth noting is that a day in the Islamic calendar begins at sundown. A consequence of this is that Islamic festivals start on the evening before you would expect if going by the Western calendar, that evening assuming as sacred a character as the following waking daylight period (compare Christmas Eve and Christmas Day in Western usage).

You will be relieved to learn, however, that in all official transactions in Egypt the Western calendar and method of reckoning the day are used. The Islamic and Coptic calendars only really come into their own at festivals.

The Islamic Calendar

Sequence of months		Duration (days)
1st	Moharram	30
2nd	Safar	29
3rd	Rabei el Awal	30
4th	Rabei el Tani	29
5th	Gamad el Awal	30
6th	Gamad el Tani	29
7th	Ragab	30
8th	Shaaban	29
9th	Ramadan	30
10th	Shawal	29
11th	Zoul Qidah	30
12th	Zoul Hagga	29 (30 in leap years)

Important Muslim festivals include:

Ras el Sana el Hegira, the Islamic New Year, beginning on the first day of Moharram.

Moulid el Nabi, the Prophet's birthday, on the twelfth day of Rabei el Awal, marked in Cairo by a spectacular procession.

Ramadan, a month of fasting from dawn to sunset. As the last full meal is taken just before dawn, working hours are usually cut short to reduce afternoon effort to a minimum. Nothing is permitted to pass the lips during fasting hours nor is sexual intercourse allowed during sun up. Alcohol is not sold in Egypt during Ramadan, and while visitors are permitted to eat and smoke, you should not do so in the presence of fasting Muslims out of common courtesy. More food is consumed during Ramadan than at any other time of year, everyone making up at night for what they gave up during the day. Every Ramadan night, therefore, has the character of a festival. In 2000 the first full day of Ramadan falls on 27 November.

Qurban Bairam, 10–13 Zoul Hagga, the month of the Pilgrimage. For days before sheep, cows, goats and buffalo fill the streets waiting to be slaughtered; on the 10th, throughout the residential areas of towns, they are killed and skinned—not for the squeamish.

Coptic festivals centring around Easter do not follow the Western calendar. Other festivals fall on fixed dates: Christmas on 7 January; Epiphany, 19 January; the Annunciation, 21 March. A national holiday that is an important Coptic-pharaonic inheritance is **Sham el Nessim** ('sniffing the breeze'), on the first Monday after Coptic Easter, when the entire population of whatever religion takes a day off. This is a celebration of the advent of spring; families go into their fields or gardens, or into the country, early in the morning and eat salted fish, onions and coloured eggs. The fish and onions are said to prevent disease, while the eggs symbolize life.

Children

Egyptians are warmly indulgent towards children, and whether in hotels and restaurants or mosques and archaeological sites, you will find that they are welcomed everywhere. But this lack of fussiness about children can also expose a child to mishap. You should be alert to traffic and untended excavation sites (even around the Giza Pyramids there are some holes of terrific depth for the unwary to fall into). Be sure that your children observe careful hygiene, and protect them against the sun with sunglasses, hats and clothing. The better hotels can recommend a doctor if necessary, and if you want to leave your children for a few hours they can also provide childminders.

Children will often more readily take to the strangeness of their environment than you do. Museums and tombs will probably seem not half so much fun to them as the dress, the scent and the bustle of the bazaar. They will enjoy carriage and camel rides, and sailing in a felucca; *son et lumière* shows will seem delightfully mysterious; and something as simple as dining outdoors can be novel.

Climate and When to Visit

In the days of leisurely travel it was often the custom to spend an entire winter, from November to May, in Egypt. This was 'the season', climatically, socially, and for those in search of dry mild conditions conducive to relief from asthma, chronic bronchitis, rheumatoid arthritis, gout, Bright's disease and other diseases of the kidneys. The new millennium visitor is unlikely to come to Egypt for medicinal reasons, nor to stay so long.

Late autumn through early spring is still the most comfortable period to visit most of the country, particularly Cairo and southwards into Upper Egypt. Temperatures increase as you travel south, though in Cairo during December, January and February it can be chilly. Cairo can be very hot from June through September, though the heat is often relieved by breezes from the north. It is hotter yet in Upper Egypt where summer generally lasts from May through October, but peak temperatures are to some extent compensated for by extremely low humidity. From Cairo southwards at any time between March and May you may experience the *khamsin* ('fifty'), a hot dust- and sand-laden wind from the southwest which can be very unpleasant and can seem to last for 50 days. Everywhere in Egypt at any time of year, but mostly in the deserts, temperatures can fall off sharply at night.

But not too much emphasis should be laid on season, for a variety of reasons. Cairo and Upper Egypt are most visited from November through April and there is pressure on accommodation. From May through September prices are lower in Upper Egypt. Air conditioning is standard in the new hotels and in the better older ones. It can be very hot, especially in Upper Egypt, during summer, but seeing the sights early in the morning and late in the afternoon, and the extraordinary dryness of the air the further south you go, can make your stay more agreeable. The proof is that Egypt has become a year-round destination.

Table of Temperature °C

	Jan min	max	Feb min	max	March min	max	April min	max	May min	max	June min	max
Aswan	8.0	23.8	9.4	26.1	12.6	30.4	17.5	35.0	21.1	38.5	24.2	42.1
Cairo	8.6	19.1	9.3	20.7	11.2	23.7	13.9	28.2	17.4	32.4	17.9	34.5
Luxor	5.4	23.0	6.8	25.4	10.7	29.0	15.7	34.8	20.7	39.3	22.6	40.7

	July min	max	Aug min	max	Sept min	max	Oct min	max	Nov min	max	Dec min	max
Aswan	24.5	41.2	24.7	41.3	22.2	39.6	19.3	36.6	14.5	20.2	9.9	25.5
Cairo	21.5	25.4	21.6	34.8	19.9	32.3	17.8	29.8	19.9	24.1	10.4	20.7
Luxor	23.6	40.8	23.5	41.0	21.5	38.5	17.8	35.1	12.3	29.6	7.7	24.8

For conversion to Fahrenheit, see 'Weights and Measures', p.24.

Communications

Postal Services

The post between Egypt and abroad can be very efficient provided you use a letter box at a post office, or in a central location or in a major hotel. Elsewhere, some letterboxes appear to be visited by postal employees only rarely, if at all. Also, anything that is not a simple letter or postcard can attract the curiosity of the authorities and might therefore take a very long time to arrive. Post offices and most hotels can provide you with stamps.

For assistance dial ℰ 10 or ℰ 140

The Egyptian telephone system has been opened up to private competition and is being upgraded. A consequence is that telephone numbers, especially in Cairo, are constantly changing: a digit altered, a new one added, or the entire number replaced by a new one—which, incidentally, explains why some telephone numbers in this guide are almost bound to prove incorrect. Seek assistance by dialling ℰ 10 or ℰ 140, unless those numbers too have been changed.

Both local and international telephone services are available at better hotels throughout the country, but there will be a surcharge, sometimes as much as 100%. Local calls can also be made from public phones (when you can find them), and at some kiosks, shops and restaurants. International, long distance and local calls can be made from **telephone exchanges** (centrales); normally you pay first for a fixed number of minutes. There are 24-hour telephone exchanges, for example, in Cairo's Midan el Tahrir and in Luxor at the central telephone office on Sharia Karnak. In Aswan the *centrale* is on the corniche at the southern end of town (*open 8am–10pm daily*).

A recent innovation is the **phone card**, available at telephone exchanges in denominations of LE15, LE20 and LE30. These are used in the direct dial orange telephones found at many exchanges and at some airports and railway stations and occasionally elsewhere.

To telephone Egypt from **abroad**, first dial the international code used in your country (e.g. 00 in Britain, Ireland and New Zealand; 011 in the US; 0011 in Australia), then 20 for Egypt, followed by the area code (*see* below), omitting the initial 0, and finally the number.

Area codes: Abu Simbel 097, Alexandria 03, Aswan 097, Cairo 02, Giza 02, Luxor 095, Pyramids 02, Qena 096.

Fax, Internet and Courier Services

There are fax machines at all the better hotels. These can be used by both guests and non-residents for a fee. Some will also have Internet and email facilities for use by guests; otherwise see under listings in the Cairo, Luxor and Aswan chapters. For courier services *see* Cairo p.71, or enquire at your hotel.

Crime and Security

In terms of everyday crime, Egypt is a far safer place than Europe or North America. You can wander day or night through any part of Cairo or Alexandria, for example, without the slightest concern that you will be mugged. Egypt's strong sense of community works against all sorts of crime, and there is a deep-seated abhorrence of violence in Egyptian culture. Additionally, there is a particular regard for the welfare of visitors which is both traditional and based on the conscious awareness that tourism provides an income and employment, directly or indirectly, for millions of Egyptians.

Travellers in a strange country often feel apprehensive at first. But as you venture forth in Egypt, every experience will confirm that you are among an unusually kindly people, sometimes inquisitive, occasionally intrusive, almost never ill-intentioned or aggressive. Look after your things when in the company of fellow tourists: they are much more likely to steal from you than any Egyptian.

The exception to the above is that there have been several acts of **terrorism** by Islamic extremists. Their object has been to overturn Egypt's moderate government and to replace it with a theocratic state. Their political success has been zero, and their acts have succeeded only in turning the Egyptian population against them. Their targets have been government ministers and the security forces, and in parts of Upper Egypt (though not Luxor or Aswan) Copts have also been the victims of violence. The extremists have also attempted to damage the economy of the country by attacking tourists. Exceptional security measures have been taken, including the suspension of Nile cruises between Cairo and Qena, sometimes the accompaniment of tourist groups by armed guards and the posting of special Tourist Police at airports and at every five- and four-star hotel.

For more information on terrorism and security measures, *see* pp.50–51.

If you need help or want to report a crime, you should contact the **Tourist Police**, whose uniform (black and white in winter, white in summer) is identical to that of the ordinary police except for an armband with 'Tourist Police' written on it. They will speak at least one other language, usually English, apart from Arabic and they are there specifically to look after you. They are found at airports, ports, tourist sites, museums and at many hotels. The **Central Security Police**, who guard embassies, government buildings and the like, wear a military uniform, which is black both winter and summer, and are armed with rifles bearing fixed bayonets or sometimes more powerful weapons. They are the people you do not point your camera at, nor do you point it at the place they stand in front of, if you want to keep your film in your camera and perhaps yourself out of jail.

Disabled Travellers

Egypt is not conventionally geared up for disabled travellers, but given a sense of adventure and the helpfulness of its people, it is possible to achieve a great deal more than you might at first imagine, as this traveller's report received by the author conveys:

'We made our trip in somewhat unusual circumstances—my wife has a hip problem which limits her mobility for other than short distances and a few (low) steps and, consequently, we use a wheelchair for anything over a short walk to the shops. While planning the trip I contacted several tour operators, only to find they were unanimous in implying that our custom really would not be appreciated. Faced with this, and in view of our limited funds, I contacted Misr Travel and arranged a trip on our own. No guided tours, no coaches, we did it all ourselves and I doubt if we missed anything within our capabilities. Moreover, the total cost for the two of us for 16 days was less than the two-week tours offered by tour operators. We stayed at the Windsor in Cairo, the Etap [now the Mercure] in Luxor and the Old Cataract in Aswan, and we spent three nights on the MS *Giza*. The most valuable service, to us, was the attendant and transport at each change of location—stretched Mercedes, and knowledgeable representatives who, in each case, refused a tip. For anyone with a walking handicap, we strongly suggest, for visits such as to the Valley of the Kings, taking a taxi from the hotel onto the vehicle ferry [though now you can also cross by the new bridge upstream]. We were able to take and use the wheelchair at every location, with not too much difficulty, since our time was our own. It would have been impossible to keep up with a group. At the tombs we were limited due to the large number of steps, but we were able to visit that of Ramses VI.

Two possible items of interest, perhaps: Egyptair, for our flight from Cairo to Aswan, put us on the plane using one of those food vans with the lifting box, right to the rear entrance. The second item, a conversation with an Egyptian who spoke fluent English. When we told him how we felt completely secure on the streets, even at night, in every city, he said, "You must realize that to us Egyptians, you tourists are sacred! Five million Egyptians depend on tourism for a living." I doubt if we will visit Egypt again but we will never forget it. Particularly the people. We met with nothing but courtesy and smiles, not a single adverse memory.'

Electricity

Electrical current throughout Egypt is **220 volts AC**. Sockets take the standard continental European round 2-pronged plug. Plug adaptors and current converters, as well as dual voltage appliances, can be bought at home.

Embassies

There is a selective list of embassies in the **Cairo** chapter, *see* p.72.

Entertainment

The last 40 years or so have seen the almost complete disappearance of Egypt's cosmopolitan population and with it a marked reduction in the range, quantity and distribution of entertainment. Even in relatively flesh-pot Cairo, the mood of politically correct Islamic conservatism makes it harder for alcohol to be drunk and bellies to dance. It you are looking for a disco or nightclub, then in Cairo probably, and elsewhere in Egypt almost certainly, it will be at a hotel. Many discos are restricted to hotel guests and members. Nightclubs combine a show with dinner.

Well-off Egyptians with Western tastes might go to Cairo's new Opera House for ballet, opera and concerts, while foreign and cultural centres such as the British Council offer film, music and theatrical programmes; these entertainments are unlikely to attract the short-stay visitor. The self-conscious folkloric entertainments promoted during Nasser's time have long since succeeded in boring everyone stiff and are all but extinguished now, while television and videos are rapidly killing off what remains of popular culture. Among the few authentic entertainments still to be seen in Egypt are the moulids and other religious festivals.

In addition to referring to the listings in this guide, you can get a fairly good idea of what is going on by looking at the monthly magazine *Egypt Today*, the fortnightly *Cairo Times* and the daily newspaper *The Egyptian Gazette* (called *The Egyptian Mail* on Saturdays).

Food and Drink

Most hotels in Egypt, particularly the more expensive ones, cater to the tastes of foreign visitors by serving an international cuisine. In Cairo there are also many restaurants specializing in one or another national cuisine: French, Italian, Lebanese, Greek, Chinese, Indian. The classic Arab-Turkish cuisine of Egypt is best encountered in private houses, but venture forth to Egyptian eating places, spanning the gamut in price and sophistication, for a taste of local cooking. Dishes are usually savoury, neither too oily nor too spicy, and as fresh ingredients are almost always used the menu varies with the season. Except in the simplest places frequented exclusively by Egyptians, restaurant menus are available in English and French as well as in Arabic, and waiters speak English. In the simple Egyptian places, as at a Greek taverna, you can go into the kitchen, have a look, a taste, and then point to what you want.

Egypt's **national dishes** are *foul* (pronounced fool), a bean paste; *tamaiya*, the same beans but pressed into a patty and fried in oil; *tahina*, a sesame paste; *babaganoush*, like *tahina* but with aubergine (eggplant) instead of sesame; and *koushari*, a mixture of rice, macaroni, lentils and chickpeas, topped with a spicy sauce. Meat usually comes as kebabs or *kofta*, a spicy ground meat patty.

At **cafés**, the preparation of mint tea and coffee is a ritual. Thick and black Turkish-style coffee is ordered according to the amount of sugar: sweet (*ziyada*), medium (*mazboota*), bitter (*saada*). While sitting there, ask for a waterpipe, a *shisha* or *narghile*. The tobacco is mild and sweet (*masil salom*) and the smoke is even milder by the time it has passed through the water. You do not inhale. Payment is a few piastres.

Beer long antedates wine as the regional drink of the Mediterranean, so it is not so strange to find it reintroduced in Egypt. The commonest brand is Stella lager, in green bottles, unpredictable but usually very good. Stella Export, in brown bottles, is sweeter, more consistent, more expensive and not as good. Aswali is an excellent dark beer from Aswan, sometimes found elsewhere. Bock beer is available briefly in the spring and is referred to as Marzen (from Marzenbier, March beer). Egyptian **wines** are from formerly Greek-owned vineyards near Alexandria. Omar Khayyam is a dry red, Cru des Ptolemees a dry white, and Rubis d'Egypte a rosé. Opinion varies over whether they are drinkable or downright awful; overall quality has fallen in recent years owing to the increased salinity of the soil in the vineyard region south of Lake Maryut near Alexandria. You are better off staying with the reds, which are improved for some people by adding ice and soda water; the roses and whites go off quickly. All are inexpensive. French wines are available at better hotels and restaurants, but are very expensive. Imported **spirits** are extremely expensive. Egypt does make its own: the gin is undrinkable; the brandy compares with the Spanish variety. *Arak*, the Arab equivalent of Greek *ouzo*, Turkish *raki* or French *anisette*, and often called *zibab* in Egypt, is excellent. Beer, wines and, less readily, spirits can be purchased in shops, usually small places few and far between. When purchased at hotels and restaurants, the mark-up is considerable. If you are particularly fond of spirits, make sure you bring in several duty-free bottles.

Many middle-class Egyptians drink beer, wine or spirits, but the vociferous minority of Islamic fundamentalists have ensured that even the international-style hotels do not always flourish their alcoholic drinks lists; however, ask and you will receive. On trains (Wagons-lits excepted) only a rubbishy non-alcoholic beer is sold; on both domestic and international Egyptair flights, no alcohol is served, though you are permitted to bring your own.

Western-style **soft drinks**, including Coca-Cola and 7-Up, are available everywhere. Unfortunately they are tending to drive out the far more delicious and wholesome tropical fruit and cane juices; try also *karkodeh* (a drink made from hibiscus flowers).

Finally, it is said that if you drink from the **Nile** you will be sure to return to Egypt. You might think you would drop dead instead. But around Aswan the boatmen will assure you that it is better than the ice-cold drinks favoured by tourists, its temperature more agreeable to the stomach. The taste is fresh if somewhat organic. **Tap water** is heavily chlorinated; probably the best reason for drinking bottled spring water, which is universally available, is to avoid the chlorination rather than any disease. If Egyptian standards of bottled spring water are as low as in Europe, then it is no better than tap water anyway.

Health

Cholera and yellow fever **vaccination certificates** are required when entering Egypt from an infected area. In fact many doctors will now tell you that cholera shots are almost entirely ineffective, but they will recommend tetanus, polio, hepatitis and typhoid shots, and some might advise rabies shots and malaria tablets. **Bites** of all kinds need the immediate attention of a doctor. The bites of carnivores can be rabid, or at least can turn septic as can camel bites. If you have been bitten, get immediate attention; in Cairo contact the Hospital of the Rabies Institute, Embaba, ✆ (02) 3462042, called Maahad al Kilab in Arabic. To combat **AIDS**, Egypt has banned the importation of blood for transfusions unless it has an AIDS-free certificate. But you cannot be sure that gamma globulin, used against hepatitis, is AIDS-free, so avoid it. Otherwise, you should take the same personal precautions as you would at home.

Snakes may be encountered when you wander off the beaten path, and you should avoid turning over stones. Most Egyptian snakes are not poisonous (their bite is recognized by a double row of teeth), but some are, especially the cobra and the viper. The smaller Egyptian cobra (*Naja haje*), 120–200cm long, is normally a sandy-olive colour and is found throughout the country. The black-necked cobra (*Naja nigricollis*), 200cm long, is darker and is confined to southern Egypt. Both are capable of displaying the characteristic hood; the black-necked cobra has a dark band on the underside of the hood. Cobra bites display a single row of teeth plus fang-marks. It was *Naja haje* that appeared as the uraeus on the pharaonic crown. It was supposedly the viper that Cleopatra used to commit suicide. There are several kinds, 34–150cm long, varying in colour from sandy to reddish, or sometimes grey. The most dangerous snake in Egypt is the carpet viper (*Echis carinatus*), 72cm long, with a light X on the head. Viper bite markings are simply the two fang punctures. It is helpful when seeing a doctor if you can describe the snake.

There are two diseases associated with Egypt, trachoma and bilharzia, though neither need unduly worry the visitor. **Trachoma** is a contagious infection of the eye, specifically the conjunctiva and cornea, and causes a cloudy scar and hence blindness. In the past, though less so now, many Egyptians have suffered from it. If you notice any inflammation of the eyes, you should at once consult an ophthalmologist. **Bilharzia** (or schistosomiasis) is caused by a worm which enters the body, causing disorders to the liver, bladder, lungs and nervous system. The worm lives only in stagnant water, so avoid some irrigation channels and slow-moving parts of the Nile. The Nile is safe for swimming and drinking (or so the author has found) between the Aswan High Dam and Esna where, except possibly along its banks, it runs swiftly. If you have ventured or fallen into stagnant water, you should get a check-up when you return home. There is little risk of the visitor contracting either disease. Both can be successfully treated.

If you are unwell, your hotel can refer you to a pharmacist, doctor, dentist or hospital, and may even have a doctor on call. Your embassy will also be able to recommend medical assistance. For minor complaints a visit to a pharmacy will suffice; pharmacists are usually very able at providing the appropriate remedy for basic ailments. Particularly in the major centres, the standards of medical care are high. Many doctors will have trained in Europe or North America and will speak English. Readers have reported on the excellent standard of dental treatment at a price that defrays much of the cost of their holiday in Egypt—and indeed have said that it would make financial sense for them to return to Egypt for major dental work.

Most likely the worst you will suffer will be a brief **upset stomach**. This is an entirely normal reaction to a change of diet and passes after a few days (Egyptians travelling to the West often experience the same problem). There is no need suddenly to stop eating Egyptian food; on the contrary, after a pause, you should continue. An anti-spasmodic medicine can be taken; standard preparations are available at any pharmacy. The one rule you should observe when eating in Egypt is to be sure your food has been washed; provided even the simplest eating place has running water, there should be no problem. Tap water is generally heavily chlorinated and safe to drink, though you can always have bottled water if you prefer.

The **sun** can be hot at any time of year, and the temperature can drop sharply at night. At both times it is wise to be appropriately covered. During the day you should wear a head covering and sunglasses. It is not advisable to drink spirits before sundown, nor to consume iced drinks during the heat of the day. A high-screen suntan lotion is advisable, factor 15 or more. Also, insect repellent would be helpful.

It can pay to be medically **insured**. At hospitals, patients will not be treated without a deposit of at least LE1,000. Be prepared to pay cash for treatment, though some hospitals will accept an AMEX or VISA card. Medical insurance is not accepted, though you can reclaim costs later.

Maps

The best readily-available map of Egypt is the Kuemmerly & Frey 1:750,000. In Egypt it is published by Lehnert and Landrock and is sold widely. The same publisher also produces the best map of Cairo, which includes a street index.

Media

One initial if thin source of information is the daily (except Sundays) English-language newspaper *The Egyptian Gazette* (called *The Egyptian Mail* on Saturdays), containing agency reports and entertainments advertisements. Also in English is the *Al Ahram Weekly*, published on Thursdays, an offshoot of Egypt's distinguished daily Arabic newspaper. Its coverage includes Egyptian and Arabic affairs, the economy, culture, lifestyle, sports, fashion, entertainment and travel. The *Cairo Times* is a lively and forthright fortnightly publication with topical features on travel, restaurants, business, the media, culture and politics. The monthly English-language magazine *Egypt Today* contains well-informed background features of interest to foreign residents and visitors. Additionally, most European newspapers are available the following day, and weekly European and American current affairs magazines are also readily available.

On any radio with a medium wave band, you can tune in to the BBC World Service, which broadcasts on 639KHz 8.45am–noon, 3pm–5pm and 7pm–9pm, all times local. It also broadcasts on 1325KHz 9pm–3am, local time. Five- and four-star hotels usually pipe CNN and other television news services straight into your room. Egyptian radio has 10-minute English-language news broadcasts on 95FM at 7.30am, 2.30pm and 8pm, while Egyptian television's Second Channel presents an English-language news programme 8—8.35pm.

Money

The unit of currency is the Egyptian **pound** (LE, from *livre égyptienne*) which is divided into 100 **piastres** (PT, from *piastre tarifée*). Also, notionally, each piastre is divided into ten **milliemes**, so that there are 1,000 milliemes to the pound. But while there are coins for piastre denominations (though these are disappearing fast), and notes for both piastre and pound denominations, there are no millieme denomination coins. Nevertheless, prices may be expressed in pounds, piastres or milliemes, which can add an alarming number of digits to a bill (all the more alarming as Egypt follows the continental European practice of using a comma instead of a decimal point). So a restaurant bill for 30,550 should not send you into the kitchen to start washing the dishes, it is simply LE30 and 55PT. Usually common sense will tell you what is meant.

Notes are in denominations of 25PT and 50PT, LE1, LE5, LE10, LE20, LE50 and LE100.

At the time of going to press the approximate **rate of exchange** was **£1=LE5** and **US$1=LE3.50**, or, putting it the other way round, LE1=20p or 30¢.

There are **exchange banks** at the airports and other points of entry and at major hotels throughout Egypt. American Express and Thomas Cook also exchange money. You should hold on to your receipts to show when paying hotel bills and in the event you need to change money back out of Egyptian pounds on departure.

Cash, travellers' cheques and Eurocheques can be exchanged at many banks. **Credit cards** are accepted at all major hotels, and also at some shops and restaurants, but generally you should count on being able to use them only in obvious tourist areas.

In fact Egypt still largely runs on **cash**, so always carry a wad on you for your immediate needs. It is also a good idea when changing money to obtain a large number of one pound notes to use for baksheesh, etc.

Opening Times

Museums, Monuments and Sites

Throughout this guide and unless otherwise noted, it is safe to assume that museums, monuments and archaeological sites are open daily; also that museums and monuments are *open at least 9am–4pm*, though on Fridays they may be closed for an hour or two anywhere between 11am and 2pm. During Ramadan these opening times may be curtailed. The hours of sunlight are usually the determining factor for the opening times of archaeological sites, that is they tend to open earlier and close later in summer than in winter, but generally you can expect them to be *open at least 8am–5pm*.

Most **banks**, **post offices** and government offices are closed on Fridays, and banks are also closed on Saturdays. Banks are normally *open 8.30am–noon*, and for currency exchange may also be *open 4pm–8pm*. Foreign banks are normally *open 8am–3pm*. **Government offices** are usually *open 9am–2pm*. Private sector offices are usually *open 8.30am–1.30pm* and *4.30pm–7pm*, though more Westernized businesses will be *open 9am–5pm*. They may be closed on Fridays or Sundays and occasionally on Saturdays. Many **shops** are closed on Fridays, others on Sunday. Shop hours are usually *9am–1pm* and *5pm–8pm*, though many are open throughout the day.

During **Ramadan**, bank and government office opening hours are often reduced. Shops, however, often stay open as late as midnight.

Packing

In winter you will need at least some light woollens and sweaters; in summer light cottons. In early spring and late autumn some combination of both is advisable against warm days and cool nights, and the possibility of changeable weather. In summer especially the sun can be fierce; it is a good idea to have long-sleeved shirts or blouses with collars to protect your arms and neck. Clothes should be light in colour to reflect the sun and should be easily washable and drip-dry. You can wash a shirt at night and have it bone dry in the morning.

Although more liberal than many other Arab countries, and tolerant of foreign habits even when not shared by the local population, Egypt is nevertheless conservative by Western standards. Your dress should allow for this. This is especially true in mosques, churches and monasteries, where shorts or short skirts should not be worn, nor anything too revealing. At hotel swimming pools, however, the briefest swimwear is acceptable, not only on visitors but on Egyptians. There are now many designer store chains where you can get stylish clothing and shoes at very attractive prices. Also, Egyptian cotton is famous for its quality. Rather than overpack these things, it would be better to buy them once you are in the country.

There is too much dust and dirt for sandals to be generally useful; bring comfortable walking shoes. Sunglasses (preferably with polarized lenses) and a broad-brimmed hat will keep out the glare of the sun.

Egypt increasingly manufactures foreign-brand shampoos, soaps, toothpastes, razor blades and other **toilet items**, or otherwise imports them. All such things are readily available at the better hotels, but will be cheaper in local shops where you will also find less expensive Egyptian brands. The same applies to suntan lotions, tampons, insect repellents, batteries and film. But bring your own contraceptives. Think if you have any particular requirements which you would not want to find yourself without, and bring those too—for example high-screen suntan lotion, special contact lens solution, the right size battery for your camera, high-speed film. Bring an initial supply of toilet paper, or at least steal a roll from the first hotel you stay at, and then keep yourself stocked with it as you travel: it is amazing how useful it can be and how often it is not available. A universal-size bath and basin plug may also come in handy. You may need a travel **plug-adaptor**; Egypt has continental-style double round-pin sockets, 220 volts AC.

A **flashlight** is invaluable for exploring tombs and other nooks and crannies. **Binoculars** are also useful, especially if you are cruising along the Nile or on Lake Nasser, but also for examining the details of gargantuan ruins.

Imported **alcohol** is very expensive and not always readily available in Egypt, so if you want your favourite tipple, either bring some duty-free drink with you or take advantage of the duty-free shops on arrival (*see* p.4).

Photography

It is a good idea to bring with you a variety of both slow (low ASA) and fast (high ASA) films. Taking photographs at museums and in tombs is usually forbidden except on payment of a special fee. Often a flash may not be used. Therefore you will need very high speed film, not less than 1000 ASA (3200 ASA is the maximum normally available). You can get such films abroad, but almost certainly not in Egypt, where anything over 400 ASA is non-existent. So bring a supply of very fast film with you, or buy 400 ASA film in Egypt and uprate that by two stops to 1600 ASA. Note that you will almost certainly have to subject your film to airport X-ray or similar inspection, although it is claimed this is safe for films right up to 3200 ASA. On the other hand the skies are blue, the sun is bright, and there is much reflected light off sand and water: for the best outdoor results use a 100 ASA or even slower film.

You are unlikely to experience any objection to taking photos in mosques or other Islamic monuments, nor in churches and monasteries, though you should be courteous and unobtrusive. During prayers, however, or at moulids when people are at their most fervent and conservative, you should be much more discreet and should not be surprised if you are told not to take photographs. By and large, people do not object to being photographed on the street; indeed, if you ask first, people often charmingly compose themselves—and then ask to be sent a copy. If someone objects, however, do not insist.

Occasionally you may meet with objections to photographing a street or village scene which seems attractive to you but which an Egyptian might think poor or dirty and thereby bringing shame on his country. Again, do not insist.

No doubt Egypt's enemies have more photographs of its airports, docks, bridges, dams and military installations than they know what to do with; nevertheless, photography of **military installations** certainly, and of the other items possibly, can mean having your film confiscated at the very least. You may meet with the same reaction if you try to photograph government buildings or foreign embassies.

Shopping

At smart shops in Cairo, Luxor and Aswan you will discover that a new generation of craftsmen, designers and entrepreneurs is translating Egyptian themes into stylish and competitively priced clothing, jewellery, furnishings and so on, with an eye to international appeal. **Traditional wares** and commodities of the bazaar—spices and perfumes, brass and copperware, gold and silver jewellery, ceramics, glass and precious stones, inlay work and mashrabiyya, cottons, carpets and leatherwork—are found in Cairo's Khan el Khalili and along Aswan's Sharia el Souq. Except where fixed prices are marked, **bargaining** is customary. Note that throughout Egypt if a customer is introduced to a shop, workshop or bazaar by a tour guide, the establishment normally pays the guide a 50% commission. As the cost of the commission will be passed on to you, this of course means that you will pay a much higher price than had you gone shopping on your own.

Further details are listed under the relevant places.

Sports and Activities

The main centre for sport is **Cairo**, with its tennis and golf facilities, keep-fit centres, cycling and running clubs, and spectator sports such as football, horse racing and rowing.

The luxury hotels are the places to look for **health clubs**, **tennis courts**, **golf courses** and the like. Staying at one gives you automatic membership, but some are open to non-residents as well, offering membership on a daily or weekly basis. There are also private non-hotel-based health clubs offering short-term membership and free cycling and running groups (*see* 'Sport and Activities', Cairo p.136).

For up-to-date information on spectator sports, get a copy of the daily English-language newspaper *The Egyptian Gazette* (called *The Egyptian Mail* on Saturdays). Egypt's most popular spectator sport is **football**, the two principal teams being Zamalek and Aghly. The season is from September through May, with games played on Fridays, Saturdays and Sundays at the Cairo Stadium in Heliopolis. The **horse racing** season is from October to May at the **Gezira Sporting Club** on Gezira Island and at the Heliopolis Hippodrome. On Fridays year-round you can watch visiting American and British university **rowing** crews being routinely thrashed on the Nile by the Cairo police crew.

Students

Egypt recognizes the International Student Identity Card (ISIC) and offers discounts at museums and archaeological sites (usually 50%) and on trains (30–50%, sleepers and Wagons-lits excepted).

In Cairo the ISIC can be obtained at the Medical Scientific Centre, 103 Sharia Mathaf el Manial, Roda Island, © 3638815 (*open daily 9am–9pm*). A fee of about LE25 is payable, and you should bring your passport and a passport photograph. The MSC is located opposite the Egyptian Tourist Authority office at Manial Palace. In Luxor, an ISIC can be obtained from a placenext to the Venus Hotel on Sharia Yusef Hassan.

Time

Egypt is two hours ahead of Greenwich Mean Time. Noon GMT is 2pm in Egypt.

Toilets

In the best tradition of distant lands, and except in the better hotels and restaurants, Egypt's toilets are usually of the squat-over-a-hole variety and are generally disgusting. A bucket of water or a pipe for squirting water may or may not be provided. It is a good idea always to travel with a roll of toilet paper.

Tourist Information

In the UK: Egyptian State Tourist Office, 170 Piccadilly, London W1, ☎ (020) 7493 5283, 🖷 (020) 7408 0295.

In the US: Egyptian Government Tourist Offices, 630 Fifth Ave, New York, NY 10111, ☎ (212) 332 2570, 🖷 (212) 956 6439; 645 North Michigan Ave, Chicago, Illinois 60611, ☎ (312) 280 4666, 🖷 (312) 280 4788; 8383 Wilshire Blvd, Beverly Hills, California 90211, ☎ (310) 653 8815, 🖷 (310) 653 8961.

In Egypt: Egyptian Tourist Authority headquarters, Misr Travel Tower, Abbassia Square, Cairo, ☎ (02) 820283, 🖷 (02) 830844.
Tourist Information Office, 5 Sharia Adli, Cairo, ☎ (02) 3913454.

Misr Travel is the state-run tourist company. They are in business for themselves and so their advice is not necessarily impartial, but they are certainly helpful.

In the UK: Rooms 201–4, Langham House, 308 Regent St, London W1B 3AT, ☎ (020) 7255 1087, 🖷 (020) 7255 1089.

In the US: 630 Fifth Ave, New York, NY 10011, ☎ (212) 582 9210, or toll-free ☎ 1-800-22-EGYPT.

In Egypt: Head office at 1 Sharia Talaat Harb, PO Box 1000, Cairo, ☎ (02) 3930010, 🖷 (02) 3924440.

Otherwise, Egyptian **embassies** and **consulates**, and also offices of the national airline, **Egyptair**, may be able to provide basic information. Amid all the junk on the Internet, there are two useful websites: the privately run *www.tourism.egnet.net*, and the Egyptian Ministry of Tourism's *www.touregypt.net*.

Weights and Measures

Egypt officially employs the metric system, though sometimes traditional weights and measures will be encountered.

Temperature

°F	°C	°F	°C	°F	°C	°F	°C
122	50	96.8	36	80	26.7	40	4
113	45	95	35	75	23.9	32	0
110	43.3	93.2	34	70	21	23	–5
107.6	42	91.4	33	65	18.3	14	–10
104	40	90	32	60	15.6	0	–17.8
102.2	39	87.8	31	55	12.8		
100	37.8	86	30	50	10		
98.6	37	84.2	29	45	7.2		

°F into °C: subtract 32 from °F, then multiply by 5, then divide by 9.
°C into °F: multiply °C by 9, then divide by 5, then add 32.

Linear Measure

0.39in = 1cm	39.37in = 1m	10 miles = 16km
1in = 2.54cm	0.62 miles = 1km	60 miles = 98.6km
1ft (12in) = 0.30m	1 mile (5280ft) = 1.61km	100 miles = 160.9km
1yd (3ft) = 0.91m	3 miles = 4.8km	

Square Measure

1 sq ft = 0.09 sq m	1.20 sq yd = 1 sq m	1.04 acres = 1 feddan
1 sq yd = 0.84 sq m	1 acre = 0.96 feddans	4201 sq m = 1 feddan

Weight

0.04oz = 1gm	2.20lb = 1kg	0.45kg = 1 rotel
1oz = 28.35gm	1 ton (2000lb) = 907.18kg	100 rotels = 1 qantar
1lb = 453.59gm	0.99lb = 1 rotel	

Liquid Measure

0.22 imp gal = 1ltr	1 US gal = 3.79ltr
0.26 US gal = 1ltr	1 imp gal = 4.55ltr

Where to Stay

Hotels in Egypt are officially **rated** from five-star (luxury) to one-star. (Some have not received any rating at all, in some cases but not always because they fall off the bottom of the scale.) The system is meant to indicate the level of amenities in each hotel, but its application can seem erratic and you may find that a three-star hotel is just as good as a four-star one, or that two four-star hotels charge markedly different rates. In this guide, hotels have been arranged according to price: very expensive, expensive, moderate, inexpensive and cheap. This system too has its faults, as price alone may not indicate quality, ambience or location. But taken together with the star-rating and the accompanying description, you should have enough information to help you form your own preliminary judgement.

As a rule of thumb, any three-star hotel will do; below that, you should have a look for yourself. Youth hostels are generally not worth bothering with; it is usually possible to find more congenial accommodation without damaging the most exiguous budget.

If possible you should make **reservations**, especially if you have your heart set on a particular hotel. Pressure on accommodation is most acute in Luxor and Aswan during winter. Reservations can be made through an experienced travel agent, or you can contact the hotel directly (addresses, telephone and fax numbers are included). The international chain hotels can be booked by contacting one of their hotels in your own country.

The **rates** that follow are indicative only and are for double rooms. (Note that upper category hotels set their prices in US dollars, lower category ones in Egyptian pounds, and that this has been followed in this book.) To these must be added **service** and **tax** which put at least another 20% on top in Cairo, and 25% in Luxor and Aswan. Also, **breakfast** is often an obligatory extra. **Single rooms** or single occupancy of a double room costs about 20% less than the rate for a double. Hotel bills must be paid either in foreign currency (the better ones will accept credit cards) or in Egyptian pounds accompanied by an exchange receipt from a bank. Rates in Cairo are higher than elsewhere in Egypt and are the same year-round; in Upper Egypt they areabout 10% lower in summer—except at some five-star hotels, whose rates remain the same year-round. Some hotels will have rooms with and without bathroom, air conditioning, balcony, or whatever, and this can also affect the rate. If custom is slack, you may be able to bargain the rate down. You can often get staggering **reductions** if you book your hotel through an agent/operator like Misr Travel as part of a ready-made or tailor-made package. However, the following is what you can expect to pay for a double at full whack (not including tax and service).

very expensive	$140+
expensive	$70–$140
moderate	$40–$70
inexpensive	LE40–LE120 ($14–$40)
cheap	LE40 (under $14)

Remember to add 20% in Cairo and 25% in Upper Egypt for tax and services.

Women

Westerners going to Egypt, whether men or women, are to some extent putting themselves in a position of contrast to the conventions of social life there. This is especially true of Western women. Family is extremely important in Egypt and an Egyptian woman's life is very much bound up with, indeed bounded by, her family relationships, as daughter, wife or mother. The entwined moral, religious and legal systems of the country enforce this. Even an educated woman would be most circumspect in her relationship with a man; both families would be involved and meetings would usually be limited to public situations.

Your Western view may be that that is their business and your business is your own. Some Egyptians will make an effort to see it that way, especially as you are only passing through. A great many more will not agree.

Therefore, dress and behave conservatively, but nevertheless be prepared for some hassle. Look confident and keep cool. It would be utterly unacceptable for an Egyptian woman to be molested, so there is no reason for you to put up with it. If, at worst, you are touched up, you can first say '*sibnee le waadee*', which means 'leave me alone'. If something stronger is called for, shout '*imshee!*', which means 'get lost!' By this time people should be coming to your assistance, and the man will be thoroughly ashamed and probably on the run.

History and Chronology

The Pharaonic Period

5000–3000 BC: Predynastic Period

During this period, two kingdoms developed in Egypt, a northern one in the Delta, a southern one in the Nile valley. Though in frequent conflict with each other, they shared many features of a common culture. Hieroglyphic writing and monumental brick architecture were initiated.

3000–2647 BC: Early Dynastic Period (1st and 2nd Dynasties)

The king of the south, called **Menes**, known also as Narmer, triumphed over the north and established his capital at **Memphis**, near the juncture of the Nile valley and the Delta, from where he ruled over a united Egypt. The country's southern border was pushed southwards as far as Elephantine, in Nubia. Pharaohs and nobility alike were buried in substantial mud brick mastabas.

2647–2124 BC: Old Kingdom (3rd to 8th Dynasties)

The Old Kingdom began with the widespread use of stone, not only in the burial mastabas of the nobility but also to realize a wholly new conception, the pyramid. The purpose of the pyramid was to provide an indestructible container for the ka, a vital force possessed by the king alone, but upon which the nobles and priests depended for their lives and afterlives. The pharaoh, in short, possessed absolute temporal and spiritual power and ruled over a highly centralized and rigidly hierarchical society.

The Step Pyramid of the 3rd Dynasty pharaoh **Zoser** (2628–09 BC) was the first; the 4th Dynasty pyramids of **Cheops** (2549–26), **Chephren** (2518–2493) and **Mycerinus** (2488–60) at Giza marked the apogee of the Pyramid Age and of Old Kingdom pharaonic authority.

Zoser   Cheops Chephren Mycerinus

RE-HARAKHTI

Throughout the Old Kingdom, Egypt extended its spheres of trade, sending expeditions into Sinai, Libya and Nubia. But during the 5th Dynasty, pharaonic authority began to decline; the construction of sun temples such as those at **Abu Ghurab** indicate that the priesthood of **Re** was becoming more important than the pharaoh himself, while inscriptions in the Pyramid of Unas (2341–11 BC) are early evidence of the rising cult of Osiris, with its message of universal redemption.

From the 6th Dynasty onwards, power increasingly passed out of royal hands and into that of the nobles, who often set up almost independent courts in their own localities.

2123–2040 BC: First Intermediate Period (9th to 11th Dynasties)

Low Niles, bad harvests, foreign incursions and a weakened royal authority led to the collapse of the central administration. Northern Egypt was ruled from Heracleopolis, near Beni Suef, while southern Egypt was ruled from Thebes. The Thebes-based 11th Dynasty pharaoh **Mentuhotep II** (2050–1999 BC) reunited the country in 2040 BC, inaugurating the Middle Kingdom.

2040–1648 BC: Middle Kingdom (11th to 13th Dynasties)

OSIRIS

Following the reunification of Egypt by Mentuhotep II, the powerful kings of the 12th Dynasty established their capital at or near Memphis. Nevertheless, the supremacy enjoyed by Re, patron of the Old Kingdom pharaohs, was increasingly challenged by the worship of **Osiris** who could promise immortality not only to kings but to all believers who could demonstrate pious and worthy lives. This religious democratization was reflected in the architecture and distribution of tombs. Though pharaohs continued to build pyramids, such as those at Hawara and Lahun, these were of inferior quality, nor did nobles any longer feel obliged to build mastabas close by. Instead provincial nobles were interred in local rock-cut tombs, as at Beni Hasan.

Major building works and hydrological programmes were undertaken in the Fayyum by **Ammenemes I** (1980–51 BC) and his successors. Trade flourished with the Aegean islands, Byblos (present-day Jubail in Lebanon), whence cedarwood was obtained, and Punt, probably corresponding to present-day Somalia, while Nubia was invaded and garrisoned to control its supplies of gold and hard stone. Egypt again prospered and became a great power. Central authority weakened, however, during the 13th Dynasty.

1648–1540 BC: Second Intermediate Period (14th to 17th Dynasties)

The collapse of central authority during the 14th Dynasty brought invasion from the northeast by the **Hyksos**, who comprised the 15th and 16th Dynasties. They gradually extended their rule over most of Egypt from Avaris, their Delta capital, and introduced the use of horses and chariots. Contemporaneous with Hyksos rule were the 17th Dynasty princes ruling at Thebes who eventually drove the Hyksos out of Egypt.

1540–1069 BC: New Kingdom (18th to 20th Dynasties)

In defeating the Hyksos and then pursuing them to extinction in western Asia, **Amosis I** (1540–25 BC), founder of the 18th Dynasty, initiated the aggressive policy towards Palestine and Syria that characterized the New Kingdom, a period of power, luxury and cosmopolitanism. As royal residence and the religious and political capital of Egypt, Thebes and its necropolis were adorned with those monumental temples and magnificent tombs still seen today, as well as with palaces and homes which, because they were made of mud brick, have long since disappeared.

Tuthmosis I (1504–1492 BC) abandoned the pyramid and began the practice of royal burials in the Valley of the Kings, which owing to its constricted space required separate mortuary temples on the plain. His daughter **Hatshepsut** (1479–57) initiated Egypt's artistic revival; her mortuary

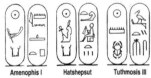

Amenophis I   Hatshepsut   Tuthmosis III

temple at Deir el Bahri is one of the finest architectural achievements of all time. Her co-ruler and successor **Tuthmosis III** (1479–25) conquered and organized the petty states of

Amenophis III

western Asia into the world's first imperial system: Egypt prospered from their tribute and trade, and gained their loyalty by educating and acculturating their young princes to Egyptian ways. Under **Amenophis III** (1391–53), who built most of the **Temple of Luxor**, the New Kingdom reached its apogee of opulence.

A major beneficiary of imperial wealth was the priesthood of the god **Amun** at the great **temple of Karnak**. Attempts to limit their power, which rivalled that of the pharaohs, came

to a head during the reign of Amenophis IV, who, as **Akhenaton** (1353–37 BC), established the worship of Aton and built a new capital at **Amarna**. Nothing so vividly portrays the break with past conventions than the sculpture and reliefs of the Amarna period, which are among the most striking

artistic works of ancient Egypt. At the death of Akhenaton and his wife

Akhenaton

Nefertiti, however, the priesthood of Amun re-asserted its authority over the young pharaoh **Tutankhamun** (1336–27 BC).

Tutankhamun

The 19th Dynasty began with the brief reign of **Ramses I**, an aged general whose son **Seti I**

(1294–79 BC) and grandson **Ramses II** (1279–13) restored royal prestige with their Asian campaigns, whose booty ensured accommodation with the Amun priesthood. Seti reverted to Old Kingdom artistic canons and produced coloured reliefs of exquisite taste, most

Seti I   Ramses II

notably at Abydos. Ramses was a prodigious builder, adding to the temples at Luxor and Karnak and constructing the Ramesseum, though his finest work is at Abu Simbel. Despite his bombast, Ramses II was not as successful a warrior as his father; he was nearly defeated at Kadesh in Syria against the Hittites. Iron weaponry was one reason why the Hittites were so formidable; the Egyptians had only bronze.

The Exodus under Moses may have taken place during the reign of Ramses II or that of his son **Merneptah** (1213–03 BC). During the following century or so Egypt finally entered the **Iron Age**. But iron could only be obtained in western Asia, and partly because Egypt was short on iron weaponry, its hold on western Asia was slipping. Instead iron had to be bought with gold, which caused Egypt enormous economic difficulties. One reason why tomb robbing became so common during the 20th Dynasty and after was the rocketing value of gold, which the country could no longer afford to leave buried with its dead. The outstanding pharaoh of the 20th Dynasty was **Ramses III** (1184–53), who recorded on the wall of his mortuary temple at Medinet Habu how he repelled an invasion by the Sea Peoples, marauders from across the Mediterranean who had already destroyed the Hittite empire. It was the last great Egyptian victory.

Ramses III

1069–332 BC: Late Dynastic Period (21st to 31st Dynasties)

This was a period of decline during which division and foreign rule were common. Native kings ruled as much of Egypt as they could from various capitals in the Delta, high priests of Amun often ruled Thebes and its surrounding area, and from time to time foreign dynasties, Libyans and 'Ethiopians' (in fact from the Sudan), controlled all or part of Egypt. Foreigner was sometimes compounded upon foreigner: during the 25th Dynasty (712–663 BC), when the massive First Pylon at Karnak was built, the Ethiopian king Taharka provoked the Assyrians who subsequently sacked both Memphis and Thebes, while the Assyrians in turn were ejected during the 26th Dynasty (663–525 BC) with the help of Greek mercenaries. This **Saite Dynasty**, as it is also known, after Sais, its Delta capital, was a period of prosperity and cultural revival, and also a time of large-scale Greek settlement in the country. The Greek city of Naucratis in the Delta was granted the privilege of being the only port through which goods could be imported into Egypt.

The Persians invaded Egypt in 525 BC and were only removed in 399 BC, again with Greek help, though the Persians returned in 343 BC and remained until **Alexander the Great** entered Egypt in 332 BC.

Alexander

The Graeco-Roman Period

332–30 BC: The Ptolemaic Period

In 331 BC, the year after he entered Egypt, Alexander founded Alexandria, though he did not stay long enough to see a single building rise. At his death in 323 BC, his new Hellenistic empire, which extended as far east as India, was divided between three of his Macedonian generals, Ptolemy taking Egypt. As **Ptolemy I Soter** (323–282 BC), he established a dynasty which ruled the country for 300 years in the guise of pharaohs, albeit Greek-speaking ones. Egypt was colonized by the Greeks, who nevertheless respected and in some measure merged their own culture with the customs and religion of the Egyptians. Through the Ptolemies' control of trade—wheat, for example, was a royal monopoly—the dynasty became spectacularly wealthy and famous as great benefactors.

Ptolemy I Soter added Cyrene, Palestine, Cyprus and parts of the Asia Minor coast to his realm, and at Alexandria, its capital and geographical centre, he founded the Museion and Library. The Pharos, the lighthouse that was reckoned one of the seven wonders of the world, was built during the reign of **Ptolemy II Philadelphos** (282–46 BC), who also first invited the Jews to settle in the city. Within 100 years of her founding, Alexandria had reached the height of her splendour and was the greatest commercial, cultural and scientific centre of the age.

In Upper Egypt, **Ptolemy III Euergetes** (246–21 BC) built at Karnak and began the temple at Edfu. The temples at Dendera, Esna, Kom Ombo and Philae were also Ptolemaic works. Though these archaic temples were built to please the priests, the Ptolemies otherwise tied Egypt to the Mediterranean. Inevitably they encountered the rising power and rapacity of Rome, and through incompetence abroad and strife at home the later Ptolemies relied on the Romans for their very thrones. The last in the line was the great **Cleopatra** (51–30 BC), who with Mark Antony attempted to create a new Hellenistic empire in the east. Their defeat by a Roman fleet in the battle of Actium off Greece in 31 BC and Octavian's victory outside Alexandria the following year led to their suicides.

30 BC–AD 642: Roman and Byzantine Periods

After seizing Alexandria in 30 BC, **Octavian** (Augustus) incorporated Egypt into the **Roman Empire**. The Roman emperors followed the example of the Ptolemies in representing themselves to the Egyptian people as successors of the pharaohs and in maintaining the appearance of a national Egyptian state. They completed and added to many of the temples the Ptolemies had begun. The dominant culture of the country remained Greek, but whereas the colonizing Greeks had had a stake in the country and made it flourish through trade, the Roman administration increasingly ran Egypt as a command economy, milking it for taxes and grain entirely for the benefit of Rome. By the third century AD, living standards were falling and the infrastructure was in decline, and in places like the Fayyum, which the

Ptolemies had raised to a level of prosperity that it has not regained even to this day, the sands washed in over once fertile fields and busy towns.

Alexandria, however, remained a great city, and to her eminence in science, mathematics and the arts she added philosophy and theology. Her mixed Greek, Jewish and Egyptian population provided the early cult of Jesus with much of its symbolism and intellectual underpinning, and during the first three centuries AD the new religion extended throughout the country, first among the Greeks themselves, but eventually among the native population. In AD 204 the Romans felt obliged to issue an edict prohibiting Roman subjects from embracing **Christianity**, and half a century later the Emperor Decius (AD 249–51) instituted a brief but severe persecution. During the reign of Diocletian (AD 284–305), persecution of Christians reached its peak, so many thousands dying that his accession marks the beginning of the 'Era of Martyrs' from which the Egyptian (that is Coptic) Church dates its calendar.

Christianity, which resonated so well with old symbols and beliefs, including the expectation of an afterlife, became the basis of a reawakened popular culture, expressed with an exuberance not found in the pharaonic or Graeco-Roman canons. Nor were native Egyptians content to follow the subtleties of Alexandrian theologians imbued with an alien Greek philosophy. Despite the **Edict of Milan** in AD 313, which granted toleration to Christianity, a gap in nationalist feeling opened up between native Egyptians and the Roman Empire.

In the West, that empire was in decline. In the East, the **Emperor Constantine** founded a new, Christian capital at Constantinople in AD 330, the beginnings of what historians now call the **Byzantine Empire**. Also at about AD 330 the first monasteries were founded in Egypt's deserts, and from them the imperial and religious authority of Constantinople and its representatives in Alexandria were opposed. In AD 451, at the **Council of Chalcedon**, the supposed Egyptian belief that Christ has only a single divine nature (monophysitism) was branded a heresy, and the Coptic Church was effectively expelled from the main body of Christianity. The bitterness felt at this decision, and grievances towards Roman and then Byzantine misrule, persuaded Egyptians to offer little resistance to the **Arab invasion** of AD 640–2.

The Arab and Turkish Period

AD 642–969: Umayyads, Abbasids, Tulunids and Ikshidids

By the time Mohammed, the founder of Islam, died at Mecca in 632, the whole of Arabia had been united under his new religion. Within a further ten years, the Arabs had destroyed the Sassanian (Persian) Empire and had defeated the Byzantines in Syria, taking Damascus and Jerusalem. Under the leadership of **Amr**, 3,500 Arab horsemen invaded Egypt in 640 and in the following year founded **Fustat** near the Byzantine fortress of **Babylon** (now in Old Cairo), which surrendered to them. In 642 Alexandria put the seal on the Arab conquest by opening its gates to them in welcome.

Though the rapidly expanding Arab empire was first ruled from Medina, from 661 it was governed by caliphs of the Umayyad dynasty at Damascus. After a violent transfer of dynasty in 750, the caliphate was moved to Baghdad. As far as Egypt was concerned, however, Arab policy always remained the same. There was little interest in making converts, for the poll tax could be imposed only on non-Muslims. During this first period of Arab rule, a succession of 80 governors was sent to milk the country, the level of taxation soon proving more oppressive than it had been under the Byzantines. The irrigation system further deteriorated, agriculture declined, prices rose and native Egyptians suffered growing impoverishment. Some converted to Islam, others rose in vain revolt during the 8th and 9th centuries.

In 870 the Abbasids sent **Ibn Tulun** to Egypt as governor. Instead he asserted his independence and soon restored the country's economy. His magnificent mosque, which owes an architectural debt to his native Mesopotamia, is the largest in Cairo and, apart from Amr's much rebuilt mosque at Fustat, the oldest. In 905 the Abbasids regained Egypt from Ibn Tulun's less able descendants, but Baghdad's authority was both nominal and brief, as another governor, Ikhshid, had barely established his own dynasty when it was swept away by the Fatimid conquest.

969–1171: The Fatimids

In 909 an Arab dynasty claiming descent from Mohammed's daughter Fatima established its own Shi'a caliphate centred on Tunisia. Opposing themselves to the Abbasids' Sunni caliphate in Baghdad, in 969 the Fatimids under their caliph al-Muizz invaded Egypt where they founded **Cairo** and, to propagate their version of Islam, the great mosque of al-Azhar. During the reign of the second Cairo caliph, al-Aziz (975–6), the Fatimid empire reached its apogee, extending beyond North Africa and Egypt to Sicily, western Arabia and Syria. Egypt's foreign trade was expanded and its taxation reduced. The empire declined after the death of the third Cairo caliph, the mad al-Hakim (996–1021), though its tradition of architectural excellence continued unabated, not least in the late 11th-century Fatimid city gates of Bab Zuwayla, Bab al-Nasr and Bab al-Futuh.

Two external events contributed to the extinction of the Fatimid empire. In 1055 the Seljuq Turks took Baghdad, their energy leading to a resurgence of Sunni Islam in Mesopotamia, Persia and Syria. Then in 1099 the First Crusade took Jerusalem.

1171–1250: The Ayyubids

When the Crusaders attacked Egypt in 1168, **Saladin**, a Kurd and son of Ayyub (from whom Saladin's dynasty took its name), successfully defended the country on behalf of the Sunni caliphate, overthrew the enfeebled Shi'a caliphate of the Fatimids and in 1171 made himself master of the country. Then after completing the Citadel in Cairo, he recaptured Jerusalem in 1187. Realizing that Egypt was the key to their control of the Holy Land, the Crusaders twice more attacked the country after Saladin's death in 1193. In a remarkable incident on the occasion of the Fifth Crusade siege of Damietta in 1218, **St Francis of Assisi** crossed the Egyptian lines in a personal attempt to convert the Sultan al-Kamil. St Francis was sent away with gifts in a kindly way and thereafter confined his preachings to birds. In 1249 the Seventh Crusade, led by the French king St Louis, also landed at Damietta but was repulsed by an army of Turkish slaves, called Mamelukes, which had been built up by the Sultan al-Salih Ayyub. The campaign was in fact conducted by **Shagarat al-Durr**, Ayyub's wife, who kept it a secret that the sultan had meanwhile died in Cairo. She proclaimed herself sultan in 1250, but found she could rule only through the chief Mameluke, whom she married.

1250–1517: The Mamelukes

The Mamelukes discovered their power during the reigns of al-Salih Ayyub and his wife Shagarat al-Durr. At her death in 1257, they raised sultans from their own ranks. Until 1382 it was the **Bahri Mamelukes**, named for their barracks on Roda island in the Nile (*bahr* means river), who ruled Egypt. They were mostly Kipchak Turks from the steppes north of the Black Sea. The most celebrated of these Mameluke sultans were **Baybars** (1260–77), **Qalaun** (1279–90), **al-Nasr** (1309–40)—the beautiful mausolea of these last two are on Sharia Muizz in Cairo—and **al-Hassan** (1347–51, 1354–61), builder of the great madrasa bearing his name. The Mamelukes were the most formidable fighting force of their time, and almost immediately, under Baybars in 1260, they won a stunning victory against the Mongols in Syria, who until then had seemed unstoppable. Qalaun in turn reduced the Crusaders holdings in the Holy Land to the port of Acre, from which they were driven in 1291, a year after his death.

The Bahri Mamelukes gave Egypt security and prosperity, at least until the end of al-Nasr's reign. Thereafter their rule descended into incompetence and vicious rivalries. From 1382 their place was taken by the **Burgi Mamelukes**, named for their barracks in the Citadel (*burg* means tower, referring to the towers of the Citadel), who were mostly Circassian Turks from the Caucasus. The outstanding architectural works of the Burgi Mameluke sultans are owed to **Barquq** (1382–9, 1390–98), whose mosque is on Sharia Muizz, his mausoleum in Cairo's City of the Dead; **Baybars** (1422–38), whose mausoleum is in the City of the Dead; **Qaytbey** (1468–95), known for his fortress on the site of the Pharos in Alexandria, and his mausoleum in the City of the Dead; and **al-Ghuri** (1500–16) whose monuments stand near al-Azhar.

In the late 14th century, Barquq deflected **Timur** (Tamerlane) from Egypt by keeping him at bay in Syria, but the cost of the campaign ruined Egypt's finances. Famine, plague and Portugal's discovery of a sea route round Africa into the Indian Ocean combined to weaken Egypt's economic position during the 15th century.

Egypt's **Christians** paid the price. The Copts had remained in the majority at least until the Crusades, but the Latin capture of Jerusalem in 1099, the Mongol sack of Baghdad in 1258 and the internecine struggles of Egypt's Mameluke rulers from the mid-13th to the 16th century produced an atmosphere of insecurity and distrust which, combined with the growing impoverishment of the country, had sultans and mobs alike turning against the Christians. In the early 14th century, fanatical Muslims looted and destroyed all the principal churches of Egypt. In revenge the Copts fired many mosques, palaces and private Muslim houses, whereupon Christians suffered wholesale massacre. Copts were expelled from official positions and subjected to a range of indignities, such as being forbidden to ride horses or asses unless they sat backwards, and being forced to wear distinctive clothing, and even to have a bell tinkling round their necks when entering a public bath. Mass conversions to Islam followed.

1517–1798: The Ottomans

When **Selim**, the Ottoman sultan, entered Cairo in 1517, he had Tumanbay, the last Mameluke sultan, strung up at Bab Zuwayla. In fact the rope twice broke and Tumanbay had to be hanged three times before he was dead. It might have been an omen, for the Ottomans never controlled Egypt absolutely, and the Mamelukes were far from being a spent force. But officially, and usually so nominally that nobody noticed or cared, Egypt remained part of the Ottoman Empire until 1914.

At first the Ottoman Pasha (governor) was successful in the usual activity of drawing off Egyptian revenues, and indeed the Egyptian Bazaar in Istanbul was not so called because it sold Egyptian goods but because it was maintained out of a small part of the heavy taxes imposed on Egypt. In return, the Ottomans allowed Egypt to rot. Cairo ceased to be an important cultural centre and Alexandria nearly disappeared altogether. As opposed to the bold forms and magnificent volumes of earlier Cairene architecture, the Ottomans contributed a few rather prissy minarets and several Baroque public fountains and indulged their taste for tiles by slapping up some third-rate indigo and turquoise examples on the 14th-century **mosque of Aqsunqur**, accounting for its popular name of Blue Mosque.

Throughout the 17th and 18th centuries the Ottoman Pashas were no more than straw men, and Egypt muddled along on shifting alliances between Mamelukes, merchants, guilds and religious functionaries. Indeed, by the second half of the 18th century certain Mamelukes had gathered up so much power that they became almost absolute masters of Egypt, and from that time all payments of revenue to Istanbul were stopped.

The Modern Period

1798–1914: Egypt's Encounter with the West

In 1798 Napoleon landed in Egypt with the aim of controlling the land and sea route between Europe and India. In the **Battle of the Nile**, fought that same year, Nelson met this threat to British interests by destroying the French fleet. Napoleon absconded to Paris in 1799; the British compelled his army to follow in 1801. But the brief expedition was to have profound effects. Egypt was exposed to the full impact of Western technology, while Western curiosity worked at turning Egypt's mysterious past into an open book. Napoleon's expedition had included a number of France's leading scholars, whose exhaustive survey of the country, *Description de l'Egypte*, was published in 20 volumes between 1809 and 1828. Their activities had included collecting antiquities and making detailed drawings of monuments and sites. Because their activities were well known to the army at large, the scholars were immediately notified when a soldier found an inscribed stone at **Rosetta**. The decipherment of its hieroglyphics by Champollion in 1822 opened up three millennia of ancient Egyptian history.

After the departure of the French, the Ottomans attempted to assert their authority. One of their Albanian commanders, **Mohammed Ali**, was made viceroy (khedive) in 1805; after massacring the Mamelukes in 1811 he became, effectively, the independent ruler of Egypt. Before his death in 1849, he placed his mark on the Cairo skyline with his Ottoman imperial-style mosque atop the Citadel. During his decades of power he began the modernization of Egypt. An improved strain of cotton, new industries and a massive public works programme laid the basis for a rise in population and prosperity which, by the end of the century, reached levels unknown to Egypt for 2,000 years. In 1820 he completed the **Mahmoudiya**

Canal which linked Alexandria to the Nile and brought the city back to life. With a powerful fleet and a highly trained army under the brilliant command of his son Ibrahim, Mohammed Ali held sway over the Eastern Mediterranean and the Middle East, and nearly overturned the Ottoman Empire itself. Checked only by the superior power of the British, and in return for recognition of his dynastic claims, Mohammed Ali confined his ambitions to Egypt.

The opening of the **Suez Canal** in 1869, during the reign of **Ismail**, returned Egypt to the crossroads of international trade, a position it had lost in the 15th century when the Portuguese opened up the route around southern Africa to the Indian Ocean. The venture was more than Ismail could afford, however, and in selling his shares to the British in 1875 he not only gave them a controlling interest in the canal but a considerable stake in Egypt's security. Therefore in 1882, when **Colonel Ahmed Arabi** led a nationalist uprising against his own government in protest at its susceptibility to British, French and Turkish influence, and when hundreds of Europeans in Alexandria were massacred in consequence, the **British** occupied the country. The final word in Egyptian affairs was now that of British consul-generals, men like Evelyn Baring, later **Lord Cromer**, who between 1883 and 1907 was typical in encouraging the development of the country's railways, public services, agriculture and irrigation system, including the **first dam at Aswan**, while at the same time failing to understand Egyptian resentment and desire for independence.

1914–present: War and Peace

In 1914, after Ottoman Turkey allied itself with Germany in the First World War, Egypt was declared a British Protectorate. At the war's end Saad Zaghloul, leader of the **nationalist movement**, demanded British withdrawal but was sent into exile. Continued nationalist activity, however, forced Britain to recognize Egypt as a sovereign state in 1922. Nevertheless, Britain retained responsibility for Egyptian defence, its foreign community and the Suez Canal, and maintained an army in the country until 1936, when it was withdrawn to the Canal Zone. But the **Second World War** (1939–45) brought the British army back in force, and after initial reversals it won a great victory at **Alamein** in 1942 over an invading German army commanded by General Rommel.

Relations in the Middle East became bitter, however, with the end of the British Mandate for Palestine in 1948. Egypt, together with other Arab countries, went to war against the new state of Israel but was defeated. Many Egyptians blamed corruption in the army, weak government, favouritism in high places and purchases of obsolete arms for the debacle, all of which implicated **King Farouk** and his ministers. **Gamal Abdel Nasser**, a young colonel who had been wounded in the fighting, gathered round him a group of dissident army officers who vowed to overthrow the monarchy. The coup came on 23 July 1952, and on 26 July Farouk abdicated and left the country. With a decade or so to run before the foreign-owned Suez Canal Company reverted to Egyptian ownership, the British were persuaded to evacuate their troops from the Canal Zone. But Nasser's plans to help Egyptian agriculture and industry by building the **High Dam at Aswan** became a new source of international friction when the Americans, angry at his nonaligned policy, refused to lend the money. In July 1956 Nasser nationalized the Suez Canal to use its revenues to pay for the dam's construction, but in October that year Israel invaded Sinai to provide a pretext for France and Britain to reoccupy the Canal, supposedly thereby to keep Egypt and Israel from fighting.

America, which was playing its own long-term game in the Middle East, and did not want the boat rocked, obliged the invaders to withdraw. For Nasser, it was a great moral victory, and on the back of nationalist fervour he threw most foreigners and Jews out of the country, and from 1961 introduced sweeping socialist measures, limiting incomes, nationalizing banks and the cotton industry, and further redistributing land.

Enormously popular and genuinely concerned for the welfare of his people, Nasser's policies nevertheless stifled enterprise, encouraged corruption and cynicism, and contributed to falling standards in education and services. In the 1967 '**Six Day War**' against Israel Egypt suffered a defeat even more humiliating than under Farouk 20 years earlier. Though the Canal was blocked and Sinai occupied, Nasser's offer to resign was rejected by an outpouring of national sentiment. But three years later he was dead.

After 1970, when **Anwar Sadat** succeeded Nasser as president, Egypt edged away from its pro-Soviet policy and its economy was gradually liberalized. Egypt's attempt to regain Sinai in the 1973 war was repelled, yet it was a triumph. Israel had been taken by surprise and was no longer seen as invincible, while Egyptian pride had been restored. Sadat could make his dramatic visit to Jerusalem in 1977, which led to a peace treaty between the two countries.

Hosni Mubarak became president after Sadat's assassination in 1981, since when the country's economy has continued to be liberalized, with controls and subsidies lifted and virtually all its nationalized industries returned to private ownership. Egyptian stability is being tested as the country endures the strains of this transition while attempting to make its economy grow faster than its rapidly rising population eats into it, a situation that has been exploited by Islamic fundamentalists.

Chronology

Pharaonic Dynasties

The following is a list of the royal dynasties ruling Egypt. The priests drew up long lists of monarchs, attaching to the years of a pharaoh's reign the events they wished to record. An example is the list of Seti I's predecessors in his mortuary temple at Abydos. Working from such lists, Manetho, an Egyptian priest under the early Ptolemies, arranged all the rulers of Egypt from Menes to Alexander into 31 dynasties. Egyptologists have relied on Manetho's list, and have been able to confirm its essential correctness. Egyptologists have in turn divided pharaonic history into periods, such as Old Kingdom, Middle Kingdom and New Kingdom, though there are competing classifications.

Dates for the Late Period are regarded as certain; otherwise the margin of error should not exceed 15 years for the New Kingdom, 40 years for the Middle Kingdom, 60 years for the Old Kingdom and about 100 years for the first two dynasties.

This dynastic arrangement has historical validity, for Egypt's fortunes were closely linked to the rise and fall of the various royal houses. Throughout this guide the dynasty of each pharaoh is mentioned after his name so that his place in the scheme of things can readily be ascertained. Only the most important pharaohs have been mentioned below within their dynasties.

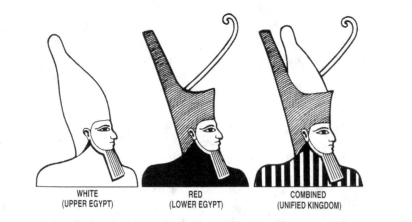

WHITE (UPPER EGYPT)	RED (LOWER EGYPT)	COMBINED (UNIFIED KINGDOM)

Predynastic Period: 5000–3000 BC

Early Dynastic Period: 3000–2647 BC

1st Dynasty and 2nd Dynasty

Menes (Narmer)   Unification of Egypt; capital at Memphis.

Old Kingdom: 2647–2124 BC

	BC	
3rd Dynasty	2647–2573	Period of stability. Start of the Pyramid Age.
Zoser	2628–09	
4th Dynasty	2573–2454	
Snofru	2573–49	
Cheops	2549–26	
Chephren	2518–2493	
Mycerinus	2488–60	Effective end of the Pyramid Age.
5th Dynasty	2454–2311	
Userkaf	2454–47	
Neferirkare	2435–25	
Unas	2341–11	Pyramid Texts.
6th Dynasty	2311–2140	Period of decline.
Pepi I	2280–43	
7th and 8th Dynasties	2140–24	

First Intermediate Period: 2123–2040 BC

	BC	
9th and 10th Dynasties	2123–2040	Collapse of central authority. Capital at Heracleopolis.

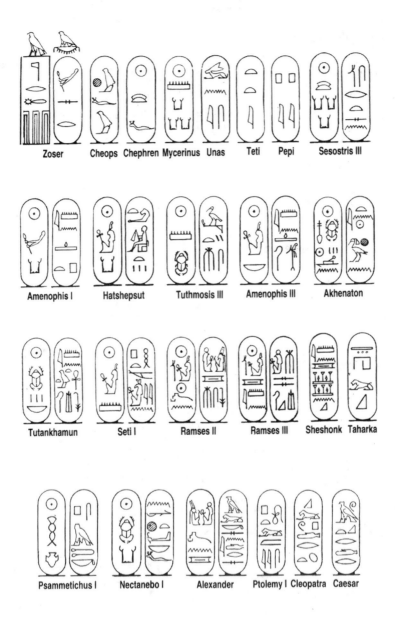

Zoser Cheops Chephren Mycerinus Unas Teti Pepi Sesostris III

Amenophis I Hatshepsut Tuthmosis III Amenophis III Akhenaton

Tutankhamun Seti I Ramses II Ramses III Sheshonk Taharka

Psammetichus I Nectanebo I Alexander Ptolemy I Cleopatra Caesar

| *11th Dynasty (first part)* | 2123–2040 | Capital at Thebes. |
| Mentuhotep II | 2050–40 (pre-reunification) | |

Middle Kingdom: 2040–1648 BC

	BC	
11th Dynasty (second part)	2040–1980	Conquest of Nubia.
Mentuhotep II	2040–1999	Reunites Egypt; capital at Thebes.
12th Dynasty	1980–1801	Royal residence moved to Memphis; major building works and hydrological programmes in the Fayyum.
Ammenemes I	1980–51	
Sesostris I	1960–16	
Ammenemes III	1859–14	
13th Dynasty	1801–1648	

Second Intermediate Period: 1648–1540 BC

Collapse of central authority.

14th Dynasty, and the (Hyksos) 15th and 16th Dynasties	All in Lower Egypt; introduction of the chariot by the Hyksos.
17th Dynasty	Contemporaneous with the Hyksos but ruling at Thebes.

New Kingdom: 1540–1069 BC

Period of power, luxury and cosmopolitanism.

	BC	
18th Dynasty	1540–1296	Period of greatest contribution to the splendour of Thebes and Karnak.
Amosis I	1540–25	Expels Hyksos; establishes royal residence, and religious and political capital at Thebes.
Amenophis I	1525–1504	
Tuthmosis I	1504–1492	Burials begin at Valley of the Kings.
Tuthmosis II	1492–79	
Hatshepsut	1479–57	
Tuthmosis III	1479–25	Struggle with Hatshepsut; after her passing, he lays foundation of Asian and African empire.
Amenophis II	1427–01	
Tuthmosis IV	1401–1391	
Amenophis III	1391–53	Apogee of New Kingdom opulence.

Amenophis IV	1353–37	Assault on priesthood of Amun; establishes (as Akhenaton) worship of the Aton.
Smenkhkere	1338–36	
Tutankhamun	1336–27	Return to orthodoxy.
Ay	1327–23	
Horemheb	1323–1295	Military dictatorship.
19th Dynasty	1295–1186	Restoration of royal power.
Ramses I	1295–94	
Seti I	1294–79	New building work in Old Kingdom style.
Ramses II	1279–13	Prodigious builder: Ramesseum, Abu Simbel.
Merneptah	1213–03	Considered, along with Ramses II, possible pharaoh of the Exodus.
20th Dynasty	1186–1069	Dislocations as Egypt enters Iron Age.
Ramses III	1184–53	Defeats Sea Peoples; succeeded by incompetent rulers.
Ramses VI	1143–36	
Herihor	1098–90	Priest-pharaoh at Thebes; rival ruler at Tanis.

Late Dynastic Period: 1069–332 BC

Period of decline; often foreign rule.

	BC	
21st Dynasty	1069–945	Capital at Tanis.
22nd Dynasty	945–745	Warriors of Libyan origin; capital at Tanis.
Sheshonk I	945	Loots Jerusalem (*1 Kings 14, 25–26*).
23rd Dynasty	745–18	Ethiopian kings control Upper Egypt.
24th Dynasty	718–12	Ethiopian kings control all Egypt.
25th Dynasty	712–663	
Taharka	695–71	Ethiopian king defeated by Assyrians; they sack Memphis and Thebes.
26th Dynasty	663–525	Delta rulers, their capital at Sais; Assyrians ejected with Greek help.
Psammetichus I	663–10	
Necho	610–595	Attempts to link Red Sea and Mediterranean by a canal; circumnavigation of Africa.
Psammetichus II	595–89	Nubian expedition recorded in Greek at Abu Simbel.
27th Dynasty	525–404	Persian rule.
Cambyses	525–22	

Darius I	522–486	
Xerxes the Great	486–66	
28th Dynasty	404–399	Persians ejected with Greek help.
29th Dynasty	399–80	Delta remains the vital centre of power.
30th Dynasty	380–43	
Nectanebos I	380–43	Great builder, e.g. at Philae.
31st Dynasty	343–32	Persian rule.
	332	Alexander enters Egypt.

The Ptolemies

BC

323   The death of Alexander.

323–282   Ptolemy I Soter (Saviour). He added Cyrene, Palestine, Cyprus and parts of the Asia Minor coast to his realm, and at Alexandria, its geographical centre, he founded the Museion and Library.

282–46   Ptolemy II Philadelphos (Lover of his Sister). To the shock of the Greeks, though with Egyptian precedent, he married his sister. He was a patron of poets, first invited the Jews to settle in Alexandria, and constructed the Pharos.

246–21   Ptolemy III Euergetes (Benefactor). A soldier with a taste for science; during his rule Alexandria reached its height of splendour. In Upper Egypt he began the temple at Edfu. Abroad, he nearly reached India, and earned the title Conqueror of the World.

221–05   Ptolemy IV Philopator (Lover of his Father). Setback in Syria, revolt at Thebes; he began construction of the temples at Esna and Kom Ombo.

205–181   Ptolemy V Epiphanes (God Manifest). Child-king. With a revolt at Alexandria and the interior in a state of anarchy, Epiphanes was placed under the protection of the Roman Senate, but by the time he came of age Egypt had lost most of her overseas possessions.

181–45   Ptolemy VI Philometor (Lover of his Mother). Seleucid invasion, Memphis captured, Egypt saved by Roman intervention.

145–4   Ptolemy VII Neos Philopator.

145–16   Ptolemy VII Euergetes II. Also known as Physcon (Fatty): when he came puffing along the quay to greet Scipio Africanus the younger, the Roman sniggered, 'At least the Alexandrians have seen their king walk'. This Roman contempt applied to Egypt's sovereignty as well.

116–07, 88–80   Ptolemy IX Soter II. Competed with his brother, Ptolemy X Alexander I, for the throne, both borrowing money from the Romans to raise arms.

107–88   Ptolemy X Alexander I. To cover his debts he bequeathed Egypt to the Roman people. As he had by then lost the throne his offer could not be accepted. But it was remembered.

80	Ptolemy XI Alexander II. Forced by Sulla to marry his (Ptolemy's) elderly step mother, he then killed her and was killed in turn by an Alexandrian mob.
80–58, 55–1	Ptolemy XII Neos Dionysos. Also known as Nothos (Bastard), he rushed back from Syria so that the vacant throne should not attract Roman annexation, and bolstered his pedigree by adding Philopator (lover of his father) to his official names. He was the son of Ptolemy IX and father of Cleopatra VII. He built at Dendera, completed the temple at Edfu and left his mark on Philae. His reign was briefly interrupted by internal disruption.
51–49, 48–30	Cleopatra VII. Ruled jointly with her younger brother Ptolemy XIII who banished her (48 BC), but that year she received the support of Julius Caesar and Ptolemy was drowned in the Nile. Another brother, Ptolemy XIV, succeeded to the co-regency (47 BC); assassinated (45 BC) at Cleopatra's instigation. Bore Caesar a son (47 BC), named Caesarion, who never ruled. Caesar assassinated (44 BC). Met Antony (41 BC). The battle of Actium (31 BC). Suicide of Antony and Cleopatra; Octavian (Augustus) makes Egypt a province of the Roman Empire (30 BC).

Roman and Byzantine Periods

BC

| 30 | Octavian (Augustus) incorporates Egypt into the Roman Empire. The Roman emperors follow the example of the Ptolemies in representing themselves to the Egyptian people as successors of the pharaohs and in maintaining the appearance of a national Egyptian state. |

AD

c. 30	Crucifixion of Jesus of Nazareth at Jerusalem.
45	Legend has St Mark make his first convert to Christianity in Egypt, a Jewish shoemaker of Alexandria.
98–117	Trajan. The canal connecting the Nile with the Red Sea reopened (AD 115).
117–38	Hadrian. Visits Egypt.
204	Edict prohibiting Roman subjects from embracing Christianity. The Delta is studded with Christian communities.
249–51	Decius. Severe persecutions.
c. 251–356	St Antony becomes the first hermit.
284–305	Diocletian. His accession marks the beginning of the 'Era of Martyrs' from which the Copts date their calendar. Persecution of the Christians.
312	Constantine the Great becomes emperor in the West.
313	Edict of Milan: Christianity tolerated throughout the Roman Empire.
324–37	Constantine the Great becomes sole ruler of the Roman Empire. Founds Constantinople (AD 330). Converts to Christianity on his deathbed.
c. 330	Founding of the first monasteries at Wadi Natrun.

379–95	Theodosius I. Declares Christianity to be the religion of the Roman Empire (AD 392).
395	Partition of the Roman Empire into East (Constantinople) and West (Rome). Notional date for the beginning of the Byzantine Empire.
451	Council of Chalcedon declares monophysitism a heresy, effectively expelling the Egyptian (Coptic) Church from the main body of Christianity.
476	Fall of the Roman Empire in the West.
622	Mohammed's flight from Mecca, the *hegira*, from which the Muslim calendar is reckoned. His death (AD 632).
636	Arabs defeat Byzantine army and take Damascus.
637	Arabs destroy the Sassanian (Persian) Empire.
638	Arabs take Jerusalem.
640–42	An Arab force under Amr enters Egypt. Fortress of Babylon taken (AD 641). Fustat founded; Alexandria surrenders and welcomes Arabs as liberators from Byzantine oppression (AD 642).

Arab and Turkish Periods

All dates are according to the Western calendar

AD

661	Murder of Ali, son-in-law of the Prophet; the caliphate passes to the Umayyads.
661–750	The Umayyad caliphate, with its capital at Damascus, rules over a united Arab empire stretching from the borders of China to the shores of the Atlantic, and up into France.
750–935	Abbasids and Tulunids. The Abbasids put a bloody end to the Umayyads in Syria and succeed to the caliphate, ruling the Arab world from Baghdad. Ibn Tulun, an Abbasid governor of Egypt, makes himself independent of Baghdad and establishes a dynasty (870–935).
c. 820	The Copts, resentful of their Arab conquerors, rise in revolt several times during the 8th and 9th centuries.
909	Establishment of Fatimid caliphate in North Africa.
935–69	A Turkish dynasty, the Ikhshidids, seizes power through the governorship.
969–1171	The Fatimid caliphate in Egypt, which now follows Shi'a rather than Sunni Islam. Cairo, its capital, founded (969). Al-Azhar founded (971). The Fatimid empire reaches its peak under Caliph Abu Mansur al-Aziz (975–96). He introduces the practice of importing slave troops, the forerunners of the Mamelukes. His successor, al-Hakim (996–1021), is an all-powerful psychotic; the decline of the Fatimid empire begins with his death.
1055	The Seljuq Turks take Baghdad, leading to a resurgence of Sunni Islam in Iraq, Syria and Iran.
1099	The Crusaders take Jerusalem.

1171–1250	The Ayyubids. the dynasty of Saladin, a Kurd from Iraq. He converts Egypt back to Sunni Islam. Drives the Crusaders from Jerusalem (1187). The Mamelukes rise to power during the rule of Shagarat al-Durr (1249–57).
1250–1382	The Bahri Mamelukes. The most celebrated of these Mameluke sultans are Baybars (1260–77); Qalaun (1279–90); al-Nasr (1309–40); and al-Hassan (1347–51, 1354–61). During the early 14th century, severe persecution of Christians who until this time are still perhaps half the population; mass conversions to Islam follow.
1382–1517	The Burgi Mamelukes. The most celebrated of these Mameluke sultans are Barquq (1382–9, 1390–98); Baybars (1422–38); Qaytbey (1468–95); and al-Ghuri (1500–16). Tumanbay (1515–17) was the last of the Burgi sultans; he was hanged three times by the Turks outside Bab Zuwayla in Cairo.
1517	The Rule of the Ottoman Turks begins in Egypt and continues, if only nominally, until 1914.

The Modern Period

1798–1801	French occupation of Egypt. Napoleon lands at Alexandria; Battle of the Pyramids; Battle of the Nile (1798). Napoleon departs from Egypt (1799). A British army compels the French to evacuate the country (1801).
1805	Mohammed Ali becomes viceroy of Egypt and after massacring the Mamelukes (1811) becomes, effectively, the independent ruler of Egypt, establishing a dynasty that was to end with Farouk.
1822	Champollion deciphers hieroglyphics.
1869	Opening of the Suez Canal during the reign of Ismail.
1882	Nationalist uprising led by Arabi. British occupation of Egypt begins.
1883–1907	Evelyn Baring (Lord Cromer) is British consul in Egypt and effective ruler of the country.
1902	British complete construction of dam at Aswan.
1914	Britain declares Egypt to be a British Protectorate.
1918	Saad Zaghloul, nationalist leader, demands British withdrawal.
1922	British recognize Egypt as a sovereign state, but maintain an army in Egypt.
1936	Anglo-Egyptian Treaty, formally ending British occupation. British army withdraws, except from the Canal Zone.
1939–45	Egypt nominally neutral during the Second World War, but British Army invited to return to fight the encroaching Germans. Battle of el Alamein (1942); Rommel repulsed.
1948	End of British Mandate for Palestine. Establishment of the state of Israel. Arab-Israeli war; Arab debacle. Resentful of political corruption, Gamal Abdel Nasser (1918–70) gathers round him a group of dissident army officers.
1952	25 January, British soldiers kill several Egyptian police in the Canal Zone. 26 January, rioting in Cairo at British action and Egyptian government's inaction.

	23 July, Nasser's group stages a coup. 26 July, King Farouk abdicates and leaves the country.
1953	Egypt declared a republic.
1954	Nasser becomes head of state.
1954–56	British evacuate the Canal Zone.
1956	United States cancels loan to Egypt for construction of the High Dam at Aswan. Nasser nationalizes the Suez Canal to use its revenues to pay for High Dam's construction. Israel invades Sinai in collusion with a British and French troop landing in the Canal Zone. Britain, France and Israel withdraw after international protest.
1961	Nasser introduces sweeping socialist measures, limiting incomes, nationalizing banks and the cotton industry, further redistributing land.
1967	The June 'Six Day War'. Israel attacks and defeats Egypt, occupies all of Sinai. The Suez Canal is blocked.
1970	Nasser dies. Anwar Sadat becomes president.
1971	Egypt's official name becomes the Arab Republic of Egypt (ARE).
1973	October, Egyptian forces cross the Canal and drive back the Israeli army. Israeli forces continue to occupy the Gaza Strip and most of Sinai.
1975	Suez Canal reopened.
1977	Sadat visits Jerusalem in a dramatic peace bid.
1980	Egypt and Israel exchange ambassadors.
1981	6 October, Sadat assassinated. Hosni Mubarak becomes president.
1982	Israel evacuates Sinai.
1984	Egypt's first relatively free elections since 1952.
1991	Liberalization and privatization of the Egyptian economy.
1993	September, Israel and the Palestine Liberation Organization agree upon mutual recognition.
1995	After the assassination of Israeli prime minister Yitzak Rabin by a Jewish fundamentalist and the election of Binyamin Netanyahu's hard-right government, Israel drags its feet on negotiations with the Palestinians, provoking and some say manipulating Arab unrest.
1997	Not that true believers of any kind need an excuse for murdering people to achieve paradise on earth…in that holy cause Islamist terrorists had by the end of 1997 killed 100 foreign tourists in Egypt, including 58 at the Temple of Hatshepsut in Luxor in November 1997
2000	With tight security measures in force throughout the country, tourism to Egypt reaches record levels.

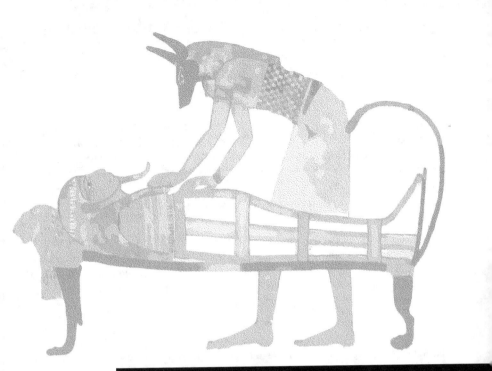

Egyptian Essays

The Egyptian Condition

About 10,000 years ago a dramatic change in climate caused the once fertile lands of northern Africa and the Middle East to turn to dust. Rock drawings in the Sahara depict ancient man hunting herbivores where now there is only sand. The inhabitants of this great belt of arid land migrated towards the few remaining rivers.

The Nile provided water and its annual flood covered the fields with rich alluvial soil. The ancient Egyptians called their country 'The Black Land', and the Nile valley and the Delta is still today the most fertile land in the world. Were it not for the existence of the Nile, no part of Egypt would be capable of agriculture. But it was not entirely a gift. The river had to be regulated, swamps drained, canals dug, fields planted and irrigated, the entire complex system maintained. To this task the fellahin gave their unremitting labour, and the state provided direction.

During the Ptolemaic period Egypt reached a level of prosperity and population that it was not to enjoy again until the 19th century when the dynasty of Mohammed Ali reversed the country's long decline under Arab and Turkish rule. In 1882 Egypt's population stood at just under seven million—equivalent to the number of Cleopatra's subjects. But since then, the ten-fold increase in population has worked against economic advance.

Though Egypt is larger than any European country except Russia, 93 per cent of its area is dry and barren desert where only a few oasis-dwellers and nomadic Bedouin can survive. In pharaonic times Egypt was likened to a lotus plant. The river was the stem, the Fayyum the bud, the Delta the flower. Within this figure of fertility today lives 95 per cent of the nation's population, its density one of the highest in the world.

Problems and Changes

Since the construction of the Aswan High Dam in the 1960s the Nile no longer floods. Instead the river flows evenly throughout the year, the harvests have multiplied, deserts have been brought to life. And Egypt gained the energy that would lead, it was hoped, to wholesale industrialization, releasing the fellahin from drudgery and the nation from poverty.

But as fast as the High Dam has helped bring new land under cultivation, other land has been swallowed by urban expansion. Fellahin seeking an improved existence have been abandoning their diminishing plots in the desperate hope of a better life in the cities, which now hold the majority of Egypt's population. In the 1970s Egypt was self-sufficient in food and even had a thriving export trade; now two-thirds of foodstuffs are imported.

Egypt's children are being born at the rate of one every 24 seconds. The population numbers well over 60 million and is increasing by a million every nine months. Though the birth rate has been falling, it has not been falling fast enough: only 30 per cent of married women practise birth control, and the earning potential of additional children is seen as a way of augmenting family income and providing for parents in old age. Meanwhile, the death rate has fallen even faster, a reflection of improved health services. The strain that the rising population puts on Egypt's food supplies, housing, jobs and services—indeed on its political stability—is a part of the country's problem.

Whatever Nasser's nationalist ideals, his socialist and centralizing policies added to the problem. Though the lands and wealth of pashas and foreigners were redistributed, the creation of new wealth was neglected. Industry and commerce were nationalized. Free education was given to all and every university graduate was guaranteed a government job by law. The result was a collapse in investment and a bloated, inefficient bureaucracy. The wait for a guaranteed job rose to six years, and the proportion of the population in employment fell. The standard of teaching is now so low that in some places free education is not worth having. There is a grave housing crisis, illustrated by those three million Cairenes who live in the city's necropolises among the dead.

A quarter of a million foreigners, most of them highly skilled and their families resident in Egypt for generations, were forced to leave the country during the 1950s and 60s. In recent years three million Egyptians have followed in their footsteps, seeking opportunities in the Gulf and the West. Before King Farouk was deposed in 1952, the 2,000 richest people owned as much land as the 1½ million poorest fellahin. Now the fellahin are deserting the land if they can, and if they can find a factory job they will earn in a lifetime only as much as Egypt's top 100,000 people spend on a luxury car.

Agriculture remains the basis of the Egyptian economy, and its main crops are cotton, sugar cane, maize, rice and wheat, while the raising of cattle and poultry is increasing. But the country's main foreign currency earners are oil, Suez Canal fees, remittances from Egyptians working abroad and tourism—and all these are peculiarly sensitive to political conditions in the Middle East. Of crucial importance are World Bank, International Monetary Fund and foreign government (principally United States) loans, on the repayments of which Egypt routinely defaults. Then there is foreign aid; for example Egypt is the second largest recipient of United States foreign aid (Egypt gets 19 per cent, Israel 21 per cent).

In the past few years, under pressure from foreign lenders, Egypt has abandoned nearly all subsidies and has privatized almost all industries and commercial organizations. The result has been a promising boom in economic growth. Nevertheless, the transition from traditional or state-guaranteed employment to a modern market economy has been a source of social anxiety, reflected in a growing conservatism, often expressed in religious terms.

Tourism and Security

The early 1990s saw an outbreak of Islamic fundamentalist terrorism in Egypt, conducted principally by El-Gamaa El-Islamiya (Islamic Group) which targeted government ministers, the security forces, Copts and intellectuals, including Naguib Mahfouz, winner of the Nobel Prize for Literature, who was stabbed and wounded by members of the group in 1994.

Their aim was to overthrow the Mubarak regime with its policy of peace in the Middle East and its openness to the West, its adherence to a measure of secularization and its attempts at economic liberalization, and instead to replace it with a theocratic state. Tourism could easily be identified with everything El-Gamaa El-Islamiya opposed; nor is tourism merely symbolic: four million tourists a year bring in two billion dollars in foreign exchange which directly or indirectly supports a fifth of the Egyptian population. What is more, it is very easy to turn off the flow: dead tourists make headlines around the world.

So the group turned its sights on foreign tourists, murdering about a hundred in all, mostly in three incidents during 1996–7: one taking place outside a Cairo hotel where the victims, eighteen Greeks, had been mistaken for Israelis; another outside the Egyptian Museum, where the nine victims were all Germans; and the worst in November 1997 at the Temple of Hatshepsut across the river from Luxor, where of the fifty-eight dead, thirty-six were Swiss, nine were Japanese, six British, four German, and the remaining three a Bulgarian, a Colombian and a Frenchman. Two policemen and two temple guards were also killed, as were all six of the El-Gamaa El-Islamiya terrorists who carried out the attack.

Already in the mid-1990s the Egyptian authorities had cracked down hard on terrorism and believed they had rounded up the entire leadership of El-Gamaa El-Ismaliya, but the perpetrators of the Luxor massacre were members of a newly-recruited splinter group. Their leader was the 32-year-old Medhat Abderrahman, who liked to call himself 'Moustache Samy'. He had committed a dozen violent attacks against Copts and the local police around his native Assiut during 1992–3, for which he served a brief prison term before joining the American-funded Afghan jihad against the occupying Russians.

The other members were unknown to the police and hardly seemed to fit the terrorist image. All were middle-class students at the Islamic University of Assiut, who ranged in age from 18 to 24 and were variously studying for degrees in agriculture, medicine and veterinary medicine. But Assiut, midway along the Nile between Cairo and Luxor, is a city bubbling with frustration. Important enough to be difficult to leave but lacking the horizons to make staying worthwhile, its lack of antique sites has contributed to its problems, for without tourism Assiut is excluded from one of the most dynamic sectors of the Egyptian economy.

Abderrahman re-entered Egypt secretly and returned to Assiut, where his simplistic certainties, bound up with the aura of the Afghan jihad, quickly won him his five recruits. It is a mystery to their parents why that should have been so, but many point to a sense of hopelessness and emptiness among Egyptian youth, who may show ambition, be very intelligent, achieve success in their studies and feel that they have earned the right to a good job, only to realize how limited their prospects are. Even so, it takes an unfathomable twist of mind to put sixty-two corpses, as well as your own, on your CV.

Egyptians were shocked and shamed by the Luxor killings and gave immediate and public expression of their apologies and condolences, as when government officials, members of parliament, actors, writers and celebrities of all kinds walked through the streets of Cairo, calling at the embassies of the dead, and again gathered at the Temple of Hatshepsut in remembrance of the massacre victims and to denounce those responsible for the murders.

All the same, Egypt could not escape the consequences. Tourist numbers immediately fell and took two years to recover, and meanwhile the people of Luxor especially suffered. But one Englishwoman who was there at the time simply refused to leave: to do so, she said, would 'double the misery this tragedy has caused the Egyptians we have met'. Not everyone plays into the hands of the terrorists.

For their part, the Egyptians are determined to reassure you and if possible to stop it from ever happening again, and this accounts for the security measures you encounter up and down the country. When travelling around Egypt these days, you may find your freedom of movement restricted, not within Cairo, Luxor or Aswan, but if attempting to wander in between. At Luxor, roadblocks have been set up on all incoming routes, while in theory foreigners are only meant to travel outside the town in armed police convoys that leave at regular hours from the corniche. This can make it a nuisance to visit Dendera and Abydos to the north of Luxor, or Esna, Edfu and Kom Ombo on the way to Aswan in the south. Nile cruises have been suspended between Cairo and Luxor, but with the precaution of a machine gun mounted on the stern they continue to operate between Luxor and Aswan, while when sailing on Lake Nasser you will find yourself accompanied ashore by men with black and shiny hardware.

It is all rather embarrassing, not to mention inconvenient. But fortunately you often find that you can hop on a bus and go wherever you like; only at Abydos does the armed presence become really intrusive, while northwards from there to Cairo you may not be permitted to travel by road at all.

Islam

The principal belief of Islam is the existence of one God, the same God worshipped by Christians and Jews, whom the Muslims call Allah. *Islam* means submission. *Muslim* means one who submits to monotheism as interpreted by the religion's founder, Mohammed (AD 570–632).

Muslims must hold six beliefs: that Allah exists, is unique and is omnipotent; that the Angels of Allah are his perfect servants, and intercede for man and are his guardians; that there is only one true religion and the Koran is the only tangible word of Allah; that there have been many prophets of Allah, among them Ibrahim (Abraham), Nuh (Noah), Musa (Moses), Isa (Jesus) and Mohammed who was the last, his message uncorrupted; that everyone will live in eternity and will be judged; and that whatever has been or will come has been predestined by Divine Will—and that it is forbidden to question or investigate this point.

There are five practical devotions, the five Pillars of Faith, that all Muslims must perform: pronounce publicly that 'I bear witness that there is no god but Allah and Mohammed is His Prophet'; pray at five specific times of day (noon, afternoon, sunset, night and daybreak); pay a tithe, which is dispersed to the poor, to needy debtors, for the ransom of captives, to travellers, and for the defence of Islam; fast during the month of Ramadan; and at least once in a lifetime make a pilgrimage to Mecca.

In addition, Islam is based on laws found in the Koran, in the Sunna (the actions of the Prophet), decided by the unanimous agreement of Muslim scholars (Ijma), and arrived at by reasoned analogy (Qiyas)—in order of descending authority.

Mohammed was a merchant in Arabia. He often contemplated in the desert and at the age of 40 had a vision of the Angel Gabriel who commanded him to proclaim monotheism to the pagan Arabian tribes. In Arabic, 'to proclaim' is *Qur'an*, and so the Koran is the word of Allah as given to Mohammed. The merchants of Mecca, concerned by the unsettling effects of this new religion, drove Mohammed out of the city in 622. His flight (the *hegira*, though literally this means 'withdrawal of affection') from Mecca to Medina, where Islam first took root, is the event from which the Islamic calendar begins.

The Arab conquest of Egypt in AD 640–2 introduced Islam to the country, though until the 14th century the majority of the population remained Christian. Today nearly 90 per cent of the Egyptian population is Muslim, adherents of the Sunni sect.

The Copts

About 95 per cent of Christian Egyptians are Coptic Orthodox, and these represent about ten per cent of the Egyptian population as a whole.

Copt comes from the Greek word for Egypt, *Aigyptos*, and those who remain Copts today, having never intermarried with later peoples, can lay claim to being the pure successors of the ancient Egyptians. But it is also true that 90 per cent of Muslim Egyptians were once Copts, making it impossible to distinguish any physical difference between the two, though some Egyptians will say Copts have higher cheekbones or almond-shaped eyes.

Copts may choose to distinguish themselves by wearing a cross around their necks, for example. Some have a cross tattooed on the inside of the right wrist—to ward off evil spirits or, in the past, to commit them to their faith during persecution. One possible identifier is choice of name: for example, George (Girgis), Antony (Antunius) and Ramses; though Gamal, Nasser and Anwar could be either Coptic or Muslim. For both groups the mother tongue is Arabic. In fact the difference between Coptic and Muslim Egyptians is neither ethnic nor cultural, except that the Copts adhere to the old religion.

That Christianity was introduced to Egypt by St Mark is entirely legendary. Nevertheless it almost certainly was introduced during the 1st century AD and came from Jerusalem, appearing first among the Jewish population of Alexandria and then spreading among the Greeks of both the city and the country.

There is evidence that at the beginning of the 3rd century Christianity had taken root among native Egyptians, and by AD 300 most of the Bible had been translated from Greek into Coptic (antedating the translation of the Bible into Latin by a century). With the end of the Roman persecutions early in the 4th century there was a sudden flowering of Christianity which, as a walk through the Coptic Museum in Cairo shows, was expressed in a vigorous folk art. Expressed in the form of monasticism, Egyptian Christianity also made a deeply spiritual impact on the wider world.

But political and theological disputes between Alexandria and Constantinople facilitated the Arab conquest of Egypt during 640–2. The Copts, that is the Egyptian people, several times rose in revolt during the 8th and 9th centuries. Though some converted to Islam, the majority of Egyptians remained Christians until the 14th century, when the Crusader threat and Mameluke misrule combined with the accelerating impoverishment of the country, turned sultans and mobs alike against the Copts, who suffered massacre, the widespread destruction of their churches and the loss of official positions. Under such conditions there was little opportunity to develop Christian thought; instead, the need was for unquestioning faith and social solidarity, even as the Copts slowly accepted a new culture.

As Arab civilization from Baghdad to Cordoba achieved its apogee in the 9th, 10th and 11th centuries, men of talent and ambition gravitated in its direction. Coptic artists began to serve the tastes of their Muslim patrons, and Arabic became the language of administration and learning. At some time between the 11th and 13th centuries the Coptic language, repository of the demotic tongue of pharaonic times, ceased to be spoken; it survives now only in church liturgy.

Egypt's contact with European influences in the 19th century improved the condition of the Copts, who went on to play an important role in and to benefit from the growing secular nationalist movement. Over the same period the Coptic Church has gradually reformed itself, initially to meet the challenge of foreign missionaries. Under the last two popes especially, Kirollos VI and Shenouda III, the Church has experienced a renaissance, attracting highly educated young men into the monasteries and the hierarchy, and reaching out into the community with schools and welfare programmes.

Today, Copts officially enjoy all civil, political and religious rights and occupy high posts in government, the military and in business. Boutros Ghali, recently Secretary General of the United Nations and formerly Egyptian foreign minister and deputy prime minister, is a Copt (and his wife, incidentally, is Jewish).

Both Copts and Muslims are proud to call themselves Egyptians, and have fought shoulder to shoulder against the Crusaders and more recent opponents. Yet the gulf between the Copts and the Western churches has often seemed unbridgeable. The West has incorrectly called the Copts monophysites and from the Council of Chalcedon in 451 to nearly this day has dismissed the Coptic Church as heretical.

It is not unusual when walking around Cairo or elsewhere in Egypt to come upon Christian celebrations, the streets festooned with decorations and lights, pictures and icons of Christ and Mary and the various saints. If you are in Egypt for the Coptic Christmas (7 January) or the Coptic Easter (moveable), it is worthwhile visiting a Coptic church for midnight mass (arrive no later than 11pm) on the eve.

The Invisible Pharaoh

There is a pharaoh whose name is mentioned frequently throughout this book, but except at the Cairo and the Luxor museums you will encounter no direct evidence of his existence: no statue, no inscription, no tomb, no mummy—after his death his memory was obliterated. Even his colossal statues in Cairo's Egyptian Museum came to light only in the 1930s, when Egyptologists found them buried near Karnak, close by the great temple of Amun.

The name of this invisible pharaoh was Amenophis IV, but he is better known as Akhenaton—his change of name explaining why his successors treated him as though he had never been born. The all-powerful god of the New Kingdom was Amun (also transliterated as Amen), and frequently pharaohs incorporated his name in theirs: Amenophis, Tutankhamun, Ramses II in his full nomen, Ramses-Miamun, and Ramses III, whose praenomen was User-Maat-Re-Meramun. In changing his name to Akhenaton and turning his back on Thebes for his new capital of Akhetaton (at Amarna, about 300km to the north), the former Amenophis IV was rejecting Amun and his priesthood (*see* p.206) in favour of Aton.

Aton was the sun's disc, the life force, indeed nothing less than an attempt at a complete remaking of the Egyptian spirit. To understand that, you must look back to the Old Kingdom, the beauty of whose art and architecture lay in its restraint, in its simplicity and its confident mastery of form. There was a moment of discovery, of harmonization and integrity, and if the First Intermediate Period had marked the termination of pharaonic civilization we might now more eagerly respond to what had been lost. But the centuries rolled on and too often carried with them only the embalmed culture of the past, integrity reduced to repetition, mastery to facility, the spirit salved with interminable formulae, authority justified and reassured with bombast. Even when using the old forms, there were brilliant exceptions, but the general impression of tedium can weigh heavily on the traveller. The breathtaking impact, then, of the Amarna period, is all the more powerful, the sense of something wonderful, tragic and lost all the more acute.

At Amarna (the present-day name for the site of Akhetaton) the tomb decorations do not concern themselves with the afterlife: the Judgement of Osiris, for example, is absent, while instead there are vivid scenes of the everyday. Also found there is the *Hymn to the Sun*, thought to have been written by Akhenaton himself, which conveys in remarkable detail and variety the cumulative incidents that give wonder to life. Convention, myth and abstraction are dispensed with, replaced by the sensate reality of Aton which creates, embraces and expresses existence.

> *At dawn you rise shining in the horizon, you shine Aton in the sky and drive away darkness by sending forth your rays. The Two Lands awake in festivity, and men stand on their feet, for you have raised them up. They wash their bodies, they take their garments, and their arms are raised to praise your rising. The whole world does its work.*
>
> *The cattle are content in their pasture, the trees and plants are green, the birds fly from their nests. Their wings are raised in praise of your soul. The goats leap on their feet. All flying and fluttering things live when you shine for them. Likewise the boats race up and down the river, and every way is open, because you have appeared. The fish in the river leap before your face. Your rays go to the depths of the sea.*
>
> *You set the germ in women and make seed in men. You maintain the son in the womb of the mother and soothe him so that he does not weep, you nurse in the womb. You give the breath of life to all you have created. When the child comes forth from the womb on the day of his birth, you open his mouth and you supply his needs. The chick in the egg can be heard in the shell, for you give him breath inside it so that he may live. You have given him in the egg the power to break it. He comes out of the egg to chirp as loudly as he can; and when he comes out, he walks on his feet.*

For a moment, Egypt was offered spiritual and philosophical renewal. Akhenaton broke with a past whose search for stasis was leading to sterility. The sun and soul were recovered from their long dark voyage through the underworld and set in brilliant transit across the horizons of this life. Whether it was monotheism, as some say, is uncertain and probably irrelevant; the universe was alive again.

But there is also the question of whether Atonism was ever anything more than a royal cult. Akhenaton's hymn, phrased in demotic, suggests that his intention was to place his revelation before all mankind. Yet, when he died, his religion was soon suppressed and, what is more, all mention of the heretic pharaoh was proscribed from the king lists, and he went unknown until the nineteenth century of our era. Can it have been just a political reaction? Dynastic infighting led Tuthmosis III to erase all images and cartouches of Hatshepsut, but her memory remained. It seems as if Akhenaton offered something far more than a political threat—and more than the military and administrative failures he has been accused of. Possibly Egypt had so far lost its faith in life that it could accept no substitute for its long investment in death.

With Akhenaton's death the counter-revolution quickly set in. Nefertiti, his exquisite wife, continued to live at Amarna, but her stay there became an exile. Tutankhamun, whose name had been Tutankhaton, and who may have been Akhenaton's son by a secondary wife, returned or was brought back to Thebes and to the authority of the priesthood of Amun. There are traces of the Amarna style of art in his tomb and a suggestion of it too, though straitjacketed and reduced to mannerism, in the works of Ramses II. You see it especially in the fluid beauty accorded the female form, a touch of Nefertiti's Florentine elegance in those portraits of Nefertari, Ramses' queen, on the tomb walls in the Valley of the Queens at Thebes and inside the Temple of Hathor at Abu Simbel.

But it was Ramses II and his father Seti I who most emphatically restored Amun to his supremacy in the Egyptian pantheon, as the former in particular never lets you forget on his wall reliefs and inscriptions. Akhenaton had vowed never to leave Amarna, not in his life nor after his death, but his body has not been found. The Great Temple of Aton at Amarna, however, was deliberately desecrated and destroyed after his death and its foundations quarried by Ramses II. Perhaps he was the last to see Akhenaton's body before consigning it to the flames.

Grand Hotels

One of the glories of Egypt was its grand hotels, cavernous places with louvred doors and mosquito nets over the beds, offering an atmosphere of worn elegance. Too many of these have disappeared, replaced by modern nondescript hotels. Where grand hotels survive they have lost much of their old Egyptian charm, but they are worth knowing about all the same.

Only one has survived in its full decrepitude, the Windsor in Cairo, where the atmosphere is literally peeling off the walls. The lift is more like one of those medieval iron cages in which bodies were hung from a gibbet to rot, and the most modern thing in the place is a calendar advertising BOAC. With an eye for a time-warp, Michael Palin stayed here while making his own attempt at travelling *Around the World in 80 Days* (alas, his visit has spurred the Windsor to tart itself up a bit). British publishers, known for their parsimony and taste, also take rooms here. They and other peculiar people gather in the comfortable old bar-cum-lounge, one of the friendliest in town.

In truth, the Windsor was never grand, rather solidly serviceable like a British railway station hotel, but it has bearing. In the 1920s Baedeker ranked it just after Shepheard's Hotel, which was burnt down during nationalist riots in 1952. The present-day Shepheard's carries the name but none of the character of the original.

But the Mena House, out by the Pyramids, has an authentic pedigree, built by the Khedive Ismail as a hunting lodge, then put into service as a rest house for the Empress Eugénie, wife of Napoleon III, when she came to Egypt to open the Suez Canal. Since then it has been a hotel, though only the wing directly facing the Pyramids is original. This is now taken up with 'honeymoon suites', where during nuptial interludes you can step out onto your balcony and ogle at more ancient wonders.

Churchill's meeting with Roosevelt at the Mena House late in 1943 to plan the D-Day landings at Normandy the following year is well known. Less celebrated is the time when King Farouk picked Churchill's pocket. It was August 1942, between the first and second battles of Alamein, and an anxious Churchill had come to give the campaign some zip by replacing General Auchinleck with General Montgomery. Farouk invited the British prime minister to the Mena House for dinner. While sitting next to one another, Churchill discovered that his pocket watch, a gift from Queen Anne to his ancestor the Duke of Marlborough for winning the Battle of Blenheim, was missing. It must have seemed an ill omen, but after much searching, Farouk 'found' it; he had, in fact, been taking pickpocketing lessons from a master thief.

In Luxor, avoiding the soulless block of the New Winter Palace that has been tacked alongside, you should book into a Nile-facing room at the Old Winter Palace, preferably making sure that you have a balcony on which to breakfast or enjoy an evening drink. Built in 1886, care was taken with the restorations in 1993 not to spoil its atmosphere or its architectural details. A carriage drive sweeps up to the main entrance through which you enter a voluminous lobby from which ascends a grand staircase with art nouveau balusters. Curling up past towering windows through which you can already see the palms which fill the garden beyond, it is a staircase that invites an easy pace and elegance.

In the old days, the hotel closed for the summer; winter was the season, 'its portico heavily embowered with verdure, its terrace overhung by palms', as Olivia Manning described it during the war years in *The Levant Trilogy*. Now it is open throughout the year, and though you can still sit out front drinking tea, in summer you can pass through the garden filled with birds and monkeys and sit half immersed around a bar that rises like an island from the swimming pool.

The finest of all hotels in Egypt is the Old Cataract at Aswan, mounted upon a granite outcrop opposite the southern tip of Elephantine Island. At the hotel's official opening in 1902, the Daily Telegraph described its dining room as 'unmatched even in Europe'. Beautifully restored, the splendour of the Old Cataract makes it one of the chief sights of Aswan. Nor is there a more magical place than its terrrace from which to fascinate yourself with the movement of feluccas and the shifting of colours on the Nile.

Cairo

What one can imagine always surpasses what one sees, because of the scope of the imagination, except Cairo, because it surpasses anything one can imagine.

Ibn Khaldun, 14th century

From the air Cairo is a city of circles and radiating avenues at the head of the Nile Delta, its buildings dull brown as though camouflaged to blend with the impinging desert. The colour is of the local stone, but is also the result of the sandstorms that sometimes dust the city. At sundown you can see a thin layer of sand clinging to the dome of the Mohammed Ali Mosque atop the Citadel, and as you walk along the cracked pavements the desert wells up from below.

Like a great lung the Nile breathes through the city, but away from the broad slow-flowing river Westernized Cairo can have a heavy, airless feeling, an architectural jumble of fake pharaonic, blocklike modern, unnoticed Art Deco and ponderous Victorian. Yet further east against the Moqattam Hills minarets like tall blades of grass rise against the sky, marking the old medieval city of hidden beauty and palpitating energy which lends all Cairo its excitement.

In spirit Cairo remains as it began, an Arab encampment on the edge of the desert: hot, dry, the smell of dung, glowing coals and musk, lively with throngs of people. To this sprawling caravanserai come visitors from all over the Arab, African and Asian world, fantastically varied in colour, dress, characteristics, yet easily talking, mingling, bargaining like distant villagers meeting again in their market town.

For Cairo is the largest city in Africa and the political and cultural fulcrum of the Arab world. The treasures of three great civilizations await you at the Islamic, Coptic and Egyptian Antiquities museums, while you can immerse your senses at Khan el Khalili, a vast bazaar as intricate as inlay work, sharp with spices, sweet with perfumes and dazzling with brass and gold and silver. You can ride in the desert, sail on the Nile, enjoy belly dancing or opera, smoke a hubbly-bubbly at a street corner café, and feed yourself on every cuisine from traditional to nouvelle.

The population of the metropolis is about 18 million, a six-fold increase over the past 30 or so years. It owes its staggering growth to Egypt's exploding birthrate, pressure on the land, and the fellahin's desire to transform their lives in a city which, for all its seeming desperation, still offers at least the hope of opportunity. At rush hours Cairo threatens to burst or collapse with the pressure of Cairenes squeezing themselves into buses and noisily jamming the roads with cars.

But as the sun sets over the Nile the present slips away into timelessness: from a high window over the river you can hear the call of the muezzins float across the darkening city and see the Pyramids at Giza glow gold against the Western Desert as they have done for one million, seven hundred thousand evenings past. The monuments of pharaohs and sultans lie within your compass, making Cairo and its environs one of the greatest storehouses of human achievement in the world.

Cairo and the Pyramids

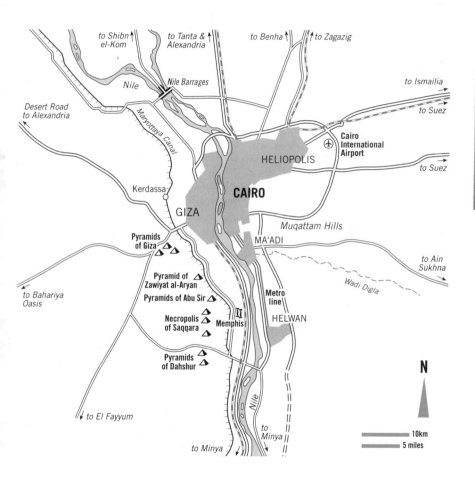

History

Orientation about the city is helped by a knowledge of its history, and its history, as with so much else in Egypt, is linked to the Nile. (*See* map on inside front cover.)

Antiquity

During the Old Kingdom the political capital of Egypt was at **Memphis**, which was 20km to the south of present-day Cairo, so that it stood between the Delta to the north and the valley of the Nile to the south, thereby controlling the whole of the country. In this strategic sense Cairo, though founded 4,000 years later, is heir to Memphis.

Ancient **Heliopolis**, the city of the sun god, whose scant ruins are near the modern suburb of that name in northeast Cairo en route to the airport, was once the religious centre of Egypt. Travellers between Heliopolis and Memphis would have taken a ferry from the east bank of the Nile where Old Cairo stands today, opposite the southern tip of the island of Roda. In pharaonic times a settlement, perhaps even a town, sprang up on the spot. The Greeks were later to call this **Babylon in Egypt**, probably a corruption of Roda's ancient name of Per-Hapi-en-Yun, House of the Nile of Heliopolis. The settlement's role was that of fortress rather than administrative centre, and Babylon never amounted to much. In the last centuries before Christ, Egypt was ruled by Alexander's successors, the Ptolemies, from their Mediterranean capital, Alexandria.

The Arab Conquest

It was the Arabs, for whom the desert and not the sea provided familiar lines of communication, who developed the logic of the site. In AD 641, Amr arrived in Egypt at the head of a small army and both Alexandria and Babylon opened their gates to him. Amr was enchanted with Alexandria and wrote back to the caliph at Medina that this should be the Muslim capital of the conquered country, but Omar, referring to Alexandria's position on the far side of the Nile Delta, replied, 'Will there be water between me and the Muslim army?' Amr returned to Babylon where only sand separated him from Arabia; the tent (*fustat*) he had pitched there before marching on Alexandria was still standing and a dove had nested in it with her young. On this spot Amr built his mosque, the first in Egypt, and **Fustat**, the City of the Tent, grew up.

Fustat was the first of several planned developments which over the centuries contributed to the growth of the medieval city. The Nile in those days lay further to the east, along what is now Sharia el Gumhuriya which runs up into Midan Ramses, where the railway station is. All of what is now modern Cairo then lay on the west bank of the river, if not beneath it. An ancient canal that once joined the Nile with the Red Sea lay still further to the east, along the line of Sharia Bur Said (Port Said), built when the canal, called the Khalig by the Arabs, was filled in during the 19th century. So the city developed along the narrow corridor of land between the canal to the west and the Moqattam Hills to the east, and extended northwards as successive rulers were intent on catching the cool summer breezes blowing in from the Mediterranean.

When Ibn Tulun, Abbasid governor of Egypt, made himself virtually independent of the Baghdad caliph in AD 870, he built his palace, government buildings, a hippodrome and the famous mosque bearing his name to the north of Fustat. The **mosque of Ibn Tulun** apart, little survives of his city, and still less of Fustat. The heart of what grew into the Cairo of today was established by the Fatimids.

Cairo Founded by the Fatimids

On 5 August AD 969, with Mars in the ascendant, the first stone of the Fatimid capital was laid to the north of the Tulunid city. The city took its name, al-Qahira, the Triumphant, from the warrior planet. Our name for the city, Cairo, derives from this al-Qahira found on maps, though as often as not Egyptians call it **Misr**. Of vague and haunting meaning, far antedating Islam, Misr is emotionally the more important name of the two and refers to both city and the country as a whole. An Egyptian abroad who says 'I am going to Misr' means he is returning to Egypt. If he says the same thing in Luxor, he means he is returning to Cairo. In either case, 'going to Misr' carries the sense of going home. For the fellahin, Cairo is *Misr um al-dunya*: Misr, Mother of the World.

The Fatimids, of the persistent though minority Shi'ite sect of Islam, invaded Egypt from Tunisia where their caliphate declared its legitimacy through descent from Ali, husband of the Prophet's daughter Fatima. They imposed their Shi'ite doctrines (those same followed today in Iran) on Egypt which, apart from the Fatimid interlude, has kept within the orthodox Sunni fold. The al-Azhar Mosque, though now Sunni, dates from this period and is still the centre of Koranic studies for the whole Muslim world.

The Medieval City

This walled city (*see* map on p.83), centred on the popular market area known as **Khan el Khalili** and extending from the gate known as Bab Zuwayla in the south to Bab al-Futuh in the north, remains astonishingly intact both in structure and in atmosphere, the medieval city *nonpareil* in all the world. Its walls and area were extended by Saladin, a Kurdish general in the service of the Abbasid caliph in Baghdad. Foreign failures and the failure of the Nile itself led to the weakening of the Fatimid dynasty which trembled in confusion before the onslaught of the First Crusade. In triumphing over the armies of the West, Saladin established his own empire in Egypt and Syria and his own Ayyubid dynasty which ruled from 1171 to 1250. Orthodoxy was re-established and the **Citadel** begun, the redoubt of power and the centre of government throughout the troubled centuries of Mameluke and Ottoman rule.

Saladin's Ayyubid successors, however, relied increasingly on their slave militia, the **Bahri Mamelukes**. (*Mameluke* means white slave, while *bahri* means riverine and refers to their barracks on the island of Roda; these were mostly Turks and Mongols. The later **Burgi Mamelukes**, mostly Circassian, were quartered in the Citadel, hence *burg*.) The Mamelukes soon became an indispensable elite and successive sultans rose from their number, legitimizing their authority more by the blood on their hands than the blood in their veins. The Mamelukes ruled Egypt until the Ottoman domination in 1517. In spite of the violent and repressive character of Mameluke rule, they enriched the city with their architecture, their most outstanding monuments being the **mosque of Sultan Hassan** and the **mausoleum of Qaytbey.**

Around 1300 the island of **Gezira** was formed as the Nile shifted westwards but the city remained largely within its old boundaries throughout the **Ottoman period**, its architecture following traditional styles with only a few baroque exceptions inspired by the mosques of Istanbul. As a province of the Ottoman Empire, Egypt was ruled by a Turkish governor housed in the Citadel who delegated most of his authority. Though no longer providing sultans, the Mamelukes perpetuated their slave aristocracy by levees of Christian youths from the Caucasus. But their power now was chaotic and rapacious. What the Turks did not take, the Mamelukes did, and Cairo was further impoverished when Western merchants discovered how to bypass the troublous region altogether by sailing around the southern cape of Africa to India and the Far East. Egypt suffered from famine and disease, its population falling to two million compared to eight million in Roman times.

The Westernization of Cairo

The brief French occupation of Egypt, from 1798 to 1801, had a profound effect on Cairo. **Napoleon** stayed in what was then a country district, on the site where the old Shepheard's Hotel was later built, overlooking the Ezbekieh lake, subsequently the Ezbekieh Gardens, now ruined by having a main street cut through the middle and a flyover amputate one side. Along with reorganizing the government, introducing the first printing press, launching a balloon and installing windmills on the Moqattam Hills, Napoleon also planned Parisian boulevards.

When **Mohammed Ali** finally massacred the Mamelukes in 1811, founding a dynasty which ended only with the abdication of Farouk in 1952 and the proclamation of a republic the next year, he continued with the Westernization of Cairo which saw the canal filled in and the great swaths of **Sharia el Muski** and **Sharia el Qalaa** (formerly Sharia Mohammed Ali) mow down long rows of the medieval city. Fortunately, however, most of the modernization of Cairo took place on the virgin land that the Nile provided when it settled in its present bed.

Highlights of Cairo

For those with very limited time in Cairo, you should make an effort to visit the **Egyptian Antiquities Museum** and the **Coptic** and **Islamic museums**. But you should also see some of the great Islamic monuments of the city. The two outstanding **mosques** are those of Sultan Hassan and Ibn Tulun, which can both be combined with a visit of the **Citadel**. Going to the famous bazaar of **Khan el Khalili** brings you to the heart of medieval Cairo, from where it can be especially evocative to walk south along **Sharia Muizz** to Bab Zuwayla, and north along the same street at least as far as Bayt al-Suhaymi, the finest old house in the city.

By Air

Cairo Airport (**Matar al-Qahira**), 20km northeast of the city, has two terminals 3km apart. Terminal 1, the old terminal, handles Egyptair and other Egyptian airlines, as well as El Al and most Arab, Middle Eastern, African and East European airlines. Terminal 2, the new terminal, handles American and Western European airlines. A free shuttle bus runs between the two terminals.

The 356 **bus** runs between the airport (stopping at both terminals) and Midan Abdel Moneim Riad behind the Egyptian Museum in the centre of Cairo. The service operates every 20mins between 5.45am and 11pm and costs LE2 plus LE1 for each large item of luggage. You will find the bus stand in the car park opposite each of the terminals. The buses themselves are easy enough to spot when they come along: they are large, white and modern, and also air-conditioned.

Also there is the 400 **city bus** which costs 25pt and the 27 **minibus** costing 50pt. These also stop at the car parks and operate half-hourly, less frequently at night. Like the 356, both go to Midan Abdel Moneim Riad behind the Egyptian Museum.

For speed, comfort and convenience, take a limousine or taxi. **Taxi** drivers will be lurking in the background somewhere and it is usually possible to get a better price out of them; but you will first be presented with a rank of **limousines** (Mercedes and Volvos in fact) whose drivers will demand at least LE50 to anywhere in town, more to hotels out by the Pyramids. Though you can find out at the limo desk inside the arrival halls what the correct price should be, you will still have to bargain. Depending on your bargaining skills you should end up paying LE25–35 for a limousine, less for a taxi (Egyptians will pay about half).

Airline Offices

Most airline offices are either on Midan el Tahrir or downtown, with some in Zamalek:

Air France	2 Midan Talaat Harb, downtown, ✆ 2758899.
British Airways	1 Sharia al-Bustan, on the corner of Midan el Tahrir, ✆ 5780743.
Egyptair	Nile Hilton, Midan el Tahrir, ✆ 5765200; 9 Sharia Talaat Harb, downtown, ✆ 3932836.
KLM	11 Sharia Qasr el Nil, downtown, ✆ 5747004.
Lufthansa	6 Sharia al-Sheikh al-Marsafi, Zamalek, ✆ 3420471.
Olympic	23 Sharia Qasr el Nil, downtown, ✆ 3931459.
Swissair	22 Sharia Qasr el Nil, downtown, ✆ 3921522.
TWA	1 Sharia Qasr el Nil, on the corner of Midan el Tahrir, ✆ 5749904/5/6/7/8.

Cairo's main train station is Ramses Station (**Mahattat Ramses**) at Midan Ramses (Ramses Square). All trains for Luxor and Aswan depart from here, as well as most trains for other destinations in Egypt. The station is about 2km north of Midan el Tahrir and plenty of taxis are always available; there is also a **metro** station here (Mubarak) from which you can get to Midan el Tahrir (Sadat). First-class bookings should be made at least a day in advance.

Negotiating Ramses Station is simple. Entering from Midan Ramses, you will see platforms 1–7 for trains to Alexandria, the Delta and the Canal cities on your right; platforms 8–11 for trains to Upper Egypt (e.g. Luxor and Aswan) are straight on, beyond the main concourse. There is a round information booth on the far side of the main concourse where helpful English-speaking staff can direct you to your platform, tell you where to buy tickets, etc.

Buying **tickets** might require some patience. First you must go to the right place. On the left as you enter the station from Midan Ramses are the tourist information office, the tourist police and the ticket offices for Wagons-lits and sleeper services. Straight on across the concourse are the ticket counters for trains to Alexandria, the Delta and the Canal cities. The ticket office for non-sleeper or non-Wagons-lits trains to Upper Egypt is beyond platform 11. You may find that some windows will only sell tickets for reserved first- and second-class air-conditioned services (which can be booked up to a week in advance), others only for second- and third-class non-air-conditioned services, so ask first.

When buying **Wagons-lits** tickets bring the passports of all those travelling; the tickets can also be bought, and with greater ease, at their office in the Helnan Shepheard's Hotel, *open 8.30–4*. There is a good Wagons-lits **café** to your right as you enter the station from Midan Ramses.

It is wise to buy your ticket for reserved services (Wagons-lits, sleepers, air-conditioned first and second class) to whatever destination a day in advance. At busy times of year, and for Wagons-lits and sleeper services especially, you should buy your tickets at the earliest possible moment, if possible at least a week in advance.

Students with an ISIC are granted a discount of 30–50% on all services except sleepers and Wagons-lits.

By Long-distance Service Taxi

Long-distance service taxis have their different termini according to destination. Most departure points are near Ramses Station—ask and you will find. However, under the current security situation, taking a service taxi to Upper Egypt will probably not be practical.

By Long-distance Bus

Long-distance bus services are operated by various companies, and also depart from various termini according to destination. The **Upper Egyptian Bus Company** operates several services a day to Luxor and Aswan from the Ahmed Helmi terminal across the tracks (north) from Ramses Station. Book a day or preferably two in advance. You have to do this at the terminal, where you can also get up-to-date departure times.

Nile Cruises

The time-honoured way of making a progress through Egypt is to cruise along the Nile. Though for the time being there are no full-Nile voyages between Cairo and Upper Egypt, there are sailings between Luxor and Aswan, many of them taking in Dendera and Abydos too, and usually lasting four days and five nights. Several international **hotel chains** offer cruises, e.g. Oberoi (the best), Mövenpick, Hilton and Sheraton—bookings can be made at their hotels in Egypt or abroad. There are also many **local operators**, good and generally less expensive, with whom bookings can be made through travel agents abroad or by contacting them directly in Cairo. Try:

Jolley's Travel and Tours, 8 Sharia Talat Harb, ✆ 5794619.

Seti First Travel, 16 Sharia Ismail Mohammed, Zamalek, ✆ 3419820, ✉ 3402419.

Orientation

See map on inside front cover.

South from Midan el Tahrir

What now passes for the centre of town—for foreigners, anyway—is **Midan el Tahrir**, or Liberation Square, on the east bank of the Nile. The square is bounded by the **Egyptian Museum** to the north and the **Nile Hilton** to the west, and has a new **metro station** beneath. Hot, noisy, characterless and thick with exhaust fumes from traffic jams, Midan el Tahrir is among the more recent schemes to bring Cairo up to date. It was created after the 1952 revolution on the site of a British barracks, the Qasr el Nil, and at the same time powers of compulsory purchase were used to cut the Corniche el Nil through the many embassy and villa gardens to the south, the new roadway extending down to Maadi and Helwan.

Immediately to the south of Midan el Tahrir is the **Mugamaa**, the suitably massive headquarters of the state administration (which you will have to visit if you need to extend your visa), and next to it are the **American University** in Cairo and the **National Assembly**. Going east beyond the campus and the station you come to **Abdin Palace**, formerly the royal residence and now the offices of the President of the Republic. A short walk south along the Corniche el Nil are the **Semiramis Inter-Continental** and **Shepheard's**—though the famous Shepheard's Hotel of the past, whose guest list included General Gordon and Sir Richard Burton, and where everyone who was anyone was seen on the terrace drinking four o'clock tea, was located near the Ezbekieh Gardens and was burned down by demonstrators in 1952. Further south along the river is the convoluted pattern of **Garden City**, a pleasant residential district of tree-lined streets.

North from Midan el Tahrir

The main local **bus terminus** is on Midan Abdel Moneim Riad, behind the Egyptian museum. To the north of Midan el Tahrir, beyond the overpass leading to the new **6 October Bridge** (named after the 1973 war), is the **Ramses Hilton** and past that the one-time slum districts of **Bulaq** and **Shubra**, now redeveloped with skyscrapers along the river. On this stretch of the Corniche el Nil are the **Television Tower Building**, housing radio and television studios and the press office, while the taller building beyond it is the new **Ministry of Foreign Affairs**. Continuing north along the corniche, past the **26 July Bridge**, is the brand new **World Trade Centre**, filled with trendy shops.

Sharia Ramses runs out from the top of Midan el Tahrir and turns northeast, leading to **Midan Ramses** with a colossal statue of Ramses II brought in 1955 from Memphis where his twin still resides. (The square is scheduled to undergo comprehensive renovation, and there is talk of removing the statue, which is suffering from traffic vibration and pollution, to various other sites, possibly back to Memphis. A concrete clone has been erected on the way to the airport.) Here you will find **Mahattat Ramses**, the main Cairo railway station for trains north to Alexandria and south to Luxor and Aswan.

Downtown Cairo

Around Midan el Tahrir and along the streets radiating out from it are numerous **airline offices** and **travel agencies**, and extending into the downtown area to the northeast several less expensive **hotels**. This downtown area is bordered by Sharia Ramses to the northwest, Sharia Tahrir to the south and Sharia el Gumhuriya to the west. Parallel to Sharia Ramses is Sharia Champollion; the **Thomas Cook** office is on the first street to intersect this, Sharia Mahmoud Basiony. Sharia Qasr el Nil heads more eastwards in the direction of the Ezbekieh Gardens, though not quite reaching that far; soon after leaving Midan el Tahrir you will find **American Express** on the right-hand side. Further on, this street intersects several others at Midan Talaat Harb. Along Sharia Talaat Harb, beginning at Midan el Tahrir and ending at Midan Orabi, are numerous **shops**, **cinemas** and **eating places**—also along Sharias Adli and 26 July running east–west. This is the liveliest area of modern Cairo, particularly on a Thursday night (preceding Friday's day of rest).

Until the creation of Midan el Tahrir, the **Ezbekieh Gardens** were the focal point for foreign visitors. The old Shepheard's Hotel stood on the corner of Sharias el Gumhuriya and Alfi at the northwest corner of the gardens, while at the southwest corner stood the old Opera House. It was built in 1869, and the Khedive Ismail commissioned Verdi to write *Aida* to celebrate here the opening of the Suez Canal and Egypt's return to the crossroads of the world. In the event, *Aida* was late and *Rigoletto* was performed instead before a glittering international audience which included the Empress Eugénie, wife of Napoleon III. The old Opera House mysteriously burnt down in 1971, but has been replaced by a handsome new one on Gezira Island. This area around Ezbekieh, though not what it used to be, is—along with the downtown area closest to it—one of the best places to stay for anyone who is serious about exploring the city on foot. It enjoys the ambivalence of being on the edge of modern Cairo and within easy walking distance of the medieval city to the east.

Medieval Cairo

The development and layout of the medieval Islamic city has already been outlined (*see* pp.60–1), and the details of its sights are provided later. Suffice to say, for the purpose of orientation, that if you walk through the Ezbekieh Gardens you will come to **Midan Ataba** with its central **post office**, *open 24 hours a day*. From here you can press on into the heart of the **bazaar** area along Sharias el Muski or al-Azhar; or if instead you leave the square along Sharia al Qalaa (formerly Sharia Mohammed Ali and still called that by many) running south you come to the **Islamic Museum** at the intersection with Sharia Port Said, and still further down you reach the **Sultan Hassan Mosque** and the **Citadel**. West of the Citadel is the **mosque of Ibn Tulun**.

Northwest from Midan el Tahrir and View North from the Cairo Tower

Returning again to Midan el Tahrir for bearings, there is the **Tahrir Bridge** which crosses the Nile to the island of **Gezira** (*gezira* is in fact Arabic for island). The central part of the island is taken up with the **Gezira Sporting and Racing Club**, next to it rising in lotus motif the 187m **Cairo Tower**, completed in 1962. There is an open observation deck up top, and below it an enclosed coffee lounge and a revolving restaurant. There are sweeping **views** of the city and beyond, and this is a good place (easy on the feet too) to establish the topography of Cairo's outlying areas in your mind.

The north part of the island is called **Zamalek**, a mostly modern, upper class and cosmopolitan residential area, though with the occasional fine old home amid leafy streets. The **Marriott Hotel** is located here. This part of Gezira can be reached directly from Midan Orabi along Sharia 26 July and across an old metal bridge.

Following Sharia 26 July (the date on which King Farouk abdicated in 1952) across to the west bank of the Nile you see the suburb of **Embaba**, the site where Napoleon defeated the Mamelukes in the so-called Battle of the Pyramids. Far to the north you can see the dark fan of the Delta. The suburb of **Heliopolis** is nearer, to the northeast, though the ancient site of Heliopolis is a bit to the north of it. There is nothing to see at the site except an **obelisk of Sesostris I** (XII Dynasty), and nearby at Matariya the **Virgin's Tree**, its predecessor much visited by medieval pilgrims in the belief that under its branches the Holy Family paused for shade before continuing their journey to Babylon (old Cairo).

View South towards Memphis from the Cairo Tower

Below your viewpoint atop the Cairo Tower, barges, feluccas and small motor craft pass up- and downstream, the prevailing north wind giving the impression by the ripples it causes on the surface of the river that the Nile flows south, though of course it is flowing north, one of the few rivers in the world to do so. At the southern tip of Gezira is the **El Gezirah Sheraton**, while the island to the south is **Roda** with the **Meridien Hotel** magnificently perched like a figurehead upon its northern prow. At its southern tip is a **nilometer** constructed by the Ummayads in AD 716.

About as far down but on the east bank of the Nile is **Old Cairo** with its **Coptic Museum**, **Coptic churches** and a **synagogue**. Much further south is **Maadi** (along with Zamalek and

Garden City, one of the residential areas favoured by Cairo's more prosperous inhabitants), and further on still the industrial town of **Helwan**, both on the east bank. The indiscernible remains of Egypt's ancient capital, **Memphis**, lie on the west bank opposite Helwan.

Views East and West from the Cairo Tower

From the Cairo Tower you can sweep your gaze round to east and west and see how the city is bounded on either side by desert. The **Moqattam Hills** are to the east and beyond them the plateau of the Eastern or **Arabian Desert**. On a spur of the hills is the **Citadel**, distinguished by the dome of the **Mohammed Ali Mosque**, and spread before it in dark sand-brown confusion is the **medieval city**, as though lurking in past centuries behind the higher, more lightly dusted buildings of the new. Away to the west is the plateau of the **Western Desert**.

Along the west bank of the Nile, opposite Gezira and south of Embaba, are the new suburbs of **Agouza**, **Medinat el Mohandiseen** (Engineer's City) and, around the Cairo Sheraton, **Dokki**. Mrs Sadat continues to live in a villa here overlooking the Nile, just south of the hotel, once President Sadat's official residence. Sharia el Giza runs southwards from the Sheraton to the **Zoological Gardens** and **Cairo University**. This is **Giza**, here long before the suburbs began their sprawl along the west bank to the north and out towards the desert escarpment, obliterating the once extensive fields of the fellahin. From the Cairo Tower you can still make out some arable land but it is fast disappearing beneath the furious antlike progress all round you. It is best to be up in the tower in the early evening as the sun sets over the Western Desert, the sharp outline of the **Pyramids** as ever marking the great divide between the distant haze of the void and the nearer ephemeral activity of the hive.

Getting Around

Although there is an extensive bus system, buses are usually extremely crowded and it is better to head for the general area you want by metro, riverbus or taxi, and then walk about. Any further information about how to reach a particular sight is given with the description of it.

by metro

The great boon to visitors (not to mention Cairenes) is the city's new metro (*see* p.74 for map). It is the first underground railway in Africa or the Arab world and it is excellent. From about 40PT, according to distance, you can travel quickly, cleanly and in comfort between important points like Midan Ramses (metro station Mubarak), Midan el Tahrir (Sadat) and Old Cairo (Mari Girgis). A further intersecting line is under construction. Services operate from about 5am to 11.30pm. Note that the front carriage is always off-limits to men.

by taxi

Taxis, which are usually black and white Fiats or Peugeots, and have meters, are in theory a cheap way of getting about within Cairo. But Cairo taxi drivers hold to an opposite theory when giving rides to foreigners. Occasionally you will get into a **metered taxi** and the driver will actually turn the meter on, in which case you will be amazed at how cheap it is, amazed at the man's innocence, and can leave it to your conscience whether you will pay him according to the metered reading. More often than not the driver will 'forget', or say his meter is broken, or simply refuse to turn it on. You have the right to insist. In fact you will soon learn not to bother about arguing or even raising the matter, and will instead devise your own rule of thumb. If, say, from Midan el Tahrir you go to Zamalek, Khan el Khalili or Midan Ramses (2km to 2.5km), pay LE3–4; from Midan el Tahrir to Old Cairo (5km), pay LE5–6; and from Midan el Tahrir to the Pyramids (11km), LE12–15. You can feel generous in knowing you are paying well over the proper fare. Your driver of course will have a fit. You then make noises about calling the police. Your driver will calm down, but even if he does not, ignore him. Taking taxis in Cairo is like bargaining in Khan el Khalili; you will soon get a feel for arriving at a fare acceptable to both of you.

by bus and minibus

The cheapest way of getting about within and around Cairo is by public bus. There are the large red and white or black and white buses which rarely cost more than 25PT a ride. Their major terminus is in **Midan Abdel Moneim Riad**, behind (north of) the Egyptian Museum. They are crowded, uncomfortable, difficult to get on, even more difficult to get off, and the main value they hold for the visitor is the entertainment derived from watching Cairenes embark and disembark through the windows.

Also from the same terminus there are the small orange and white **minibuses** at about 60PT a ride.

by limousine

Costing somewhat more than taxis are the unmetered limousines (Volvos and Mercedes usually) which charge fixed fares. They are found at the airport and at major hotels, where their fares are posted. These posted fares can serve as a guide to how much less you ought to pay the taxi driver who brings you back or takes you from one point to another during the day.

car hire

If you are planning to drive extensively in and around Cairo or further afield, it could be worth hiring a car. It is often cheaper to arrange car hire from abroad. You need to be at least 21, must have an International Driver's Licence, and should have a sense of adventure: Cairenes, you will have observed, meander from one side of the road to the other as the fancy takes them, and the only way to survive is to meander with them. Both international and local car hire firms are represented; most of the major hotels will have agency desks, and there are offices downtown and at the airport.

It is worth checking that everything essential (like brakes) actually works and that a record is taken beforehand of any dents or scratches in the bodywork. It is advisable to book a day in advance.

by riverbus

Riverbuses make frequent runs from **Maspero Station** (on the Corniche in front of the Television Tower Building which is just north of the Ramses Hilton) down to Old

Cairo, with stops at either side of the river along the way. There are also boats from Maspero Station north to the Nile barrages from 7am to 5pm daily.

tours

The alternative to public transport or car hire are tours by car or bus with guide. There are morning, afternoon and evening tours to the Egyptian Museum, the Pyramids and Sphinx, Memphis and Saqqara, medieval or Islamic Cairo, Old Cairo, and Cairo by night, incorporating a visit to a nightclub. **Thomas Cook**, 17 Sharia Mahmoud Bassiouni, near Midan Talaat Harb, ✆ 5743955, has a comprehensive list of tours by car with driver/guide. The more passengers, the less expensive it is per person. **American Express** (15 Sharia Qasr el Nil, a short walk from Midan el Tahrir, ✆ 5747991–6, and with branches at the Meridien, Marriott, Cairo Sheraton, and the Nile and Ramses Hiltons) does coach tours which for one or two people will work out about 40% cheaper than Cook's tours. These companies also offer tours throughout Egypt by rail or air.

Possibly cheaper and more comprehensive is Egypt's own tourist company, **Misr Travel**, 1 Sharia Talaat Harb, ✆ 3930010, with an office also at 43 Qasr el Nil, and branches elsewhere. They are efficient, and can arrange accommodation, cruises, tours, and air, sea, road and rail travel.

Tourist Information

There are **Tourist Information Offices** at both airport terminals, ✆ 667475 and ✆ 2914277, downtown (head office) at 5 Sharia Adli, at the Ezbekieh end, ✆ 3913454, and at the Pyramids on Sharia al-Ahram, ✆ 3850259. They can provide brochures and a good free **map** of Cairo (with practical information on the reverse).

The people working at their offices are charming and helpful (most helpful is the head office), but they are used to tourists going to the obvious places by the slickest means, and so have to be pressed for alternative information. If you do not want a tour and do not want to take taxis everywhere, then make it clear that you do not mind taking the local bus or train to Memphis, Saqqara, Meidum or wherever, and they will come up with the information you require.

The **Tourist Police**, ✆ 3919144 or ✆ 126, are found browsing about the airport, the railway station, in the bazaars and at tourist sights, and are recognized by a small blue strip on their left chest and an armband with 'Tourist Police' written in Arabic and English. Otherwise they wear the normal police uniform, which is black in winter and white in summer. They usually speak at least two foreign languages and are helpful with information while doing their best to ensure that tourists are not excessively importuned. They are based at the airport, at the Midan Ramses railway station, at the Pyramids near the Mena House, in Midan el-Hussein on the edge of Khan el Khalili, and downtown at 5 Sharia Adli, towards Ezbekieh Gardens, as well as in all tourist areas in the rest of the country.

Courier services: Federal Express, the international courier service, has two customer hotlines in Cairo, ✆ 3571304 and ✆ 3516070. Also there is **DHL**, ✆ 3029801, and **TNT**, ✆ 3488204.

Fax: All the better hotels have fax services which can be used by guests and others. They can also be sent and received at the Midan el Tahrir, Sharia Alfi and Sharia Adli telephone exchanges (*see* below).

Email and Internet: Some hotels will have online facilities for use by their guests. Otherwise the most centrally located Internet café is the **Nile Hilton Cybercafé**, ✆ 5780444, extn 758, Midan el Tahrir. It is in the basement of the shopping mall. *Open 10am–midnight, on Fri closed noon–2.*

Postal services: The **Central Post Office** is at Midan el Ataba, near the Ezbekieh Gardens. *Open 7am–7pm daily except Fri, 7–noon.* The Poste Restante is here, down the side street to the right of the main entrance (*open 8am–6pm daily, on Fri open only 10am–noon*). Other post offices are *open 9am–4pm, closed Fri.* Most hotels have letter-boxes and can supply you with stamps for cards and letters. Do not use letterboxes in the street unless you want to arrive home before your postcards.

EMS Mail is a new express service offered at all post offices. It is faster and safer than the usual postal service, while slower but a quarter of the price of a courier service.

To send a **parcel** out of Egypt requires an **export licence**. You must obtain this at the Post Traffic Centre, Midan Ramses (*open 8.30–3, closed Fri*). The building is to the right of the main entrance to Ramses railway station. Go there with your parcel unwrapped; here it will be inspected and, for a small fee, wrapped for you; for a further small fee you will be guided through the remaining formalities and paperwork. Your parcel must not weigh more than 20kg if going to Europe or Africa, 30kg if going to North America. Its dimensions must not exceed 1m x 1m x 50cm. If sending home fabrics or souvenirs you have bought, ask first at the shop whether they will do it for you. Most shops catering to tourists have export licences and are reliable.

You can **receive mail** at your hotel, or care of American Express (if you have their travellers' cheques or card), or care of your embassy (the envelope should be marked 'Visitors Mail'). American Express will forward mail arriving after your departure for about LE3.

Telegrams in English or French can be sent from the **PTT** offices on the north side of Midan el Tahrir (*open 24 hours*), or in Sharia Alfi or Sharia Adli—or from major hotels.

Telephones: For local calls, some shops, restaurants and hotels will have payphones for public use, or you may encounter a public phonebox at a public place or in the street. For long-distance and international calls you can phone from most hotels (at the better hotels it does not matter whether you are a guest or not), but you will pay a hefty premium, as much as 100%. Or you can phone at the normal rate from a telephone exchange.

Telephone exchanges (PTT), called *centrales*, are on Midan el Tahrir (north side), Sharia Alfi by the Windsor Hotel and on Sharia Adli. The one at Midan el Tahrir is *open 24 hours*. You can buy phonecards here and use them in the orange direct-dial phones located at the exchanges (and sometimes elsewhere, e.g. airports and railway stations).

You can make reverse charge (collect) calls from some of the luxe hotels, e.g. the Marriott and Semiramis Intercontinental, or British Airways in Midan el Tahrir (to the UK only).

For more information on telephone services and area codes within Egypt, *see* p.14.

embassies

Your embassy can assist you by holding onto your mail, advising on emergency financial and medical problems and effecting emergency communications home. Embassies also encourage visitors, especially those not travelling in large groups, to register with them. It should be noted, however, that embassies cannot lend money to stranded travellers—though they can find ways of helping you.

Australia	World Trade Centre, 11th Floor, Corniche el Nil, ℂ 575 0444, ℗ 5781638.
Canada	5 el Saraya el Kubra, Garden City, ℂ 3543110, ℗ 3563548.
Ireland	3 Abu el Feda Tower, Zamalek, ℂ 3408264, ℗ 3412863.
New Zealand	handled by the UK, *see* below.
UK	7 Sharia Ahmed Raghab, Garden City, ℂ 3540850, ℗ 3540959.
US	5 Sharia Latin America, Garden City, ℂ 3557371, ℗ 3573200.

health and emergencies

Police ℂ 122
Tourist Police ℂ 126
Ambulance ℂ 123
Fire service ℂ 125
Telephone enquiries ℂ 140

In an **emergency** you can phone the Tourist Police, ℂ 126, or the police ambulance service, ℂ 123, which will take you to the nearest hospital, but if you need urgent treatment the best thing is to get yourself (by taxi or whatever means) to the nearest hospital as quickly as possible. Only two (private) hospitals send ambulances with on-board professional paramedics or life-support equipment:

As Salam International Hospital, Corniche el Nil, Maadi, ℂ 3029091, and 3 Sharia Syria, Mohandiseen, ℂ 3638050.

Nil Badrawi Hospital, Corniche el Nil, Maadi, ℂ 3638684, 3638688, ambulance ℂ 3638168.

In addition to the above, these centrally located private hospitals are often recommended:

Anglo-American Hospital, al-Burg (meaning the Cairo Tower; it is just west of it), Zamalek, ℂ 3406162/3/4/5.

Italian Hospital, 17 Sharia Bayn el Sarayat, Abbassia, northeast of Midan Ramses, ✆ 2821581-2.

All of these are modern and fully equipped. But note that private hospitals may not accept you simply because you may have medical insurance; not only should you be prepared to pay cash, but a substantial deposit will be required before you are admitted, though in some cases payment can be made by credit card.

For **medical care**, ask at your hotel. Most will be able to refer you to a doctor or dentist, while some of the major hotels will have a doctor on call. Most Egyptian doctors have been trained in Europe or North America and speak English. Your embassy can also recommend doctors and dentists.

There are several **pharmacists** around Midan el Tahrir and downtown with a wide range of medications not requiring prescriptions—describe your symptoms and, if the ailment is minor, the pharmacist will prescribe on the spot. Both imported medicines and those locally licensed are heavily subsidised by the government. You will probably be able to obtain your favourite medicine at a fraction of its usual price. Cosmetics, perfumes and toiletries are also stocked.

If **stranded**, you can go to Thomas Cook, American Express, Barclays International or the Nile Hilton and have them send a telegram or fax requesting your bank or persons at home to arrange the transfer of money to you in Egypt. This can be accomplished in 2–3 days. Western Union offers its faster Money Transfer service ('in minutes'), ✆ 3571375 or ✆ 3571385. Or you can go to an airline office and ask for a pre-paid ticket, the airline faxing or cabling whomever you suggest to pay for the ticket home. Authorization to issue you with a ticket can be received back in Cairo within 2 days.

maps

Tourist Information Offices (*see* p.70) can provide you with a good free **map** of Cairo. A still better Cairo map, which includes a street index, is published by Lehnert and Landrock (*see* p.19) and sold at most hotel kiosks.

money

To exchange money, go to **Thomas Cook, American Express**, or to the banks in the **major hotels**—all the 5-star hotels have 24-hour banks. For a full-scale commercial banking service, there is **Barclays Bank International**, 12 Midan el Sheikh Youssef (PO Box 2335), Garden City, Cairo, ✆ 3549415/3542195, ✉ 3552746.

If you have Egyptian pounds which you want to **convert back** into foreign currency before your departure, you can go to any bank (including the one at the airport) and show them a receipt indicating that you had previously converted at least such an amount from foreign currency into Egyptian pounds. They will then subtract what they reckon you should have spent per day, with the result that you will probably be stuck with a load of unwanted Egyptian currency. Moral: never change too much at any one time, and what you do change, spend. This is made easier by the new regulation allowing you to spend up to LE1,000 at the airport duty-free shops on departure.

To extend your **visa** while in Cairo you must go to the Mugamaa, a huge government building (a gift of the Soviet Union in the 1960s) on the south side of Midan el Tahrir, not far from the Nile Hilton. It is *open 8am–3.30pm daily, closed Fri*, but you should nevertheless go early if you hope to get anything done. Go to the first floor and to the section marked 'forms' to obtain a visa application form; you will also need a photograph and may be asked for pink bank exchange receipts showing that you have changed at least $180 into Egyptian currency within the last month. These you take with your LE15 fee to one of the appropriate windows, normally 23 to 29. **Re-entry visas** are dealt with at windows 16 and 17, while fines for overstaying your visa are paid at window 40 (a 15-day grace period is allowed, beyond which at least LE60 is payable). The whole process should take an hour. Visas can also be extended at Luxor and Aswan.

Cairo Metro

═══════════ Projected metro line

Old Cairo, and particularly the **Coptic Museum** there, should be high on your list of places to visit in Cairo—you should allow two to three hours. Otherwise, the circular tour below is really a stroll of two or three hours, which the visitor short on time can skip. The highlights are the **Manyal Palace** on Roda Island and the **Cairo Tower** on Gezira Island—you could simply go direct to the Cairo Tower for its magnificent 360° view over Cairo.

Getting There

Old Cairo and Fustat are about 5km south of Midan el Tahrir from where you can take the **metro**, though you can also go by **bus**, **riverbus** or **taxi**. There are several places on either side of the Nile and on the islands of Roda and Gezira which can be visited as a circular tour or combined with a visit to Old Cairo.

The Nile

A Circular Tour

Immediately south of Midan el Tahrir on the left (east) side of Sharia Qasr el Aini is the **American University** in Cairo, a pleasant enclave that seems a world away from the heat, clatter, dust and swirl of the city. The library is excellent, the AUC Press publishes some of the best English-language material on Egypt and the bookstore is first rate. A block further on, a square opens on the right (west) and leads via Sharia Lazugali to the American and British embassies, which are at the north end of the fashionable residential and diplomatic quarter (rivalled by Zamalek at the north end of Gezira) called **Garden City**. The area, developed by British planners early in the 20th century, is a latticework of winding tree-shaded streets in contrast to the geometrical regularity of downtown Cairo, which was laid out by the French. From here you can make your way to the Nile corniche (where feluccas are tied up and can be hired for sailing on the river) and walk south to Roda island.

The **Meridien Hotel** at Roda's northern tip can be reached across its own bridge from Garden City: stop for a drink and a commanding view of the Nile. A quarter of the way down Roda, set in a garden of banyan trees overlooking the smaller eastern branch of the Nile, its entrance however on Sharia Sayala facing the approach road to El Gama'a Bridge, is the oriental-rococo **Manyal Palace**. Built in 1903 by Prince Mohammed Ali, brother of Khedive Abbas II and uncle of King Farouk, it is now a museum (*open daily 9–4; adm LE5*) worth visiting for the opulence of its decorations. On view is a reception palace, the palace proper, a private mosque and the prince's private hunting museum. Displays include a thousand-piece silver service, a table made of elephants' ears and a stuffed hermaphrodite goat. That pretty much sets the tone of the place, which is bizarre kitsch.

Continue south to the Nilometer at the southern tip of Roda or cross to the east bank of the Nile to the Fumm el Khalig (in either case, *see* below). Or cross over El Gama'a Bridge to the west bank of the Nile, in which case ahead of you are the **Zoological Gardens**, while heading north brings you to **Dokki**. On a houseboat tied up along the west bank corniche road, Sharia el Nil, just south of the Cairo Sheraton, is the **Papyrus Institute** (*open daily*

10–7). Founded by Professor Hassan Ragab, this is a workshop, research centre and small museum demonstrating the manufacture and use of this first flexible writing material. Only *cyperus papyrus*, the same plant used by the ancients, is used here (the institute has several commercial imitators, but they use the modern *cyperus alopecuroides* of inferior quality). The institute grows at least some of its own papyrus, exhibits copies of ancient papyri and sells others. (As you go down the quayside steps, notice on your left the plaque marking the highest level of the Nile during the flood of September 1887.)

At the west end of 6 October Bridge in Dokki, in gardens planted with specimen trees off Sharia Abdel Aziz Radwan, is the **Agricultural and Cotton Museum**, which concentrates on all aspects of present-day Egyptian rural life, especially the country's single most important crop (*open daily 9–3, closed Mon; adm cheap*). The handsome new **Opera House** is also here, built in 1989 with Japanese assistance; in its grounds, also in a fine modern building, is the **Museum of Modern Egyptian Art** (*open daily exc Mon 10–1 and 5–9.30; adm*).

Towards the lower end of the island of Gezira is the **Cairo Tower**, which rises 187m and offers marvellous panoramas (*see* 'Orientation', p.67) from its enclosed 14th-level restaurant and 15th-level cafeteria and its open 16th-level observation platform (*open daily 9am–midnight; adm for the ascent*).

You can now complete the circle by returning to Midan el Tahrir.

South along the East Bank of the Nile

Coming down the corniche from Midan el Tahrir towards Old Cairo, at a point two or three blocks south of your view across to the Manyal Palace on Roda, is a traffic roundabout called **Fumm el Khalig**. This is where the canal, now covered by Sharia Bur Said (Port Said) and its southern extension, left the river. There is a large octagonal tower of stone here, once housing great waterwheels which lifted water from the Nile to the level of the Mameluke aqueduct which can still be followed almost all the way to the Citadel. At this end, the **aqueduct** dates only from 1505 and was an extension made necessary by the westward-shifting Nile; the main part of the aqueduct, further east, was built by al-Nasr around 1311.

A few blocks further south is the Malek al-Salih bridge crossing over to the southern end of Roda. At the lower tip of the island is the **Nilometer** (*open daily 9–4, closed Fri; adm cheap*), dating from the 9th century, though the superstructure with its Turkish-style conical roof dates from Mohammed Ali's time. The stone-lined pit goes down well below the level of the Nile, though the water entry tunnels have been blocked up and you can descend by steps. At the centre of the pit is a graduated column for determining whether the river would rise enough, not enough, or too much, so announcing the expected fertility of all Egypt over the coming year. A reading of 16 ells (8.6m) ensured the complete irrigation of the valley; then the Nile crier would broadcast the *Wafa el Nil* or superfluity of the Nile, and the dam to the Khalig would be cut amid great festivity. The Nile used to reach its flood in mid-August, but the High Dam at Aswan now regulates its flow and it keeps a steady level year-round.

Immediately north of the Nilometer is the former **Monasterly Palace**, built in 1851, noteworthy for its architectural detail and painted ceilings; it is now the **Centre for Art and Life** (*open daily 10–2, closed Fri*), a cultural institute devoted to Egyptian art from ancient to modern times, where students' work can be purchased.

> *The angel of the Lord appeareth to Joseph in a dream, saying, Arise,*
> *and take the young child and his mother, and flee into Egypt, and be*
> *thou there until I bring thee word: for Herod will seek the young child*
> *to destroy him.*

Matthew 2:13

The Coptic Museum here is a must, and a delightful one at that. After spending an hour or two wandering around its rooms, you should look at the remains of the Roman fortifications, visit the Hanging Church which sits on top of them, and then visit the church of Abu Sarga and the Synagogue. Allow three hours in all.

Getting There

If taking a **taxi** to the fortress of Babylon in Old Cairo, ask first for Misr (also pronounced Masr) el Qadima (Old Cairo), and then specify Mari Girgis (St George), and he will bring you right to the walls outside the Coptic Museum. By **metro**, get off at Mari Girgis station; by **riverbus** the landing stage is also called Mari Girgis. There is also a **bus** from the main city terminus behind the Egyptian Museum.

Old Cairo describes the general area, but specifically you want to arrive at the Roman fortress (known in Arabic as Qasr el Shamah, fortress of the Beacon) opposite the Mari Girgis metro station.

Qasr el Shamah (Fortress of the Beacon)

The section of wall and two towers here formed part of the Roman fortress of Babylon, first built in the time of Augustus, added to by Trajan and remodelled by the Byzantines. The technique of dressed stone alternating with courses of brick is typically Roman. The portal between the towers was a water gate and excavation has revealed the original quay 6m below present street level, but the Nile has since shifted 400m to the west.

The Coptic Museum

Now the towers of the fortress mark the entrance to the Coptic Museum (*open daily 9–5; adm LE16*), pleasantly set in gardens. It is a charming building, decorated with wooden mashrabiyyas from old Coptic houses, embracing green courtyards, airy and light within, its spirit in keeping with its collection. The exhibits cover Egypt's Christian era, from AD 300 to 1000, and are both religious and secular, linking the art of the pharaonic and Graeco-Roman periods with that of Islam. The museum is arranged in sections, covering stonework, manuscripts, textiles, icons and paintings as well as decorated ivories, woodwork, metalwork, pottery and glass. Often, as in stone carving and painting, the work is crude, though agreeably naïve. High artistic achievement, however, is found in the textiles, and there are many fine chemises, tapis and clothes here embroidered with motifs of St George, or graceful women and gazelles. Throughout, the museum has beautifully carved wood ceilings and beams. Some highlights are described below.

New Wing: Ground Floor

Room 1. Pre-Christian reliefs and architectural fragments, 4th and 3rd century BC. The themes are pagan gods, such as Pan and Dionysus.

Room 2. Again reliefs and fragments, but of the 4th to 6th centuries and so early Christian. The cross is incorporated at every opportunity, often surrounded by flowers or backed by a shell forming the half-dome of a niche—see exhibit 7065, a shell with dolphins on either side. Technically the work is similar to the pre-Christian, but there is a sense of excitement at working with the new imagery—Pan and other pagan motifs had become hackneyed.

Room 3. Reliefs and frescoes, 6th century AD. See 7118 showing Christ ascending to heaven in a flaming chariot. **Rooms 4–8** contain more of the same, including work from Abu Jeremias Monastery at Saqqara.

Room 9. Reliefs and frescoes, from the 6th to the 10th centuries AD. See exhibit 3962, 10th-century Fayyum frescoes, showing Adam and Eve before and after the Fall. On the right they are naked, enjoying the fruit; on the left they clasp fig leaves to their genitals and Adam points accusingly at Eve as if to say 'You made me do it'.

New Wing: First Floor

Rooms 10, 11 and 12 all contain textiles. Room 10 also displays manuscripts and ostraca; note especially Case 4, exhibit 7948, the tapestry showing a musician and dancers (3rd to 4th centuries AD), beautifully observed, fluid, rhythmic, happy. The Copts were at their best in textiles, which they developed from an ancient Egyptian tradition, adding to it Graeco-Roman and Sassanid (Persian) influences. Plants, animals, birds and human beings blend in sumptuous decorative patterns that have a liveliness that Byzantium itself could not rival.

Room 13 contains icons and ivories. **Rooms 14, 15** and **16** display metalwork (including armour and weapons). **Room 17** has objects and several striking frescoes from Nubia.

Courtyard

You step out from the main museum building into a courtyard like that of a grand Cairo house, planted and with mashrabiyyas round the walls. Across the court is part of the Roman wall and a gate of Babylon; you can descend to the level of the seeping Nile and step along concrete gangways beneath great arches and vaults where once were prisons, stables and a grain mill.

Old Wing

Entered through the courtyard, the rooms here contain items of wood, pottery and glass. Most agreeable are the mashrabiyyas, fixed together without glue or nails, admitting a diffused light through their intricate Christian patterns.

Old Cairo's Churches and Synagogue

The churches close at 4pm; the synagogue keeps irregular hours and usually Rabbi Cohen or Ahmed is there after 4pm to show you around. Admission to the buildings is free, but all are in need of donations.

Alexandria was the Coptic Rome. Old Cairo was never a city, never a place of monuments, and it is not a ghetto. Copts live throughout Cairo and all over Egypt, and are particularly numerous in Upper Egypt. But especially within these walls it is an old and holy place, to Jews as well as Copts, and although Muslims are in the majority in the environs of Old Cairo, there are tens of thousands of Copts as well as a number of Jewish families living in the area.

The oldest Coptic churches sought security within the fortress walls, and usually they avoid facing onto the street and so are indistinguishable from neighbouring houses. Their main entrances were long ago walled up against attack, entry being through a small side door. Their plan is basilical, with a narthex or porch admitting to an aisled nave with an iconostasis placed across the sanctuary. In seeking out the five churches within the fortress precincts, and also the synagogue, there is interest too in the winding little streets, glimpses within windows and doors, the decorations of the houses, the domes of some (as in Upper Egypt), and the atmosphere of remove, of an almost rural village.

The church of **El Muallaqa, the Hanging Church**, is so named because it rests on the bastions of the southwest gate into the fortress, its nave suspended above the passage. It is reached by going out from the museum grounds between the two great towers and turning left. Though the church claims origins in the 4th century AD, it is unlikely that the present structure, which in any case has been rebuilt, would have been built on the walls until the Arab conquest made them redundant. Certainly, it is known to have become the seat of the patriarchate when it was moved from Alexandria to Cairo in the 11th century. The interior of El Muallaqa, with pointed arches, cedar panelling and translucent ivory screens, is intricately decorated—the carved white marble pulpit inlaid with marble of red and black is the finest in Egypt. Services are held in the dead Coptic language and in Arabic. On the right as you come in is a 10th-century icon of the Virgin and Child: Egyptian faces, Byzantine crowns. On the same wall is an ancient icon of St Mark, by tradition the founder of Christianity in Egypt. El Muallaqa is dedicated to the Virgin and is properly called Sitt Mariam, St Mary. Its central sanctuary is dedicated to Christ, its left sanctuary to St George, its right sanctuary to St John the Baptist, scenes from the saints' lives decorating their iconostases.

Now walk back out to the street and turn right so that you pass by the entrance to the museum. Atop one of the Roman towers is the circular Greek Orthodox **church of St George** (Mari Girgis), rebuilt in 1909 after a fire; the adjoining **monastery** of St George is the seat of the Greek patriarch. Further along, steps on your right lead down to a narrow street at the level of the early settlement. Walking along this, the Coptic **convent of Mari Girgis** is on your left. Still further along, you are obliged to turn left or right. If you turn left into the narrow lane you pass (on the right) the Coptic **church of Mari Girgis**, built originally in the 7th century but burned down in the 19th, only a 14th-century hall surviving. The modern church is of no interest. At the end of this lane you come to **al-Adra**, the Coptic **church of the Virgin**, first built in the 9th century but destroyed and rebuilt in the 18th century. It is known also as Kasriyat el Rihan, 'pot of basil', a favoured herb of the Greek Orthodox Church. Al-Hakim's mother had been of that faith and for the duration of his reign it was transferred to Orthodox use. (For more on Al-Hakim, *see* pp.114–15.)

If where you turned left for al-Adra you had instead turned right, you would at once be at **Abu Sarga**, the Coptic **church of St Sergius** (which can also be reached by steps down from the ticket kiosk in front of the Coptic Museum). This is possibly the oldest church within the fortress, thought to date from the 5th century AD, though it was restored and partly rebuilt in the 12th century. European pilgrims are recorded as visiting the church from at least the 14th century because of its associations with the Flight into Egypt; steps to the right of the altar lead down to the crypt, once a cave, where according to tradition the Holy Family found refuge after fleeing from Herod.

Abu Sarga is typical of early Coptic churches, being a basilica with aisles separated from the nave by two rows of columns which support a high timbered roof. One column is granite, the other 11 are marble, and some bear faded paintings of the apostles, probably dating from the 8th century AD. Paintings of saints, probably 11th- and 12th-century, can also be made out within the central apse. A usual feature of early Coptic churches was a basin set in the floor of the narthex, used for Epiphany blessings. It is now boarded over. The central altar screen, inset above with ebony and ivory panels, is 13th-century, but a century or so older are the carved wooden panels, probably once the leaves of a door, depicting (right) three *warrior saints* and (left) the *Nativity* and the *Last Supper*. There is an icon in the south sanctuary of the *Flight into Egypt*. The marble pulpit is modern; the original rosewood pulpit and the canopied altar are now in the Coptic Museum.

Turning right out of Abu Sarga and then right at the corner, at the end of the street you see **Sitt Barbara** (St Barbara's) to the left, a synagogue to the right. The Coptic church of Sitt Barbara was built in the 7th century AD in a similar pattern to Abu Sarga and like the latter was restored in Fatimid times. The central screen is 13th-century; the icons atop it are 18th-century. The marble pulpit is very fine. The relics of St Barbara are in the right-hand sanctuary; she had the misfortune to be born into the 3rd century AD, daughter of a pagan father who, discovering that she was a Christian, turned her over to the Roman authorities to be tortured and beheaded. Off to the left, as though an annexe, is the separate Church of SS Cyrus and John, also beheaded in the 3rd century.

The **synagogue of Ben Ezra** is a neighbourhood temple whose neighbourhood has gone away—left the country or gone to other parts of Cairo. It is a forlorn place, a forgotten outpost, yet it claims a more ancient history than anything else in Old Cairo. The synagogue is the oldest in Egypt and resembles in its basilical arrangement an early Christian church. The Coptic church of St Michael did stand here from the 4th to 9th centuries AD, but the Copts had to sell it to the Jews to pay Ibn Tulun's tax towards the erection of his mosque. Sources differ as to whether the original church was destroyed or if its fabric remains in what the Rabbi of Jerusalem, Abraham Ben Ezra, at least renewed in the 12th century. But the Jews say the site has far older associations than that: in the 6th century BC Jeremiah preached here after the destruction of Jerusalem under Nebuchadnezzar, and it was the presence of their community here, they say, that drew the Holy Family to Babylon. For the same reason, say the Copts, the apostles Peter and Mark came here; as proof of this they cite Peter 5:13: 'The church that is at Babylon elected together with you, saluteth you; and so doth Marcus my son.' The rest of Christendom argues that Babylon is here a metaphor for Rome; but there is the suspicion that this interpretation is ingenuous, serving to appropriate Peter to Rome in order there to crown him pope and martyr, legitimizing the Vatican's claim to apostolic supremacy.

Ben Ezra's synagogue sits in a small shady garden, its exterior plain, a Star of David in wrought iron over the gate. Inside there is an arch of ablaq masonry and a small stained-glass window towards the far end above the sort of intricate stone inlay work you would expect to see around the mihrab of a mosque. The synagogue has recently undergone extensive restoration, paid for by the Egyptian government and foreign donors.

Nathan Abraham Moishe Cohen lives opposite, and is often found sitting outside passing the time of day with his friend Ahmed. For decades now, Rabbi Cohen (who must be a rabbi by default, as he is illiterate) has been selling charmingly awful postcards of himself at wickedly high prices. Buy one and he may show you exactly where Pharaoh's daughter plucked Moses from the bulrushes (you might have mistaken it for a sewer), identify the Miracle Rock beneath which Jeremiah is supposed to be buried, and tell you how the synagogue once possessed a library of 100,000 books, all gone. Discovered hidden in a genizah in the walls at the end of the 19th century was an ancient Torah, now dispersed throughout the great libraries of the Western world.

Turning right out of the synagogue gate, a lane passes an abandoned Jewish school on the right and leads into a **Coptic cemetery**, a complete town of bungalows for the dead.

Fustat

Emerging from the garden of the Coptic Museum, or back up the steps from the warren of streets where you have been visiting churches within the fortress walls, turn right (that is walk two or three blocks north of the fortress with the railway line on your left) and you will come to the **mosque of Amr**, so restored and expanded that nothing remains of the original built here in AD 642, the first mosque in Egypt and the point from which the country's conversion to Islam began. Except for its associations, the present mosque is without interest. Its dimensions date from AD 827 when it was doubled in size: it has several times since been restored, and has recently been restored yet again. It is a pedestrian reminder of a cheaply won victory, and you pause to wonder what it would take to reverse the effect of Amr's 3,500 men.

Behind the mosque extends what appears to be a vast and smoking rubbish dump. The curious should wander into its midst and be amazed and rewarded with one of the most fascinating sights in Cairo. Among the smouldering heaps is a community of **earthenware manufacturers** whose seemingly rubbish houses (you should be careful not to fall through their ceilings as you walk over them) stand, or settle, amid a complete and complex process for the making of fine clay and the fashioning of narghile stems, drums, small pots, large amphoras and road-sized drainage pipes—indeed these people could equip a band, a kitchen or a city, and probably meet the earthenware needs of a large part of Cairo. There are vats dug into the ground for mixing and refining clay, subterranean workshops where potters draw from shapeless lumps beautifully curved vessels with all the mastery and mystery of a fakir charming a thick brown snake, and there are enormous beehive kilns like Mycenaean tombs fired from below with mounds of wood shavings shovelled in by Beelzebub children.

At evening these mud-covered people wash themselves off, the women appear from out of their hovels in bright dresses, flowers are arranged in soft-drink bottles, a television—wired up to a car battery—is switched on, tea is made, chairs set out, and if you are there then you will be invited to join them in watching the setting sun.

Beyond this potters' community (the easiest way is to return towards the fortress of Babylon but turn left up the road running alongside the cemetery wall) lie the dismal remains of **Fustat**, the foundations and lower walls of the first Arab city in Egypt, the true beginnings of Cairo. Once famous for its glassware and ceramics, with water supply and sanitation facilities far more advanced than anything in Europe until the 18th century, the city was destroyed and abandoned in 1168 rather than allowed to fall into the hands of the Christian king of Jerusalem. Fustat's destruction fell most heavily on the Copts, who had been the majority here and lost everything. When the threat had passed, the Muslims turned their attention to their new city of Cairo, which you can see rising to the north, and filled it with some of the greatest monuments of medieval civilization.

Medieval Cairo

He who has not seen Cairo cannot know the grandeur of Islam.

Ibn Khaldun, 14th century

Islam in Egypt began at Fustat and flowered into a great civilization, many of whose most beautiful monuments survive throughout the medieval quarters of Cairo. The following nine sections tour this Islamic city, progressing generally from south to north and concluding with the City of the Dead.

The Islamic monuments of Cairo, and there are hundreds of them, are each marked with a **small green enamelled plaque** bearing an Arabic number. These numbers are given after the name of each monument covered in the following itineraries to ensure identification. Although these are historical monuments, they are often places of current worship and when touring this most conservative part of the city you should **dress** and act with decorum. Women should not wear short dresses or too-revealing blouses. Inside mosques you must remove your shoes, or shoe coverings will be provided. For this, and also if you accept the services of a guide, or sometimes if you ask to be shown the way up a minaret, **baksheesh** of 50PT to LE1 will be expected. Whenever local assistance is solicited, not only is baksheesh expected, it is usually demanded; avoid paying until you have seen everything you want to, otherwise the demand for baksheesh will be made again and again, at each stage. There is also an **entry fee**, usually LE12, to many of the monuments, which, unless they are places of community prayer, are *likely to close at 4pm*. In short, it is a good idea to carry around a lot of small change.

You may sometimes find yourself in a mosque at prayer time, and then, though visitors are otherwise welcome, you might be asked to retreat into an alcove or out onto the street. Normally though, the atmosphere is relaxed.

Comfortable **walking shoes** are recommended. Though you might rely on a taxi or other transport to get you to the beginning of the itinerary or to some of the major monuments along the route, walking is preferable for a sense of leisure and atmosphere, and also because some places are difficult to get at or to discover, even once you are in the vicinity. There are occasional **kahwehs** along the way: that is, places to sit—perhaps just a few chairs beneath

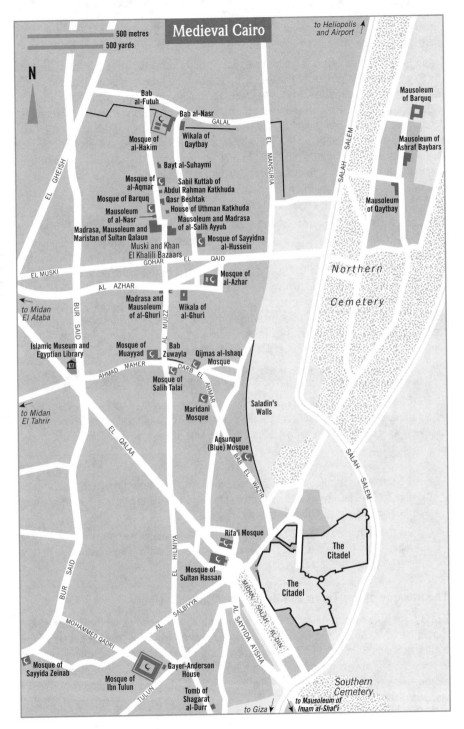

Medieval Cairo

500 metres
500 yards

N

to Heliopolis
and Airport

Bab
al-Futuh

Bab al-Nasr

GALAL

Mausoleum
of Barquq

Mosque of
al-Hakim

Wikala of
Qaytbay

Mausoleum of
Ashraf Baybars

Bayt al-Suhaymi

Mosque of
al-Aqmar

Sabil Kuttab of
Abdul Rahman Katkhuda

Mosque of Barquq

Qasr Beshtak

Mausoleum
of al-Nasr

House of Uthman Katkhuda

Mausoleum
of Qaytbay

Madrasa, Mausoleum and
Maristan of Sultan Qalaun

Mausoleum and Madrasa
of al-Salih Ayyub

Muski and Khan
El Khalili Bazaars

Mosque of Sayyidna
al-Hussein

GOHAR

EL
QAID

EL MUSKI

AL   AZHAR

Mosque of
al-Azhar

Northern

Cemetery

Madrasa and
Mausoleum
of al-Ghuri

Wikala of
al-Ghuri

Islamic Museum and
Egyptian Library

Mosque of
Muayyad

Bab
Zuwayla

Qijmas al-Ishaqi
Mosque

to Midan
El Ataba

BUR
SAID

AHMAD   MAHER

AL   MUIZZ

DARB   EL   AHMAR

Mosque of
Salih Talai

to Midan
El Tahrir

EL   QALAA

Maridani
Mosque

Saladin's
Walls

Aqsunqur
(Blue) Mosque

BAB   EL   WAZIR

SALAH   SALEM

EL   GHEISH

EL   MANSURIA

SALAH   SALEM

Rifa'i Mosque

EL   HILMIYA

The
Citadel

Mosque of
Sultan Hassan

BUR   SAID

MIDAN   SALAH   AL-DIN

The
Citadel

MOHAMMED QADRI

AL   SALBIYYA

AL   SAYYIDA   AISHA

SALAH   SALEM

Mosque of
Sayyida Zeinab

Gayer-Anderson
House

Southern
Cemetery

Mosque of
Ibn Tulun

TULUN

Tomb of
Shagarat
al-Durr

to Giza

to Mausoleum of
Imam al-Shafi'i

the shade of a tree or awning—for a coffee or more likely a refreshing cup of mint tea. Then there is immediate tranquillity; give your feet a rest and let the city parade by before you.

In the 14th century the great Arab historian Ibn Khaldun wrote of Cairo: 'It is the metropolis of the universe, the garden of the world, the nest of the human species, the gateway to Islam, the throne of royalty: it is a city embellished with castles and palaces and adorned with monasteries of dervishes and with colleges lit by the moons and the stars of erudition.' Along with Cordoba and Baghdad, it was one of the great centres of the Arab world, but while Cordoba fell to the Reconquista and Baghdad was destroyed by the Mongols, medieval Cairo survives. The erudition Ibn Khaldun refers to was more the Muslim version of how many angels could dance upon the head of a pin, but otherwise many of the marvels he describes still wait for you, often so unobtrusively that you could pass a façade a hundred times and never guess at the grandeur within.

The streets may be ancient, narrow and dusty, full of strange colour and smell. People may be curious, children occasionally a nuisance and merchants in the tourist bazaars importunate, but generally the inhabitants of these quarters, like Egyptians throughout the country, will be friendly and helpful. This is the heart of Cairo, a heart that anyone with the least sense of adventure will come to love. After sometimes centuries of neglect, there is a new Egyptian and international appreciation of Cairo's Islamic monuments, and a recent drive has been very ably restoring these treasures. The earthquake of late 1992, however, caused some fresh damage, and in recent years rising groundwater has been a serious problem. Further funds will be necessary on a considerable scale if the monuments are to be preserved.

Around the Citadel

The Citadel and its mosque of Mohammed Ali sitting on the Cairo skyline seem irresistibly to attract tourists. But truly magnificent are the mosques of Ibn Tulun and Sultan Hassan; if you have time to see only two of Cairo's Islamic monuments, these should not be missed.

Getting There

To reach the starting point of this tour you can take a **taxi** direct to the mosque of Ibn Tulun. The Sayyida Zeinab **metro** stop is 500m west of Midan al-Sayyida Zeinab; the mosque is then 600m further east.

All the monuments in this chapter are quite close together with the exception of the mausoleum of Imam al-Shaf'i—to reach this take the **tram** from Midan Salah al-Din, which terminates just short of the mausoleum.

The Mosque of Ibn Tulun and the Gayer-Anderson House

If you have time to visit only one Islamic monument, the **mosque of Ibn Tulun** (220) should be your choice. The mosque is midway between Midan al-Sayyida Zeinab at the bottom of Sharia Bur Said (Port Said) to the west and Midan Salah al-Din below the Citadel to the east. The area is poor and rundown, but behind its outer courtyard or ziyadah the mosque achieves an isolation which heightens the dramatic effect of the inner courtyard's bold simplicity.

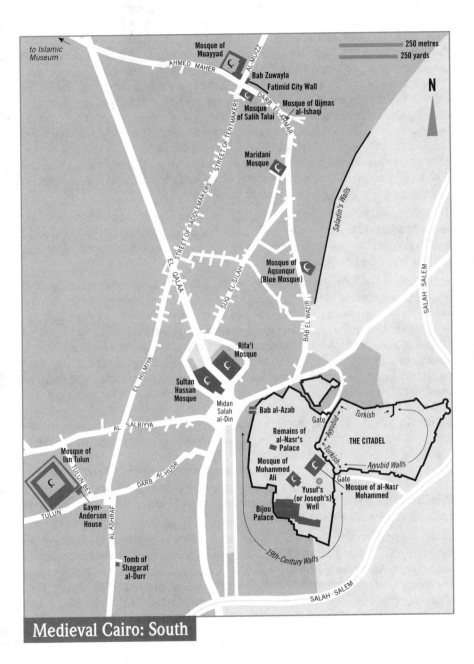

to Islamic Museum

Mosque of Muayyad

AHMED MAHER

AL-MUZZ

Bab Zuwayla

Fatimid City Wall

DARB EL-AHMAR

Mosque of Salih Talai

Mosque of Qijmas al-Ishaqi

STREET OF TENTMAKERS

Maridani Mosque

STREET OF SADDLEMAKERS

Saladin's Walls

EL QALAA

SUQ EL-SILAH

Mosque of Aqsunqur (Blue Mosque)

BAB EL WAZIR

SALAH SALEM

250 metres
250 yards

N

Rifa'i Mosque

EL HILMIYA

Sultan Hassan Mosque

Midan Salah al-Din

AL SALBIYYA

Bab al-Azab

Gate

Turkish

THE CITADEL

Ayyubid

Remains of al-Nasr's Palace

Turkish

Ayyubid Walls

Mosque of Ibn Tulun

TULUN BEY

DARB AL-HUSR

Mosque of Mohammed Ali

Yusuf's (or Joseph's) Well

Gate

Mosque of al-Nasr Mohammed

TULUN

Gayer-Anderson House

AL ASHRAF

Bijou Palace

19th-Century Walls

Tomb of Shagarat al-Durr

SALAH SALEM

Medieval Cairo: South

Ibn Tulun was sent to govern Cairo by the Abbasid caliph at Baghdad and the mosque, built in AD 876–9, displays strong Mesopotamian influence. A congregational mosque with an inner courtyard or sahn of parade-ground proportions, it strives to fulfil the ideal of accommodating all the troops and subjects of the fortress capital for Friday prayers. Arcades run round the sahn on four sides, deeper along the qibla wall facing Mecca. Brick piers support the pointed horseshoe arches which have a slight return (that is, they continue their curve inwards at the bottom), and the arches are decorated with carved stucco (restored on the outer arches but original on the others within the arcades), a technique Ibn Tulun introduced to Cairo. The windows along the qibla wall (to your left as you enter the mosque) have stucco grilles (the fifth and sixth from the left are original), permitting a faint light into this deeper arcade with its prayer niche or mihrab and beautifully carved pulpit or minbar, 13th-century restorations. The roof, like the repaired stucco work, is owed to the efforts of 20th-century restorers. Original, however, is the Koranic inscription carved in sycamore running at a height round the interior of the four arcades.

The effect as you enter the sahn is of severe simplicity, yet these details of carved stucco and sycamore and returning arches offer subtle relief. You should walk round the sahn under the arcades to appreciate the play that is made with light and shadows, the rhythm of the arches, the harmony of the ensemble.

At the centre of the sahn is a 13th-century fountain. All these 13th-century restorations and additions were undertaken by Sultan Lajin, who had assassinated the incumbent sultan and hidden in the then decrepit mosque: he vowed that if he survived to be raised to the sultanate he would restore his hideaway. Also to him belongs an explanation for the striking minaret opposite the qibla wall. The original was Tulun's, in the form of a spiral, and there is a story of Tulun, normally of grave demeanour, absentmindedly twiddling a strip of paper round his finger to the consternation of his audience, excusing himself with the explanation that it was the model for his new minaret. In fact its prototype, still standing, was the minaret of the Great Mosque of Samarra in Iraq. But Lajin had to rebuild it and out of taste or for stability gave it a squared base. It succeeds in being extraordinary and along with the merlons along the parapets of the arcades, like a paperchain of cut-out men, it has the alertness of the surreal. You can climb the minaret right to the top, although as you round the spiral there is nothing to steady you and a high breeze adds to the vertigo. There is little close by but tenements with views into bedroom windows, though to the west you can see the Pyramids, to the north pick out the major landmarks of the Fatimid city, and below you again contemplate the forthright plan of the mosque.

At the southeast corner of the Ibn Tulun Mosque is **Bayt al-Kritliyya**, the House of the Cretan Woman (in fact it is two 17th-century houses knocked together). It is better known as the **Gayer-Anderson House** (*open daily 8–4, closed Fri noon–1; adm LE16; entrance tickets are valid on the same day for the Islamic Museum*), named after the British major who restored and occupied it during the first half of the twentieth century. He filled it with his eclectic collection of English, French and oriental furniture and bric-a-brac, which can be disconcertingly anachronistic, but does give the place a lived-in feeling. Its tourist reputation must be founded on this and its proximity to the Ibn Tulun, for otherwise it is not half as fine as the Bayt al-Suhaymi, between Khan el Khalili and the northern walls.

Overlooking its large reception room is a balcony enclosed in a wooden mashrabiyya screen from which the women of the harem could discreetly observe male visitors and their entertainments. Edward William Lane in his *Manners and Customs of the Modern Egyptians*, which describes Cairo in the 1830s, says the women 'have the character of being the most licentious in their feelings of all females who lay any claim to be considered as members of a civilised nation... What liberty they have, many of them, it is said, abuse; and most of them are not considered safe unless under lock and key, to which restraint few are subjected. It is believed that they possess a degree of cunning in the management of their intrigues that the most prudent and careful husband cannot guard against.' Indeed, Lane believed that Egyptian women were under less restraint than those in any other country of the Turkish Empire, with those 'of the lower orders flirting and jesting with men in public, and men laying their hands upon them very freely.' As for those of the upper classes: 'They generally look upon restraint with a degree of pride, as evincing the husband's care for them and value themselves upon their being hidden as treasures.' The only man allowed into the harem, the female domestic quarters, was the husband—and so the strictures also worked against men, the only unveiled women they could see being their wives or female slaves.

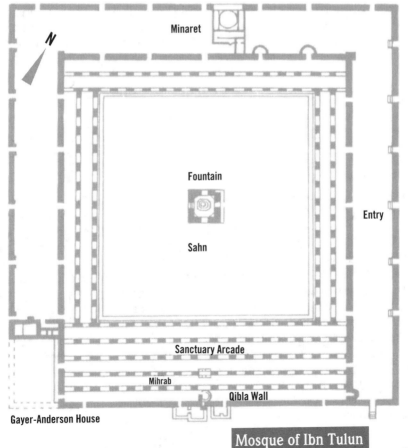

N

Minaret

Fountain

Sahn

Entry

Sanctuary Arcade

Mihrab

Qibla Wall

Gayer-Anderson House

Mosque of Ibn Tulun

The Mausoleum of Shagarat Al-Durr

Those interested in making a romantic pilgrimage to the tomb of Shagarat al-Durr (169) should walk southwards along the medieval city's main street, here called Sharia al-Ashraf, which passes just to the east of Ibn Tulun's mosque. The tomb is at the edge of the Southern Cemetery in one of Cairo's poorest areas; it stands within iron railings and is kept locked to prevent neighbourhood encroachment. Built in 1250, it is small and simple, though in allusion to her name, Tree of Pearls, the prayer niche inside bears fine Byzantine-style mosaics of the tree of life inlaid with mother-of-pearl. Until Pakistan's Benazir Bhutto and Turkey's Tansu Çiller each became prime minister of their countries, Shagarat al-Durr and a near-contemporary at Delhi were the only two Muslim women rulers in history. It can be a dangerous game and Shagarat al-Durr played it fast and loose, coming to a sticky end: only part of her body lies within her tomb—the rest was eaten by dogs. Her story is told in conjunction with a visit to the mausoleum and madrasa of al-Salih Ayyub near Khan el Khalili (*see* pp.109–10).

Midan Salah Al-Din

Walk to Midan Salah al-Din; to your left (north) are two large mosques pressed against each other like the walls of a canyon, Sharia el Qalaa cutting between them. The mosque on the right (east) is the **Rifa'i**, a modern imitation of Bahri Mameluke style, where members of the late royal family, including King Farouk, are buried, as is the ex-Shah of Iran. The best thing about the Rifa'i is its near-abutment with the mosque of Sultan Hassan on the left (west), the canyon enhancing the massiveness of the latter. Both mosques are lit by orange lights at night, as though the light itself was old, not bright and white, and had been lingering on the façades for some long time until it darkened with age. But then in the darkness is the booming call to evening prayer, not mysterious but electrically amplified, saving the muezzin not only his voice but the long trudge up to the top of the minaret. It is a regrettable practice.

Sultan Hassan Mosque

The **mosque-madrasa of Sultan Hassan** (133) is genuinely of the Bahri Mameluke period and was built of stone (reputedly from the Great Pyramid)—unlike the brick of Tulunid and some Fatimid mosques—in 1356–63. Its short distance from the mosque of Ibn Tulun allows a ready comparison between these exemplars of the two principal forms of Cairo mosque. The purpose of the congregational is to gather in, and architecturally the emphasis is on the rectangular and the horizontal. But the Sultan Hassan served as a theological school, a madrasa. The madrasa was first introduced to Egypt by Saladin as part of his effort to combat and suppress the Fatimid Shi'ites. Classrooms and dormitory space required a vertical structure, most functionally a cube. The central courtyard remains a feature, but opening onto each of its sides are four enormous vaulted halls or liwans, creating a cruciform plan. The doctrinal justification for four liwans was that each served as a place for teaching one of the four Sunni, that is orthodox, Muslim rites (Shafite, Malikite, Hanefite and Hanbalite), though the origins of the liwan are found at Hatra in Iraq, an Arab city flourishing at least 400 years before Mohammed. But it was the Mamelukes who arranged them with magnificent effect in the cruciform plan and who also added domed mausolea to their

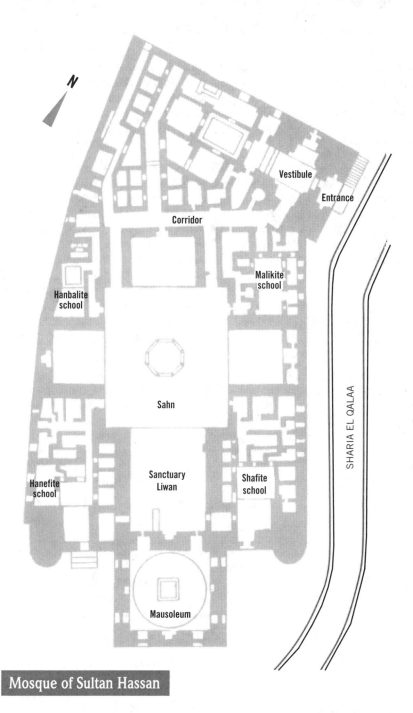

N

Vestibule

Entrance

Corridor

Malikite
school

Hanbalite
school

SHARIA EL QALAA

Sahn

Sanctuary
Liwan

Hanefite
school

Shafite
school

Mausoleum

Mosque of Sultan Hassan

mosque-madrasas. Hassan's mausoleum is appended to the south end of the mosque but his tomb is empty; he was executed two years before its completion and his body disappeared.

There are many who regard the Sultan Hassan as the outstanding Islamic monument in Egypt, and certainly it vies with the Ibn Tulun. Though entirely different in type, the two mosques share a boldness of conception and clarity of execution, gathering still more strength in restraining decoration to the minimum necessary solely to underline architectural form. There is self-confidence, and at the Sultan Hassan even architectural insolence, but rarely indulgence.

The Sultan Hassan already impresses from the outside. Though it stands beneath the glare of the Citadel it holds its own, its great cornice and the strong verticals of its façade rising to the challenge. Notice how the broad surfaces along the east and west sides are relieved by blind recesses into which are set the paired arched windows of the dormitories. Height is especially emphasized as you enter on Sharia el Qalaa the towering portal with its stalactite decorations—a favourite Mameluke motif. The portal is at an angle to the main east flank of the mosque and the west flank too is bent, though at first sight the building had seemed more regular. Earlier periods had enjoyed more space, but as Cairo grew and became more dense the Mamelukes had to squeeze in their buildings where they could, though they had a fetish for achieving a cubistic effect no matter how irregular the plot. The liwans had also to be cruciform, regardless of the exterior and in the Sultan Hassan this has been neatly done, all hint inside of the irregularity of the outer walls suppressed except for the slight angle of the door in the west liwan.

The portal leads to a domed cruciform vestibule and you turn left into a dark angled passage. It empties suddenly into the north end of the brilliantly sun-filled sahn, certainly a deliberate effect and a preparation for the play of light and shadow, concrete and void, intended for the courtyard and its liwans. It is important that you do not come too late in the day; indeed it is best to visit the Sultan Hassan in the morning, when the sun lights up the mausoleum and west liwan and begins its long and rarely accomplished reach into the full depth of the sahn. Its depth is considerable, for the liwans lift about as high as the sahn is long. The sun soon passes, illuminating hardly more than the merlons by late afternoon, and much of the architectural effect of direct sunlight and strong shadows is lost so that the mosque can then seem a disappointment. The stucco is pasty brown with sand and dirt, and other details need cleaning.

The gazebo at the centre of the sahn has been rebuilt in Ottoman style and is used now for ablutions. The original fountain is met later on at the Maridani Mosque. Hundreds of chains hang down from the liwans, the glow of their oil lamps at night a delight reserved for the imagination as they are all gone, though some can be seen in the Islamic Museum. The sanctuary liwan is opposite the entrance passage, a Kufic band running within it and an unfortunately fussy marble decoration on its qibla wall. The columns on either side of the mihrab are from some Christian edifice, possibly Crusader—they do not seem Byzantine. Further on either side of the mihrab are doors leading into the mausoleum. The right-hand door is panelled with original bronze inlaid with gold and dazzles when polished. The mausoleum dome collapsed in the 17th century and was rebuilt in the 18th century in the lofty imperial style of Istanbul, though it rests on the original stalactite squinches. Rich though the restored decorations are, the atmosphere is sombre and Hassan's cenotaph, surrounded by a wooden screen where women pray for the sultan's intercession, is very simple. From the grilled windows there are views of the Citadel.

The Citadel

Open daily in winter 8–5, in summer 8–6; museums close at 4.30; adm LE20.

Returning towards the Citadel you once more enter **Midan Salah al-Din**, extended by clearances at the instruction of General Kitchener. It was here that the annual pilgrimage to Mecca gathered before winding through streets lined with thousands of spectators and leaving the city at the northern Fatimid gates of Bab al-Futuh and Bab al-Nasr. The long park to its south was a parade ground and polo field for the Mamelukes. Up a ramp at the front of the Citadel is a gate, closed to the public, **Bab al-Azab**. The crooked lane behind the gate, enclosed by high walls, was the scene of the massacre of nearly 500 Mamelukes by Mohammed Ali in 1811. Only one escaped, leaping on horseback through a gap in the wall into a moat. During the Ottoman occupation and even under Napoleon the Mamelukes had survived and were a power to be reckoned with. Mohammed Ali invited them to dinner at the Citadel, bidding them homewards via this cul-de-sac and cutting them down with their bellies full.

The entrance to the Citadel is round to the left, on the north side. The military still occupies part of the Citadel, an echo of its role as stronghold of the city from 1176 when Saladin built his fortress here to the reign of Mohammed Ali. For almost 700 years nearly all Egypt's rulers lived in the Citadel, and held court, dispensed justice and received ambassadors here. A

The Citadel and the Mosque of Mohammed Ali, 1856.

succession of palaces and elaborate buildings thrown up during the Mameluke period were mostly levelled by Mohammed Ali when he built his mosque and the **Qasr al-Gawharah** (the Jewel or Bijou Palace) in their place. The palace, to the south of the mosque, now serves as a museum, and houses 19th-century royal portraits, costumes and furnishings in its French-style salons.

The **mosque of Mohammed Ali**, a Turkish delight on the Cairo skyline, proves disappointing close up—though perhaps not for those who have never visited an imperial Ottoman mosque in Istanbul. Half-domes rise as buttresses for the high central dome and the two thin minarets add an ethereal touch, possibly more in tune with our oriental dreams than the robust Arab minarets of Cairo. But the alabaster cladding, a gesture of baroque luxe, has cheapened with time, while the pretty courtyard with its gingerbread clock (given by Louis Philippe in exchange for the obelisk in the Place de la Concorde in Paris) suggests a folly rigged up for fashion and amusement. That could explain why the mosque is so popular with tourists: also the interior is vast and agreeably cool, the dome huge and the decorations in opulent bad taste. Principally, though, the architecture is routine; there is none of the feeling of lift or weightlessness to the dome that you find in the better Istanbul mosques, nor an appeal to spiritual contemplation. Mohammed Ali, whose tomb is on the right as you enter, meant this more as a symbol of the Ottoman power he had snatched.

From the parapet to the southwest there is a good view of the mosques of Sultan Hassan and Ibn Tulun and a panorama of the city which will be more or less impressive depending on the cinereous haze in which Cairo is smothered by heat and Helwan, the industrial area to the south.

Across from the entrance to the courtyard of the Mohammed Ali Mosque is the **mosque of al-Nasr Mohammed** (143), not much visited, dating from 1318–35. Once the principal mosque of the Citadel, it was built in the congregational style with an arcaded courtyard, many of the columns re-used from pharaonic, Roman and Byzantine buildings. Plain though it is outside, it is beautiful inside, all the more so as Turkish vandals stripped it of its marble panels, revealing its simple elegance. The two minarets are unique for the pincushion shape of their tops and their Mongol-inspired faïence decoration, of which only traces remain.

Just beyond the southeast corner of the mosque of al-Nasr is a tower which stands over **Bir Yusef** (305), Joseph's Well, also known as Bir al-Halazun, the Well of the Snail, for the spiral staircase leading 88m down the great central shaft to the level of the Nile. Yusuf was one of Saladin's names and the well was dug during his time by Crusader prisoners, providing a secure source of water in case of siege. The water reaches the well by natural rather than artificial channels, and was brought up by donkeys, the rock steps covered with earth to provide them with a foothold.

Passing through the Bab al-Qullah, which is northeast of al-Nasr's mosque, you enter the northern enclosure where the Burgi Mamelukes were quartered and where there are still military barracks. Here there is both the **Carriage Museum**, which includes a golden state carriage presented to Khedive Ismail by Napoleon III, and the **Military Museum**, its collection of weapons and costumes illustrating warfare in Egypt from ancient times to October 1973.

The Southern Cemetery

At this point you can interrupt your progress north with a visit to the Southern Cemetery (al-Qarafah al-Kubra, the Great Cemetery), a vast, confusing and dilapidated Muslim necropolis stretching as far as Maadi. The Eastern Cemetery (the City of the Dead) generally offers the more impressive monuments (*see* pp.117–19), but if you avail yourself of transport (or make the long walk there and back), the **mausoleum of Imam al-Shaf'i** (281) in the Southern Cemetery would more than repay an excursion.

The mausoleum is most easily reached by heading south from the Citadel along the street bearing the Imam's name, a distance of about 2km from Midan Salah al-Din. A descendant of an uncle of the Prophet, al-Shaf'i was the founder of one of the four rites of Sunni Islam and died in AD 820. The cenotaph was put here by Saladin and the mausoleum built by his brother-successor's wife who is also buried here. The mausoleum is covered by a large wooden dome sheathed in lead and is the largest Islamic mortuary chamber in Egypt. Inside you may see a couple of cats, some birds chirping, men lying about or reading the Koran, and above this the magnificent dome painted red and blue and gold, a pattern of flowers rising to the highest sound of birdsong. The original lighting system of lamps suspended from carved beams is intact—the only one to be seen in Cairo.

The spot itself is of significance: here Saladin founded the first madrasa in Egypt to counter the teachings of the Fatimid Shi'ites, and it became a centre of Shafite missionary work, the orthodox rite predominant even today in southern Arabia, Bahrain, Malaysia and East Africa. The majority of Cairenes, too, are Shafites, and the Imam is revered as one of the great Muslim saints (achieved by popular acclamation, as there is no formal notion of sainthood in Islam). Because of this, the mausoleum is annually the site of a great **moulid**, an anniversary birthday festival in honour of Shaf'i, which takes place in the eighth month of the Muslim calendar and lasts for a week from, usually, the first Wednesday. Atop the dome, like a weathervane, is a metal boat in which about 150 kilos of wheat and a camel-load of water for the birds used to be placed on the occasion of the moulid. The boat is said to turn sometimes when there is no wind to move it, and according to the position it takes to foretoken various events, good or evil: plenty, scarcity, or the death of some great man.

Darb el Ahmar

The road issuing from the northeast end of Midan Salah al-Din and passing by the entrance to the Citadel is Sharia el Mahga. Branching north off this road, between the midan and the Citadel and plunging downhill, is Sharia Bab el Wazir, the Street of the Gate of the Vizier; later as it runs up to Bab Zuwayla it becomes Darb el Ahmar, the Red Road. This entire district is known as **Darb el Ahmar**, a name which nowadays epitomizes a poorer, broken-down section of the city. At the Citadel end, which is entirely residential, the street is fairly quiet and fairly filthy; it becomes livelier, and you do not notice the filth so much, as you enter the bazaar area further north. Apart from the ruins of many old houses and some fine intact monuments, you may also encounter the gaiety of a marriage procession, a great noise of motor scooters, car horns, tambourines, ululations, whistling, chanting and cries, an amazing public racket by no more than two dozen people escorting the bride and groom through the streets.

The pleasure of this itinerary is the slow **walk** and the occasional pause at the **mosques** along the way—enjoyment of atmosphere. At the end of it, in 1.5km, you will arrive at the square before the **mosque of Salih Talai** and **Bab Zuwayla**. From there, subsequent itineraries take you to the Islamic Museum and continue your walk northwards from Bab Zuwayla to the Northern Walls via Khan el Khalili. The mosques visited in this chapter are still very much places of worship rather than tourist sights and they are usually open throughout the day and into the evening. Nevertheless, tourists may sometimes have to pay an **entrance fee**, and baksheesh should be paid for services, such as offering shoe coverings or taking you up a minaret.

Along Sharia Bab el Wazir

Soon after setting off down Sharia Bab el Wazir you come on your right to the **mosque of Aqsunqur** (143), better known as the **Blue Mosque** and much beloved for the wrong reasons by tour guides. It was built in 1347 but usurped in 1652 by the Turkish governor Ibrahim Agha who slapped up the tiles that give the mosque its popular name. The best Turkish tiles were from Iznik; these were made in Ottoman factories at Damascus and are poorly decorated and often marred in the glazing as well. They are along the qibla wall and around the walls of Agha's tomb which you enter through a door on the right side of the courtyard. The worst thing about the tiles is their inappropriateness, for the mosque is otherwise charmingly simple. A stand of palms and other trees makes the courtyard an agreeable place to linger after the hot desolate sahns of other mosques. The pillars round the courtyard, and especially the octagonal ones of the sanctuary, are crude but contribute to the rustic pleasantness of the whole. The finest work is the carved stone minbar, which is original. On the left before entering the courtyard is the **tomb of Sultan Kuchuk**, the Little One, a brother of Hassan who ruled for five months at the age of six, but was then deposed, imprisoned in the Citadel, and three years later strangled by another of his brothers.

From the street you can see behind the Aqsunqur a section of **Saladin's walls** which extended from the Fatimid city in the north to Fustat in the south, the Mamelukes using a part of its southern section to carry their aqueduct. Across the street from the mosque is a Turkish apartment building from 1625.

Into Darb el Ahmar

Continuing north, Sharia Bab el Wazir becomes Darb el Ahmar; set at an angle to this street, on the left-hand side, is the **Maridani Mosque** (120). Built in 1339–40 in the early Mameluke period, it is one of the oldest buildings in the quarter which until the 14th century had been Fatimid and Ayyubid cemeteries.

Entering from the hurly-burly of the street you are soon absorbed into the restfulness of the Maridani; a monument, yes, but no museum, no entry fee, no one to ask baksheesh for shoe covers, for there are none: leave your shoes inside the door and walk about in your socks.

Isolation from the outside world is as much a matter of tranquil ambience as it is of ritual cleanliness. The atmosphere attracts many who come not only for prayer: here you may see men sleeping, boys doing their homework leaning up against the qibla screen, a dozen women talking and their children playing at the fountain (the one removed from the Sultan

Hassan). Yet all these things are against the precepts of Mohammed. Lane reported eating, sewing and spinning as well 170 years ago, though these activities ceased during prayers; here you may see the hum of the everyday continue while men are on their palms and knees, submitting themselves to Allah.

If you stand in the open courtyard of the Maridani in the evening, you may see a crescent moon hanging from the approving sky. An easy rhythm of arches on slender columns runs round the courtyard, an inner and an outer series, a third and partial fourth (on either side of the mihrab) added to the qibla arcade. A wooden screen separates the qibla from the court-yard, a unique feature in Cairo, and, inside, the arcade is agreeably dark. The mihrab and the minbar wall have had their mosaic decorations well restored. The dome above the mihrab is supported by two pink granite pharaonic columns. The merlons along the parapet of the courtyard are at intervals topped by curious pots. Try, if you can, to climb up the minaret for a more immediate view of the medieval city than you can get from the Citadel.

Rituals and Prayers

Not that you need worry about form, but as a matter of interest a Muslim will carry his shoes in his left hand, sole to sole (the left hand being for unclean uses), and he will put his right foot first over the threshold. If he has not already performed the ablution outside, he will at once go to the inner fountain. Before praying, he will place his shoes on the matting, a little beyond the spot where his head will touch the ground, and again, to avoid contaminating the mosque, he will put his shoes one upon the other, sole to sole.

Prayers are performed five times a day, though mostly at home, with better-off people rarely visiting a mosque except for Friday prayers. But wherever they are performed, prayers follow the same procedure, which is quite involved. First the worshipper will stand, facing Mecca, and inaudibly propose a prayer of so many rek'ahs, or inclina-tions of the head. He then says 'Allahu Akbar', God is great, and recites the opening chapter of the Koran, followed by three or more other verses, again says 'Allahu Akbar' and makes an inclination of the head and body. Next he drops gently to his knees, places his palms upon the ground, his nose and forehead touching the ground between them, and during this prostration says 'I extol the perfection of my Lord, the Great', three times. Though still kneeling, he raises his head and body, again says 'God is great', and bends his head a second time to the ground and repeats what he has said before. This—and it is a simplification of the full litany—completes one rek'ah and will take about a minute. Several rek'ahs will be performed and there must be no wandering of the mind, no irregular movement and no interruptions, otherwise the procedure must be gone over from the beginning. Islam literally means submission and that is what the procedure achieves. The concentration required explains why mosques are often so austere: architecturally they should be conducive to prayer, but should not distract with decorations. That does not explain why, nowadays, in some mosques, women should be chattering in the corner and children splashing in the fountain, yet it does all fit together most agreeably.

Another 150m up the street is the **mosque of Qijmas al-Ishaqi** (114), built in 1480–1 during the Burgi Mameluke period. It has been squeezed into a triangular plot where a street joins Darb el Ahmar from the right, yet despite this the Mameluke fashion for rectangular illusion succeeds, at least at first glance. Inside, however, a sacrifice has been made in the cruciform plan: the north and south liwans are merely vestigial. So restricted was the space that the kuttab, the Koranic school usually part of the mosque, had to be sited across the street joining from the right; it is now derelict.

But the mosque itself has been very well restored and though around this period—only a few decades before the Ottoman domination—Mameluke architecture began to deteriorate, there was a last bravado of decorative artistry with fine marble inlays and beautifully carved stone and stucco. Within this covered mosque is a feast of detail, yet all of it harmonious and restful; nothing jitters, jumps or jars. The east and west liwans are supported by arches with a slight return, the stonework in alternating red and white, the vaults very fine and the stucco windows excellent. The inlaid marble floor is covered with mats (the mosque is in daily use), but the keeper will lift these if you ask; the best section to see is the mosaic flooring of the east liwan. You can also ask to go up the minaret from which there is a clear view of Bab Zuwayla.

The **tomb chamber** by the entrance is plain and dignified beneath a lofty dome. But Qijmas, Master of the Sultan's Horse and officer in charge of the yearly pilgrimage to Mecca, died in Syria and is buried at Damascus; the chamber contains the more recent tomb of a 19th-century holy man. Mamelukes and Turks of Qijmas' rank built not only for Allah or themselves, but also for the community, and a *sabil* or public watering fountain was often provided. This was in keeping with Mohammed's reply when asked what was the most meritorious act: 'To give people water to drink.' You can see its grille outside at what was a convenient height for drawing water 500 years ago, though it's now well below street level.

Outside the Gate of the Fatimid City

Darb el Ahmar now bends to the west, a surviving section of Fatimid wall concealed by the building on your right, and opens into a square dominated by **Bab Zuwayla** (*see* p.100), the massive southern gate into the Fatimid city. The place has long had a reputation for being unlucky, perhaps because it led out to the cemeteries now built over by the Darb el Ahmar quarter, though it was also the site of public executions. Tumanbay, the last independent Mameluke sultan, was hanged here by the Turks. Twice the rope broke, but the third time his neck.

The street running directly south from Bab Zuwayla is the continuation of the principal Fatimid street to the north and extends all the way down, past the mosque of Ibn Tulun and through Saladin's walls to the vicinity of the mausoleum of Imam al-Shaf'i. This was the longest thoroughfare of the medieval city and along here amid great festivity the Mecca pilgrims would begin their arduous journey. It changes its name several times and can be worth following for its own sake a little to the south where it is first the Street of the Tentmakers, becoming less colourful as the Street of the Saddlemakers before crossing Sharia el Qalaa.

On the corner of this street and Darb el Ahmar, facing the square, is the **mosque of Salih Talai** (116), built in 1160 towards the close of the Fatimid period. A congregational mosque, perfectly rectangular in the Fatimid pattern, it is one of the most handsome in Cairo. A lower level of shops, again once at street level, was part of Salih Talai's *waqf* or endowment, as other mosques might have had fields or adjacent apartment buildings, the rents contributing to the mosque's upkeep. The façade, therefore, would have been higher, its effect still more imposing. Its five keel-arches, supported by classical columns linked by wooden tie-beams, are flanked by sunken false arches or panels topped by stylized shell niches—the whole a perfect expression of the Fatimid style. The arches, however, form a narthex or porch unique in Cairo. Along its interior wall another set of panels, each one immediately behind an open keel-arch, runs in muted harmony. In its proportion and reserve the narthex is a fine composition in classical measure. The mosque interior is spacious, an agreeable rhythm of keel-arches and tie-beams running around the arcades.

The Islamic Museum

Open daily 9–4, Fri 9–11.30 and 1.30–4; adm LE16. Entrance tickets are valid on the same day for the Gayer-Anderson House.

The **Islamic Museum** lies to the west of the Bab Zuwayla, and is at the intersection of Sharias el Qalaa and Port Said. Its entrance on the latter is through a garden to which you should return later. Of course the museum could be visited before you explore any part of medieval Cairo, but for the neophyte a visit at this point, halfway through the tour, might be best: you will already have seen enough to make you conversant with form and curious about detail, and you will explore the Fatimid city with greater appreciation.

A revelation, met especially here, is how much you miss human and animal representation in Islamic art and architecture. This is a museum without statues or paintings, where nearly every object is beautifully worked design. A different sort of attention is required, and perhaps you wish sometimes, more here than at other museums, that the exhibits could have remained *in situ*, admired as parts of a whole. But then the collection began precisely because the monuments from which they mostly came had suffered a long period of neglect—it was only then, in 1880, in part at European instigation, that the Egyptian government first seriously undertook preservation of Cairo's Islamic treasures.

The museum is not visited nearly as much as it deserves to be, so that you often receive personal attention from the attendants. The exhibits are well presented and lit and are arranged in 23 rooms which proceed chronologically for the most part, though some rooms specialize in examples of a single subject, such as textiles, from several periods. Though no guide book is available, the exhibits are numbered and labelled, often in English and French as well as in Arabic. A satisfying tour can be accomplished in an hour and a half. With one exception, all the rooms are on one floor. A brief outline follows, but some rooms may be closed and their contents either inaccessible or found in another nearby room.

Note that because the entrance used to be along the side of the building facing Sharia Port Said, the room numbers start from there; but because you now enter through the north garden (reached also from Sharia Port Said) you find yourself first in Room 7 and so should walk straight through rooms 7, 10, 4B and 2 in order to begin at Room 1.

The Islamic Museum is at Midan Ahmed Maher, where Sharia Bur Said (Port Said) and Sharia el Qalaa intersect. A **taxi** can take you here or to nearby Bab Zuwayla (the driver may know it better as Bab al-Mitwalli).

A Tour of the Museum

Room 1 contains recent acquisitions, though it also holds some permanent exhibits, including a magnificent **14th-century lantern** of bronze chased with silver from the Sultan Hassan Mosque.

Room 2 deals with the Ummayad period (7th–8th centuries AD), whose art was representational and drew on Hellenistic and Sassanid (Persian) sources.

Room 3 is Abbasid (8th–10th centuries AD) and includes Tulunid works (from the 9th–10th centuries AD). Here there is greater stylization, with the emphasis on decoration rather than representation, with great use of stucco, characterized by its slant cut. There are stucco panels from Samarra in Iraq, and tombstones, of which 3904, dating from AD 858, has fine Kufic inscriptions.

Room 4 displays works of the Fatimid period (10th–12th centuries) with examples of very fine woodwork, carved with human and animal figures and foliage. The Fatimids, who were Shi'ites, did not observe the Sunni prohibition on representation of high living forms, and were much influenced by the Persians, whose craftsmen they imported.

Room 4B, off Room 4, has fine wood, marble and stucco carving of the Ayyubid period (12th–13th centuries).

Room 5. Before entering, note above the dividing arch the windows of openwork plaster filled with coloured glass (16th–18th centuries, Ottoman period). The attendant will turn off the main lights and illuminate the coloured windows for effect. The room contains works of the Mameluke period (13th–16th centuries). There is a beautiful 14th-century fountain sunk into the floor (the attendant will turn it on). Despite the bloody succession of Mameluke sultans, Egypt during much of this period enjoyed peace and the decorative arts flourished. A Chinese influence was felt in Mameluke ceramics and pottery. Soft woods were inlaid with ivory, bone, tin and ebony, usually in star-polygons, the Naskhi cursive supplanted the squat Kufic style of decorative inscription, and arabesque floral designs found favour. A 13th-century wooden door (602) at the far end of the room shows both square Kufic and cursive Naskhi calligraphy. It is from the mausoleum of al-Salih Ayyub.

Rooms 6–10 are devoted to woodwork, illustrating the development of the art. On the far wall of **Room 6** is a carved frieze, originally from the western Fatimid palace (10th-century), showing scenes of hunting, music and other courtly activities rarely found in Islamic art. In **Room 7** are mashrabiyyas, wooden screens which preserved the privacy of the house from the gaze of the street while still admitting refreshing breezes. They were also used to screen off interior harem rooms from courtyards and reception halls. The projecting niches were for placing porous water jars for cooling. **Room 8** has examples of inlaid wood, while **Room 9** displays wood and bronze work.

Room 10, off Room 9. Here you will be asked to sit down on a lattice-backed seat round a column fountain which will be turned on for you and illuminated. This is a restful and eye-filling place to linger: gaze up at the exquisite woodwork ceiling, carved and coffered, with three dome recesses, the centre one with windows round it for ladies of the harem to see below. The period is 17th and 18th century.

Room 11 is hung with 14th-century bronze chandeliers, and in the cases are various metal-work objects, such as a perfume brazier (15111, Case 7).

Room 12 contains armour and weapons, many of them chased and inlaid. In Case 7 are swords belonging to Mehmet II (4264), who conquered Constantinople, and Suleiman the Magnificent (4263). In the same case, opposite the windows on the right, is the sword of Muradbey, commander of the Mamelukes, which has had a remarkable history. It was taken by the French general Murat after he had chased the Mamelukes up the Nile, and was presented to Napoleon who in turn wore it when calling on the Directory shortly before seizing power on 18 Brumaire 1799. He had it with him also at Waterloo and left it in his carriage which he abandoned in haste after the battle; it was then presented to Wellington.

Rooms 13–16 contain pottery of various periods from Egypt, from as far west as Spain and as far east as China.

Room 17 is up the stairs on your right as you enter from the garden. It displays textiles and carpets of various periods from Egypt and elsewhere in the Islamic world.

Room 18, off Room 19, is an outdoor court which contains principally Turkish headstones and tombs, but also other stonework objects, including a sundial and water-level measures.

Room 19 is devoted to the art of the book, its changing exhibits sometimes including illuminated Korans, at other times manuscripts such as those of Avicenna on anatomy and botany. Avicenna (which is the westernized version of Ibn Sina) lived from AD 980 to 1037 and was one of the greatest physicians of the Middle Ages. Chaucer mentions him in *The Canterbury Tales*. He was an example of the way in which the Islamic world passed on the medical theory of the Greeks, enriching it by practical observation and clinical experience.

Room 20 exhibits Turkish art since the 15th century, including tapestries, china and jewellery. Between Rooms 20 and 21 are enamelled glass lamps which the attendant will illuminate.

Room 21 has more glass lamps in cases round the walls, and in the centre a fine Isfahan carpet that once belonged to King Farouk. The lamps are from mosques (and include some of those now entirely missing from the liwans of the Sultan Hassan) and are arranged chronologically from left to right covering the 12th to 15th centuries.

Room 22 contains Persian objects, mostly pottery, some of which (Cases 1 and 2) have been copied from Chinese models.

Room 23 is for temporary exhibitions.

The **garden** can now be enjoyed on your way out; there are welcome refreshments for sale in a flower-planted setting with a shaded gazebo, a fountain, columns and other large stone pieces. Particularly fine are the large marble panels bearing Fatimid figurative reliefs of plants, birds, fish and animals. The fountain comes from the Monasterly Palace, now the Centre for

Art and Life, on Roda Island. Its purpose was to run a stream of water through channels decorated with creatures of the Nile, the channels encircling a large dining table, the flowing water keeping the diners cool.

In the same building but on the upper floor is the **Egyptian Library** with its entrance on Sharia el Qalaa. It contains over 750,000 volumes; a vast collection of manuscripts of the Koran dating back to the 8th century AD; and, most outstanding visually, a collection of Persian manuscripts adorned with miniatures of imaginative conception and frequently employing living forms as distinct from the purely ornamental art of the Korans.

Bab Zuwayla to Khan el Khalili

Though the distance covered by this walk is less than 1km, you should allow at least an hour, and that does not include wandering about Khan el Khalili itself, for you are now entering the heart of the medieval city, where streetlife as much as monuments will hold you spellbound in fascination. The most impressive thing to do is to climb one of the minarets above Bab Zuwayla.

Getting There

It's easiest to get a **taxi** to take you direct to Bab Zuwayla (the driver may know it better as Bab al-Mitwalli).

The City Gates

Bab Zuwayla was built at the same time (11th century) and in a plan similar to Bab al-Futuh and Bab al-Nasr to the north. These three are the last surviving of the 60 gates that once encircled medieval Cairo and which, well into the 19th century, were shut at night, enclosing the city's then 240,000 population. But Bab Zuwayla had long since found itself outflanked by the growth of the city to the south (where it was delimited by Saladin's walls), and in fact marked the city centre. The architects of all three were Armenians from Edessa (present-day Şanliurfa in what is now Turkey), and their work is contemporary with and resembles the fortifications of the former Armenian capital of Ani in eastern Turkey. Certainly here at Bab Zuwayla the projecting round towers connected by a walkway and an arch repeating the curve of the gateway below show Armenian or Byzantine rather than Arab inspiration. Springing from the massive towers are the elegant minarets of the mosque of Muayyad, its serrated dome further back seeming to rise between them.

The gate was named after the al-Zawila, a Berber tribe whose Fatimid soldiery were quartered nearby. But most inhabitants know it as the **al-Mitwalli** after El Kutb al-Mitwalli.

The Story of a Saint

El Kutb al-Mitwalli was the holiest man alive at any one time, who would assume a humble demeanour and simple dress, and station himself inconspicuously, even invisibly, at certain favourite places. Bab Zuwayla was the most famous of these in Egypt, though he could flit to Tanta in the Delta, or to Mecca and back, in an instant. His

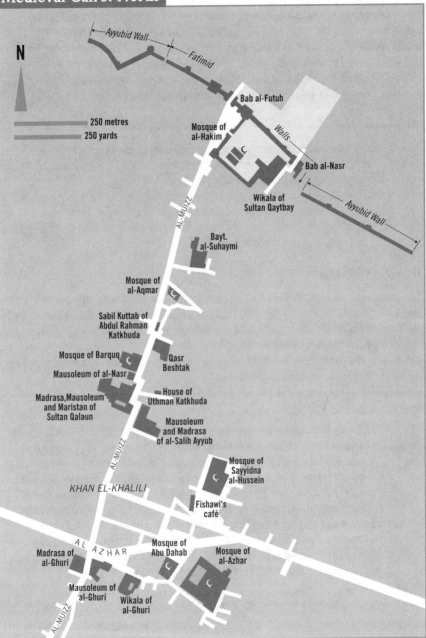

N

250 metres
250 yards

Ayyubid Wall

Fatimid

Bab al-Futuh

Mosque of al-Hakim

Walls

Bab al-Nasr

Wikala of Sultan Qaytbay

Ayyubid Wall

Bayt. al-Suhaymi

Mosque of al-Aqmar

Sabil Kuttab of Abdul Rahman Katkhuda

Mosque of Barquq

Qasr Beshtak

Mausoleum of al-Nasr

House of Uthman Katkhuda

Madrasa, Mausoleum and Maristan of Sultan Qalaun

Mausoleum and Madrasa of al-Salih Ayyub

Mosque of Sayyidna al-Hussein

KHAN EL-KHALILI

Fishawi's café

AL-MUIZZ

AL AZHAR

Madrasa of al-Ghuri

Mosque of Abu Dahab

Mosque of al-Azhar

Mausoleum of al-Ghuri

Wikala of al-Ghuri

service was to reprove the impious, expose the sanctimonious, and to distribute evils and blessings, the awards of destiny. Into the earlier part of the twentieth century, passers-by would recite the opening of the Koran, while those with a headache would drive a nail into the door, and sufferers from a recent toothache would fix their tooth to it as a charm against recurrence. Locks of hair and bits of clothing would also be attached by the sick in search of a miracle—indeed they still are; and, it is said, the saint still makes his presence known by a gleam of light mysteriously appearing behind the west door.

Passing through the gate, you should enter the **mosque of Muayyad** (190) on your left, noting the magnificent doors, removed here from the mosque of Sultan Hassan. You enter less for any intrinsic interest, though the Muayyad is restful and has a garden, than for access to the top of Bab Zuwayla or even up one of the minarets. This is a view of medieval Cairo from its heart and it is splendid. The last of the great open courtyard congregational mosques, the Muayyad was built in 1416–20 by the Burgi Mameluke Muayyad Shaykh, who had been imprisoned on the spot before becoming sultan.

Souks and Wikalas

This street running north from Bab Zuwayla is **Sharia Muizz** (named after the caliph of the Fatimid conquest), though over its distance between Bab Zuwayla and Bab al-Futuh it enjoys successive traditional names, each one demarcating a **souk** reserved to a particular trade or the sale of a particular type of merchandise—ensuring, subject to proper bargaining, price control by competition between neighbours. Hence alongside Muayyad's mosque the street is Shari'es-Sukkariya, the sugar bazaar.

Spot Checks and Punishments

In Mameluke times competition was not the only control on market prices: the mohtesib, an officer on horseback, would regularly ride through the souks, preceded by a man carrying a pair of scales and followed by the executioner. If spot checks revealed short weights, a butcher or a baker would have his nose pierced with a hook and a piece of meat or loaf of bread suspended from it as the poor man was himself tied to the grilled window of a mosque and left to endure the heat of the sun and the indifference of passers-by. One butcher who sold short was deprived of that much flesh from his own body, while a seller of kunefeh, a sweetmeat made from the vermicelli pasta (atayif) you still see prepared along the streets at night, was fried on his own copper tray for overcharging.

Continuing up to the intersection with the modern Sharia al-Azhar, you find yourself between two Mameluke buildings, the **madrasa of Sultan al-Ghuri** (189) on the left and his **mausoleum** (67) on the right. **Al-Ghuri** was the penultimate Mameluke sultan and the last to reign for any duration (1500–16). A keen polo player into his seventies, a grandiose builder, an arbitrary despot, a torturer, murderer and thief, in short no less than what you would expect a Mameluke sultan to be, he inaugurated his madrasa in May 1503 with a great banquet attended by the Abbasid caliph and all the principal civil, military and religious officials, the souks down to Bab Zuwayla magnificently illuminated and decorated. But though agreeably exotic at first impression, with strong lines and bold ablaq (that red and white pattern of the minaret with its curious topping of five small bulbous domes), on closer inspection there is lack of elegance in the details, and in climbing up to the roof you see that the ablaq is not contrasting stone but crudely painted on.

Across the street, the mausoleum dome, now collapsed, had to be rebuilt three times during al-Ghuri's reign and, as though shrewdly realizing that this might be an unsafe place to be buried, he got himself killed outside Aleppo in a losing battle against the Turks. His luckless successor, that same Tumanbay who was hanged three times at Bab Zuwayla, is buried in his mausoleum (*see* p.96). Nowadays the Ghuriya Cultural Centre is housed here, and during some times of year there are Wednesday and Saturday night performances by **Whirling Dervishes**, Egyptian adherents of the Sufi sect founded in Konya in Turkey during the 13th century by Celâleddin Rumi, known as Mevlâna.

Heading east along Sharia al-Azhar you come after about 100m to the **wikala of al-Ghuri** (64) on your right, unmistakably Mameluke with its ablaq masonry and strong, square lines. Built in 1504–5, this is Cairo's best preserved example of a merchants' hostel or caravanserai, the animals quartered on the ground floor and their masters above. The courtyard would be the scene of unloading aromatic cargoes, with buyers and sellers sitting round and bargaining. This wikala was built just at the time that the Portuguese were dealing a blow to Egypt's overland trade with the East by their discovery of new routes round the Cape to India. Even so, as late as 1835 there were still 200 wikalas serving Cairo's bazaars. The wikala of al-Ghuri now serves as a permanent exhibition of fellahin and Bedouin **folk crafts**, and those of Nubia and the oases. Folk music and dancing troupes sometimes perform in the courtyard.

The Religious Heart of Medieval Cairo

The famous **mosque of al-Azhar** (97), 'the most blooming', is 100m east of al-Ghuri's wikala, the first mosque of the Fatimid city (completed in AD 971), the oldest university in the world and the foremost centre of Islamic theology. Its age and importance have caused it to be rebuilt and added to many times, the result confusing and unremarkable. The court and arcades are basically Fatimid, but their interest lies in the people gathered here, students and teachers at lessons, some pacing back and forth, mumbling to themselves, memorizing religious texts, others dozing.

Throughout the millennium of its existence, al-Azhar has offered free instruction and board to students from all over the Islamic world, from West Africa to the East Indies, its courses sometimes lasting 15 years. Riwaqs or apartments are set aside around three sides of the court for specific nationalities or provinces of Egypt, and students have traditionally studied religious, moral, civil and criminal law, grammar, rhetoric, theology, logic, algebra and calculations on the Muslim calendar which is based on the moon, its festivals changeable but always advancing against the secular solar calendar. The **chapel of the Blind** at the eastern angle of al-Azhar accommodates blind students, once notorious for their outrageous behaviour. Fanatical in their belief and easily thinking themselves persecuted, they would rush out into the streets, snatching at turbans, beating people with their staves and groping about for infidels to kill.

Al-Azhar's religious curriculum has remained unchanged since the days of Saladin, who turned al-Azhar from a hotbed of Shi'ism to the home of orthodoxy, though Nasser obliged the university to include, too, schools of medicine, science and foreign languages, so that in many ways it is now competitive with other institutions of higher education in Egypt. The modern university buildings are behind the mosque proper.

You enter the mosque through the double-arched **Gate of the Barbers** (the only one open to visitors) where students once had their heads shaved, and for a bit of baksheesh can ascend the minaret of Qaytbey. Passing into the courtyard, on the left is the library, worth a visit, and to the right a 14th-century madrasa with a fine mihrab. The sanctuary hall directly opposite the entry gate is very deep, though in Fatimid times it did not extend beyond the fifth row of columns (that is, five rows beyond the two of the east arcade); the original mihrab remains. These columns were taken mostly from early churches. The sanctuary was extended to eight rows in the 18th century and a new mihrab placed at its furthest, qibla, wall.

Leaving al-Azhar and walking north, you pass under the busy Sharia al-Azhar and stand before the **mosque of Sayyidna al-Hussein**, a modern structure with slender Turkish-style minarets built on a Fatimid site. This is the main congregational mosque of Cairo and the President of the Republic comes here on feast days for prayers, while the open square before it is the centre for popular nightly celebrations throughout the month of Ramadan—well worth seeing.

The Hussein, named for a grandson of the Prophet, is supposedly forbidden to non-Muslims, though if you show interest you may well be invited inside. The claim is that Hussein's head was brought to Cairo in 1153 in a green silk bag and was deposited in the mausoleum (it is also said to be in the Great Mosque in Damascus), a relic of one of the most critical events in Islamic history, the schism between the Sunni majority and the Shi'ites. It is remarkable that it is here in the old Fatimid city, by the mausoleum supposedly containing the very head of the Shi'ite martyr, that the president of thoroughly Sunni Egypt should come to pray.

Shi'ite and Sunni

Mohammed was more than a prophet; he organized the Arab tribes into an enduring political and military force that within a hundred years or so of his death in AD 632 advanced as far west as Morocco and Spain, as far north as Poitiers and as far east as the Indus. But Mohammed died without naming a successor. His son-in-law Ali, husband of the Prophet's daughter Fatima, advanced his claim but after some argument Abu Bakr, one of Mohammed's companions, won acceptance as Khalifat rasul-Allah or Successor to the Apostle of God. Abu Bakr was succeeded by Omar who was succeeded on his death by Othman, an old, weak and vacillating man, but a member of the powerful Umayyad family of Mecca. Tribal tensions within the ever-expanding Arab Empire led to revolt and his murder in AD 656. Again Ali put himself forward as the natural inheritor of the caliphate, for not only was he related to Mohammed through Fatima, but he was a man of considerable religious learning and sincerity, while his supporters claimed the Umayyads were no more than power-seeking opportunists. To some extent both sides cloaked political and economic aspirations in religious arguments. Ali, however, was opposed by Aisha, who had been Mohammed's favourite wife, along with her Umayyad family and many of Mohammed's surviving companions. He took to arms and won his first battle, but later saw his authority dissolve when rebels advanced on his army with copies of the Koran fixed to the points of their spears and his troops refused to fight. Ali was assassinated and the Umayyads were installed once again in the caliphate.

The real wound to Islam occurred, however, when Ali's son—no mere in-law of the Prophet but of his blood—led a revolt against the by now overwhelming forces of the Umayyads and after a fanatical struggle was slain with all his men. In a sense the Prophet's own blood had been shed—excusable, said the Ummayads, for Hussein was no more than an outlaw; martyrdom, replied those who had supported Ali and Hussein. It was on this matter of succession—divine right versus might—that Islam was riven, for the partisans or *Shia* of Ali refused to accept as caliph any but Ali's descendants, while the Sunni, followers of the *sunna*, the Way, barred the caliphate to the Prophet's descendants for all time.

In fact, the Shi'ites went on to win some notable victories as when the Fatimids took Egypt, and to this day one-tenth of all Muslims (Iranians, most Iraqis and significant numbers in Yemen, Syria, Lebanon and eastern Arabia) still hold to the Shi'ite conviction that with the deaths of Ali and Hussein the greater part of Islam was stained with betrayal. All the same, this division within Islam is much less important than the doctrinal rifts within Christianity.

Muski and Khan el Khalili

See map of Khan el Khalili on pp.106–7.

Muski and Khan el Khalili are used interchangeably by both foreigners and Egyptians alike to describe what are historically two different **bazaars**. **Muski** lies astride Sharia el Muski, a street of Mohammed Ali's period running east from Midan Ataba, pots, pans, plastic bowls and other prosaic wares sold at its western end but blending with the oriental atmosphere of Khan el Khalili which it joins to the east. Both are lively throughout the day and well into the night, especially on Thursdays and Fridays, but most shops are closed on Sundays.

Khan el Khalili is the larger and older of the two, and grew round a khan or caravanserai built in 1382 by Sultan Barquq's Master of Horse, Garkas el Khalili. It became known as the Turkish bazaar during the Ottoman period and has always attracted foreign merchants—Jews, Armenians, Persians and Arabs—and so it is not surprising that today, along with the Muski, it is Cairo's tourist bazaar, selling souvenirs, perfume oils, jewellery, leather goods and fabrics. Of course the sight of so many tourists invites relentless importuning, but there is adventure all the same. Escape down back alleyways where an artisan sitting in his hole in

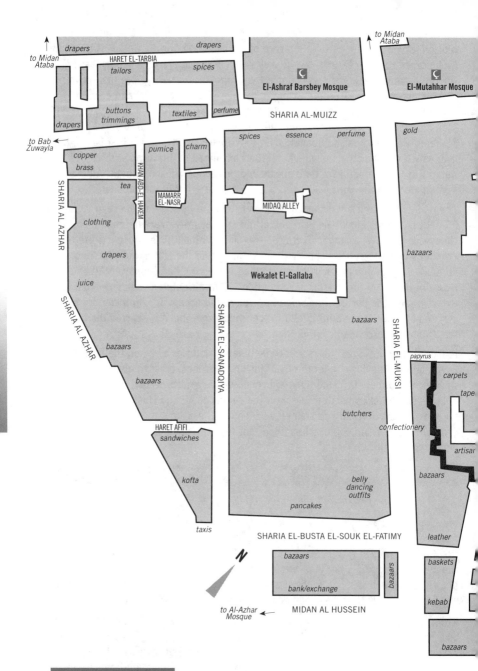

Khan el Khalili

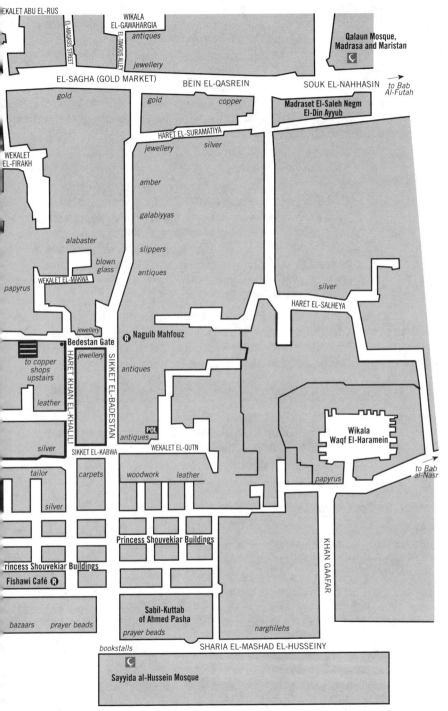

EKALET ABU EL-RUS

WIKALA EL-GAWAHARGIA

antiques

jewellery

Qalaun Mosque, Madrasa and Maristan

EL-SAGHA (GOLD MARKET)   BEIN EL-QASREIN   SOUK EL-NAHHASIN

to Bab Al-Futah

gold   *gold*   *copper*

Madraset El-Saleh Negm El-Din Ayyub

HARET EL-SURAMATIYA

jewellery   *silver*

WEKALET EL-FIRAKH

amber

galabiyyas

alabaster

blown glass   *slippers*

WEKALET EL-MAKWA

papyrus   *antiques*

silver

HARET EL-SALHEYA

jewellery

Bedestan Gate   *jewellery*   ® Naguib Mahfouz

to copper shops upstairs   *antiques*

leather

silver   *antiques*

SIKKET EL-KABWA   **POL**

WEKALET EL-QUTN

Wikala Waqf El-Haramein

tailor   *carpets*   *woodwork*   *leather*

to Bab al-Nasr

silver   *papyrus*

Princess Shouvekiar Buildings

KHAN GAAFAR

Princess Shouvekiar Buildings

Fishawi Café ®

Sabil-Kuttab of Ahmed Pasha

bazaars   *prayer beads*   *prayer beads*   *narghilehs*

bookstalls

SHARIA EL-MASHAD EL-HUSSEINY

Sayyida al-Hussein Mosque

HARET KHAN EL-KHALILI   SIKKET EL-BADESTAN

Khan el Khalili   107

the wall may be patiently making beads one by one from rough bits of stone, turning them on a spindle by means of a bow. Or start in bargaining and then break off—an accepted, indeed the expert, pattern—and instead sip a proffered glass of tea, idling for hours if you like upon a pile of carpets without there being any sense of the need for business. Or go into **Fishawi**'s, the famous café just off Midan Sayyidna al-Hussein. Here you can have the chance of easy conversation and a gentle smoke of a water pipe ('Do not inhale, it is not hashish'), and open the pages of *Children of the Gebelawi* (banned in Egypt for being blasphemous) or *Midaq Alley* by Naguib Mahfouz, Egypt's Nobel Prize-winning novelist, who found the settings for these books around this area:

> *Many things combine to show that Midaq Alley is one of the gems of times gone by and that it once shone forth like a flashing star in the history of Cairo. Which Cairo do I mean? That of the Fatimids, the Mamelukes or the Sultans? Only God and the archaeologists know the answer to that, but in any case, the alley is certainly an ancient relic and a precious one... Although Midaq Alley lives in almost complete isolation from all surrounding activity, it clamours with a distinctive and personal life of its own. Fundamentally and basically, its roots connect with life as a whole and yet, at the same time, it retains a number of the secrets of a world now past.*

Khan el Khalili extends in part over the site of the now vanished Fatimid palaces which covered an area of 400,000m² and housed 12,000 domestics. The palaces, al-Muizz on the east side of Sharia Muizz and al-Aziz on the west, loomed like mountains when seen from afar; near to, they could not be seen at all, so high were the surrounding walls.

To the Northern Walls

Allow two to three hours for this walk of about 1.5km from Khan el Khalili to the northern gates of the Fatimid city, **Bab al-Futuh** and **Bab al-Nasr**. Along the way, you should not fail to visit **Qalaun's mausoleum** and **Bayt al-Suhaymi**, the finest of the old Cairene houses open to the public. It is also good to walk here at night when the stones still seem to breathe the tales of the beautiful Shagarat al-Durr and the crazed Caliph al-Hakim.

Street of the Coppersmiths

Sharia Muizz, as you leave the awning-covered alleyways of Khan el Khalili and walk north along it, is the Street of the Coppersmiths, with some bashing of metal and much flashing of sunlight. Some reminders of the Fatimid period survive, though mostly the monuments are Mameluke. There should be a mosque on every street, it is said, but here mosques fight for every corner, their domes and minarets bunched like palms in an oasis grove. The scene is still that of the *Thousand and One Nights*, ostensibly set in Baghdad, though Baghdad by then had been razed by Tamerlane and it was the Cairo of the Mamelukes that was described. Sweet juices and cool water are sold in the street by a waterseller who has a large flask slung under one arm like a bagpipe, and the cups round his waist. He leans forward to pour, and for a moment you imagine this to be an obeisance to a passing sultan; in the sweep of robes, the clattering of donkey carts, the bursts of reflected light from the coppersmiths' stalls, you easily imagine a triumphal entry, a parade of state, singers and poets preceding the royal appearance, celebrating the achievements of his reign. You see fluttering banners of silk and gold thread, then, carried before the sultan himself, the jewelled saddlecloth, symbol of his sovereignty; held aloft by a prince of the blood above his head is a parasol of yellow silk surmounted with a golden cupola on which perches a golden bird. A band of flutes, of kettle-drums, trumpets and hautboys is passing now, their music mingling in the clamour of the street and then lost.

There is spectacle enough in Sharia Muizz and behind its façades to remind you that this was a city of beauty and mystery. Ruthless for power, cunning in government, often brutal and barbarous, the Mamelukes at their best were resourceful and vital, with an incomparable flair for architecture. Their grandiose designs, bold, vigorous and voluminous, were gracefully decorated with the play of arabesques, the embroidery of light through stained-glass windows.

Al-Salih Ayyub and Shagarat al-Durr

You come first, on the right, to the mausoleum and madrasa of al-Salih Ayyub, diagonally opposite the Maristan of Qalaun. Where the street now presses its way was once, in Fatimid times, a broad avenue, so broad it served as a parade ground, the great palaces looking down upon it from either side. Throughout the Fatimid and Mameluke periods, this was the very centre of Cairo.

The **mausoleum and madrasa of al-Salih Ayyub** need to be searched for. You turn right off Muizz into a lane—there is a tiny teashop on the corner with some round brass tables outside, an agreeable place to sit for a while. A short distance along the lane is an arch set into a façade with a Fatimid-style minaret rising from it. This is the madrasa, and you enter what remains of it by turning left into what is now used by neighbourhood youths as a playing field, liwans to east and west. The mausoleum is reached by returning to the Street of the Coppersmiths and turning right. You will see the dome on your right, and the door will be locked, but ask (or gesture to) anyone nearby for the key: they will find the keeper.

The interest of this place is historical, for it marks a political and architectural transition. **Al-Salih Ayyub** (38) was the last ruler of Saladin's dynasty. His wife, who completed his madrasa and mausoleum after he died in 1249, was **Shagarat al-Durr**, a beautiful Armenian or Turkish slave girl who ushered in Mameluke rule. While it has Fatimid elements, the madrasa was also the first to provide for all four schools of Sunni Islam, and was the first also to link madrasa and mausoleum—in short, it was the prototype for the Mameluke mosque-madrasa-mausolea to follow. Throughout the Mameluke period it was used as Cairo's central court (the schools teaching, among other things, law as at al-Azhar), and the street outside, Sharia Muizz, served as the place of execution.

The Story of Shagarat al-Durr

Shagarat al-Durr, whose name means Tree of Pearls, shares with Hatshepsut and Cleopatra that rare distinction of having been a female ruler of Egypt (1249–57). She rose to power at a critical moment, when St Louis at the head of the Sixth Crusade seized Damietta in the Delta. Ayyub, dying from cancer, was too weak to dislodge him, and St Louis was content to await the sultan's death and what he imagined would be the collapse of government and all resistance to Christian occupation of the country.

But Shagarat al-Durr was of independent and possibly nomadic stock, whose women went unveiled and were the equals of their men. She hid her husband's corpse in the Mameluke barracks on Roda while pretending he was merely ailing, and for three months ruled Egypt by appearing to transmit orders from Ayyub to his generals.

Egypt played for time and offered the Crusaders Jerusalem if they would abandon Damietta. St Louis refused. Meanwhile, in the heat, and fed bad fish by the Delta people, the Crusaders became sick with scurvy and plague. St Louis then accepted the offer of Jerusalem, but now it was the Egyptians who refused, and the Mameluke general Baybars fell upon the Crusaders, capturing St Louis, who had to buy his freedom with a vast indemnity and the renunciation of all claim to Egypt.

Shagarat al-Durr now openly proclaimed herself sultana and for 80 days was (until 1993 when the Turks elected a woman as prime minister) the only female Muslim ruler in Middle Eastern history, but the Abbasid caliph refused to recognize her, quoting the Prophet who had said, 'The people that make a woman their ruler are past saving.' So she married the leader of her Mameluke slave-warriors, Aybak, ruling through him; but when she heard he was considering another marriage, she hired assassins to murder him in his bath. Hearing his screams, seeing his body hacked at with swords, at the last moment she tried to save his life, but the assassins went on: 'If we stop halfway through, he will kill both you and us.'

When the murder was discovered, Shagarat al-Durr offered to marry the new Mameluke chief, but instead she was imprisoned and is said to have spent her last days grinding up all her jewels so that no other woman should wear them. The Mamelukes had discovered their power to make and unmake rulers; in future they ruled themselves. Shagarat al-Durr was turned over to the wife whom she had forced Aybak to divorce and who instructed her female slaves to beat Shagarat al-Durr to death with bath clogs. They tossed her naked body over the Citadel wall to be devoured by dogs. Her few remains were deposited in her tomb (*see* p.88) on the edge of the Southern Cemetery not too far from the mosque of Ibn Tulun.

Qalaun, al-Nasr and Barquq

Looking up and across Sharia Muizz you see on its west side the splendid cluster of domes and minarets that are the madrasa and mausoleum of Qalaun, the mausoleum of al-Nasr, his son and successor, and the mosque of Barquq. **Qalaun**—the name means duck and has an absurd ring in Arabic—was one of the ablest, most successful and long-lived (1220–90) of the notoriously short-lived Mameluke sultans, and moreover founded a dynasty lasting nearly 100 years. His name suggests Mongol origins, and he is known to have been brought from the lower Volga region, ruled at the time by the Golden Horde. It was al-Salih Ayyub, buried across the street, who first began importing slaves from the Volga, employing them as body-guards. Qalaun served the country of his purchase well: Damascus and Baghdad had fallen to the Mongols, Egypt and Arabia being the sole remaining bulwarks of Islam; Baybars checked the threat, Qalaun eliminated it, and then marched against the Crusaders at Acre, their last stronghold in the Holy Land, but died en route. An outstanding builder, his tribute to his Christian enemies was the adoption of Gothic elements in his complex here, the **maristan**, **madrasa** and **mausoleum** of Qalaun (43).

First you go through the gate and down a wide tree-shaded walk, the heat and noise of the Street of the Coppersmiths falling away behind you. At the end is a modern hospital, built within the vaster limits of **Qalaun's maristan** or hospital and insane asylum—a hospital has stood on this spot for 700 years. Three great liwans of the original remain, the windows of the east liwan still displaying their carved stucco surrounds. The north liwan, it seems, is now used as a dump for surgical dressings.

Islam was a wonder of enlightened medical care at a time when the ill, especially the mad, were pariahs in Christian Europe. From Spain to Persia, hospitals flourished, were divided into clinics, surgery was perfected, such delicate operations as the removal of cataracts were performed, musicians and singers entertained the sick, and upon their discharge patients were given sums of money to enable them to live until they could again find employment.

Returning to the street and turning left, the wall on your left-hand side is that of **Qalaun's madrasa**. At the far corner the line of the building then retreats and you come to what was the original entrance to the maristan. This great marble Gothic arch is in fact a magnificent piece of booty, taken by Qalaun's son and successor al-Ashraf Khalil from the church of St Andrew at Acre after its capture in 1291 and placed facing the street for all to see, a reminder to the Mamelukes' subjects of the triumph of Islam over the Crusaders. The arch opens onto a corridor, blocked at the far end, which runs between the mausoleum on the right and the madrasa on the left. During recent reconstruction of the madrasa the opportunity was taken to excavate for clues to the Fatimids' western palace which once stood here. The plan is a courtyard with a liwan at either end, the sanctuary or eastern liwan suggesting a north Syrian basilical church, with three aisles and classical columns. The stucco work further in from the arch is original.

Qalaun's mausoleum is off the other side of the corridor. The plan has been influenced by the Dome of the Rock at Jerusalem, well known to the sultan: an octagon approaching the circular within a square, the arches supported by square piers and classical columns. The dome has been restored. The structure perhaps does not seem light enough, the decorations too rich, and the mashrabiyya screen obstructs a total view (the best is from the entrance)—though it also has the effect of making the relatively small interior seem endless. But there is splendour all the same, in carved stucco, the stone inlay, the wood ornamentation, slowly revealed as your eyes get used to the filtered coloured light from the stained-glass windows—those high, double round-arched windows with *oculi* above, framed (from both inside and out on the street) by deeply recessed pointed arches inspired once again by the architecture of the Crusaders.

On your way out through the corridor, have a look at its beamed and coffered ceiling, which is marvellous. The street is just before you, yet in this complex all has been private, cool and quiet, birds chirping, trees and shade and shafts of sunlight. The buildings and their purpose reveal a dignity and humanity; they provide the peace by which you recognize an unexpected civilization.

The next building on the left, continuing north on Sharia Muizz is the **mausoleum of al-Nasr Mohammed** (44), now ruinous except for the façade with its Gothic doorway, removed from the Crusader church of St John when al-Nasr completed his father's work and took Acre. Al-Nasr's reign marked the zenith of Mameluke civilization; his principal monuments are the mosque on the Citadel and the aqueduct bringing water there from the Nile. He is in fact buried next door in Qalaun's mausoleum.

The third of this group is the **mosque of Barquq** (187), the first Burgi Mameluke sultan. It dates from 1386, about a century later than Qalaun's buildings, and the change in style is evident: the minaret is octagonal and, compared to the square blocks of Qalaun's, slender; the high monumental entrance is topped with stalactite decorations, seen also at the Sultan Hassan, which became typical of Mameluke architecture. This mosque-madrasa, in cruciform plan, was in use until the twentieth century and has been well maintained and restored. The portal is of black and white marble, the doors of bronze inlaid with silver. The sanctuary liwan is flat-ceilinged, not vaulted like the others, and receives support from four pharaonic columns of porphyry quarried in the Eastern Desert. The exquisite domed tomb chamber with marbled floors and walls of varying colours, painted ceiling, latticed and stained-glass windows and ornate wooden stalactites in the corners, contains the grave of one of Barquq's daughters—he himself was removed to his mausoleum in the Eastern Cemetery, the City of the Dead.

Some Grand Cairene Houses along the Way

Nearby are two houses of the Bahri Mameluke period (there should be someone selling tickets outside each). The **house of Uthman Katkhuda** (50) is in the street running east from Sharia Muizz, opposite Qalaun's mausoleum. It is about halfway down on the left-hand side. Katkhuda was an 18th-century lieutenant governor of the city who made what in fact was a mid 14th-century palace into his home. Only a part of the whole remains, but it is an impressive example of Mameluke domestic architecture. Suddenly you are in a narrow hall of enormous height, its bare stone walls rising to support a wooden dome, distant sunlight streaming through the windows of its octagonal drum. This was the reception room, and guests sat in the raised area at the south end. The walls were once wainscotted with marble; the woodwork remains, though the consoles within the arches date from the 16th century. Ask to go up to the roof for a view of the quarter, and look at the malqaf or ventilator, a rectangular scoop common to old Cairene houses, always facing north to catch the Mediterranean breeze. One of the best things about this place is that you will almost certainly be the only visitor; its fresh bareness invites pleasing, undisturbed thoughts of moving in and where to put the furniture.

The other house, even more a palace, is the **Qasr Beshtak** (34). This is back on Sharia Muizz, just to the north of Barquq's mosque and on the right-hand side. The entrance is the second door along the little street of the north façade. The Emir Beshtak was married to the daughter of al-Nasr and was a man of great wealth. He built his palace on part of the foundations of the eastern Fatimid palace and it once rose to five storeys, with running water on all floors. You pass though a courtyard, up some stairs, and enter the harem reception room, even more vast than Katkhuda's, with mashrabiyya screens along the galleries. From these there is a perfectly medieval view of the streets below.

The **Sabil Kuttab of Abdul Katkhuda** (21) was built in 1744 by Uthman Katkhuda's son and is one of the most charming structures in Cairo. It stands on a triangular plot at a fork in the street, the kuttab's porches overhanging the roadways on either side, the great grille of what was the fountain at its base facing south towards you as you approach. The kuttab is still used as the neighbourhood Koranic school, while the rest of the block is taken up with a renovated 14th-century apartment building.

Continue along the left-hand fork and eventually at the next block, on the right-hand side, discover a rare surviving Fatimid structure in this Mameluke-dominated part of the city, the **mosque of al-Aqmar** (33). *Aqmar* means moonlit: it was so named for the pale stone—the Fatimids, who meant to stay, building in stone rather than the earlier brick and stucco. The mosque dates from 1125 and displays a typically Fatimid keel-arch portal. The niche ribbing, used here for the first time, was to become a favourite Cairene motif. The medallion set into the niche ribbing is very finely executed. The recesses on either side of the portal have stalactite decorations, also appearing here for the first time and later taken up by the Mamelukes. The interior is original, but the slapdash minaret is modern. The mosque has been restored by the Bohra sect of India (*see* p.114), their work including modern damp-proofing against the rising groundwater.

The **Bayt al-Suhaymi** (339) is neither a palace nor a refuge for an English major's bric-a-brac. It is a merchant's house of the Ottoman period, built in the 16th and 17th centuries, and completely furnished to the age. It is the finest house in Cairo and wonderfully achieves the ambition of Islamic secular architecture—the anticipation of paradise. You reach it by taking the first right a block after the mosque of al-Aqmar. The street is called Haret ed-Darb el Asfar and the house is at No.19 (in case you do not notice the little green and white plaque) on the left-hand side. There is a broad wooden door. If there is no guardian selling tickets outside, knock.

Nothing on the façade prepares you for what lies within. The house consists of numerous rooms on irregular levels, mashrabiyya screen windows looking out onto the streets at one side, screened and latticed windows and arched galleries giving onto a garden courtyard on the other. You will want to wander, to enjoy the perspectives across the court from every possible angle and elevation, though you will probably be guided—by well-informed students. They will take you to the women's bedroom which faces the street but is closely latticed, to the women's chapel outside it, a malqaf, air conditioner, above your head. You will then be deposited in the harem reception room overlooking the garden, its floors of marble, its walls covered with the most delicate green and blue plant-patterned enamel tiles, and with carved and painted wood decorations. Here you can rest and begin taking it all in. For it is not the plan, not the details, but the ambience of the place that seduces you, and you want some time.

Though this house was built in later centuries, in ambience it cannot be different from Cairene houses of earlier times, and it becomes obvious why Crusaders crusaded—the East offered such a luxuriously pleasurable life for those with the means, far exceeding anything back in Europe. Medieval western architecture and certainly domestic living (with the possible exception of Provence) was crude in comparison, and uncomfortable. In Europe there were the seasons of cold and wet to contend with; in Egypt the heat. But here in this house they so easily defeated heat and burning sun, creating shadows and breezes, bringing plants and birds into their home, embracing a nature they had made kinder.

The Mosque of al-Hakim and the Northern Gates

Return once again to Sharia Muizz and turn right (north). It is wonderful to walk along this seemingly humble street, learning its secrets, the treasures offered in this guide only a sample of the many more that would require a far longer exploration. You are heading towards Bab al-Futuh and the walls which limit the Fatimid city. But first, on your left, is the clean, pencil-like minaret of the **Silahdar Mosque**, a Turkish-style structure of Mohammed Ali's time. Though centuries out of place for this quarter, the minaret is a graceful landmark that never fails to draw your attention as you pass by.

After about two blocks, the street broadens into a **market** area where garlic and onions are transported into the city and sold. The trucks that rumble in and out of Bab al-Futuh are painted with eyes as talismans against the evil eye. It is an appropriate place for superstition: on your right and leading to the Fatimid wall is the **mosque of al-Hakim** (15), completed in 1010. For centuries this mosque's aura meant that it was avoided by Cairenes who rarely used it for worship and let it crumble. It was used as a prison for Crusader captives, as a stable by Saladin and as a warehouse by Napoleon. As recently as 1980 it was ruinous, its roofless arcades haunting, dominated by its massive brooding minarets in keeping with the Fatimid wall. These minarets proved unsound soon after construction and needed buttressing by great trapezoid bases that project out into the street, so that they seem like ziggurats (especially when viewed from outside the walls), with pepperpot domes, placed there by Baybars II at the begining of the 14th century.

The mosque has now been entirely restored—perhaps over-restored—by the Indian-based Bohra sect of Ismailis who claim spiritual descent from the Fatimid imams. They will tell you that al-Hakim was not mad, that these are the lies of his enemies. And here certainly they have erased the darkness: there is the bright glitter of white marble and gold leaf, and at night the once forbidding arcades are illuminated by the warm glow of suspended glass oil lamps.

The Legend of al-Hakim

Al-Hakim was the third of the Cairo Fatimid caliphs who ruled with absolute political, military and religious authority. He was a paranoic who declared himself God and answered objections by inciting mobs to burn half the city while he lopped off the heads of the well-to-do, claiming the assistance of Adam and Solomon in angel guise. Jews he made walk about Cairo wearing clogs round their necks and Christians he made carry heavy crosses.

In the company of only a mute slave, he would spend his wary nights riding a donkey into the Moqattam Hills to observe the stars for portents. Then, exchanging clothes with his slave, he would secretly descend into the city and mix with the people to learn their complaints, though assuming the role of a cadi to punish infractions with summary decapitations. One night, returning from the hills, he was assassinated—at the instigation, it is thought, of his sister Setalmulq, whom he had intended to marry.

Some say he survived the attack and retreated to the desert. The Copts claim that Christ appeared to him, and that he begged for and was granted pardon. Others say he withdrew to the sanctuary of Ammon at the Siwa Oasis deep in the Western Desert, where more than a thousand years earlier Alexander had heard himself declared the son of Zeus. There, it is said, al-Hakim formulated his doctrine of a tolerant religion, similar to Islam, which was carried by Darazi, his disciple, to Lebanon where the Druze view al-Hakim's life as a kind of Passion, giving him his due as their messiah.

It was at **Bab al-Futuh**, the Gate of Conquests, that the great caravan of pilgrims returned each year from Mecca and then made its way along Sharia Muizz and Sharia Bab el Wazir to the Citadel. Nowadays the journey is made by jet. The gate is similar to Bab Zuwayla, with projecting oval towers, though the masonry is finer and the impression greater, for the space outside it has been cleared and there is a magnificent view of the ensemble of Bab al-Futuh, Bab al-Nasr (the Gate of Victory, to the east), the linking Fatimid wall and al-Hakim's minarets. The **Fatimid wall** extends to the west; beyond that, where it retreats, and also to the east of Bab al-Nasr, the wall dates from Saladin. You can walk both within and along the top of the wall between the gates: to do this you should make yourself obviously interested at either gate and eventually someone will come along with the key.

Re-entering the medieval city through Bab al-Nasr, the immediate area is noisy with metal workshops. On the right (west) against the east façade of al-Hakim's mosque is the **wikala of Sultan Qaytbey** (11), built in 1481. Until recently inhabited by tinsmiths and their families, with women scrubbing, washing strung across the courtyard, children beating a kitten and throwing it into the air, the caravanserai has now been cleared and is, apparently, in line for renovation.

The Return of Pilgrims from Mecca

As many as 30,000 people were about to swell the population of Cairo. I managed to make my way to Bab al-Futuh; the long street which leads there was crammed with spectators who were kept in place by soldiers. The procession advanced to the sound of trumpets, cymbals and drums; the various nations and sects were distinguished by their trophies and flags. The long files of harnessed dromedaries, which were mounted by Bedouins armed with long muskets, followed one another monotonously, but it was only when I reached the countryside that I was able to appreciate the full impact of a spectacle which is unique in all the world.

A whole nation on the march was merging into the huge population which adorned the flanks of the Moqattam on the right, and, on the left, the thousands of usually deserted edifices of the City of the Dead; streaked with red and yellow bands, the battlements on the walls and towers of Saladin were also swarming with onlookers. I had the impression that I was present at a scene during the Crusades. Further ahead, in the plain where the Qalish meanders, stood thousands of chequered tents where the pilgrims halted to refresh themselves; there was no lack of dancers and singers; all the musicians of Cairo, in fact, competed with the hornblowers and kettledrummers of the procession, a monstrous orchestra perched upon camelback.

Late in the afternoon, the booming of the Citadel cannons and a sudden blast of trumpets proclaimed that the Mahmal, a holy ark which contains Mohammed's robe of cloth of gold, had arrived within sight of the city. From time to time the Mahmal came to a halt, and the entire population prostrated themselves in the dust, bending their foreheads low upon their hands. An escort of guards struggled to drive back the negroes who, more fanatical than the other Muslims, aspired to the honour of being trampled to death beneath the camels, though their only share of martyrdom was the volley of baton blows showered upon them. As for the santons, who are even more wildly devout than the dervishes and whose orthodoxy is more questionable, several of them pierced their cheeks with long sharp daggers and walked on, dripping with blood; others devoured live serpents, while a third group stuffed their mouths with burning coals.

Gérard de Nerval, Journey to the Orient, 1844

Nerval was a precursor of surrealism; he enjoyed going over the top. But in this case that sober chronicler Edward William Lane, author of *Manners and Customs of the Modern Egyptians*, who observed the arrival of the caravan ten years before, is hardly less fantastic in his description, though he says the swallowing of serpents went out with the Mamelukes. The journey from Mecca took 37 days across rocky desert, the caravan moving at night. Not everyone survived: 'Many of the women who go forth to meet their husbands or sons receive the melancholy tidings of their having fallen victim to privation and fatigue. The piercing shrieks with which they rend the air, as they retrace their steps to the city, are often heard predominant over the noise of the drum and the shrill notes of the hautboy which proclaim the joy of others'.

Lane mentions that the Mahmal was empty; its purpose was entirely symbolic, dating back to the reign of Shagarat al-Durr. She went on the pilgrimage one year, travelling in a magnificent hodag or covered litter borne by a camel, and for several successive years her empty hodag was sent with the caravan merely for the sake of state. The practice was continued by Egypt's rulers till 1927, when the puritanical Saudi king, on the pretext of objecting to the soldiers accompanying it, forbade passage of this 'object of vain pomp'. These days, alas, you wait in vain for pomp at Bab al-Futuh.

You may already have noticed the **City of the Dead** as you drove in on the Heliopolis road from the airport; it did not seem inviting. It has the look of a *bidonville*—hot, dusty, dilapidated, with a quantity of domes. It is in fact the burial ground of the Mameluke sultans and of others who aspired to their end, and some of its mausolea are as wonderful as anything in the city of the living. Nor is the cemetery without life. There were monasteries and schools, part of the mausolea. The poor have always made their homes here, as have the keepers, and relatives visit the family plots on feast days for a picnic. This is reminiscent of the ancient Egyptian practice of feeding the dead, though it is practized elsewhere in the Mediterranean, for example in Greece where it is more a cheerful popping of the cork and celebration of life.

Getting There

The Eastern Cemetery (Qarafat al-Sharqiyya) or City of the Dead lies to the east of the Fatimid city. The mausoleum of Barquq is 1.5km from Bab al-Nasr and Qaytbey's mausoleum is 1km from al-Azhar. So a **walk** from Bab al-Nasr, visiting these two mausolea as well as that of Ashraf Baybars—the three most outstanding buildings— and then back to al-Azhar, will cover about 3km. You may prefer to make a separate journey of it, hiring a **taxi**.

The Three Most Outstanding Mausolea

Follow the road that runs east outside Bab al-Nasr and on reaching the cemetery you will see ahead of you a broad building with two domes and two minarets. This is the **mausoleum of Barquq** (149), completed in 1411. Its plan is similar to that of a cruciform madrasa, but the liwans are not vaulted: instead there are multi-domed arcades. You enter nowadays at the southwest corner and pass through a corridor into the sahn, its vastness once relieved by a pair of tamarisk trees, now only by the fountain. On the eastern side is the sanctuary liwan with a beautifully carved marble minbar, dedicated by Qaytbey. At either end of the liwan are domed tomb chambers: Barquq (removed here from his mausoleum in Sharia Muizz) and

The City of the Dead, from Description de l'Egypte, 1809–28

his two sons buried in the left chamber, women of the family in the right. These domes are the earliest stone domes in Cairo; the zigzag ribbing on their exteriors was to develop into the elaborate polygons of Qaytbey's domed mausoleum. From the outside, the domes are minimized by the surrounding structure, so once inside their marvellous shape and soaring height comes as a surprise.

Go back across the courtyard to the northwest corner and up the stairs. These lead you to the khanqah or dervish monastery, its four storeys a warrren of rooms, cells and corridors. For some extra baksheesh the keeper will usually let you go up the northern minaret for a sweeping view of the necropolis itself and all of Cairo from Heliopolis to the Citadel.

The **mausoleum of Sultan Ashraf Baybars** (121)—he is also known as Barsbey—is south down the paved but dusty road that passes along the front of Barquq's mausoleum. This building is less visited than the other two and finding the keeper may be more difficult than usual; apprehend the first child or lounger you see and make it known you want the key—the keeper will normally appear quite quickly. Baksheesh is then of course expected all round. This mausoleum was originally planned solely as a *khanqah* and so is unusually elongated; also it is recognized by its ungainly minaret which comes to a point too soon. Baybars, whose mausoleum dates from 1432, was a Burgi or Circassian Mameluke and is not to be confused with his namesake who held St Louis to ransom. He neither drank nor swore, though he was martial enough and took Cyprus from the Franks in 1426. The appeal of the place is in its few but well-chosen elaborations—the polygonally decorated dome rising above the simple façade through which you pass by a doorway with trefoil arch. The tomb chamber is at the north end of the mosque, dimly illuminated by stained-glass windows subsequently introduced, though the mihrab of mother-of-pearl and marble mosaic is original. But really you have come for the interior view of the dome and its impression alone is sufficient: it ascends effortlessly upwards, almost losing itself to infinity.

It is a longer distance down this same dusty road to the **mausoleum of Qaytbey** (99), completed in 1474 and a jewel of Mameluke architecture. First, from across the square, look at the ablaq masonry of the façade, the intricate polygonal relief on the exquisitely proportioned dome, and the slender minaret of three tiers (the Mameluke fashion), each tier ornately decorated with columned recesses or raised arabesques or stalactite clusters. Along with the mosques of Ibn Tulun and Sultan Hassan, this rates as one of the great buildings of Cairo. Unlike them it is free with decoration, but like them it uses its decoration to the great effect—the frequent play of filigree flowers upon star-shaped polygons which has been described as 'a song for two voices', a geometrical base with floral melody. The perfection of this mausoleum, however, like the splendour of Qaybey's reign, marked the final apogee of Mameluke vigour. Decadence ensued; two decades later the Turks were in the city and Bab Zuwayla was ornamented by the last Mameluke sultan, a rope round his neck. Inside is a cruciform madrasa with vestigial liwans to east and west. The decoration of ceilings, pavings, arches and windows is breathtakingly variegated, yet overall it is measured and subdued. There is deliberate though sensitive contrast with the scale of the courtyard and sanctuary in the immense height of the tomb chamber, its walls drawn into the ascending dome. From the sanctuary, you should climb the **roof** to enjoy at closer hand the tracery of stone carving on the dome and minaret, as delicate as previous periods had managed in wood and stucco.

Qaytbey

He is an old man of about 80, but tall, handsome and as upright as a reed. Dressed in white, he was on horseback, accompanied by more than 2,000 Mameluke soldiers... Whoever wishes can have access to the sultan: there is in the town a great and splendid fortress at the entrance of which he sits publicly on Mondays and Thursdays, accompanied by the governor of the city; a guard of more than 3,000 Mamelukes surrounds him. Whoever has been manhandled or robbed by one of the Mameluke princes or emirs can there complain. Thus the nobles refrain from actions that might carry condemnation.

Meshullam ben Menahem

This description of Qaytbey by an Italian Jew portrays him in a sympathetic light. Along with al-Nasr, Qaytbey was the grandest of Mameluke builders, emblazoning his cartouche on buildings religious and secular throughout the Middle East, as well as in Cairo and Alexandria. He was also the last Mameluke ruler of strength. He came up through the ranks, having been bought by Ashraf Baybars, and apart from al-Nasr ruled longer than any other sultan.

The Egyptian Museum

Open daily 9–4.45, closed Fri noon–2 in summer, 11.30–1.30 in winter in summer; adm LE20 plus LE40 for the Mummy Room. Note that tickets used Fri morning are not valid on Fri afternoon.

The **Museum of Egyptian Antiquities**, to give it its proper name, is housed in a rose-coloured neoclassical building in what was one of the quietest areas of Cairo when the museum was built in 1902; now, in their brainlessness, the authorities have created Cairo's busiest traffic intersection on its doorstep and a fume-filled bus depot behind. Within the ill-lit, leaking museum, which relies on open windows for ventilation, 120,000 catalogued objects, of which 44,000 are on display at any one time, bathe in pollution levels reaching 80 per cent of those outside (as compared to 0.5 per cent in environmentally controlled Western museums). During peak periods it can be murder trying to barge your way round the collection. Unfortunately, proposals to modernize and enlarge the building have been shelved owing to lack of money.

Allowing one minute for each exhibit on display, you could see everything in about four months. The average guided tour lasts two hours. The selection offered here would take one hard-working day to cover, though it would be better to break that down into two or three half-day visits. The exhibits are numbered and some carry background notes in English, French and Arabic. The rooms are also numbered, as shown on the plans. The collection is arranged more or less chronologically, so that starting at the entrance and walking clockwise round the ground floor you pass from Old Kingdom to Middle and New Kingdom exhibits, concluding with Ptolemaic and Roman exhibits. The first floor contains prehistoric and early dynastic exhibits and the contents of several tombs, including Tutankhamun's. Not every room is mentioned in the tour below. Please note that some objects may have been moved elsewhere, and that some rooms close early.

Getting There

The museum is on the north side of Midan el Tahrir, near the Nile Hilton. The **metro** station is Sadat.

The Ground Floor

Immediately upon entering (from the south), you walk into a rotunda that is **Room 48**. Apart from the monumental Sphinx at Giza, the colossal head to the left of Userkaf (V Dynasty) is the only large sculpture surviving from the Old Kingdom. The rotunda contains other giant works (out of chronological order), including three colossi (1, 2, 4) of Ramses II (XIX Dynasty) and a statue of Amenhotep son of Hapu (3), architect to Amenophis III (XVIII Dynasty).

The Old Kingdom

Room 47 contains IV, V and VI Dynasty items. The walls are lined with sarcophagi. Most interesting are the figures in the central aisle cases, including, in Case B, statuettes of the dwarf (160), the man with a deformed head (6310) and the hunchback (6311), but also, in Case D, those of people grinding corn, kneading dough and preparing food (a goose about to be gutted and plucked).

Room 41. The V Dynasty bas-relief (79) with scenes of country life is particularly worthy of close observation. Farm tasks and crafts are carried on through a series of registers. The women wear ankle-length chemises, but the men wear only a cloth or are sometimes entirely naked. They are circumcised as was the Egyptian custom. There is also one episode of a malefactor being held and brought before a court.

Room 42. The very fine statue of Chephren (138) in black diorite with white marbling was found in a shaft at his valley temple at Giza where he built the second of the Great Pyramids. The falcon god Horus embraces Chephren's head with his wings, at once transferring the ka and protecting the pharaoh. The remarkably preserved wooden statue of **Ka-aper** (140) is vividly executed. You feel you would recognize the face in the original, and indeed when Mariette found it at Saqqara his workmen immediately dubbed it Sheikh el Beled because of its resemblance to their village headman. The living eyes are copper inlaid with quartz. It is said of some paintings that the eyes follow you; in this case it is uncanny how they fix you with their sure and level gaze when faced head on, but as soon as you shift even an inch they gaze off—not inert, but reflectively, into an internal dream world of their past.

Room 31. Outstanding here are the six wooden panels of the II Dynasty priest Hesire (88). This was the brief period in ancient Egyptian history when moustaches were fashionable.

Room 32. One gets so used to the rigid frontality of Egyptian sculpture that it is a surprise to see the wooden statue in the far right corner with its slight twist. At the centre of the room are the IV Dynasty statues (223, 195) of Prince Rahotep and Princess Nafrit; her skin painted yellow, his ruddy brown. He has short back and sides and sports a natty moustache. In his white waist cloth he looks for all the world like an advertising executive taking a sauna. The group representing the dwarf Seneb, Chief of the Wardrobe, with his wife and two children

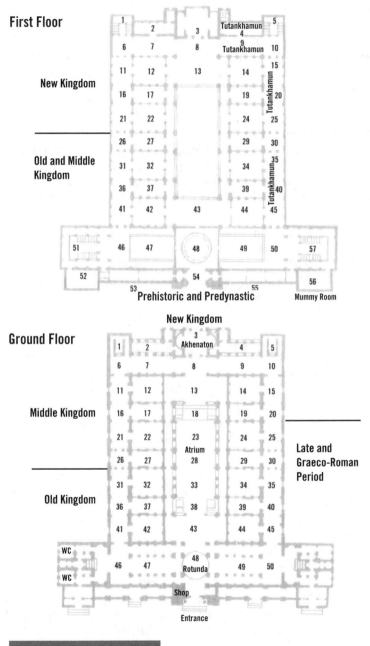

First Floor

New Kingdom

Old and Middle Kingdom

1				Tutankhamun	5
6	7	8		9 Tutankhamun	10
2		3	4		
11	12	13		14	15
16	17			19	20
21	22			24	25
26	27			29	30
31	32			34	35
36	37			39	40
41	42	43		44	45

Tutankhamun

Tutankhamun

| 51 | 46 | 47 | 48 | 49 | 50 | 57 |
| 52 | | 54 | | | | 56 |

53 55
Prehistoric and Predynastic   Mummy Room

Ground Floor

New Kingdom

3
Akhenaton

1	2		4	5
6	7	8	9	10
11	12	13	14	15

Middle Kingdom

16	17	18	19	20
21	22	23	24	25
		Atrium		
26	27	28	29	30
31	32	33	34	35
36	37	38	39	40
41	42	43	44	45

Late and Graeco-Roman Period

Old Kingdom

WC

WC

| 46 | 47 | 48 Rotunda | 49 | 50 |

Shop

Entrance

The Egyptian Museum

(6055) deserves close attention. It is delightful, but also a puzzle. Despite his small size, Seneb is a man of importance; he looks pleased with himself, sure of his position, his family and his wife's proud affection. Notice his legs: they are too short to hang over the edge of the chair; instead his children stand where his legs would be—is this a mere compositional nicety or has it a symbolic intention? And look at the children, their right index fingers to their lips as though they were keeping a secret. The III/IV Dynasty '**Geese of Meidum**' (136) are vividly coloured. The copper statues (230, 231) of Pepi I and his son are the first metal statues known, and that of Pepi the largest of its kind. He is a great striding figure, reminiscent of an archaic Greek kouros.

The Middle Kingdom

With **Room 26** you pass into the Middle Kingdom. Here (or hereabouts, as he is unusually peripatetic) is a rare and astonishing wooden ka statue (280) of the Pharaoh Hor (XII Dynasty) stepping out from his naos. It actually stands on a sliding base to demonstrate the wanderings of Hor's double. That it is his ka is clear from the ka hieroglyph of upraised arms on his head, and his nakedness.

Room 22. Generally sculpture and stone monuments of the Middle Kingdom. At the centre is the burial chamber of Horhotep (300). The walls are painted with oil jars and offerings are closely listed. The decorated doors, like patchwork curtains, were for the ka to flit in and out at will. Around the chamber are ten statues of Sesostris I (301). On the sides of each throne are reliefs of the gods of Upper and Lower Egypt entwining the lotus and papyrus, symbolizing the unity of the country.

The New Kingdom

Room 11. Here you pass into the New Kingdom, with a fine statue of Tuthmosis III (XVII Dynasty) in grey schist (400).

Room 12. XVIII Dynasty sculpture. The brightly decorated chapel built for Amenophis II or his predecessor Tuthmosis III once contained Hathor as cow (445, 446)—she now stands before it in a glass case. To the right is a pink granite statue (952) of Hatshepsut. Look also for the case containing a small statuette (6257), delicately carved out of Sudanese ebony, of Thay, a royal equerry.

Room 8. It is unusual for mud brick houses, even palaces, to survive, and so our impression of ancient Egypt is largely determined, often distorted, by rock tombs and stone mortuary temples. But the Egyptians did concern themselves with this world and at the centre of this room is a model of a typical house as excavated at Amarna, Akhenaton's brief capital on the Nile near Minya.

The Akhenaton Room

Room 3 contains perhaps the most astonishing works in the museum, from the reign of Akhenaton (*see* pp.53–5). Some find the Amarna style—particularly when applied in its most exaggerated form to Akhenaton himself—grotesque. Others think it powerful and often beautiful. Staring down at you are four colossi of the pharaoh: the glare of revolution, elongated face, narrow eyes, long thin nose with flaring nostrils and full, perhaps sardonic lips.

The belly and thighs protrude like some primitive female fertility figure. These are from the temple he built, at Karnak, later destroyed, its blocks serving as foundations and pylon filler for others' works. In its own glass case there is a magnificent head, probably of Nefertiti, and this is not distorted at all—though examples of Amarnan distortion applied to Nefertiti are seen on the stele in Case F, and the centre stele in Case H.

This distortion is sometimes called realism; there is a theory that Akhenaton was indeed deformed and that some of his family may have been also—hence the Amarna style was a mass acquiescence to this misfortune. But you might prefer to think that this style was deliberately experimental, calculated for effect, indeed to illustrate opposition, and as readily dispensed with (as with the bust of Nefertiti, above) when sheer beauty rather than shock value was desired. There is a note of realism, indeed intimacy, in the centre stele in Case F. Instead of showing the royal family in formal adoration of the sun disc Aton, Akhenaton is seen playing with his eldest daughter Meritaten, while Nefertiti holds their other two daughters on her lap. This expression of family joy, or any personal feelings whatsoever, was never before and never again seen in depictions of the pharaohs.

Coins

Room 4 contains a collection of Greek, Roman, Byzantine and Arab coins. Quite a few bear the head of Alexander, and on the left side of the first case on the right are several coins bearing the head of Cleopatra VII.

The Ramessids

Room 15. Items from the reign of Ramses II, including a painted limestone statue of a XIX Dynasty queen from the Ramesseum (Case A).

Room 14. On the right is a statue (743) of Ramses VI (XX Dynasty), unusual for its attempt at movement, dragging a doubled-up Libyan by the hair. A painted sunk relief (769) in the left near corner shows Ramses II similarly apprehending three prisoners, one black, one red, one brown. At the centre (unnumbered, but catalogued as 765) is a unique freestanding coronation group sculpture, Ramses III at the centre, Horus on the left, Seth on the right. Though it has been greatly restored, enough was found to determine that the figures stood on their own legs without supports.

The Late Period

The New Kingdom, in any case tottering since the end of the XX Dynasty, ended with the XXI Dynasty. Objects from the Late Period begin with **Room 25**. One ruler of the XXV Dynasty, Taharka, left his mark at several sites in Upper Egypt, for example the remains of his kiosk in the Great Court at Karnak. Here you see his sculpted head (1185) with curled hair—he was from the Sudan (which the Greeks called Ethiopia). He enjoys the distinction of being mentioned in the Bible (II Kings 19:9).

Room 24 contains a green schist statue of the goddess Tweri (791)—finely finished, though an utterly ridiculous image of a pregnant anthropomorphic hippopotamus. Otherwise, the most interesting items are the Osiris, Isis and Hathor group (855, 856, 857) at the centre, and to the left 1184, an attempt at portraiture of the Mayor of Thebes.

Room 30. At Medinet Habu are the mortuary chapels of the Divine Adorers of Amun. Amenardis, in white stone (930), was one of these princesses of the XXV Dynasty.

The Graeco-Roman Period

Room 34. Note the colossal bust (1003) of Serapis. This god, an invention of Ptolemy Soter, combined Osiris with Apis, the bull god of Memphis, but with Greek features and dress.

Room 44. The contents of royal tombs of a Nubian people, the Blemmyes, who lived just south of Abu Simbel during the Byzantine period and were under the dominion of Meroë in the Sudan. Their aristocracy was strongly negroid. Long after Christianity came to Egypt, they worshipped Isis, Horus and Bes. The burial of kings and queens was accompanied by strangled slaves and servants, and gaily caparisoned horses which were led into the tombs and axed to death. Crowns, the skeleton of a horse and the models of two others, complete with trappings, along with spearheads, jewellery, pottery and other artefacts form this fascinating exhibit. The artefacts of the Blemmyes have a strong, handsome look, similar to Celtic work—a fine brutality. (At least some of the exhibits in this room are being transferred to the new Nubian Museum in Aswan.)

Room 49. An exceptional piece is the coffin of Petosiris (6036), a high priest of Thoth at Hermopolis (c. 300 BC). The hieroglyphics are beautifully inlaid with stone and enamel. From Saqqara during the Persian period is the stone sarcophagus (on the right, near the rotunda) of a dwarf dancer at the Serapeum Apis ceremony. He has been well rewarded: his true-to-life figure is cut on the outside of the adjacent lid, while on the inside of the lid and at the bottom of the sarcophagus is carved a sex-bomb (the goddess Nut) for him to lie on and stare up at for eternity.

The Atrium. On the ground floor there now remains only the atrium to visit. At the centre of **Room 43** is the Palette of Narmer (3055), possibly the oldest record of a political event, the unification of Egypt, c. 3000 BC. Narmer was probably one of the names of Menes, the founder of the I Dynasty, from which Egypt's historical period is dated. Writing was not yet able to convey complex sentences and this slate palette tells its story by means of pictures which are easily translated into words. On the obverse, Narmer is shown braining an enemy, and to the right is a complex symbol relating the significance of this action. The falcon is Narmer, holding a rope attached to the head of a bearded man. The head protrudes from a bed of papyri, representing Lower Egypt. Therefore the symbol reads, 'The falcon god Horus (Narmer) leads captive the inhabitants of the papyrus country.' Narmer came from Upper Egypt, as the crown he wears on this side shows. On the reverse, Narmer wears the crown of Lower Egypt as he reviews the spoils of his victory, which include the decapitated bodies of his foes. The centre panel shows two fantastic beasts, their necks entwined but restrained from fighting by bearded men on either side: Upper and Lower Egypt joined, if not yet altogether at ease. On either side of the room are two large wooden boats for solar sailing from the pyramid of Sesostris III at Dahshur.

Room 38 is really a stairway leading down into the well of the atrium and contains the rectangular stone sarcophagus (624) of Ay, at first an adviser to Akhenaton, then to Tutankhamun, and later his successor. Four goddesses at each corner extend their wings protectively: Isis, Nephthys, Neith and Selket.

Room 33 displays various pyramidions from Dahshur, the capstones to pyramids. Under 6175 you can see the stone peg which slotted into the pyramid top. The sarcophagus (6337A) of Psusennes I, a XXI Dynasty pharaoh ruling from Tanis in the Delta after Egypt had split in two, has its lid (6337B) raised over a mirror so that you can see the lovely raised relief of the goddess Nut suspended from its underside. Stone sarcophagi in fact represented the goddess, for just as the sun god Re entered her mouth at sunset to be reborn at dawn, so the deceased was symbolically engorged within his sarcophagus and awaited his own rebirth. Indeed the symbolism goes further, for Nut was mother to Osiris with whom the deceased was also identified. Stone sarcophagi, therefore, which first came into use with Cheops (IV Dynasty), combined ancient Egypt's two greatest cults, of the sun and of Osiris. To the left, from the XVIII Dynasty, are the stone sarcophagi of Tuthmosis I (619), that of his daughter Hatshepsut made before she came to the throne (6024) and her final sarcophagus (620).

Room 28 at the centre of the atrium has a painted floor with a river scene (627) from the palace of Akhenaton at Tell el Amarna.

Room 23 contains two interesting lintels, the one on the left (6189) showing the Heb-Sed of Senusret III (XII Dynasty) very finely cut in sunk relief, while the one on the right is a tenth-rate copy by a later pharaoh.

Room 18 (the stairway leading out of the atrium well) has the colossal group (610) of Amenophis III and his wife Tiy with three of their daughters (XVII Dynasty). They are serene, almost a portrait of Victorian contentment but for the play of a smile on their lips and the physicality of their bodies. Despite the formality of the work and its size, there is a great sensuality to it. The reign of Amenophis was marked by luxury and a sudden eruption (or at least recording) of fashion consciousness: note particularly Tiy's full wig, the hair falling down to her breasts, a style associated almost exclusively with this reign.

Room 13. On the right is a fascinating document, a stele (599) inscribed on the reverse during the reign of Amenophis III with all that the pharaoh had done for Amun, but later inscribed on the obverse by Merneptah, pharaoh at about the time of the Exodus, with the sole known reference in Egyptian texts to the Israelites: 'Israel is crushed, it has no more seed.'

Corridors on each side of the atrium (allowing communication between Rooms 43 and 8 but not with the atrium itself) are lined with pottery, wall paintings and inscription fragments.

Here and there throughout the museum you may notice a curiosity resembling one of those cookie-cutters used for making gingerbread men, but life-size. It is in fact a vegetating Osiris, a wooden silhouette of the god with his image again carved out within this; the depression was once filled with earth from which grass would sprout with symbolic effect.

The First Floor

To see the first-floor rooms in approximate chronological order you should start at Room 43 overlooking the atrium from the south and follow the corridors in a clockwise direction.

Old and Middle Kingdom Tomb Contents

Room 42. Outside, there is a panel (6278) inlaid with blue faïence, from Zoser's Step Pyramid at Saqqara. Inside the room you should spend time with the alabaster vase (3054) on the right, beautifully round and smooth and yet criss-crossed in raised stone with ropes from which it would have been suspended. In Case Q is the black Palermo Stone which bears a list of pharaohs from the I to mid-V Dynasties along with important events during the period and annual measurements of the Nile flood, thus adding much to our knowledge of the Old Kingdom.

Room 37 is full of wooden coffins and sarcophagi of the Middle Kingdom. The coffin of Sepi (3101 in Case C), a XII Dynasty general, is particularly well-painted. This is the oldest anthropoid coffin in the museum. The dismantled panels of his sarcophagus (3104, Cases A and L) are finely painted and extensively inscribed. Artefacts from the tomb of General Mesah at Assiut are displayed in several cases and include his sandals, mirror and neck pillow, and models of Egyptian soldiers (3345), black soldiers (3346) and a pleasure barge (3347).

Room 32 contains models (Case E: 3246, 4347) of solar boats. The solar boats are unmanned, operating on autopilot. They are the abstraction of the other boats displayed: funerary boats for carrying the dead man on a canopied bier, or for transport of the living. There is a delightful model of a boat (3244 in Case F) with its mast down, its rowers pulling at full strength, one rower taking a quick sidelong glance at you as the boat shoots by.

Room 27 contains marvellous models (6077–86) from the XI Dynasty tomb of Meketre at Thebes, including a plantation owner reviewing a parade of his cattle and workers (6080); a carpenter's workshop (6083); a pleasure garden with pool, lined with sycamore-figs, at one end a columned verandah (6084); and two boats dragging a net between them, taking fish from the Nile (6085).

New Kingdom Tomb Contents

Room 22 contains many interesting small figures, including XII–XXX Dynasty ushabtis (Cases I and J: 6062–72), and women, perhaps concubines of the dead man, lying on beds (Case C: 9435, 9437). Cases O, P and R contain New Kingdom funerary gear, painted linen or woven cloth for covering the chest, body and feet, beautifully designed and all the more fine for being highly perishable materials that have survived.

Room 17 is particularly interesting for the papyri on its walls from the Book of the Dead.

Room 12 contains artefacts from royal tombs: a chariot of Tuthmosis IV (3000); the mummies of a child and a gazelle (Case I: 3776, 3780); and a collection of priestly wigs and wig boxes (Case L: 3779).

Room 13 at the north end of the atrium displays furnishings from the intact Theban tomb of Yuya and Tuyu, parents-in-law of Amenophis III, with beds, chairs, whippet-like chariots, mummified food and time-serving ushabtis.

Gold, Dung and Jewels

Most of the north end of the first floor and all the outer rooms along its east side are devoted to Tutankhamun's treasures. Their profusion is described separately, pp.130–1.

Room 2 has material from the Late Period royal burials at Tanis, including gold masks and a falcon-headed sarcophagus of silver, a treasure as exquisite as Tutankhamun's.

Room 6, nearby, contains a collection of scarabs. This black dung beetle, running everywhere about the desert sands, pushing a ball of dung before it, symbolized the self-creator, the morning sun.

Room 4 *closes a quarter of an hour before the rest of the museum* and is specially guarded: it contains jewellery from the I Dynasty to the Byzantine period: necklaces, pectorals, diadems, daggers and much else in gold, silver and precious stones. The most splendid sizeable object is the VI Dynasty gold falcon head (case 3: 4010). The best workmanship is found in the jewellery of the XII Dynasty, and the stones are real (carnelian for red and orange, amethyst for purple and violet, lapis lazuli for blue, feldspar for green)—in Tutankhamun's time, as you will see in the nearby rooms containing objects from his tomb, paste and glass were used instead and though the settings are gold it is mere costume jewellery.

Graeco-Roman Burials

Room 14 holds portraits—among the most affecting exhibits in the museum. These people, Greeks from the Fayyum, continued the Egyptian practice of mummification, yet from their portraits, so lifelike and modern, you cannot imagine they would have accepted the ancient belief. The encaustic portraits (colours mixed into molten wax) were bound onto the mummies—there are shelves of these. A collection of panels is against the south wall (4310): the technique is superb, with shading, highlighting and perspective, two or three of them qualifying as masterpieces in their own right. Their garbage bodies contrast with these living faces in which you can read whole lives. All are marked by a seriousness, rarely pompous, occasionally sad, a faint smile on one man's lips. They have steadfastly faced the passing millennia and now look at you as you look at them, as though suddenly we might recognize one another.

Room 19 displays the main gods of the Egyptian pantheon, from various periods.

Sketches, Papyri, and Fixtures and Fittings

Room 24 is full of painted ostraka, limestone fragments. Case 18 contains interesting representations of animals: a monkey eating, a man leading a bull and a lion devouring a prisoner. There are people too: an intriguing picture of a woman relaxing and playing a stringed instrument. In the east doorway is a plan of a Theban tomb (4371), with what appear to be doorways shown in elevation.

Room 29 contains further ostraka, but written on, and papyri—6335 is especially worthwhile: a Ptolemaic Book of the Dead in finest detail, showing the 'Weighing of the Heart' ceremony.

The corridor outside Room 34 has an Amarna toilet seat. Is this the loo on which Akhenaton sat?

Room 44 displays decorative details, most interesting the faïence from palaces of Ramses II and III.

Room 57 is around the southeast staircase. The square red and green leather tent (3848) belonged to a XXI Dynasty queen and was used at her funeral.

Room 48, at the centre of the south wings, contains a model of a funerary complex, showing how a river temple linked with the pyramid on the desert's edge. There is also a cross-sectioned pyramid showing the internal buttressing. A case to the north contains beautifully worked statuettes from various periods.

Prehistoric and Predynastic Periods

Rooms 54, 55 and **53** are devoted to prehistoric and pre-dynastic artefacts, such as pottery and tools, and are generally dull, except that in Room 53 are mummified animals: baboons, a dog, a crocodile and the skeleton of a mare. Egyptian religion grew out of animal worship, totemism and an admiration of their qualities (strength, swiftness, beauty), or a desire to appease; wild dogs, the 'Egyptian wolf', prowled the cemeteries by night in search of bones and bodies that the Egyptians hoped would remain unmolested, and so this predator of their eternal life was transformed into their funerary deity, Anubis. Animal cults proliferated towards the end of the pagan period and were extremely popular, religious societies collecting the sacred animals (from shrew mice to hippopotami) which died in the district, mummifying them and burying them in special cemeteries (*see* pp.186–7).

The Mummy Room

> *The more I walk along, the more I listen, the more I move around the columns, the more do I experience the feeling of a dark world which fastens on to ours and which will not loosen the suckers through which it takes its life. Whatever it may cost, they find it necessary to confirm their existence, to perpetuate themselves, to incarnate, to reincarnate, to hypnotise nothingness and to vanquish it... They did not hide themselves in order to disappear, but in order to await the cue for their entry on the stage. They have not been dragged from the tomb. They have been brought from the limbo of the wings with masks and gloves of gold... Seti the First! How beautiful he is, with his little nose, his pointed teeth showing, his little face which belongs to death, reduced to one requirement alone—not to die. 'I! I! I!' This is the word which the rafters throw back.*

> Jean Cocteau, *Maalesh, A Theatrical Tour of the Middle East*

Room 56 (*closes 15 mins early*) is the Mummy Room where some of the mightiest men in ancient history lie half-naked and bird-boned in glass cases. Jean Cocteau believed that the pharaohs did not intend to hide away, but Sadat decided in 1981 that visitors should be forbidden entry. It was meant as a gesture to fundamentalist Islamic sensibilities, but to no avail: the same year they made a mummy of him.

The mummies had been kept in Room 52 under indifferent conditions, though the poor state of preservation of some was not so much due to that, nor to any failure of the embalming process (*see* below), as to early exposure by grave robbers (*see* pp.223–4). Various initiatives to rebury the royal bodies either in their original tombs or in a chamber built for the purpose were overcome by inertia. Then, after some sprucing up, which in the case of Ramses II meant a trip to Paris where he was received with the full honours due to a visiting head of state in need of urgent medical treatment, it was announced in 1993 that some of them at least would again be presented to the public gaze. Here in Room 56 eleven royal mummies, not all those previously on display (some were quite gruesome, while some of the women were perhaps too fetching), lie like cigars in sealed humidity-controlled cases under a dim sepulchral light where, under strict injunction not to take photographs or chatter (thankfully no guides are permitted), you circle round them along a ramp in chronological order.

Among those permitted out for an airing is Sequenenreta'a, otherwise known as Sekenenre (XVII Dynasty), who died of an axe wound in the forehead (clearly visible) received in the heat of battle. He was probably mummified on the spot—his lips scream with agony, his legs are contracted with pain. Tuthmosis II and IV (XVIII Dynasty) seem to lie sleeping, though the latter seems to be forever weeping silently at his death. There is Seti I (XIX Dynasty), serene and majestic, his profile exactly as you see it on the reliefs at Abydos. His son Ramses II (XIX Dynasty) looks as though he is straining to awaken, his arms rising from his chest, his hands opening, his fingers uncurling—this happened as he was unbandaged. Whatever uncertainty there may be that Merneptah (XIX Dynasty) was the pharaoh of the Exodus, there can be no doubt that he was his father's son, bearing as he does Ramses II's unmistakable conk.

Making Mummies

Not only royalty and the nobility were mummified but all classes of ancient Egyptian society according to their ability to pay, the practice continuing well beyond the pharaonic age, as demonstrated by a mummified Christian in the Graeco-Roman Museum at Alexandria. Herodotus, who visited Egypt in the mid-5th century BC, noted the varieties of mummification on offer from embalmers in his day:

> The embalmers, when a body is brought to them, produce three specimen models in wood, painted to resemble nature, and graded in quality. After pointing out the differences in quality, they ask which of the three is required, and the kinsmen of the dead man, having agreed upon a price, go away and leave the embalmers to their work.

> The most perfect process is as follows: as much as possible of the brain is extracted through the nostrils with an iron hook, and what the hook cannot reach is rinsed out with drugs. Next the flank is laid open with a flint knife and the whole contents of the abdomen is removed. The cavity is then throughly cleansed and washed out, first with palm wine and again with an infusion of pounded spices. After that it is filled with pure bruised myrrh, cassia and every other aromatic substance with the exception of frankincense and sewn up again, after which the body is placed in natrun for seventy days. When this period, which must not be exceeded, is over, the body is washed and then wrapped from head to foot in linen cut into strips and smeared on the under side with gum. In this condition the body is given back to the family, who have a wooden case made, shaped like the human figure, into which it is put.

> When, for reasons of expense, the second quality is called for, no incision is made and the intestines are not removed, but oil of cedar is injected into the

body through the anus which is afterwards stopped up. The body is then pickled in natrun for the prescribed number of days, on the last of which the oil is drained off. The effect is so powerful that as it leaves the body it brings with it the stomach and intestines in a liquid state, and as the flesh, too, is dissolved by the natrun, nothing of the body is left but the bones and skin. After this treatment it is returned to the family without further fuss.

The third method, used for embalming the bodies of the poor, is simply to clear out the intestines with a purge and keep the body seventy days in natrun. It is then given back to the family to be taken away.

When the wife of a distinguished man dies, or any woman who happens to be beautiful or well known, her body is not given to the embalmers immediately, but only after the lapse of three or four days. This is a precautionary measure to prevent the embalmers from violating the corpse, a thing which is said actually to have happened in the case of a woman who had just died. The culprit was given away by one of his fellow workmen.

The Tutankhamun Exhibition

At the north end of the first floor you can see the astonishing plenitude of objects found buried with Tutankhamun in the Valley of the Kings. Yet this king was a minor figure who died young and was stuffed into a small tomb; imagine the impedimenta that Seti I tried to take with him. Rooms 3, 7, 8, 9, 10, 15, 25, 30, 35, 40 and 45, and part of Room 13, contain 1,700 items in all. The eyes jadedly search for the highlights of the highlights, or otherwise fix on curiosities.

Tutankhamun's mummy, his outermost coffin of gilded wood and his granite sarcophagus are all in his tomb in the Valley of the Kings, but the second **coffin** of gilded wood and the third of solid gold are in **Room 3**, along with the **gold mask**. Each of these, placed one within the other like Russian dolls, in turn were placed within a gilded wood shrine—which again fitted within three more (**Rooms 7** and **8**). The ancient Egyptians employed these gold casings in part because gold was thought to be the flesh of the gods, but also because they believed it warded off all outside contamination.

Among the finer or more curious items in the east gallery (Rooms 15 to 45) are a jewellery casket of gilded wood (**Room 45**, Case 54, 447) in the form of a naos with the figure of Anubis on top; a chest (**Room 35**, Case 20, 324) for the pharaoh's clothes, decorated on the lid with a desert hunt, on the large panels with Tutankhamun waging war, and on the small panels with the royal sphinx trampling on his enemies; and the famous **small throne** (**Room 1**), its back richly decorated with a scene of Tutankhamun's queen placing her right hand on his left shoulder. This is often interpreted as a relaxed domestic scene, though probably the gesture confirms the young pharaoh's position: she was the daughter of Akhenaton and his wife Nefertiti, and, though Akhenaton may also have fathered Tutankhamun (by a different wife), the royal ka was transferred through the female line (explaining the frequent sister and daughter marriages of pharaohs). The armrests too are beautiful, the lovely shape of falcons' wings extending in protection, the birds' heads wearing the crown of Upper and Lower Egypt.

As you leave the gallery, on either side of the doorway are **statues of the two guards** who were found standing in Tutankhamun's tomb. It was a job they quietly performed for well over 3,000 years until Howard Carter caught them napping. In penance they must stand here in the Cairo Museum for a few more years yet.

Shopping

While shopping at the bazaar stalls is a matter of haggling over **prices**, shops and department stores in the modern part of Cairo sell at fixed prices. Except in shops found in the arcades of major hotels, prices are usually marked in Arabic numerals, and are often stated in piastres (100PT = LE1). So an item priced at 1,000 is likely to be 1,000PT or LE10. Usually, common sense will tell you whether piastres or pounds are intended.

Department stores and shops are generally *open from 9am to 1pm* and *from 5pm to 8pm* or later, though some may remain open continuously throughout the day, particularly in Khan el Khalili. Some shops will close on Fridays, others on Sundays. During Ramadan, shop hours are likely to be *from 9.30am to 3.30pm* and *from 8pm to 10pm* or even later.

Bargaining

In the bazaars, price is usually what you agree on after a bout of bargaining. A stallkeeper will always ask more than he expects to get; the traditional response is to offer half as much. After several minutes, perhaps half an hour, a price midway between the extremes is agreed. That is the traditional way, but the visitor's impatience or foolishness can spoil the market, traders asking for and getting far more than their goods are worth. This is particularly true of hawkers at places like the Pyramids, and every now and again it is worth making a ridiculous counter-offer, perhaps only one-tenth of the asking price...and finding it immediately accepted.

Hawkers at tourist sights are taking advantage of their isolation and yours in demanding exorbitant amounts. The virtue of a bazaar is that there is plenty of competition. In Khan el Khalili you will find all the copperware, all the spices, all the wood and mother-of-pearl inlay in the same area, and you should browse around, examining the goods, asking the prices, getting a feel for the market. Try to be dispassionate; the more you want something the more you are likely to pay for it.

A good technique is to bargain first over something you do not want and then casually to start bargaining over what you do want—almost as though you did not want anything and just bargained for the sport. It is a sport and there are rules as well as tricks of the game. Your first extreme counter-offer will be laughed at and you may feel silly; do not worry, this is part of the game. After a few offers and counter-offers, walk out. If the shop or stall owner stops you, it means he thinks there is still a deal to be made; if he does not, you may have learnt you are aiming at too low a price—go back later, or go to another shop, with an adjusted view of the item's worth.

The essence of a bargain, of course, is not to arrive at some formula fraction of the original asking price, but to feel that you have paid the right price, a price you could not have bettered elsewhere, a price that makes the item worth it to you.

antiquities

Antiquities offered to you on the street are bound to be fake. Which is not to say there are not any genuine pharaonic, Coptic and Islamic artefacts around, but they will cost a lot of money and your only guarantee of their authenticity is to buy them from a shop displaying a licence from the Department of Antiquities. The shop will also give you a certificate of authenticity. You will also need a **permit** from the Department of Antiquities to export your purchase. Try Ahmed Dahba, 5 Sikket el Bedestan, in the heart of Khan el Khalili, and Lotus Palace, 7 Sharia Khan el Khalili, who both also sell reproductions.

antiques

Zamalek is the main hunting-ground in Cairo, both for genuine antiques and repro-ductions: try Atrium, 4 Sharia Mohammed Mazhar, ✆ 3406869, and Nostalgia, 6 Sharia Zakaria Rizk, ✆ 3420880, both very smart, the former mainly for furniture, the latter good for accessories. In Khan el Khalili there is the Old Shoppe, 7 Sharia Khan el Khalili, ✆ 924976, like a great dusty warehouse and fun to rummage about in. If you are an expert, try your luck at the Osiris Auction House, 15 Sharia Sherif, downtown, ✆ 3926609. But note that anything over one hundred years old requires an export permit.

books and prints

Books on Egypt and Egyptology, but also light holiday reading in paperback, are found in the major hotel bookstalls, which also sell magazines and newspapers.

For a more extensive selection, the following bookshops are recommended: **The American University in Cairo** (AUC) Bookshop at the university, 113 Sharia Qasr el Aini (entrance through Mohammed Mahmoud Gate), not far from Midan el Tahrir, ✆ 3542964. This is probably the best general bookshop in Cairo (*closed Aug*). **Lehnert and Landrock**, 44 Sharia Sherif, ✆ 3935324, downtown near Sharia Adli (they also run the bookshop at the Museum of Egyptian Antiquities) is a good general bookshop and a publisher as well: they sell (under their own imprint) the excellent Kuemmerly & Frey map of Egypt, and they do a map of Cairo, some-what better than the one issued free by the Tourist Office, and with the virtue of a street index. **L'Orientaliste**, 15 Sharia Qasr el Nil, downtown, ✆ 5753418, special-izes in old and rare books, maps, lithographs and postcards. There will be no bargains, however: much of their stock is bought in London and can be obtained more cheaply there.

Brass and copper work has long been a Cairo tradition, and the standards are still high today. The best place for it is in **Khan el Khalili** along or just off Sharia Muizz, south of the Madrasa of Qalaun. Small plates intended as ornaments and candlesticks, gongs, lamps, mugs and pitchers are the easiest to carry off—though be sure that anything you intend to drink out of is coated on the inside with another metal, like silver, as brass or copper in contact with some substances can be highly poisonous. The finest items are the big brass trays which can serve as table tops (wooden stands are available).

camels

The camel market, Souk el Gimaal, has recently moved from Embaba to the village of Birqash, 30km northwest of Cairo, where it is open Monday and Friday mornings from dawn. You should be there no later than 7am–8am; it is pretty much over by late morning. A taxi will cost about LE25 each way, or you can take a bus from the terminus behind the Egyptian Museum to Manashi by the Nile Barrage at Qaratir, from there taking a service taxi. On your return you ought to be able to find a service taxi to bring you back to Cairo—unless you have bought a camel: docile females make the best mounts; expect to pay LE2,000.

There is also a small camel market in a little square not far from the southern section of the City of the Dead.

carpets, tents, tapestries and weaving

Weavings, carpets, tents and tapestries require further adventures if you want the best. In fact, Egypt is not particularly well known for **carpets**, and if you are going to Aswan you should look around there first, rather than Cairo, for small rugs and weavings. Old rugs are auctioned off from time to time, and you should look in the *Egyptian Gazette* for announcements. Carpets and rugs are found in Khan el Khalili and elsewhere around town.

Tent-making, on the other hand, is a Cairene speciality, and you should go to the Street of the Tentmakers immediately south of Bab Zuwayla. There are six or seven workshops along this covered section of medieval Cairo's major north–south street, creating beautiful appliqué tents used at mosques or street festivals (and funerals). Some are decorated with scenes of pharaonic or Islamic themes, but the best have abstract arabesque designs or intricate calligraphy. Not that you have to buy a tent; they are made in sections and you can buy a piece about big enough to serve as a pillow cover.

Two villages outside Cairo are centres of the best **tapestry-weaving** in Egypt. Harraniyya, about 3km along the canal road from Giza to Saqqara, was developed by the late Ramses Wissa Wassef; he taught the children how to card, dye and spin their own wool, and weave it into tapestries of their own design, usually village scenes, primitive and boldly coloured. Harraniyya's tapestries are now world-famous, and the workshop, on the right of the road, continues to be run by Wassef's daughter. The other village is Kardassa (*see* p.168).

Clothing will be found in the hotel shops, shops in the downtown area (Sharias Talaat Harb and 26 July, for example), boutiques in Zamalek, Heliopolis and downtown, at the new World Trade Centre on Corniche el Nil north of the 26 July Bridge and in the big department stores: Chemla, 11 Sharia 26 July, where low prices are more important than quality; Cicurel, 3 Sharia 26 July, for quality and higher prices; Omar Effendi, a good department store with several branches—on Sharia Talaat Harb just off Midan el Tahrir, on Sharia Adli near Sharia Talaat Harb, and also at Heliopolis and Dokki. Sizes are continental.

A fairly new phenomenon is **designer fashion** with international appeal, with stylish clothing costing a fraction of what it would at home. Have a look at On Safari, 10 Sharia Lutfalla, Zamalek, and at the World Trade Centre, 1191 Corniche el Nil, Boulaq. Nomad at the Marriott Hotel, Zamalek, ✆ 3411917, and at their nearby shop, 14 Serai el Gezira, ✆ 3412132, has adapted Bedouin designs to Western styles; similarly Ed-Dukkan, with a branch at the Ramses Hilton.

The **galabiyya**, the full-length traditional garment of Egyptian men, is popular with both male and female visitors as comfortable casual wear. Fancier versions can also serve as evening wear for women. There are three basic styles: the baladi or peasant style, with wide sleeves and a low rounded neckline; the saudi style, more form-fitting, with a high-buttoned neck and cuffed sleeves; and the efrangi or foreign style, looking like a shirt with collar and cuffs but reaching all the way down to the floor. Several shops sell galabiyyas along Sharia Talaat Harb between Midan Talaat Harb and Sharia 26 July, and also the department stores. Fancier ones are at Ammar, 26 Sharia Qasr el Nil, and at Atlas with branches in Khan el Khalili and the Semiramis Intercontinental. Both are fixed price. Atlas is on Sikket el Bedestan, the main east–west street through the bazaar, ✆ 5906139. For better-quality work, find Abbas Higazi, also in Khan el Khalili, ✆ 924730, who sticks to traditional patterns, though he will tailor your galabiyya to your choice of material and decoration.

Shoes are found in many of the shops mentioned above; also there is a plethora of shoeshops along Sharia Qasr el Nil, Talaat Harb and 26 July.

fabrics

Fabric is found in variety and quality at Omar Effendi (*see* 'Clothing', above); Salon Vert, Sharia Qasr el Nil; or Ouf in el Mashhad el Hussein—heading south along Sharia Muizz and approaching Sharia al-Azhar, take the first right after Sharia el Muski/Sharia Gohar el Qaid and the first left; Ouf is on the right down this alley. Each of these stores also sell off-the-peg galabiyyas.

glass and narghilehs

Muski glass, usually turquoise or dark brown and recognizable by its numerous air bubbles, has been handblown in Cairo since the Middle Ages, and is now turned out as ashtrays, candlesticks and glasses. It is inexpensive, but also very fragile. Try Sayed Abd al Raouf, 8 Khan el Khalili, ✆ 933463. The best **nargilehs** (hubbly-bubblies) will have glass, rather than brass, bottoms. For these, try around the Street of Coppersmiths, south of the madrasa of Qalaun.

jewellery

There are numerous jewellery shops in Sharia Abdel Khalek Sarwat (near Garden Groppi) and in the small street leading off it, Sikket el Manakh. And of course, there are numerous jewellers in Mouski and Khan el Khalili. Too often, Egyptian jewellery is disappointing, much of it mimicking the more obvious pharaonic motifs (cartouche, ankh, Eye of Horus), and those of Islamic motif showing little popular imagination—hands and eyes for warding off evil, or as pieces inscribed with 'Allah'. At first it may seem exotic, but it is limited and grows tiresome, while much outside these two motifs is usually conceived in bad taste.

Nor is there much, if any, genuine Bedouin jewellery around anymore; almost all old and traditional pieces have been sold and taken out of the country, while the Bedouin themselves come to Cairo and Alexandria and other towns and buy glittering junk. However, for a selection of handsome pieces, often based on Bedouin designs, go to Nomad at the Marriott Hotel, Zamalek, ✆ 3412132, and to their shop near by at 14 Serai el Gezira, ✆ 3411917.

musical instruments

Sharia Qalaa between Midan Ataba and the Islamic Art Museum has several shops selling traditional instruments. These include the *oud* (lute), the *rabab* (viol), the *nai* (flute), the *kanoon* (dulcimer), the *mismare baladi* (oboe), the *tabla* (drum), and the *riq* and *duf* (forms of tambourine).

scents and spices

One of the most enjoyable excursions, whether you intend to buy or not, is to wander through the **spice market** which lies off Sharia Muizz between Sharia el Muski (Sharia Gohar el Qaid) and Sharia al-Azhar. There are bottles of perfume essences, boxes of incense and bags of herbs and spices. Also there is kohl, a black eye cosmetic. The fragrances, and the quality of the light in awninged alleyways, awaken sensation.

woodwork and leatherwork

Inlay of wood and mother-of-pearl, and also leatherwork, are also plentiful in the **bazaar**. Egyptian leather is not the best, however. The most common items are handbags, suitcases and hassocks. More interesting than useful or comfortable are camel saddles (for buying a camel, *see* p.133). Wooden trays, boards (including backgammon and chess boards) and boxes inlaid with mother-of-pearl and coloured bits of wood are not quite as good as those made in Syria, but are intricate and beautiful enough. Mashrabiyyas, those intricate screens found in old Cairene houses, made from bits of wood fitted together without nails or glue, occasionally come on sale in the bazaars.

One of the most effortless and pleasurable things to do is to sail up and down the Nile in a **felucca**, especially in the evening. These can be hired by Shepheard's Hotel and at the Meridien.

For greater exertion, all the luxe hotels have **health clubs**; staying at the hotel gives you automatic membership, but many are also open to non-residents on a daily or weekly basis. There is also the excellent World Trade Centre Club, Corniche el Nil, north of 26 July Bridge, ✆ 764425. Typical facilities at these places include a gym with rowing and cycling machines, tennis courts, pool, sauna, jacuzzi and health food bar.

Cycling, running and similar activities are organized by groups composed of both foreigners and Egyptians resident in the city. Contact telephone numbers are usually home numbers, and the latest are given below, but you should check the back pages of *Egypt Today* where the most up-to-date announcements appear. The **Cairo Cyclists**, ✆ 3526310, meet every Friday at 8am at the front gate of the Cairo American College, Midan Digla. The route, distance and pace is decided by those joining the ride. A second group, devoted to fast-paced training rides, meets at 7am on Saturdays.

The **Hash House Harriers**, ✆ 3476663, meet every Friday afternoon at about two hours before sunset for non-competitive fun runs at the Pyramids, in the desert and through the more traffic-free parts of Cairo. Members include people of all abilities, nationalities, sexes and ages.

The **Cairo Divers Group**, ✆ 2907112, meets at 7pm on the first Monday of each month at the Helnan Shepheard Hotel. Its more than 300 members, representing 11 nationalities, have joined together to promote the exploration of the Red Sea, and their meetings are open to all.

For **skiing** and **golf**, *see* p.168.

For **spectator sports** like football, horse-racing and rowing, check the daily *Egyptian Gazette* (on Saturdays called the *Egyptian Mail*). The national craze is football, and anyone who recalls the performance of the Egyptian team during the 1990 World Cup will know that the standard of play is very high. The season is from September to May, with the two main teams, Ahly and Zamalek, playing at the Cairo Stadium, Heliopolis, on Fridays, Saturdays and Sundays.

There is **horse racing** from October to May at the Gezira Sporting Club and the Heliopolis Hippodrome. On Fridays year-round you can watch **rowing** on the Nile, the premier crew being the Cairo police who routinely thrash visiting Oxford, Cambridge and other foreign crews.

If you have not already made a reservation, then on arrival at Cairo Airport you can go to the **Tourist Information Office** or **Misr Travel** and see if they can help. Alternatively, do your own hotel hunting, probably running no greater risk than having to visit a couple of hotels before finding something suitable. Often a hotel will volunteer or can be prevailed upon to telephone ahead on your behalf, saving legwork and fares.

All hotels in the *very expensive* and *expensive* categories will have air conditioning and colour televisions, normally with satellite stations, and usually the *moderate*-category hotels will too. Many of the hotels in the *moderate, inexpensive* and *cheap* categories are survivors from an earlier age; while some of these have been modernized, and others at least maintained in good order, yet others, if they were ever up to much in the first place, have sunk into decrepitude. Some of these hotels may have style, but they may not have air conditioning or heating or hot water, and rooms and bathrooms should be checked for cleanliness and comfort. If you are not satisfied with the first room you are shown, ask to see another; in these categories, rooms can vary greatly from one another within the same hotel.

For hotels in the area of the Pyramids, *see* p.169. These are ideal when visiting the Pyramids themselves, but note that it can be difficult to return the 11km to Cairo as the bus service is infrequent.

The following is a selective list of hotels in and around Cairo itself. For rates and tipping, *see* p.26.

very expensive

Near Midan el Tahrir

★★★★★**The Helnan Shepheard's**, Corniche el Nil, Garden City, ℗ 3553800, ✆ 3557284, is not the famous Shepheard's; that was near Ezbekieh Gardens and was burnt down in the nationalist riots of 1952. This Shepheard's, south of Midan el Tahrir, was built in 1956 and has recently been refurbished. Unlike the newer 5-star hotels, it is sedate, possesses some architectural charm, and has spacious rooms. The 24-hour café is very comfortable and the top-floor bar and restaurant have good views of the river. The preferred Nile-side rooms have ceiling-to-floor picture windows and balconies. Shops, travel agent, car hire, but no pool.

★★★★★**The Nile Hilton**, Midan el Tahrir, ℗ 5780444, ✆ 5780475, is right next to the Egyptian Museum and overlooks the Nile. This was the first international hotel built in Egypt (opening ceremonies in 1959 were attended by Nasser and Tito) and was the first Hilton in the Middle East. It has become something of an institution. The Nile Hilton Centre, a 1981 extension, provides further rooms as well as a concentration of travel agencies, airline offices, banks, shops and business facilities in addition to those already in the main building. American Express, Avis and Egyptair are among those represented. It is in the main building with its larger rooms that you should try to stay, insisting on a Nile view. Pool, tennis courts, disco, nightclub, casino, sauna, plus numerous shops and a variety of eating places are among the facilities. The Ibis Café is open 24 hours; its pizzeria is good; the Taverne du Champ de Mars, imported stick by stick from Brussels, is also very agreeable. All rooms are air-conditioned and have colour television.

★★★★★**The Ramses Hilton**, Corniche el Nil, ✆ 777444, ✆ 5757152, is a 1981 tower, all rooms with balconies, many with a Nile view, a short walk north of the Egyptian Museum. The rooms are a bit small. The best thing about the hotel, which guests and non-guests alike can enjoy, is its top-floor cocktail lounge with sweeping night-time panorama. Facilities include a pool, health club, casino, business centre, shops, Hertz and travel agent.

★★★★★**The Semiramis Inter-Continental**, Corniche el Nil, ✆ 3557171, ✆ 3563020, is central Cairo's newest luxury hotel, on the Nile, a short walk from Midan el Tahrir. Its jumble of tiered reception area-cum-bar-cum-café is a good example of how not to design a hotel, but it has a high reputation for service and is particularly favoured by businessmen. Pool, health club, business centre, shops, travel agent and car hire desk are among the usual facilites.

★★★★★**The Meridien Le Caire**, Roda Island, ✆ 3621717, ✆ 3621927. Access is by private bridge from the Corniche el Nil, Garden City. The hotel perches like a figurehead on the northern prow of the island and commands a sweeping view down the Nile. It has a French flavour: boutiques and bidets; good coffee and pastries in the 24-hour café and gourmet French and Italian cuisine at its restaurants. Its pool and health centre contribute to its well-run resort-style atmosphere. All rooms are soundproofed and have a Nile view.

On Gezira Island or the west bank of the Nile

★★★★★**The Cairo Marriott**, Serai el Gezira, Zamalek, ✆ 3408888, ✆ 3406667, is on Gezira Island overlooking the Nile. The public areas of the Marriott inhabit with effortless vulgarity an 1869 royal palace (which was purchased soon after by the Lebanese magnate 'Prince' Lutfallah, and its parkland sold off to make the Gezira Club), while the rooms are in new, purpose-built towers. There is a pleasant garden with swimming pool, and there are tennis courts, health club, casino, business centre, shops, car hire and travel agent. Unless you like long walks, it is a taxi-ride to almost anywhere.

★★★★★**El Gezirah Sheraton**, Gezira Island, ✆ 3411333, ✆ 3405056, is a 1980s-built circular tower at the southern tip of the island, offering wonderful views up and down the Nile and towards the Pyramids. All the usual luxury-class facilities are available, while the uppermost storeys contain suites and amount to a hotel within the hotel, with separate reception, bar and lounge.

★★★★★**The Cairo Sheraton**, Midan el Galaa, Dokki, ✆ 3465782, ✆ 2918520, was the first Sheraton in Egypt; it opened in 1970, was renovated in 1986, and a second tower was added in 1990. The hotel is located on the west bank of the Nile across the Tahrir Bridge, with upper-storey views either over the river or towards the Pyramids.

All rooms have air conditioning and colour television. It is a lively place, with a good nightclub; also two pools, health club, casino, business centre, many shops, a good 24-hour café and an Avis desk.

expensive

★★★★**The Manyal Palace**, Roda Island, ✆ 3644524, ✉ 3631737, is in the gardens of Farouk's uncle's palace—air-conditioned bungalows run by Club Méditerranée, with pool and disco. The location is beautiful and convenient.

★★★★**The Flamenco**, 2 Sharia El Gezira el Wasta, Zamalek, ✆ 3400815, ✉ 3400819, is at the northwest end of Gezira Island in a residential area. This is a Spanish-run hotel, reflected in its café and restaurant cuisine. Facilities include shops, business centre and travel agent. Some rooms have Nile views.

★★★★**The Atlas Zamalek**, 20 Sharia Gameat el Dowal el Arabia, Mohandiseen, ✆ 3465782, ✉ 3476958, is not in Zamalek at all, but just across an arm of the Nile in the west bank residential area of Mohandiseen. Despite its distance from the centre of town, it is a popular choice, offering a pool, sauna, disco and a variety of eating places.

★★★★**Novotel Cairo Airport**, Heliopolis, ✆ 2918520, ✉ 2914794, is one of several hotels in the vicinity of the airport, which is not where anyone in their right mind would want to stay unless they had to catch an early flight. If you do, this is a good choice. Frequent courtesy buses deliver you within minutes to the airport; the rooms are soundproofed, air-conditioned and provided with colour television; there are tennis courts and a pool.

★★★**The President**, 22 Sharia Taha Hussein, Zamalek, ✆ 3400652, ✉ 3411752, is in a quiet residential area of many embassies and diplomatic residences north of Sharia 26 July. Rooms are large and clean; all have private baths and television. There is a bar, restaurant and the lively Cellar Pub in the basement.

moderate

Downtown

★★★**The Windsor**, 19 Sharia Alfi, ✆ 5915810, ✉ 5921621, was ranked by Baedeker early in the 1920s as just below the old Shepheard's, since when it has not changed a jot: the character is literally peeling off its walls (*see* pp.55–6). High-ceilinged rooms for ventilation, much old wooden furnishing, a delightful bar/lounge/dining room hung with weird curios and damaged paintings, beers served by berobed and long-dead waiters—this is the place to come for Cairo as it once was, if you are prepared to enjoy class in tatters and atmosphere in abundance. It is situated towards Ezbekieh Gardens. Rooms with either shower or bath. Reservations are advisable.

★★★**The Cosmopolitan**, 1 Sharia Ibn Taalab, off Sharia Qasr el Nil, ✆ 3923845, ✉ 3933531, is an old traditional hotel, nicely refurbished in 1983, tucked away in a quiet side street. It has a restaurant, bar, coffee shop and bank. All rooms are air-conditioned with bath.

★★★**The Victoria**, 66 Sharia el Gumhuriya, ☎ 5892290, ✉ 5913008, is a 1930s-vintage but newly renovated downtown hotel towards Midan Ramses. There is a bar and good food in the restaurant, and a hairdresser and bank on the premises. The rooms are spacious, often furnished in mahogany, and air-conditioned.

★★★**The Odeon Palace**, 6 Sharia Abdel Hamid Said, between sharias Talaat Harb and Champollion, downtown, ☎ 776637, ✉ 767971, is a modern place convenient for the Egyptian Museum, its 24-hour restaurant and bar (*see* listings below) popular meeting places for the unconventional.

★★★**The Grand Hotel**, 17 Sharia 26 July, ☎ 757700, ✉ 757593, is an Art Deco survival at the intersection with Sharia Talaat Harb. Its rooms are clean and comfortable, some with shower.

★★★**The Fontana**, Midan Ramses, ☎/✉ 5922145, is a good hotel despite its grim location near Ramses Station, and conveniently welcome if you have arrived by rail at some unearthly hour. Surprisingly, it has a pool, and a lovely one at that, and there is a good café on the rooftop. Rooms have baths, air conditioning and colour television.

On Gezira Island

★★★**The Horus House**, 21 Sharia Ismail Mohammed, Zamalek, ☎ 3403977, ✉ 3403182, is a small, friendly and very pleasant hotel with restaurant, bar and café. It is set in a residential area north of Sharia 26 July near the President Hotel.

★★★**The Longchamps**, 21 Sharia Ismail Mohammed, Zamalek, ☎/✉ 3409644, is another small hotel at the same address as the Horus House, this with a disco: all its rooms have bath, air conditioning and television.

★★**New President**, 22 Sharia Taha Hussein, Zamalek, ☎ 3422780, ✉ 3422781. This is a more basic, cheaper version of its *expensive* sister establishment, The President, at the same address (*see* above).

inexpensive

★★**The Lotus**, 12 Sharia Talaat Harb, ☎ 5750627, ✉ 921621, occupies the top three floors in the building opposite the Felfela restaurant in downtown Cairo. The hardwood floors and spacious rooms with baths (those with showers are smaller) lend an extra touch of calm to this clean and well-run place.

★★**The Horris**, 5 Sharia 26 July, ☎ 5910855, ✉ 5910478, is near the Windsor, towards the Ezbekieh Gardens end of the street. Refurbished and with clean, bright, air-conditioned rooms, the hotel occupies the upper floors of the building, with its restaurant up top on the 14th floor.

★★**El Nil Zamalek**, 21 Sharia Maahad el Swissri, Zamalek, ☎ 3401846, is a modern hotel on the east side of Gezira island overlooking the main branch of the river just north of Sharia 26 July. Rooms are spacious and all have a bathroom, air conditioning and colour television, while some have balconies with Nile views. The restaurant, on a terrace overlooking the river, is very pleasant.

★★**El Nil Garden**, 131 Sharia Abdel Aziz al-Soud, Roda Island, ✆ 3653422, 📧 3685767, is a clean and small hotel with restaurant and bar but only 21 rooms, overlooking the main branch of the Nile near the Manyal Palace.

★**Zamalek Pension**, 6 Sharia Salah ad-Din, Zamalek, ✆ 3409318. Set in leafy environs, this is a small and cosy place (only half a dozen rooms) with an air of quiet and privacy. Air conditioning available as an extra.

cheap

Downtown

★★**The New Hotel**, 21 Sharia Adli, ✆ 3927033, 📧 3929555, is not far from the downtown Tourist Office. Rooms are simply furnished but large and clean, and the bathrooms are clean too.

★★**The Tulip**, 3 Midan Talaat Harb, ✆ 3939433, is a clean, old hotel facing the famous Groppi restaurant, both of a vintage, both managing a certain decency.

★**The Pensione Roma**, 169 Sharia Mohammed Farid, ✆ 3911088, 📧 5796243, is two blocks south of Sharia 26 July and just east of Sharia Talaat Harb. Its clean, airy rooms, its grand lounge and dining room, and the good service make it a popular place, so book ahead.

★**The Garden City House**, 23 Sharia Kamal al-Din Dalah, ✆ 3544969, is near the Semiramis Inter-Continental. From outside there is a small sign three storeys up: the rooms are there and on the floor above; you take the lift. The place is a bit shabby, but respectable, clean and friendly, and the food is good. Some rooms have baths. Some face the river, most have balconies. There are not many single rooms. Half-board is compulsory. It is essential to book ahead.

★**The Montana**, 25 Sharia Sherif, ✆ 3928608, 📧 3936025, is a very clean and well-run seventh-floor place two blocks south of Sharia Adli. Some rooms have bathrooms and air conditioning.

★**The Hotel des Roses**, 33 Sharia Talaat Harb, ✆ 3938022, near the intersection with Sharia Sarwat, is fine as long as you take a refurbished room. Try to get one high up with views.

★**The Viennoise**, 11 Sharia Mahmoud Bassiouni, at Sharia Qasr el Nil, ✆ 5751949, 📧 5753136, is one of the cheapest places in town. It has huge rooms and an air of comfortable decrepitude. Some rooms have showers, but you should check that there is hot water.

On Gezira Island and in Medieval Cairo

★★**El Hussein**, Midan el Hussein, ✆ 918664, in the heart of Khan el Khalili, with Fishawi's tea house next door and, with views out over the Sayyidna al-Hussein and the al-Azhar mosques, is the best hotel for those wanting to be amid the sights and atmosphere of medieval Cairo. The restaurant on the roof looks out over the medieval city. Rooms are clean, large, simply furnished and have balconies; all are air-conditioned, but insist on one with a bathroom.

★★The New Riche, 47 Sharia Abdel Aziz, off Midan Ataba, ✆ 3900145, ✆ 3906390, has good rooms, all with air conditioning, some with baths; its woman owner ensures that it is a perfectly agreeable place for women to stay.

★The Mayfair, 9 Sharia Aziz Osman, Zamalek, ✆ 3407315, is on Gezira Island. It is dilapidated but clean, simple and comfortable, with a verandah, garden, peace and quiet.

hostels and camping

There is a **youth hostel** near the Manyal Palace on Roda Island: Manyal Youth Hostel, 135 Sharia Abdel Aziz el-Saud, ✆ 3640729, ✆ 3984107. Take the metro to Sayyidna Hussein and cross over the Manyal Bridge, keeping the palace gardens on your left; the hostel is near the Salah ad-Din Mosque by the El Gama'a Bridge. There are cheap bunks in clean but noisy dorms, with lock-up facilities for your gear. Shut-out time is from 10am to 2pm and there is an 11pm curfew. It is often full up, so book ahead. For the only **campsite** in the area, *see* p.169.

Cairo ✆ 02   **Eating Out**

You can spend a fortune or a few piastres on a meal in Cairo, and choose between the world's cuisines. Not only restaurants, but coffee shops, tea rooms and snack bars are included here. You should also *see* 'Entertainment and Nightlife', below.

expensive

Cairo's **major hotels** each have a number of restaurants offering a variety of cuisines, though only a few are worth going out of your way to dine at. The best are **Champollion** at the Meridien Le Caire, ✆ 3621717, and **The Grill** at The Semiramis, ✆ 3557171, both of which offer French-international cuisine; **Aladin** at the Cairo Sheraton, Dokki, ✆ 3369700, where Lebanese cuisine is served up with a belly dancer; and the **Moghul Room** at the Mena House Oberoi out at the Pyramids, ✆ 3833222, which offers both Western and Indian dishes to a background of live Indian music.

Getting **out and about town**, the best and probably the most expensive restaurant in Cairo is **Justine**, 4 Sharia Hassan Sabri, Zamalek, ✆ 3412961, which is part of the Four Corners complex. The atmosphere is formal, the cuisine is Franco-Mediterranean; the fish is especially good.

For Japanese cuisine in a pleasant atmosphere, there is **Yamato** at The Ramses Hilton Annex, ✆ 758000. At the World Trade Centre, 1191 Corniche el Nil, north of 26 July Bridge, is **Piano Piano**, ✆ 5749556, favoured by Cairo's glitz set, offering Chinese and French cuisine, Nile views and of course live piano music.

Le Chateau, El Nasr Building, Sharia El Nil, Giza, ✆ 3485321, has a formal but pleasant candle-lit ambience with leather armchairs, wood-panelled walls and attentive service. Its continental menu includes excellent seafood dishes. **Raoucha**, fifth floor, 3 Sharia el Dowal el Arabia, Mohandiseen, just over the Zamalek Bridge and overlooking Midan Sphinx, ✆ 3030615, offers authentic Lebanese cuisine in authentic surroundings; a singer entertains after 9.30pm.

Amici, at Sahara Restaurants, Sharia Al-Ahram, ☎ 3830880, provides a spectacular view of the Pyramids while you enjoy its excellent Spanish and Italian cuisine, though avoid its bland paella; its forte is seafood.

You can float up and down the Nile for lunch or dinner in **The Nile Pharaoh**, a cruising restaurant got up like a pharaonic sailing barge. Phone Oberoi Hotels for reservations, ☎ 5701000.

moderate

An old downtown standby is **Caroll**, 12 Sharia Qasr el Nil off Midan Talaat Harb, ☎ 5746434, offering Western and Levantine dishes in ample portions. Also downtown but much brighter is **La Chesa**, 21 Sharia Adli, ☎ 3939360. Operated by Swissair Restaurants, this is a haven of Swiss cleanliness, excellent food and a very good cake and pastry section.

Arabesque, 6 Sharia Qasr el Nil, ☎ 5747898, is an elegant downtown restaurant with a small bar; adjoining it is a gallery of Egyptian artists. The cuisine is Egyptian, Lebanese and European. Prices are moderate, but imported wine will make it *expensive*. The **Naguib Mahfouz Café**, 5 Sikket el Bedestan, ☎ 5903788, in the heart of Khan el Khalili, is a classy place to which the Nobel Prize-winning novelist seems to have sold his name rather than the sort of place he would hang out, but all the same its location makes it interesting and the traditional Egyptian dishes are excellent; also it stays open fairly late, well after the souk has gone quiet and dark, making it a good starting point for an atmospheric night walk.

Peking, Sharia Saraya el Ezbekia, behind the Cinema Diana, downtown, ☎ 5912381, is a Chinese restaurant popular for its sophistication and flair, its menu varied and imaginative. **Da Mario**, Nile Hilton, Midan el Tahrir, ☎ 5780666, serves up probably the best Italian pasta and pizzas in Cairo; if you stick to those the cost will be moderate, but if you lose your head it will become *expensive*.

La Mama at the Cairo Sheraton Hotel, Dokki, ☎ 3369700, is similar and has the advantage of Nile views. **Chin Chin** is Chinese, **La Piazza** is Italian, and both are at the Four Corners complex, 4 Sharia Hassan Sabri, ☎ 3412961, the former with a mirrored ceiling, the latter brightened by white latticework hung with plants.

At the northwest end of Gezira island is **Florencia**, on the 10th floor of the Flamenco Hotel, 2 Sharia el Gezira el Wasta, Zamalek, ☎ 3400815; a charming and little known culinary treasure with an ambitious continental menu, live guitar music and pleasant views over houseboats moored in the Nile.

Cairo Cellar at the President Hotel, 22 Sharia Taha Hussein, Zamalek, ☎ 3400718, is a restaurant-cum-bar open till 2am, frequented by regulars, cosy though sometimes noisy, its changing menu written up on blackboards ranging from mezzas and omelettes through pasta, seafood and steaks. A quiet place worth seeking out is **Il Yotti**, 44 Sharia Mohi el Din Abu el Ezz, Dokki, ☎ 3494944, down a poorly-marked passage where you ring the bell at a heavy wooden door and are admitted by a man in oriental dress to a den of mahogany panels and classical statuary, its cuisine excellent Egyptian and Levantine.

Papillon, Sharia 26 July, Tirsana Shopping Centre, a few blocks west of the Zamalek Bridge and Midan Sphinx in Mohandiseen, © 3471672, is a favourite with vegetarians for its wide variety of Lebanese mezzas that make a meal in themselves but also has tender and savoury lamb, beef and chicken entrees for carnivores. **Christo's**, also known as **Vue des Pyramides**, 10 Sharia al-Ahram, © 3833582, specializes in Mediterranean seafood, Red Sea lobster and Egyptian mezzas. The kitchen is on the ground floor and you either eat outdoors or upstairs from where there is a terrific, yes, *vue des pyramides*.

Sometimes you just want to rest your feet, cool off and have a drink and a bite to eat. The **cafés** in the major hotels have the advantage of being *open 24 hours*; also, they are air-conditioned. There is a small minimum charge. **Le Café** at The Meridien is marvellous for its Nile views; the lounge at **Shepheard's** is a comfortable and civilized place for afternoon tea; while the Nile Hilton gets credit for its **Taverne du Champ de Mars**, a *fin de siècle* Brussels tavern, dismantled and reconstructed on the ground floor of the hotel. Beer, spirits and snacks are served *from noon to 2am*, and a reasonably priced buffet meal in the evening.

The Cairo Tower, Gezira Island, offers coffee, tea, beer, and snacks, all at a slight premium for having been carried up to the top, where the atmosphere is pleasant, the views wonderful.

inexpensive

In wandering around the streets, either in modern or medieval Cairo, you will encounter numerous simple establishments for having a snack, even a meal, and certainly a refreshing mint tea. There are also peripatetic **street vendors**, good for drinks though perhaps less so for food which may not be particularly clean. In buying anything to eat, always be sure the place has running water—if so, a modicum of hygiene can be counted upon. Forget the Cokes and 7-Ups for a change; instead pause for fresh guava, mango, orange, sugar cane or strawberry juice (after you have drunk it, you scoop the strawberries from the glass with a spoon).

A cheap but nutritious way to stuff yourself in Cairo is to dine on *koushari*, a plateful of lentils, onions, noodles and macaroni topped with a hot tomato sauce, and one of the best places to get it is at **Lux**, Sharia 26 July, near the intersection with Sherif, downtown. Then there is **Felfela**, 15 Sharia Hoda Sharawi, © 3922833, just off Sharia Talaat Harb near Sharia el Bustan, popular with tourists and foreign residents, but also a favourite of Egyptians. The food is certainly good and inexpensive. Tree trunks serve as tables. The speciality is fool in all its varieties of preparation, but the menu extends to meat dishes and ice creams. For Chinese, try **Fu Ching**, in a passageway at 28 Sharia Talaat Harb, © 3936184; it also does take-aways.

El Hatti, 8 Midan Halim, behind the Cicurel department store on Sharia 26 July and virtually next door to the Horris Hotel, is unusual for an Egyptian restaurant in that it sparkles—mirrors cover the walls and brilliant chandeliers hang from the high ceiling. The food (roast lamb is the speciality), service and atmosphere all make this a worthwhile place to search for.

Alfi Bey, 3 Sharia Alfi, near Midan Orabi, ✆ 5771888, is a sedate 1940s restaurant with panelled walls and chandeliers favoured by Cairenes for its excellent Egyptian cuisine, including roast lamb, fish and a good range of vegetarian dishes (no alcohol). **The Greek Club**, above Groppi's (*see* below) at Midan Talaat Harb, entrance on Sharia Bassiouni, serves decent food (hardly Greek, but then the Greeks of Cairo were hardly Zorbas) and passable alcohol *from 6pm to 1.30am*, and in summer you can dine out on its terrace.

The Odeon Palace Hotel, 6 Sharia Abd el Hamid Shahad, off Sharia Talaat Harb, ✆ 767971, offers Egyptian food at its 24-hour restaurant and bar, a favourite of journalists, artists and pseuds.

The **downtown** area also has a number of good **cafés**. **Groppi** is a famous Cairo institution with three branches, one at Midan Talaat Harb, another on Sharia Adli and a third in Heliopolis. It is Garden Groppi, as the one at the Midan el Opera end of Sharia Adli is called, that was so famous among British servicemen during the Second World War, and its outdoor café remains a pleasant place to sit by day or by night. There is a delicatessen here too, selling cold cuts, pastas, jams and bottles of wine. **Lappas**, 17 Sharia Qasr el Nil, is a Groppi-like place of Groppi-like vintage, popular among those who do not want to be disturbed.

The **Brazilian Coffee Shop**, 38 Sharia Talaat Harb and 12 Sharia 26 July, is *open from 7am to midnight* and is where to come if you care about coffee. The beans are freshly ground (unground beans can be taken away), and the espresso, cappuccino, café au lait—or almost any other way of drinking coffee—are excellent. The **Indian Tea Centre**, off the passageway at 23 Sharia Talaat Harb, is an inexpensive place where snacks are also served, though this is principally a tea room, with imported Indian teas and Indian-style pastries.

In medieval Cairo there is **El Dahan**, Sharia Muski near the El Hussein Hotel at Midan Sayyidna al-Hussein, which specializes in kofta and kebab. You can also eat at the rooftop restaurant of the hotel, but the wonderful view is spoiled by the slovenly service and awful food. In a small alley just behind the hotel is the famous **Fishawi Café**, where you can sit on cane chairs at marble-topped tables in the narrow passage lined with mirrors. As coffees pass by on brass trays you are propositioned with any number of offers including perhaps a shoeshine, a device for making catcalls, a woman's song accompanied by a tambourine, and necklaces of jasmine flowers, their scent thick on the night air.

The epitome of a good, simple Egyptian restaurant is **Abu Shakra**, 69 Qasr el Aini, ✆ 3648811, at the south end, about 3km from Midan el Tahrir, near the bridge crossing over to Roda at the Manyal Palace. This is a strict Muslim establishment, serving no alcoholic beverages and closed Fridays and daytime during Ramadan. The interior is all alabaster and marble, and the specialities are kofta and kebab, though sometimes pigeon and grilled chicken are also available. Usually (though not always) the food is excellent.

On Gezira Island, **Il Capo**, 22 Sharia Taha Hussein, Zamalek, ✆ 3413870, near the President Hotel, is cheap, casual and Italian. It also does take-aways. A more imaginative menu is on offer at **Al Dente**, 26 Sharia Bahgat Aly, Zamalek, ✆ 3409117, which also stays *open till 2am*. **Deals**, 2 Sharia el Maahad el Swissri, Zamalek, ✆ 3410502, is a tiny restaurant and bar *open till 2am* with film-poster décor, a young clientele and blasting rock and roll music, the food ranging from hamburgers and chicken drumsticks to salads and seafood, with French wine served by the glass.

On the west bank of the Nile is **Al Omdah**, Sharia Al-Gazair (off Sharia Gameat el Dowal el Arabia), Mohandiseen, ✆ 3452387, a few doors along from the Atlas Zamalek Hotel. The restaurant sign is in Arabic but features a man looking vaguely like Mark Twain. Huge portions of hearty Egyptian fare, and it stays *open until 2am*. No alcohol. Also in Mohandiseen is **Ataturk**, 20 Sharia Riyadh, off Sharia Shahab, ✆ 3475135, a cosy and relaxing Turkish restaurant, serving delicious hot bread and good mixed grills.

Cairo ✆ 02   ***Entertainment and Nightlife***

It is the popular mysteries—the man staging a backstreet show with a snake and a guinea pig or a marriage procession of loud cries and ribald song strolling down the middle of a road—that are most entertaining in Cairo. For some help in locating more conventional amusements, get a copy of *Egypt Today*, the monthly English-language magazine.

bars

The Cairo Cellar, downstairs at The President Hotel, 22 Sharia Taha Hussein, Zamalek, ✆ 3400718, is a popular meeting place for young Cairenes. Also appealing to the younger set but requiring more cash is **Matchpoint**, in the Four Corners complex, 4 Sharia Hassan Sabry, Zamalek, ✆ 3412961. **Le Pacha 1901** is a riverboat tied up at Sharia Serai el Gezira, Zamalek, ✆ 3405734, with several restaurants (the ambience vulgar, the food not very good) and two watering holes, **Johnny's Pub** and **Il Pianoforte** piano bar.

Calming and agreeable is **Taverne du Champ de Mars** at The Nile Hilton Hotel, Midan el Tahrir, ✆ 5780444, which has been rebuilt from an original Brussels bar. For fantastic night views over Cairo, go to **Windows on the World**, on the top floor of The Ramses Hilton Hotel, Corniche el Nil, ✆ 777444, ext 3231.

The Odeon, at the Odeon Palace Hotel, 6 Sharia Abd el Hamid Shahad, between Sharias Talaat Harb and Champollion, ✆ 767971, has a funky 24-hour bar (as well as restaurant, *see* p.145), a favourite hangout for Egyptian intellectuals and hacks.

nightclubs

Nightclubs in the big **international hotels** usually offer a programme of both oriental and Western acts, such as a first-class Egyptian belly dancer followed by some unemployed London showgirls pretending to be from Las Vegas or Paris. The comparison between the two can be embarrassing. The Western conception of dancing, at least as expressed in the pseudo-Folies Bergères variety, is to throw oneself about as though somehow velocity has any meaning other than to disguise a lack of sensuality. The Egyptian dancer, on the other hand, knows how to stand still, to flick and ripple her body like some night plant licking up the moonlight and starlight, curling and uncurling to the faint brush of cosmic rays so that she and all the dark sky pulse as one. **Fifi Abdou**, however, usually puts on a one-woman show, one moment the most graceful and subtle of belly dancers, the next moment a typhoon—she was last contracted to the Cairo Sheraton, but if not there then it is well worth finding out where she is now. Some other nightclubs, like those along the Pyramids Road (Sharia al-Ahram) and a few downtown will stage a more purely **Egyptian programme**, and these, even if sometimes second-rate, can be delightful.

Music and Belly Dancing

A series of singers and bands from all over the Islamic world, oriental and African rhythms, wailing and plaintive drone of male singers, marvellous squeaky violins, tinkling harpsichords, also flutes, bass and tambourines. Belly dancer comes on, a dead ringer for Rita Hayworth. Less squeaks and tinkles; now there are deep strokes of violins, pulsation of drums, the low hum of the saxophone. No bumps and grinds to detract from a performance of incredible sensuality, a slow motion of sea waves and sand dunes, the slightest flick an orgasm.

The Arab audience generally takes it with a warm, contained appreciation. The odd whistle, applause, a shout at some particular movement of the hips—or a shout sometimes when there is no movement: when almost nothing happens and she is at her most erotic. The perfectly still position: arms arabesqued, one leg extended, the hips at an angle, a continuous ripple running up and down her body, and then one flank is gyrated ever so slightly, like the minimal, most controlled movement of a toreador before the horns of the bull. The music stops, the band claps in a flamenco rhythm, Arab after Arab comes up on the stage with gifts of flowers, flower necklaces, glasses of whisky (which she knocks back in mid-movement), cigarettes and money, every one of them a desert king, but she is master of their fantasies.

Fire-breathers, circuses, puppet shows, belly dancers: this Arab patronage of the popular mysteries which imported television programmes and videos are destroying, a lack of discrimination prefigured in what happens next, for after this dance, with as much attention as it had accorded to the former, the audience watches a dull Lebanese riding a bicycle across a wire 2m above the stage.

At **Scheherazade** on Sharia Alfi, near Midan Orabi, the audience is predominantly Arab, almost all men, though a few women and even children may be present. A few Westerners go there and take their women: a great mistake as the latter sit prune-faced throughout the performance, which is indoors during winter, but on the roof (and more enjoyable for that) in summer.

For further adventures among human contortionists and laid-back finger-cymbal players, with the additional incentive of incredibly fat and ugly belly dancers of ill repute, and if you do not mind joining an audience even less respectable than the performers, then go to **Arizona** (the sign is in Arabic only, but you will know it by the photographs outside), across the road from the Scheherezade and a bit to the east.

discos

At discos you skip live entertainment, Western or oriental, and twitch instead to the vibrating recorded music. Some of the best places for this are **Jackie's** at the Nile Hilton and **Regine's** (of Paris, London and New York fame) at the El Gezirah Sheraton (but both of these are open only to members or residents and their guests); also the **Saddle Room** at the Mena House Oberoi and **Windows on the World** atop the Ramses Hilton. **After Eight** is a restaurant-cum-disco which serves excellent food; it is at the end of a passageway at 6 Sharia Qasr el Nil, downtown, but note that it is *closed July and August.*

Less stylish and cheaper discos are found at the **Longchamps Hotel**, 21 Sharia Ismail Mohammed, Zamalek, and at the **Fontana Hotel**, Midan Ramses.

casinos

Casinos (admission only to non-Egyptians) are found at the **Meridien**, the **Marriott**, the **Mena House**, the **Hiltons**, the **Cairo** and **El Gezirah Sheratons**, and the **e Heliopolis Mövenpick Hotel**. Play is in US dollars, with free drinks for punters; doors close at dawn.

cinemas

Cinemas are mostly located around midans Talaat Harb and Orabi, and several are likely to be showing English-language films, subtitled in Arabic. The *Egyptian Gazette* carries listings. The problem is that the Egyptians, being able to read the subtitles, do not have to listen to the dialogue. Instead the audience chatters throughout the film, which often has its sound turned down anyway, so that you will be lucky to hear much of it—which is, however, perhaps not so important when you consider the entertainment potential of the audience. Tickets are cheap, and all seats are reserved. You should buy your tickets several hours in advance of the performance you intend seeing, as seats go very quickly. **Women never go to cinemas on their own**.

cultural events

Many events with a Western content in the performing arts are arranged by **foreign cultural organizations** such as the British Council, 192 Sharia el Nil, Agouza, ✆ 3031514; the Goethe Institute, 5 Sharia Abdel Salam Aref, ✆ 5759877; the French Cultural Centre, 1 Sharia Madraset el Huquq el Fransia, ✆ 3553725; and the American Center at the US Embassy, 5 Sharia Latin America, ✆ 3549601. These can tell you about films, theatre and dance productions, and concerts in which they are involved or know something about.

The American University in Cairo's **Wallace Theater**, Sharia Qasr el Aini, ☎ 3542964, presents English-language plays, musicals and concerts during the academic year (*from October to May*).

The new Japanese-designed **Opera House** on Gezira Island near the Tahrir Bridge, ☎ 3420603, hosts foreign productions as well as the Cairo Opera (*from Mar*), the Cairo Ballet (*from Jan*) and the Cairo Symphony Orchestra (*throughout the year except July and Aug*).

The National Troupe and the Reda Troupe, both **folk dance** troupes, perform regularly at the Balloon Theatre, Sharia 26 July at Sharia el Nil, Agouza, ☎ 3471718. The Oum Khalsoum Arabic Music Troupe performs twice-monthly in winter at Sayed Darwish Concert Hall on Sharia Gamal al-Din al-Afghani near the City of Art, south of Sharia al-Ahram, ☎ 5602473. The **Folkloric Orchestra of Egypt**, which performs with ancient Egyptian instruments, may be found at various venues; ☎ 735153 for information.

Muslim celebrations and whirling dervishes

Moulid el Nabi, which is a nationwide Muslim celebration of the Prophet Mohammed's birthday on the 12th day of Rabei el Awal, is marked in Cairo by a spectacular procession. As at **Ramadan**, the place to be is the square in front of the Sayyidna al-Hussein Mosque in Khan el Khalili (*see* p.104).

Mevlâna, the 13th-century Sufi master who founded his sect of **whirling dervishes** at Konya in Turkey, has his followers in Egypt. Almost entirely suppressed in Turkey and suspect in most other Muslim countries, their intention is to achieve mystical union with God through ecstatic whirling. They whirl for ecstasy and tourists alike at the cultural centre inside the al-Ghuri Mausoleum on Sharia Muizz in medieval Cairo (*Wed and Sat, 8–9pm*). *See* p.103.

for children

Two fixtures appealing at the level of popular mysteries are the **Egyptian National Circus**, a good one-ring affair next to the Balloon Theatre, Agouza, by the Zamalek Bridge, ☎ 3470612 (*daily performances except Wed, 8–10.30pm; in summer the circus moves to Alexandria*); and the **Cairo Puppet Theatre** in Midan Ataba, at the southeast end of Ezbekieh Gardens, ☎ 910954 (*Oct–May, performances at 11.30am, Thurs–Sun*). The repertoire includes Ali Baba and Sindbad the Sailor, and shows are performed in Arabic, which hardly matters as it is easy to follow the action, and anyway adds to the enchantment of the productions, appealing to adults and children alike.

There is also the ersatz Dr Ragab's **Pharaonic Village** on Jacob Island, 2km south from the Giza Bridge, reached by half-hourly boats from the Corniche el Nil (*open daily in winter 9–5, in summer 9–9; tickets are LE40 per person, LE20 for children under 6*). A two-hour tour takes you round a replica temple and a nobleman's villa, and floats you down the Canal of Mythology where you encounter the ancient gods, while perfectly silly-looking Egyptians dressed in bedsheets perform various domestic and priestly duties. It is probably best to approach the **son et lumière** at the Pyramids on this level too (*see* p.159).

Over four hundred species of animal, from free-flying parakeets to wallowing hippopotami, inhabit the extensive and well-stocked **Cairo Zoo**, Sharia el Giza, on the west bank of the Nile (*open daily 8.30–4.30, last entry 3.30*). Next to it are the **El Urman Botanical Gardens**, formerly belonging to the khedives of Egypt, a good place for picnics except on Fridays when everyone else has the same idea. (*A small fee is charged at both places.*)

The Pyramids, Memphis and Saqqara

Everything fears time, but time fears the Pyramids.

12th-century Arab physician

Before taking the Giza road out to that desert escarpment where the famous Pyramids of Cheops, Chephren and Mycerinus stand, it is worth knowing something of the period in which they were built, and to know too something of that entire line of Old Kingdom pyramids which extends from Abu Roash to the north of Giza to Meidum near the Fayyum, a line that is 70km long and numbers over 80 pyramids. This introduction refers to the main pyramid clusters, and explains why and how, at the very beginning of recorded history, these most prodigious and enduring monuments in stone were built.

The First Pyramid

Around 3000 BC, Upper and Lower Egypt were united under **Menes** and the I Dynasty was established. It is not certain that Menes was an individual; he may represent a conflation of early warrior-princes, and the conquest of the Delta may not have been a single campaign but a struggle lasting over generations. There is evidence of fighting and rebellion during the I and II Dynasties, and the energies of this period would have been devoted to consolidation. Building was in mud brick and reed, though during the II Dynasty some stone was used underground in tombs.

Below ground these tombs were built like houses: rectangular and divided into chambers. Above ground they had a low, flat-topped form with sloping walls. This mud brick superstructure was sometimes faced with mud plaster and covered with white gypsum stucco. Mariette called them *mastabas*, the Arabic for those stone benches outside the shops and coffee houses of medieval Cairo.

About 350 years after unification, that is around 2650 BC, Egypt entered into a long period of security and order known to us as the **Old Kingdom**, which begins with the III Dynasty. Awareness of the two Egypts, Upper and Lower, remained acute, as can be read from the ritual of Zoser's Heb-Sed festival at Saqqara, and the village and tribal units up and down the Nile continued to worship their local gods, that prolific pantheon that never disappeared but which was eventually overlaid by a few powerful national cults.

During the reign of **Zoser** (III Dynasty) there was a sudden use and mastery of stone at Saqqara. His mortuary complex of courts and chapels, 544m long and 277m wide, surrounded by a wall 10m high, was all of stone, beautifully detailed and architectured. Dominating the whole was the first pyramid, over 62m high, built in steps. Stone had risen from the darkness of the tomb into the confident light of the sun.

The explanation is not found in technology; stone was not new and tools and construction methods remained as simple as they had been in the past—the lever was used but the wheel and pulley were unknown. Rather there was peace and stability; there was a developing theocratic doctrine that invited the use of stone; and there was a man of genius who knew how to build with it.

That man was **Imhotep**, Zoser's grand vizier, chief judge, minister of agriculture and supervisor of building works. He was also high priest at Heliopolis, centre of the increasingly important sun cult. His range of accomplishment typified the opportunities and needs of a new civilization, where everything was still to be invented and then organized. He was revered throughout pharaonic history, though recalled as a healer rather than as an organizer, statesman or architect. He became a mythical figure, a demi-god, and was eventually raised to unqualified divinity—but his contemporary existence is certain from inscriptions found at Zoser's complex.

The doctrine that begged the use of stone was that of the pharaoh's sole possession of the **ka**, the vital force emanating from the god to his son, the king, who could then dispense it to his subjects. The ka was eternal so long as it was linked to the pharaoh, and so it was essential that ka and king be given an indestructible container of stone.

A stone mastaba was built for Zoser and was twice enlarged. Then in three further stages, Imhotep made a qualitative leap, a sudden vertical thrust, and created the world's first skyscraper, the **Step Pyramid**. Political and cultural revolution in Egypt has always swept down through the valley, nomadic in inspiration. The mastaba belonged to the earthbound world of the Delta farmers; the pyramid and generally Egyptian architecture thereafter eschewed the enclosure of space and instead posed itself against the sun and the stars. Stone permitted it; Imhotep mastered the physics required; and yearning for the vast and timeless cosmos was its inspiration.

It is interesting and important, though, that Zoser's complex remains human in feeling. Zoser was the son of the god, and even if he was the god himself, he at least relished the life of man, for in the house-like arrangement of chambers beneath his pyramid, with their faïence decorations imitating domestic reeding, there is the desire to project his present life into the hereafter. This sense never again appears inside a pyramid, and rarely at any mortuary structure of a pharaoh throughout Egypt's history. Instead the savouring of the everyday was excluded, divinity insisted upon, and ritual became obsessive.

So there was a first revolution, an eruption, in stone. But the second revolution was an adventure even more astonishing and led to the perfection of the pyramid form at Giza. We think of the vastness of Egyptian history and how slowly it must have unfolded, yet from Zoser's complex to Cheops' Pyramid no more time passed than our fast-moving age took to travel from the beginnings of iron construction to the Eiffel Tower—around 75 years, in fact. What is more, the age of the great pyramids was over within 200 years. What explains its sudden coming and going, and the intensity, the phenomenal labour, with which it was pursued?

At Giza you confront the apogee, but you do not find the answer. That lies to the south of Saqqara, at Dahshur and at Meidum.

The Pyramid Production Line

The pyramid at **Meidum** is about 90km by road south of Cairo and even without visiting it you can see it, if you are alert, from the left (west) side of the overnight train back from Luxor soon after it passes El Wasta in the morning. Like all the pyramids, it stands beyond the belt of cultivation on the edge of the desert. It is an amazing sight: a steeply inclined tower rising from a low hill—and that is exactly what it was thought to be by early travellers. In fact it is a pyramid that collapsed. It did not slowly crumble over time; near the moment of its completion there was some catastrophe. Then or after further collapses only a part of the core remained clear of the mound of debris all around.

This was the first pyramid after Zoser's and it was conceived at first as a step pyramid. A second, larger stepped structure was soon superimposed and finally a true pyramidal shell was added, its smooth sides rising at an angle of about 52°. But there were serious design faults, including the badly squared stones of the outer casing which stood on horizontal limestone blocks embedded in compacted sand instead of on a bedrock foundation given an inward slope. The weight of the pyramid, instead of being directed downwards and inwards, was directed outwards; it was destroyed by its own lateral forces.

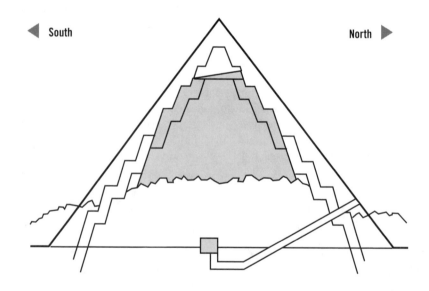

Meidum Pyramid

South   North

Pyramid Puzzles

This disaster leads to an explanation of the pyramid craze that marks the succeeding dynasty to Zoser's. An inscription at Meidum says it was built by **Snofru** (IV Dynasty). But this has disturbed Egyptologists because Snofru was known to have built two pyramids at Dahshur. If the purpose of a pyramid was to provide an indestructible container for the pharaoh and his ka, why did Snofru need three? Snofru's inscription was explained away as a usurpation of his predecessor's pyramid: 'It cannot but seem extraordinary that one and the same king should have built for himself two pyramids of vast dimensions at no great distance from one another…and since it is hard to imagine that he erected three pyramids, the one at Meidum is now tentatively ascribed to Huny,' wrote Sir Alan Gardiner, the noted Egyptologist, in *Egypt of the Pharaohs*. But that left the Bent and Red Pyramids at Dahshur. The Bent Pyramid was disposed of with the argument that it had been deemed unsafe and so Snofru decided to build another. One pharaoh, one ka and one pyramid to suit.

The **Bent Pyramid** rises for 70 per cent of its bulk at an angle of 52°, the same as at Meidum. It then abruptly alters to an angle of 43.5°. The **Red Pyramid** rises at a constant angle of 43.5°. The lower angle of the Red would clearly be safer than the steeper initial angle of the Bent, but it fails to explain why the angle of the Bent should have been changed in mid-construction. If the steep initial angle of the Bent was thought to be unsafe, why not at once abandon the project? But if changing the angle was thought to make it safe, why build the Red Pyramid? Of course, one could argue that it was thought the change of angle would make the Bent Pyramid safe and that unhappily this proved not to be true—though the pyramid has stood safe and sound for nearly 5,000 years.

Eminent Egyptologists have said that the builders of the Bent Pyramid suddenly tired of their task and decided to reduce the pyramid's volume, and hence their labour, by reducing its angle. It has also been said that the bend in the pyramid was predetermined and meant to express a 'double pyramid', that is two pyramids of different angles superimposed, and that

The Bent Pyramid

this symbolized some unexplained duality. It has also been said that the architect lost his nerve, but one reason for this tantalising possibility—the collapse of the Meidum pyramid at a point when the Bent Pyramid was 70 per cent of the way towards completion—has not been countenanced by Egyptologists because, as Sir Alan Gardiner pointed out, it would reintroduce the 'unpalatable conclusion that Snofru did possess three pyramids'. The key word is possess, for it signals the insistence that pyramids were built for the sole reason of providing a container for the pharaoh's ka, so that Snofru had no business building what he believed at that point to be two perfectly good pyramids.

The Egyptologists' evasions could have gone on indefinitely as long as they could have believed that the pyramid at Meidum had belonged to Snofru's predecessor and had merely crumbled with time. But in *The Riddle of the Pyramids* and the *Journal of Egyptian Archaeology*, Kurt Mendelssohn, Professor of Physics at Oxford, has argued that Meidum, while nearing completion, came down with a bang when Snofru was already well advanced on his second pyramid—which only then, and for that reason, was continued at a bent angle. (Mendelssohn's opponents in the *Journal of Egyptian Archaeology* argued well against a single bang, but some initial partial disaster seems likely.)

So why should several pyramids be built in overlapping succession during the reign of a single pharaoh? It is a fact that more large pyramids were built during the IV Dynasty than there were pharaohs to fill them. The answer is in the scale of the task. Herodotus says it took 20 years to build Cheops' Pyramid with 100,000 men working a three-month shift. Modern calculation of the workforce required does not vary substantially from Herodotus' figure, though it is likely that several thousand men, highly skilled in their various trades as stone-cutters, masons and surveyors, would have been employed year-round, while the larger requirement for unskilled labour would have been drawn from the fields between July and November, the period of the inundation. All these people would have needed training and organization, as well as feeding, clothing and housing, and the logistics of the operation must have been formidable.

It is not the sort of operation that would be easily or efficiently mounted on the uncertain occasion of a pharaoh's accession, nor is the size of a pyramid and so the time it will take to build readily geared to the uncertain duration of a pharaoh's reign. The suggestion is rather that pyramid construction was continuous and independent of whether or not there would be enough pharaohs to fill them. And this is what the evidence of Meidum and the Bent Pyramid suggests did happen: the overlap is accounted for by the fact that, as the first pyramid tapered towards completion, the surplus workforce was immediately engaged on starting a second pyramid.

Unification and Authority

Whether by intention or as a consequence, this pyramid production line must have had two important effects. The first was that the vast levy of men required would have cut across the division of Upper and Lower Egypt and the parochialism of villages and tribes throughout the length of the valley and the breadth of the Delta. Pyramid building would complete, down to the fibres of society, the unification of the country begun by Menes by force of arms. The second effect was that whoever was responsible for pyramid building would see their power enhanced. But production of pyramids surplus to the requirements of any one pharaoh, surplus even to the requirements of an entire dynasty, demanded a transcending organizing authority. Imhotep's own career suggests the composition of that authority: in part the power of the pharaoh, but also that of the bureaucracy and the priesthood. Pyramids created the apparatus of the state.

Symbolism of the Pyramids

There is then the pyramidal form. One can see how constructionally the pyramids began with the mastaba; Zoser's pyramid is in fact a stepped mastaba. The achievement in architecture of the pure abstract pyramidal form came, briefly, at Meidum, when before it collapsed its steps were being sheathed in planes. If anything, the disaster was a spur to the technical perfection of the pyramidal symbol. That symbol preceded construction rather than technology dictating symbol seems likely.

In Egyptian creation myths there is a primal hill which rises from the chaos of the waters. Until the High Dam at Aswan finally put an end to the annual inundation, that was very much the scene in Egypt: villages huddled on mounds to avoid the flood, then its subsidence and the sun drawing the harvest from the mud. This myth is referred to at Medinet Habu and Hermopolis. Heliopolis, centre of the sun cult where Imhotep was high priest, also claimed a primal hill, the *benben*, a tapering megalith, a word whose root, *bn*, is bound up with the notion of shining, brilliant, ascending. It is depicted in II Dynasty inscriptions, that is before the pyramid age.

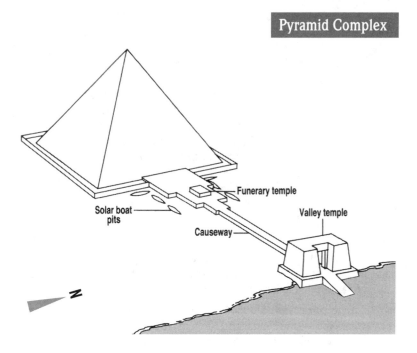

Pyramid Complex

Funerary temple

Solar boat pits

Valley temple

Causeway

N

Variations on the pyramidal form continued to be popular throughout Egyptian history, as for example the **obelisks** whose points or pyramidions were sheathed in electrum, a mixture of silver and gold. Pliny the Elder described obelisks as petrified rays of sunlight, and more than one modern writer has remarked on the pyramid-like form of a burst of sunlight through the clouds after a rare Egyptian rain.

The building of pyramids would have been no mere drudgery inflicted on the population by some megalomaniac pharaoh. The symbolism would have been appreciated throughout all levels of society, and it is quite likely that far from being built by slave-labour, as Herodotus claims, they were built willingly and with a shared sense of exalted purpose which at the time would have seemed far more important, and certainly would have been more conscious, than creating new political forms.

But here the gods died sooner than the works of men. Those works included not only the pyramids, but the creation for the first time in human history of an organizational principle, the state, that was to serve Egypt until her absorption into the Roman Empire, and is the basis of human organization to this day. Once the pyramid production line had achieved this, their symbolism could be carried on in lesser forms, such as obelisks; in any case, it was no longer politically necessary to build pyramids, and apart from some inferior examples in later dynasties, by 2450 BC the age of the pyramids was over.

The Great Pyramids of Giza

Familiarity (though at second-hand) had led me, not to despise the Pyramids, but to discount them. They had become international commonplaces, degraded to the level of the tourist souvenir. They had passed through so many million minds as one of the 'Wonders of the World' that their sharp edge of real wonder had been blunted. … But in actuality, they make an overpowering impression. It is not one of beauty, but on the other hand not one of mere bigness, though size enters into it, and there is an element of aesthetic satisfaction in the elemental simplicity of their triangular silhouette. But this combined with an element of vicarious pride in the magnitude of the human achievement involved, and with a sense of their bold novelty and their historical uniqueness, to produce an effect different from that of any other work of man.

Sir Julian Huxley, *From an Antique Land*, 1954

Getting There

Apart from taking a **taxi** or **limousine**, you could take the 355 bus, a new air-conditioned service which runs every 20mins from just outside the Egyptian Museum in Midan el Tahrir and costs LE2.

For the *son et lumière* show, hop off the bus 1km before the Mena House Hotel where you see the Sound and Light sign on your left and then walk. Almost any taxi driver will know what you mean if you say Sound and Light. Agree a per-hour or all-in rate if you want him to wait (thus avoiding any difficulty in getting a ride back, though you can walk over to the Mena House and get a taxi there); the limousines have a set rate for this.

Another alternative is to take a **tour**, which will include admission and the ride out and back. This works out at about as much as it would cost one person to take a taxi and keep it waiting; for two or more people it is better to take the taxi.

Access and Fees

Access to the **Pyramids** site is *7am–8pm daily in winter and 6.30am–midnight daily in summer; adm LE20*. Access to the interior of the Pyramids is *8.30am–5pm daily year-round; adm LE20*. Tickets are bought at the kiosk at the top of the road coming up from the Mena House Hotel towards the north side of the Pyramid of Cheops. Tickets for the **Solar Boat Museum** (*open daily 9–4 winter, 9–5 summer*) are purchased at the museum; *adm LE20*.

Touts are coming under closer control by the Tourist Police, but can still be a nuisance. Deal with them only if you want to ride on their horse or camel, or if you want to careen about in one of their horse-drawn carts.

Son et Lumière Show

There are two *son et lumière* shows nightly (*in winter 6.30pm and 7.30pm, in summer 7.30pm and 8.30pm—hours may be different during the month of Ramadan; adm LE33*). Seating is on a terrace facing the valley temple of the Pyramid of Chephren, by the Sphinx. Bring a sweater; it can get cool on the edge of the desert, even in summer.

The **language** in which the programmes are presented (English, French, Italian, German, Spanish and Arabic) varies from evening to evening and from first to second programme: for information call © (02) 3852880. If you do not understand Arabic, then the Arabic programme (usually on Thursdays) is definitely recommended; it saves you from having to listen to the drivel while giving you all the benefit of the coloured lights and booming sounds.

Tourist Information

The Tourist Office is opposite the Mena House Hotel on the approach road to the Pyramids, where you can confirm opening hours and entry charges and learn the going rate for hiring camels, horses and horse-drawn buggies (but *see* below).

riding at the Pyramids

The classic view of the Pyramids is from the south across the sands. It is easy enough to walk and indeed to go further, past the Christian and Muslim cemeteries you see in the distance and to climb the rocky outcrop beyond them. But for the fun of it you might like to ride a camel or horse (*see also* p.170), and as you walk round the Giza plateau there will be plenty of Bedouins importuning you to do so. The Tourist Office opposite the Mena House Hotel will tell you the official rates, about LE5 an hour for a camel, LE6 for a horse.

In fact you will be asked for about LE50 for the ride as from experience the Bedouins know there are enough takers at that price, though you can certainly get it down to LE30, less when business is slow. Probably you will be asked to ride two on a beast, but refuse; and no doubt you will be asked for baksheesh in addition to whatever is agreed, to which you should reply with silence and a smile, paying nothing until you have completed your ride and then only the price you originally agreed.

tours

Various agencies offer tours of the Pyramids, some including Memphis and Saqqara. **Misr Travel**'s Cairo office is at 7 Sharia Talaat Harb, downtown ✆ 3930010, ✇ 3924440, and they alo have an office at the Mena House Hotel, ✆ 3835315.

Approaching the Pyramids

There they rose up enormous under our eyes, and the most absurd, trivial things were going on under their shadow.

William Makepeace Thackeray, *Notes of a Journey from Cornhill to Grand Cairo*, 1846

Half a day should be allowed for the visit to the Giza Pyramids, though you should return again at night. They are approached along a broad straight road, originally built for Empress Eugénie so that she could cover the 11km from Cairo in her carriage. This Sharia al-Ahram or Road of the Pyramids once passed across fellahin's fields which would flood with the rising of the Nile, but nowadays the entire route has been built up. There is therefore, at first, something ordinary about the approach, as though you were off to a funfair on the edge of town, expecting at any moment the distant screams of roller-coaster passengers as they plunge down papier-mâché mountains. But even the Pyramids themselves initially conspire to deflate anticipation.

Be prepared for the hordes of touts urging you to ride their horse or camel, the numberless 'guides' and 'watchmen' who gather about you like mosquitoes, endlessly trying to lure you into ruined little temples with the promise of an undiscovered mummy or reliefs of pharaonic pornography. In the old days, for which you are bound to develop the greatest nostalgia, visitors would come with a dragoman who wielded a big stick. Mark Twain, who led a party of tourists here in the 1860s, attempted escape by climbing to the top of Cheops' Pyramid but was pursued by an Arab, to whom he offered $1 if he could race to the top of Chephren's Pyramid and back to the top of Cheops' within nine minutes, in the hope that the man would break his neck. Three dollars later an exasperated Twain, now joined by the man's mother, offered them each $100 if they would jump off the Pyramid head first.

The best times to visit the Pyramids are at dawn, at sunset and at night when they form as much a part of the natural order as the sun, the moon and the stars. Flaubert recalled the view from the top of Cheops' Pyramid: 'The sun was rising just opposite; the whole valley of the Nile, bathed in mist, seemed to be a still white sea; and the desert behind us, with its hillocks of sand, another ocean, deep purple, its waves all petrified.' Or you might visit them after the *son et lumière*, when the lights go out and the sky is black, and the great stones rise

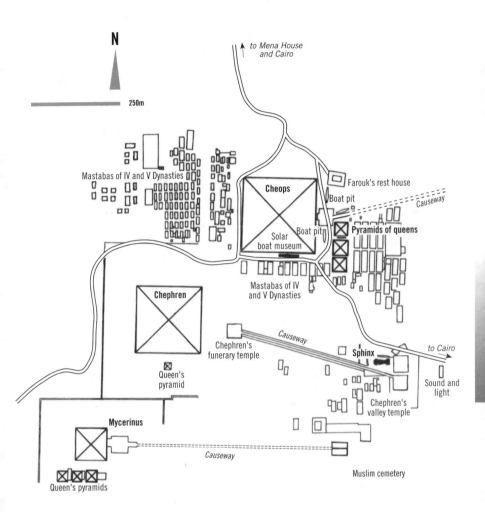

N

250m

to Mena House
and Cairo

Mastabas of IV and V Dynasties

Cheops

Farouk's rest house

Boat pit

Causeway

Boat pit

Solar
boat museum

Pyramids of queens

Chephren

Mastabas of IV
and V Dynasties

Chephren's
funerary temple

Causeway

Sphinx

to Cairo

Queen's
pyramid

Chephren's
valley temple

Sound and
light

Mycerinus

Causeway

Queen's pyramids

Muslim cemetery

on either side, picked out by the moon and stars. Then especially you get the feeling, as Napoleon said to his army, of 'forty centuries of history looking down upon us', and feel it in the most awesome way.

The road arrives at the Mena House Hotel and then curves sharply to the left, mounting a gentle slope and finishing at the north end of the plateau, almost directly opposite the **Great Pyramid**, that of **Cheops**. This is the oldest of the group and the largest, and the others, **Chephren** and **Mycerinus**, stand in descending order of age and size along a southwest axis, each identically oriented 8.5° west of magnetic north; when built they were probably aligned precisely with the North Star, their entrance corridors aiming straight at it. At first the second pyramid, that of Chephren, seems largest, but that is because it stands on higher ground and retains its casing towards its peak. Its present height is 136.4m (originally 143m) and its volume is 2,200,000 cubic metres; this compares with a height of 137.2m (originally 146.6m) for the Great Pyramid of Cheops, which has a volume of 2,550,000 cubic metres. This pyramid was built of over 2,500,000 enormous blocks of limestone cut from the Moqattam and locally, though about 170,000 have been removed by Arabs and Turks since the founding of Cairo. Mycerinus is much smaller, rising only to a height of 65.5m, though it is still imposing, and it contributes to the satisfying arrangement of the group. Napoleon astonished his officers with the calculation that the stones from these three pyramids would be sufficient to build a wall 3m high and 0.3m thick around the whole of France.

But the Pyramids do not have this rocky ledge entirely to themselves. There are smaller **attendant pyramids**, some at least for royal wives, and suburban rows of **mastabas** for nobles and princes of the blood. There are the remains of **temples** and **causeways**; there are **solar boat pits**; and there is the **Sphinx**. A pyramid was never merely a self-sufficient geometrically shaped tumulus of masonry raised above a royal burial; it was the culminating point of a vast funerary area comprising a valley temple, a funerary temple and a causeway linking the two. Near the desert edge and overlooking the cultivation so as to be accessible by boat in the inundation season was a modest valley **chapel**. From it led a walled-in causeway, as long as 500m, upwards to the funerary temple proper, this abutting the east side of the pyramid, where a false door permitted the deceased pharaoh to emerge in order to partake of the offered feasts.

Also, on several sides of a pyramid, set in pits, wooden **boats** have been found. Whether these were only symbolic or actually used is not known; some have supposed that they enabled the pharaoh to follow the sun god across the skies, but as they have been found facing all four points of the compass they could as easily have been intended to enable the pharaoh to go wherever he desired. For convenience, however, they will be referred to here as **solar boats**.

The Great Pyramid of Cheops

What are the hopes of man? Old Egypt's King
Cheops erected the first pyramid,
And largest, thinking it was just the thing
To keep his memory whole and mummy hid;
But somebody or other rummaging,
Burglariously broke his coffin's lid.
Let not a monument give you or me hopes,
Since not a pinch of dust remains of Cheops.

Byron, *Don Juan, Canto I, 219*

Cheops

The Great Pyramid of Cheops (Khufu), later regarded by the Greeks as one of the seven wonders of the ancient world (and the only one to have survived intact), has a volume of 2,550,000 cubic metres, making it the second most massive structure ever built by man (the pyramid at Cholula in Mexico, built nearly 4,000 years later and largely destroyed by the Spaniards, was 500,000 cubic metres greater in volume). The polished casing to the pyramid is entirely gone, so you are presented with the tiered courses of limestone blocks, an invitation to climb to the 10m² platform at the top. This used to be a fairly easy and entirely safe thing to do, as guides would simply haul you up, one at each arm, a third shoving from below.

Climbing the Pyramids is now **forbidden**, however, which leaves the field open to the more adventurous or the more foolhardy to make the attempt unassisted. The ascent is best made at the northeast corner, each 'step' a metre-high block, and will take 15 to 20 minutes. The footing is more difficult on the way down; also you are more prone to tiredness and vertigo (you must not look down). Recently a young man who slept on top while awaiting the dawn fell out of bed, so to speak. There is no stopping a fall; he bounced only twice before obliteration.

Inside the Pyramid

The squeamish might content themselves with going inside. Here the only thing to fear is fear itself, in the form of claustrophobia, and difficulty for some in breathing due to

Pyramid of Cheops

King's Chamber

Air shaft

Air shaft

Great Gallery

Ascending corridor

Entrance

Queen's Chamber

Unfinished chamber

inadequate oxygen. You enter at the north face through an opening made by the 9th-century caliph al-Mamun, son of Haroun el Rashid of *A Thousand and One Nights* fame; coming from Baghdad to suppress an uprising of Copts in the Delta, he took the opportunity to search for treasure (though it is probable that this pyramid had been robbed as early as the First Intermediate Period).

Soon you come to the original corridor which descends for 100m to a depth of 30m beneath the surface of the bedrock. It reaches an unfinished chamber and, as this corridor is constricted (1.3m high, 1m wide) and slippery, it is not usually open to the public. Instead, about 20m from the entrance along the descending corridor you come to a block of granite designed to prevent access to the ascending corridor, though al-Mamun merely hollowed out the rock to the left to bypass it. From here you find yourself crouching your way upwards (height again 1.3m, width 1m) for 40m. The gradient is one in two and so can be quite tiring, but arrival at the Great Gallery at least permits a stretch. Here there is a shaft (right) which winds down to the descending corridor—purpose unknown. There is also a horizontal corridor, again only 1.3m high for most of its length, which leads to the so-called Queen's Chamber (the name given it by the Arabs), nearly square with a pointed roof of gigantic blocks. But best by far is the ascending **Great Gallery**, 8.5m high, 47m long, a marvel of precision masonry, of which it has been said that neither a needle nor a hair can be inserted into the joints of the stones. This leads on to the principal tomb chamber, commonly called the King's Chamber.

Why there are three burial chambers has been one of the enduring riddles of the Great Pyramid. In 1993 an answer was proposed by Dr I.E.S. Edwards, formerly Keeper of Egyptian Antiquities at the British Museum, who noted that the subterranean chamber 'resembles a quarry in which work had come to an abrupt end owing to some unexpected development'. That development, he argued, was the new belief that the pharaoh must be buried, not in a wooden coffin as before, but in a stone sarcophagus. The pyramid shape, a stairway to the sun, had already been adopted in support of the doctrine that at death the pharaoh would be assimilated into the sun god Re. But now there was a further requirement: just as the setting sun was swallowed by the goddess Nut to be born again the following dawn, so too the dead pharaoh should be enclosed within a stone sarcophagus symbolic of the goddess, thereby ensuring his rebirth (*see* Room 33, Ground Floor, at the Egyptian Museum in Cairo).

But this new idea came after a corridor, too narrow for the huge sarcophagus now proposed for Cheops, had already been cut through the bedrock, and so the subterranean chamber was abandoned. Instead, it was intended that the sarcophagus should be placed in a new chamber—the so-called **Queen's Chamber**—which was scheduled into the building programme 'at as low a level as would be compatible with the estimated delivery date of the sarcophagus'. But for some reason, according to Dr Edwards, delivery was delayed and, so that work on the Pyramid could continue, the Queen's Chamber was roofed over but never used, and yet another chamber, the **King's Chamber**, had to be built higher up. Mystery dissolves into familiarity as you imagine the unfortunate architects pulling their hair out each time they had to redesign their building in mid-construction to suit the unpredictable desires of their clients.

The King's Chamber is 42.5m above the surface of the bedrock and is 5.22m wide and 10.44m long, that is a double square, aligned east–west. On the north and south walls, a metre above the floor, are the rectangular mouths of the two ventilation shafts (or perhaps they had a religious significance) which extend to the surfaces of the pyramid. The chamber is built entirely in pink Aswan granite and roofed over with nine huge granite slabs laid horizontally. Above these (seen by means of a ladder leading to a passage in the upper south wall of the Great Gallery) are four more granite layers, their purpose to create five relieving chambers, one on top of the other, which were meant to distribute the full weight of the pyramid away from the King's Chamber, though in fact this job is accomplished by the topmost pointed roof of limestone blocks. It was in these relieving chambers that the only inscriptions in the Great Pyramid were found—the cartouche, traced several times in red, of Khufu, Cheops. His mummy, if it found its way to this pyramid at all, would have been placed in this King's Chamber. But, as Byron observed, the sarcophagus is empty.

Though Byron was wrong about it being the first pyramid, he was right about it being the biggest, and it is here that you might think about the great weight upon you. Over your head is 95m of solid pyramid, more than enough to squash you very thin for a very long time. Unlike the Meidum pyramid, however, the Pyramid of Cheops has been shown by engineering studies to be exceptionally stable. The building blocks are far larger than those used for earlier pyramids and they are precisely fitted together, while the casing blocks overlaying the basic step structure rest upon foundations slotted into the bedrock. The weight of the pyramid itself contributes to its stability, but not simply its dead weight; the stepped inclined buttresses throw much of this weight towards the centre. At every level the pyramid's horizontal thrusts are directed towards the central core, while 35 per cent of the vertical thrusts are transmitted to the inner core (that is the line running from the top of the pyramid through you to the base), only the remaining thrusts being carried down into the bedrock. In fact the bigger the pyramid, the more stable it becomes.

Around Cheops' Pyramid

Coming out of the pyramid you can see on the north side, also on the east, the remains of the original **enclosure wall**, about 10m from the base. Backing against this wall on the east side is the basalt paving of Cheops' **funerary temple**, about all that remains of it, and occasional traces of the **causeway** that came up from the valley temple, which was discovered in 1990, 4m below street level in the village lying at the foot of the plateau. The three **small pyramids**, 15–20m high, probably belonged to Cheops' queens or sisters.

Three empty **boat pits** have been found near Cheops' Pyramid, but in 1954 a fourth pit revealed a dismantled **solar boat** of Syrian cedar. This magnificent craft has been reassembled and housed in its own specially constructed museum on the south side of the pyramid. Video cameras lowered through drill holes into a fifth pit in 1987 discovered another boat perfectly preserved in 4,500-year-old air beneath the hermetic seal of 1.5m-thick limestone slabs.

An outcrop of hard grey and soft yellow limestone, useless as building material, was left standing in the quarry from which Cheops cut many of the blocks for his pyramid. His son Chephren had the happy idea of shaping it into a figure—lion's body, god's face, though perhaps Chephren's own, and wearing the royal headdress with uraeus (sacred serpent). The Egyptians would have regarded it as a symbol of strength and wisdom combined, but the Greeks applied their word sphinx to it, recalling the creature with a lion's body but the breasts and head of a woman given to putting riddles to passers-by, and so this most famous Sphinx has acquired an air of mystery quite foreign to its intention.

Nevertheless, some mysteries are associated with it. Neither Herodotus nor any other classical writer until Pliny the Elder mentioned the Sphinx, presumably because it was buried in sand. Prints and photographs of recent times show its features looming from an engulfing sea of sand, but this is all too assiduously cleared today, some mystery swept away with it. The future Tuthmosis IV (XVIII Dynasty) dreamed here that if he was to become pharaoh he must clear away the sands: his stelae between the Sphinx' paws commemorate this first known restoration. During the Turkish period the Sphinx was used for target practice and its nose, which originally had been cemented on, fell off; 18th-century drawings show that it was missing long before Napoleon was supposed to have done the damage. The uraeus has also gone, but the beard is being pieced together and should soon be stuck back on.

In the Sound and Light programmes, the Sphinx is given the role of narrator which it performs much better in Arabic when you cannot understand a word. This is in fact one of

The Pyramid of Cheops and the Sphinx, Description de l'Egypte, 1809–28

the best times for viewing it or, after the programme, having a drink on the terrace of the Pavilion of Cheops, for then it gains in perspective against the more distant Pyramids. It may not otherwise seem as large as you had imagined: 20m high and 48.5m long, and much of its bulk is crouched within the quarry so that only its head overtops the horizon.

Chephren's Pyramid Complex

Chephren

Immediately in front of the Sphinx and associated with it is a IV Dynasty temple, one reason for believing the face on the Sphinx is a god's and not Chephren's, for the Egyptians did not build temples to their kings. Adjacent and to the south is Chephren's valley temple, facing east. This is the only IV Dynasty sanctuary to retain its grandeur. It owes its exceptional state of preservation to the fact that it was buried in the sands until it was discovered in 1853 by Mariette (though it may prove to be rivalled by Cheops' valley temple, now being excavated). The material is pink Aswan granite, majestically and simply assembled in strong verticals and horizontals, square monolithic pillars supporting massive granite architraves. It was here that Mariette discovered the magnificent diorite statue of Chephren (Room 42, Ground Floor, Egyptian Museum). The purpose of this temple is uncertain, or rather certain for some and contradicted by others. One view is that valley temples were used for mummification; others think the site too exposed and that embalming would have been done either at the pharaoh's Memphis palace or at the base of the pyramid, in the funerary temple. There is at least more general agreement that here was performed the 'Opening of the Mouth' ceremony at which the ka entered the deceased's body. The ka always required a secure residence, hence pyramids and immutable bodies, though it would also inhabit the mortuary statue of the pharaoh, such as that in the Egyptian Museum, one of 23 that sat round the main T-shaped chamber.

Follow if you can the traces of Chephren's causeway up to his **funerary temple** at the base of his pyramid. More of this temple survives than of Cheops', the walls formed of possibly the largest blocks ever used in building, one of them 13.4m long and weighing 163,000kg. To the south of the pyramid is a ruined small pyramid, probably of a queen.

The **Pyramid of Chephren** (Khafre) compares to Cheops' in size, seemingly exceeds it in height and is also capped with its original casing. Its interior is less interesting, and the outside ascent is much more difficult, requiring an hour to get to the casing. Progress then becomes very dangerous because the smooth surface offers no hold. One of the earlier explorers and snatchers of antiquities was Belzoni, born in Italy but first achieving fame for his 'human pyramid' act on the stage of the Sadlers Wells theatre in London. He was the first European to enter this pyramid, in 1818, and promptly emblazoned his name on the south wall of the burial chamber. When Flaubert entered the chamber 33 years later he recorded: 'Under Belzoni's name, and no less large, is that of a M. Just de Chasseloup-Laubat. One is irritated by the number of imbeciles' names written everywhere: on the top of the Great Pyramid there is a certain Buffard, 79 Rue Saint-Martin, wallpaper manufacturer, in black letters; an English fan of Jenny Lind's has written her name; there is also a pear, representing Louis-Philippe.'

When the Egyptians built their pyramids it was with a feeling for the sublime power of the plane, without reliefs, inscriptions or any detailing whatsoever. Once the polished limestone casings were set in place, the pyramids both literally and symbolically repulsed the touch of mortals—well, that was the idea, anyway. One of the high points of a visit to the Pyramids in Roman times was the spectacle of men from a nearby village shinning up from the ground to their very tips; one Roman woman scribbled on a casing stone, 'I saw the Pyramids without you; sadly I shed tears here', a lament copied down by a 15th-century pilgrim, when the casing was more extensive than now.

Last of the Great Pyramids

Mycerinus

The Pyramid of Mycerinus (Menkaure) has only one-tenth of the volume of the other two pyramids and effectively marks the end of the pyramid age. The last pharaoh of the IV Dynasty built a quite different sort of tomb at Saqqara, while the pyramids of the next dynasty were small and shoddy. Though the last of the great pyramids, Mycerinus' was built well, with granite used for the lower courses and a casing that remained almost entirely intact until the 16th century. An attempt was made by the sultan in 1215 to destroy all the Pyramids and his workmen started with Mycerinus'. After eight months they gave up. 'Considering the vast masses that have been taken away, it might be supposed that the building would have been completely destroyed, but so immense is the pile that the stones are scarcely missed. Only on one of its sides can be noticed any trace of the impression which it was attempted to be made,' wrote the 13th-century historian Abd el Latif.

Though you can enter, the interior is not interesting. The sarcophagus was removed early in the 19th century and put aboard ship for England, but ship and sarcophagus sank off the Spanish coast. Opposite the south face are three small pyramids, while against the east are the remains of Mycerinus' funerary temple.

Shopping

For excellent tapestry-weaving go to the village of Kardassa, about 3km off Sharia al-Ahram (turn right several hundred metres before the Mena House at the Pyramids, at the sign for Andrea's Restaurant). Here you can buy **tapestries,** and also **bedspreads**, **rugs**, **shirts**, **dresses** and black **Bedouin dresses** with bright cross-stitching—usually old, with a patchwork look after repairs, and becoming quite expensive and rare.

Sports and Activities

The best nine-hole **golf course** in the Cairo area is at the Mena House Hotel, a well-watered oasis beneath the brow of the Pyramids, ✆ 3415121. Before and during the Second World War the British would go **skiing** at Giza. 'You can eat your cake and still have it!', went a local magazine article in the autumn of 1939. 'Under the sunniest of blue skies, you will find sand dunes where you can both ski and bronze yourself to your heart's desire'—an accompanying photograph showing a tent set up just south of the Pyramids, a sort of portable chalet, with men and women wearing swimsuits and strapped into skis slipping down the desert slopes.

For accommodation in Cairo *see* pp.137–42.

very expensive

★★★★★**The Mena House Oberoi**, Sharia al-Ahram, Giza, Ⓒ 3833222, ✆ 3837777, is a historic hotel, originally a khedivial hunting lodge (converted to a hotel in 1869) where Churchill and Roosevelt initiated the D-Day plan. The Pyramids are just across the road. The one drawback is the long journey, especially at rush hours, into central Cairo (11km to Midan el Tahrir). The old wing is magnificently decorated, and its balconied suites overlook the Pyramids. Avoid being shunted into the garden wing, which was added in 1976; it is pleasant, but lacks the old style and the dramatic Pyramid views. Pool, tennis, golf, casino, nightclub, business centre, car hire and Misr Travel office make the Mena House a self-sufficient resort on the desert's edge (*see* p.56).

expensive

★★★★**The Green Pyramids**, 13 Sharia Helmiat al-Ahram, Giza, Ⓒ 537619, ✆ 537232, was until 1982 the Swiss chalet-style villa of Egyptian actor Yussef Wahby. Wings were added, creating a small hotel set back from the main road to the Pyramids and peaceful gardens. The service is superb, the facilities personalized, the rooms generously proportioned, each with garden balconies, and the food is excellent. There are two luxury suites in the villa itself, with the original furniture and round black baths with gold taps. There are several restaurants, including one by the poolside, a bar and disco. The one drawback is that it is 7km from Midan el Tahrir in Cairo and 4km from the Pyramids, so a journey is always required, which in rush hours can be tedious.

★★★★**The Siag Pyramids Hotel**, Saqqara Road, Giza, Ⓒ 3856022, ✆ 3840874, has good views of the Pyramids, 1km distant, but otherwise you are far from anywhere (10km to Midan el Tahrir). There is a heated swimming pool, two night-lit tennis courts, a Lebanese restaurant and all the usual in-room fittings.

Camping

Camping Salma, Ⓒ 3849152, ✆ 3851010, at Harraniyya, 3km along the canal road from Giza to Saqqara, is a long way from anywhere and only for people with a vehicle. Harraniyya is the village where the late Ramses Wissa Wassef established his famous tapestry-weaving school, so the way is known and easily found: turn left off the Pyramids Road towards Saqqara and then look for the signposted turning to Harraniyya. There are toilets, showers, meals and a delightful garden; pitching a tent costs about $2, renting a cabin about $12.

Eating Out

In the Mena House Hotel at the base of the plateau there is the reasonably priced **Khan el Khalili** café, with views to the Pyramids, a bar, a drinks lounge and several expensive restaurants.

Saqqara is 32km by road from Cairo and 21km south of the Giza Pyramids. The necropolis extends about 7km north to south along the desert plateau and looks down over the palm groves that cover the site of **Memphis**, about 6km to the southeast in the valley of the Nile. Memphis was the capital of the Old Kingdom, its palaces and shrines of that period built of mud brick for the span of the living and now vanished; Saqqara, built of stone to endure eternity, survives.

Getting There

You can reach Saqqara by **horse** or **camel** from the Giza Pyramids (*see* below), though as the journey takes 3 hours in each direction you will not be left with much time to explore the site, and a visit to Memphis would probably be out of the question. You can, however, ride to Saqqara and return by taxi, taking in Memphis en route, or you can hire a camel at Saqqara for a little trot round the site. There is also a **bus** from the Giza Pyramids to Badrashein, a village near Memphis; ask about it at the Mena House Hotel or the Tourist Police at the Pyramids. Also there are **tours** or a **taxi** from Cairo. Tours do not include Meidum with Memphis and Saqqara, but ask the travel agent if it can be included at an extra cost, or go to Misr Travel, who in addition to their Cairo office at 7 Sharia Talaat Harb, ✆ 3930010, ✉ 3924440, have one at the Mena House Hotel by the Pyramids, ✆ 3874999, ✉ 3875315.

If journeying **by road**, you turn left off the Pyramids Road (Sharia al-Ahram) at the traffic lights immediately after a canal about 1.5km before the Mena House Hotel. It is a pleasant country road with glimpses to the right of the Western Desert and the V Dynasty pyramids of Abusir. You come first to the turning, on your right, for Saqqara; or you can carry straight on for the left-hand turning to the Memphis site.

riding to Saqqara

You can ride on horseback or camelback across the desert from the Pyramids to Saqqara, negotiating the hire of an animal with one of the many importuning Bedouins at the Pyramids or visiting the stables. Among the better stables are **Omar Stables**, run by Mohammed Zaghloul Omar, ✆ 850301 at the stables or ✆ 621665 at home; also **AA Stables** and **SA Stables**. These are located below the Sphinx and a short walk south. First you should check at the Tourist Office opposite the Mena House to learn the official rates (though these are ignored in practice, it is nevertheless good to know them, as it will strengthen your resolve to bargain hard) and perhaps also enquire at Misr Travel, ✆ 3835315, inside the Mena House, who can organize a journey for you.

The journey will take at least 3 hours in each direction, and spending just a little time at Saqqara means an 8-hour expedition in all. For this reason you should resist offers of hire by the hour and negotiate a price for the entire journey. Expect to pay LE50 per beast for a one-way journey (remembering that you will have to pay for a taxi back, about LE20) or LE100 for the return journey plus LE20 for waiting time at Saqqara.

Out of summer take a sweater as the desert can be cold, especially in the morning and towards sundown. Omar Stables also offer a return journey with overnight camping at a palm grove near Saqqara, and will provide Bedouin-style tents and Egyptian food.

Camels can carry two people, but this is not advisable. There is some dispute as to which animal is better; most people prefer horses over longer distances. Either way, all but the most hardened rider can expect to end the day feeling pretty sore.

Access and Fees

The almost entirely buried site of Memphis can be visited without charge; the nearby statuary garden with its building sheltering the colossal statue of Ramses II is *open 7.30–4 in winter, 7.30–5 in summer; adm LE14.* The Saqqara site is *open 7–5; adm LE20.* In summer it is best to visit Saqqara early in the morning to avoid the heat, and so to call on Memphis afterwards, but for context Memphis is mentioned here first.

Lunch/Cafés

Refreshments are available at Memphis; the refreshment tent at Saqqara may still be temporarily closed.

Memphis, the Old Kingdom Capital

On the land which had been drained by the diversion of the river, King Menes built his city.

Herodotus

Memphis probably began as a fortress by which Menes controlled the land and water routes between Upper and Lower Egypt and kept the conquered inhabitants of the Delta in subjection. By the III Dynasty it must have become a sizeable capital, as the Saqqara necropolis suggests, but it may not have been fixed. The IV Dynasty pharaohs built their pyramids to the north at Giza and might well have had their palaces near there too. One can imagine Memphis developing in stages like Arab Fustat and its successors, decamping northwards. Whether it was the Mediterranean breezes that attracted, or the growing dominance of the sun cult at Heliopolis, so closely associated with pyramid development, is not known. By the VI Dynasty, however, the old site of Memphis had been reoccupied, its attraction the venerable sanctuary of Ptah. From the court of Pepi and its associated monuments came the name Men-nefru-Mire, the Beauty of King Mire (Pepi), later abbreviated to Menfe, in Greek Memphis.

Although no longer capital, in the New Kingdom Memphis rivalled Thebes in grandeur, embellished in particular by Ramses II's mania for building. During the 5th century BC when the Persians ruled Egypt from here and Herodotus visited the city, it was a great cosmopolitan centre, a foreshadowing of Alexandria, with many Greeks and Jews, Phoenicians and Libyans among its population, as full of oriental spectacle as parts of Cairo are today. Herodotus, in his hydrology of Egypt, which fascinated him, wrote that 'when the

Nile overflows, the whole country is converted into a sea, and the towns, which alone remain above water, look like islands in the Aegean. At these times water transport is used all over the country, instead of merely along the course of the river and anyone going from Naucratis to Memphis would pass right by the Pyramids... The priests told me that it was Menes, the first king of Egypt, who raised the dam which protects Memphis from the floods... On the land which had been drained by the diversion of the river, King Menes built his city and afterwards on the north and west sides of the town excavated a lake, communicating with the river.'

The decline of Memphis began with the founding of Alexandria, and the final blow was struck when the Arabs founded Fustat as their capital. Even so, as late as the 12th century Abd el Latif could write that 'the ruins still offer, to those who contemplate them, a collection of such marvellous beauty that the intelligence is confounded, and the most eloquent man would be unable to describe them adequately'. But towards the end of the Mameluke period the dikes around Memphis fell into disrepair and at every inundation the level of the ground was raised.

The Site

Today the centuries of Nile mud have swallowed Memphis entirely, so much so that it is impossible to soliloquize on how the mighty has fallen—there is, simply, so little to stir reflection. Yet even had the dikes been maintained, the more ancient stratas of Memphis would have been lost. Herodotus exactly describes those conditions, persisting until the building of the High Dam at Aswan, which annually drowned the valley and the Delta and gradually covered the past with mud, so that settlements built upon themselves, one strata upon another, to form what in Arabic are known as *tells*. The earliest mud brick houses, palaces and sanctuaries have long since disintegrated beneath the wash of the annual flood, explaining why so much is known of the Egyptian dead, who dwelt in stone on high desert ground, while so little is known of the living.

At Memphis there is a modern building erected for the sole purpose of roofing over a supine **colossus of Ramses II**, brother to the one outside the Cairo railway station. This Ramses is the victim of monumental indifference: the Egyptian government gave him to the British Museum—which failed to collect. He lies here with his right fist clenched, like a cataleptic Gulliver, bound down by brain seizure rather than ropes. Several smaller statues stand or lie in the grass beneath palms near the covered colossus. Otherwise the immediate area has been turned into a garden, and set up along the central pathway like a plaster gnome is a friendly **alabaster sphinx** dating from the New Kingdom.

If you walk a bit beyond this, no more than 100m eastwards, you can survey the shapeless mounds that cloak the ancient city. The faint remains of the vast **Temple of Ptah** lie waterlogged beside the village of Mit Rahinah. Or from the garden with its sphinx follow the road to Saqqara for 100m; off its north side are the alabaster mummification beds where the **Apis bulls** (*see* pp.184–5) were prepared for burial.

The Egypt Exploration Society is now excavating at Memphis; perhaps in a decade or so there will be more to see.

A Desert Ride

One way to reach Saqqara is by **horse** or **camel** from the Giza Pyramids. The three-hour journey in each direction takes you along the edge of the cultivation and often strikes across the desert, allowing you to see several rarely visited pyramids and sun temples along the way. There are stables behind the *son et lumière* pavilion. A camel costs more than a horse to hire and is more exhilarating to ride, but be sure there is plenty of padding round the pommel. You will be accompanied by a guide, so finding your way is not a problem.

As you leave the Giza Pyramids you pass adjoining Christian and Muslim cemeteries on the left; you then head south into the desert, though you will always be in sight of the cultivation of the Nile valley. After about 1¼ hours you come to the **Zawiyat el Aryan pyramids**, both awash in sand. The northerly **Unfinished Pyramid**, abandoned during the IV Dynasty, is surrounded by unused blocks of limestone and granite. About 15 minutes to the southeast and nearer the cultivation is the III Dynasty **Layer Pyramid**, older than the Giza group, built of small blocks and probably meant to be a step pyramid. Another 30 minutes further south and near the cultivation (where roses are a speciality) you come to the two V Dynasty **sun temples of Abu Ghurab**. In the courtyard of the northernmost sun temple, that of Neuserre, stands an altar and the base of a solar obelisk. The obelisk has vanished, but you can climb up within the base for the view. The southerly sun temple of Userkaf is utterly ruined and not worth stopping at.

At the edge of the cultivation 400m southeast and taking their name from a nearby village are the V Dynasty **Abusir pyramids**. The northernmost pyramid of Sahure is badly damaged, though you can crawl through a narrow passage into its tomb chamber. Climbing to the summit, you can gain a fine panorama of the other pyramids in this cluster, together with their attendant mortuary temples. These are the pyramids of Neuserre, Neferikare and Neferefre: neither the first nor last was ever finished, perhaps owing to the early deaths of their pharaohs. Work on the pyramid of Neferikare continued, though he too died early; but what had begun with red granite and limestone was completed in mud brick.

From Abusir you can clearly see the Step Pyramid and other structures at Saqqara, less than 30 minutes' ride further south.

Sun Temples and the Supremacy of Re

Before ascending the throne, Userkaf, the first king of the V Dynasty, had most likely been high priest at Heliopolis, and it was from this time that the cult of Re was raised to the official state religion. Userkaf together with the five kings who succeeded him, though they all built pyramids, diverted considerable resources to building sun temples. In effect a measure of royal power and wealth was being transferred to the priesthood of Re, and by comparing the dimensions of pyramids to sun temples we can see how far this process went. For example, the pyramid that Neuserre built for himself at Abusir had an 81m² base and rose to a height of 52m, but the sun temple he built near by at Abu Gharab enclosed an 87m² area within which rose a masonry-built obelisk, symbolizing Re, 53m high. The pharaoh was quite literally overtopped by the god.

The Saqqara site has a far more desert feel than Giza; the sands wash about your feet nearly everywhere. Also it is dotted with untended holes left by excavators, some of terrific depth and not always enclosed. It would be dangerous for children on the loose, and adults should mind their step. Many tombs, once discovered and examined, have been closed again and some even sanded over. The most comfortable way to explore the site is to go first to Zoser's funerary complex, visiting also the Pyramid of Unas nearby, and then to drive or walk to the refreshment tent (recently removed, though perhaps by now replaced) from where you can visit the mastaba of Akhti-hotep and Ptah-hotep, the mastaba of Ti and the Serapeum.

History

Saqqara, from Sokkar, the Memphite god of the dead, was a necropolis from the unification of Egypt throughout the Ptolemaic period, and it is the site also of a Coptic monastery destroyed by the Arabs c. 960, so that discoveries here span 4,000 years. In historical range and the quantity and value of what has been found here—monuments, works of art, texts and vases—there can be few archaeological sites in all the world, not just Egypt, to compare with Saqqara. Even so, serious examination of the site only began in the mid-19th century and what remains to be discovered is incalculable. Early in 1986 there was one of the most important finds since Howard Carter broke into Tutankhamun's tomb: the discovery here of the tomb of Maya, a close friend of the famous boy-pharaoh. (It will not be open to the public for several years.)

Except for Zoser's Step Pyramid, Saqqara was ignored, its revelations unsuspected, until 1851 when Auguste Mariette discovered the Serapeum. Even the funerary complex immediately surrounding the Step Pyramid went undiscovered until 1924, and its restoration, to which Jean-Philippe Lauer has given a lifetime, continues to this day. Cecil M. Firth's campaign of 1924–7 overturned accepted notions about the origins of Egyptian architecture in stone which, because of the gigantic blocks used at Giza, was thought to have developed from megalithic monuments. Instead, at Zoser's complex, one sees a stone architecture which replicates the use of brick in its size and courses, and which is full of imitative references to rush matting, reed and wood forms. One of the greatest achievements of Egyptian civilization was to sever stone from the rock and on a large scale to make of it a building material unsurpassed to this day. It happened here at Saqqara, the world's first city of stone, with some hesitancy in the new technology but astonishing artistic brilliance.

Zoser's Funerary Complex

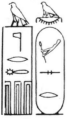

Zoser

Zoser's funerary complex, dominated by the **Step Pyramid**, is 544m from north to south, 277m from east to west, and entirely surrounded by a magnificent panelled and bastioned **enclosure wall** of fine limestone. It still survives to a height of 3.7m at some places along its south side, while on the east side, near the southeast corner, it has been rebuilt with stones found in the sand to its original height of 10.48m. This vast white wall in itself, once easily visible from Memphis, must have conferred enormous prestige on

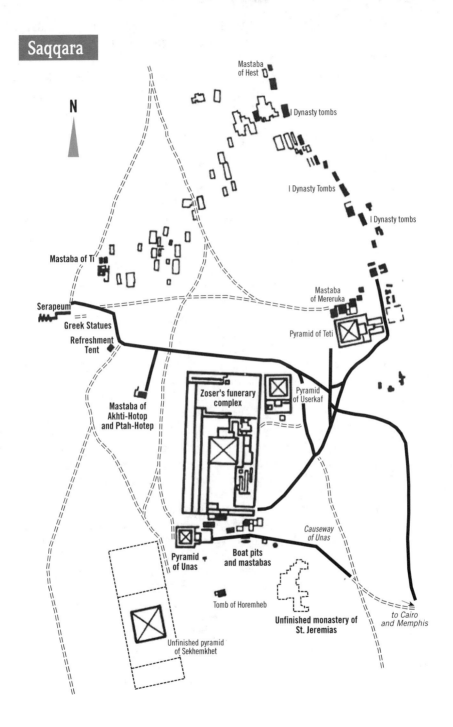

Saqqara

N

Mastaba
of Hest

I Dynasty tombs

I Dynasty Tombs

I Dynasty tombs

Mastaba of Ti

Mastaba
of Mereruka

Serapeum

Greek Statues

Refreshment
Tent

Pyramid of Teti

Mastaba of
Akhti-Hotop
and Ptah-Hotep

Zoser's funerary
complex

Pyramid
of Userkaf

Causeway
of Unas

Pyramid
of Unas

Boat pits
and mastabas

Tomb of Horemheb

Unfinished monastery of
St. Jeremias

to Cairo
and Memphis

Unfinished pyramid
of Sekhemkhet

Zoser and his architect Imhotep. Lauer was himself at first an architect and was called in by Firth when it was realized that the complex could be accurately reconstructed using the original stones.

Though there are many false doors in the enclosure wall for the ka to come and go, there is only one **entrance** (1) for the living, at the southeast corner. The narrow passage is through a fortress-like tower and gives onto a vestibule where you can see on either side the leaves of a simulated double door thrown open, complete with hinge pins and sockets. Ahead of you is a **colonnaded corridor** (2), its columns engaged and ribbed in imitation of palm stems (the protective ceiling is modern concrete). At the far end is a broad **hypostyle hall** (3) with four pairs of engaged columns, and on your right as you enter the court a half-open ka door. This is where the statue base bearing Imhotep's titles was found. Before leaving the hall, notice that the columns are comprised of drums seldom exceeding 25cm in height, one of many details of the masonry which betray Imhotep's hesitancy in working with this new material, stone.

You now emerge into the **Great South Court** (4), and along the wall to your left is a section of rebuilt wall with a frieze of **cobras** (5). The cobra, *uraeus* in Latin, was an emblem of royalty and an instrument of protection, always appearing on the pharaoh's headdress and able to destroy his enemies by breathing flames. The cobra was worshipped in Lower Egypt, and so here in this early dynasty it also emphasizes Zoser's mastery over the conquered peoples of the Delta. Near here is a shaft leading to Zoser's **southern tomb** (6), similar in its faïence decoration to that beneath the Step Pyramid. There is a relief here of Zoser running the Heb-Sed race (*see* p.178). One explanation for his two tombs is that early pharaohs thereby demonstrated their connection with the two Egypts, so needed both a southern and a northern tomb. Possibly the canopic jars containing Zoser's viscera were placed here, the body beneath the pyramid (where in fact a foot was found).

The **Step Pyramid** (7) and its place in the development of pyramid building has already been referred to (*see* p.153). Now you have a first-hand opportunity to examine its features. Despite its 62m height, it was built of fairly small limestone blocks, far smaller than those enormous blocks at Giza. Though working with stone, Imhotep was still thinking in terms of mud brick. But even in the enlargement of his monument from mastaba to pyramid (*see* illustration, p.178), you can detect signs of Imhotep's growing confidence in the new medium: at the southeast corner where the casing has come away you can see the smaller stonework of the mastaba, as you can if you walk along the east face of the pyramid. Also note how regularly the courses are laid, both of the mastaba and the pyramid as a whole, and how well shaped and fitted the stones are. In technique, Imhotep was without fault. The last enlarged mastaba measured 63m each way and a little over 8m high. Recall that the first pyramid erected over this mastaba rose four steps; the further pyramid of two additional steps increased the total volume more than fourfold. The entire monument was then sheathed in fine limestone from Tura, just to the south of modern Cairo, as were the Giza Pyramids.

The original entrance to the Step Pyramid was at the north face, but in the XXVI Dynasty, known as the Saite period for its dynasty's origins at Sais in the Delta, a **gallery** (8) was dug from the Great South Court to the chambers beneath the pyramid. Permission and keys will have to be asked for at the office of the Inspector of Antiquities to the northeast of the

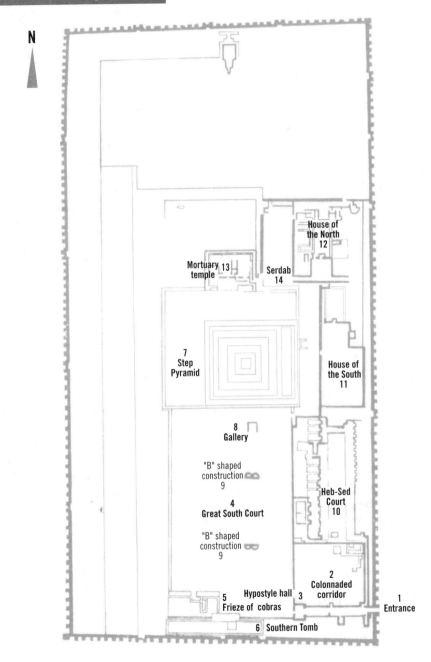

Zoser's Funerary Complex

N

House of
the North
12

Mortuary 13
temple

Serdab
14

7
Step
Pyramid

House of
the South
11

8
Gallery

"B" shaped
construction
9

4
Great South Court

Heb-Sed
Court
10

"B" shaped
construction
9

2
Colonnaded
corridor

5
Frieze of cobras

Hypostyle hall
3

1
Entrance

6 Southern Tomb

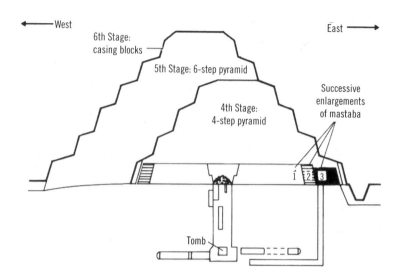

West ← | East →

6th Stage: casing blocks

5th Stage: 6-step pyramid

4th Stage: 4-step pyramid

Successive enlargements of mastaba

Tomb

Pyramid of Teti. The Saites admired the works of the Old Kingdom and it is quite possible they tunnelled their way into the pyramid out of sheer archaeological curiosity. After 60m you come to the main central shaft from where there are impressive views up into the pyramid and down towards the burial chamber which is sealed with a huge granite plug.

Emerging once again into the Great South Court, you see two **B-shaped constructions** (9) near the centre. These marked the limits of Upper and Lower Egypt, the gap between them symbolically spanned by Zoser in the Heb-Sed race. (A relief in the southern tomb shows Zoser in full stride, the two B-shaped constructions to the rear and fore.) The Heb-Sed race was one of the ceremonies during the five-day jubilee which occurred in the thirtieth year— that is, at the interval of one generation—of the pharaoh's reign. It is possible that at some earlier period power was granted for only 30 years and the chieftain then deposed, perhaps killed, to spare the land from decline because of his failing strength. This jubilee, therefore, was a renewal of the vital forces of the pharaoh and his ka, and so of all Egypt.

Also at his jubilee the pharaoh re-enacted his coronation, sitting first on the throne of Upper Egypt, then on the throne of Lower Egypt, each time presenting gifts to the various priest-hoods before they returned to their provinces. Participation in the festival obliged the priests to recognize the supremacy of the pharaoh over their own local deities. These ceremonies, however, including the ritual race, would not have taken place here but at Memphis. The funerary complex was meant as a cosmic 'stand-in' for the actual jubilee site—it perpetuated the regenerating Heb-Sed in eternal stone. This explains the extraordinary film set quality of the Heb-Sed Court.

The **Heb-Sed Court** (10) in the southeast part of the complex is rectangular and flanked to east and west by shrines, each one representing a province. They are hardly more than façades, as in the town backdrops to a Hollywood western. You gain access to the offering niches by circumventing a screen wall, which disguises the lack of depth, for the tall buildings are mere dummies, filled with rubble. Half-open doors with hinges, imitations of the wooden originals, receive immortality in stone. In actuality, these shrines would have been tents with wooden poles and cross-supports. The chapels are not uniform: some have a curved cornice, as though the underlying frame represented flexed wood; other roofs are horizontal, featuring the outward curve of the cavetto cornice that was to become so familiar a feature of Egyptian architecture, and torus moulding. Drawing on earlier building materials, Imhotep here invented the language of stone architecture. Cornices, torus mouldings, stone corner posts and columns and a variety of capitals appear for the first time in history at Saqqara. It is all the more astonishing that the effect is so delicate and beautifully proportioned. A stone platform at the south end of the court is probably where the two thrones of Egypt stood for the re-enactment of the coronation, while at the north end of the court, to the left, is a base with four pairs of feet, most likely those of statues of Zoser, his wife and two daughters.

North of the Heb-Sed Court is another spacious court and the **House of the South** (11) with engaged proto-Doric columns. These Doric-style columns were never popular in Egypt where planes and hence smoothly rounded columns were preferred to the Aegean play of light and shadow. There is the peculiarity of the door being placed asymmetrically, owing to the proto-type façade being no more than a curtain, the door therefore needing to abut a column for support. As with the shrines in the Heb-Sed Court, the House of the South and the House of the North would actually have had wooden frames. They may have been sanctuaries, or possibly they represent government buildings of Upper and Lower Egypt.

Inside the corridor are the first known examples of tourist graffiti, written in a cursive form of hieroglyphics and dating from the New Kingdom. The visitors, scribes from Thebes, express their admiration for Zoser's achievement, though here and elsewhere some settle for the ancient equivalent of 'Kilroy was here', while one pedantic crackpot, taking exception to some illiterate graffiti he must have seen, scribbled: 'The scribe of clever fingers came, a clever scribe without his equal among any men of Memphis, the scribe Amenemhet. I say: Explain to me these words. My heart is sick when I see the work of their hands. It is like the work of a woman who has no mind.'

The **House of the North** (12) is similar to that of the South except that the columns have the form of a papyrus plant, the shaft the triangular stem, the capital the fanning head.

The **mortuary temple** (13) at the north face of the pyramid is largely in ruins. The original entrance to the burial chamber beneath the pyramid led from this temple. To the east of the temple is the **serdab** (14), as startling now as it was to Firth when he uncovered it. It is a masonry box, tilted slightly back and with two small holes drilled through its north face. A window at the side, put there by the excavators, allows you to peer in. And there is Zoser! A life-size painted limestone statue, as you realize after the initial surprise, but for all the world like a strapped-in astronaut in his space capsule, his eyes fixed through the holes on the North Star, awaiting blast-off and immortality. The circumpolar stars and the North Star itself were 'those that know no destruction' or 'those that know no weariness', for they never set and so never died; this was the place of eternal blessedness for which Egyptians longed. And there is Zoser. It is absolutely convincing. It is this which impresses about the ancient Egyptians again and again, how they gave as well as they could mechanical effect to their illusions. They put California body-freezers to shame. Alas for poor Zoser, the unbelieving Mr Firth removed the original statue to the Antiquities Museum in Cairo; this is a copy. But then again, the substitution probably does not bother Zoser's ka; it lives here still, and at dark of night it rockets starwards and mingles with the universe.

The Pyramid of Unas

Unas was the last pharaoh of the V Dynasty. About 300 years mark the distance between Zoser's Step Pyramid, the Giza Pyramid, and this heap of rubble that is Unas' pyramid. These monuments graphically portray the rise and decline of the Old Kingdom sun cult.

The Pyramid of Unas was approached by a 1km causeway, part of which has been reconstructed, including a very short section of its walls and roof, for it was entirely enclosed. A slit in the roof allowed the sunlight to illuminate the inscribed walls which were lively with everyday scenes. On the north side several mastabas are arranged like village houses on either side of narrow lanes. The best is that of Princess Idut (V Dynasty) with 10 rooms. On the south side of the causeway there are impressive boat pits. About 150m to the south are the sanded-over ruins of the **monastery of St Jeremias**, founded in the second half of the 5th century AD and destroyed by the Arabs around AD 960. Practically all of its paintings and carvings have been removed to the Coptic Museum in Old Cairo.

The Pyramid of Unas looks like a pile of dirt, certainly when approached from the east. On the west side its stones are more evident, but are disarrayed. Even originally it rose only about 18.5m; its core was loose blocks and rubble, its casing alone in hewn limestone. Nevertheless, the pyramid has proved of immense historical importance, for when Gaston Maspero entered the tomb chamber in 1881 he found the walls covered with inscriptions, the **Pyramid Texts**, which are the earliest mortuary literature of Egypt. These are hymns and rituals that preceded and accompanied the interment of the body; prayers for the release of the ba or soul; another section listing offerings of food, drink and clothing for use in the afterlife. Until this time, pyramids had gone unadorned. Thereafter, funerary literature underwent considerable elaboration and embroidery, culminating in that collection—or rather genre, for no definitive compilation existed—of New Kingdom literature known to us as the Book of the Dead.

The Pyramid Texts and Osiris

The only complete account of the Osiris myth was given by the Greek writer Plutarch more than 2,000 years after the passing of the Old Kingdom, by when it represented a compendium of evolved belief. Nevertheless, aspects of the story are preserved in various Egyptian literary sources, including the Pyramid Texts. These show that by the end of the V Dynasty Osiris was described as being born of the sky goddess Nut after her union with the earth god Geb, whose other children included Isis and Seth. Osiris and Isis were the parents of Horus, who became associated with the sun cult and with whom the living pharaoh was identified, while at death he was identified with Osiris. The king therefore was linked to cults of both sky and earth, life and afterlife, and existed simultaneously and undyingly in all spheres and realms. In time the cult of Osiris would extend far beyond the royal sphere, and its message would become one of universal redemption.

Despite its exterior, the pyramid of Unas remains internally sound and you can creep down the 1.4m-high corridor, entered from the north face, past three enormous slabs of granite meant to block the way. Unlike the New Kingdom texts which were full of advice on how to steer a course clear of the forces of evil, which in effect emphasized the dangers that preceded safe arrival in the afterlife and were the tools of the trade of a blackmailing priesthood, the Pyramid Texts celebrate eternal life and identify the deceased pharaoh with Osiris. Nevertheless, there is anxiety in the prayers. The confident era of the sun cult was waning; a personal god and a note of redemption marked the rising cult of Osiris. The state was weakening; the troubled times of the First Intermediate Period were approaching.

Saqqara's Outstanding Mastabas

You can now trudge across the sands or drive to the refreshment tent (recently removed but perhaps by the time you read this replaced) which normally stands near the site of Mariette's house, where he stayed during those first serious explorations of Saqqara. The beer is cold and in the heat goes straight to your head. You can walk around the rest of the necropolis in a state of intoxication. When visiting the Serapeum, you may be grateful for that.

Viziers and Priests

But first you can visit some mastabas. The **mastaba of Mereruka**, with 32 rooms, is the largest at Saqqara. He enjoyed in death not only elbow room, but the prestigious company to which he had become accustomed in life. For Mereruka was vizier to the pharaoh Teti (VI Dynasty), whose pyramid is next door, and he married and was buried with the boss's daughter. The entry passage shows Mereruka painting a picture of the seasons and playing a board game to pass away the time, while the first three chambers are decorated with scenes of hunting, furniture-making and goldsmiths at work. At the far end of the mastaba is a chapel with six pillars, containing a statue of the vizier himself. The scenes to the left of this are interesting: they show the domestication of gazelles, goats and hyenas.

The double **mastaba of Akhti-Hotep and Ptah-Hotep** is to the southeast of the refreshment tent, along your way if you are walking between the complexes of Zoser or Unas or between Mereruka's mastaba and a beer. Ptah-Hotep describes himself as a priest of Maat and may have held other positions too. At any rate, he seems to have been a very important official during the reign of Djedkare (V Dynasty), predecessor of Unas. Akhti-Hotep, who may have been Ptah-Hotep's father, was vizier, judge and chief of the granary and treasury. Their mastaba is smaller than that of Ti's, which we come to next, but is more developed and is particularly interesting for the reliefs which are in various stages of completion.

You enter from the north and come into a corridor. On its left wall are preliminary drawings in red with corrections by the master artist in black. On the right wall are various stages of low relief. The background is cut away first to yield a silhouette and then the details are pencilled in and cut. In the lower registers, servants carry fowl in their arms towards Ptah-Hotep who stands at the far end of this right-hand wall. Though somewhat stylized, with his shoulders squared but with head and limbs in profile, this detailed musculature shows the artist's sound sense of anatomy.

At the top end of the corridor you turn right into a pillared hall and then left, passing through a vestibule, into **Ptah-Hotep's tomb chamber**. The ceiling imitates the trunks of palm trees while the mural reliefs, still retaining some colour, are the finest preserved of the Old Kingdom, surpassing even those in the more famous mastaba of Ti.

Food and Entertainment for the Ka

On the right wall are two door-shaped stelae, representing the entrance to the tomb. Between them is Ptah-Hotep, depicted in the panther-skin of a high priest, seated at a cornu-copian table of offerings, a goblet raised to his lips. In the upper register, priests make offerings; in the lower three rows, servants bear gifts. They are lucky to get off so lightly; during the I Dynasty they were sacrificed and interred around their master's mastaba. On the far wall Ptah-Hotep is again at table, this time with a stylized loaf of bread before him and copper basins and ewers alongside so that he may cleanse himself before eating. In the upper register women representing various estates bring him the products of his farms, while in the second register animals are being thrown and slaughtered. The reliefs on the left wall are the finest and most interesting, a catalogue of events in the life of the deceased. On the right, according to the text, Ptah-Hotep is inspecting the 'gifts and tribute that are brought by the estates of the North and South'; boys are wrestling and running, caged animals (lions, gazelles, hares and hedgehogs) are drawn up, and a cow is giving birth, a peasant guiding the calf into the world. The bottom register shows domestic poultry and the text claims that Ptah-Hotep possessed '121,000 geese of one variety, 11,210 of another variety, 120,000 small geese, 111,200 goslings and 1,225 swans'. On the left of this wall Ptah-Hotep 'witnesses all the pleasant activities that take place in the whole country'. In the top regis-ters, boys and girls are playing; there is one episode of two boys seated and facing each other as their friends vault over them. This game, called *Khaki la wizza*, is still played today by Nubians. The third register is devoted to aspects of viticulture; the fourth shows animal life (note the hare emerging from its hole with a cricket in its mouth); the fifth is a hunting scene, the cow tied as bait for the lion; the fifth and sixth show marsh and boating scenes.

Above the entrance is a faded mural, but you can make out Ptah-Hotep preparing for his day, a manicurist at his hands, a pedicurist at his feet, musicians entertaining him, greyhounds beneath his chair and a pet monkey held by his valet. The sophistication of this scene is all the more striking when you recall that it depicts daily Egyptian life, albeit at the very top of the social ladder, nearly 4,500 years ago, at a time when Europe and most of Asia were still in the Stone Age. The purpose of these reliefs was to provide food, indeed a complete experience of life, for the ka. They began during the IV Dynasty as it was realized that relatives and descendants did not always provide fresh offerings; the reliefs were imitative magic against default. But one can also imagine the great pleasure they must have given the tomb owner, an assurance that he was going to take it all with him, and to his relatives when they did gather in his tomb. Think of some of the more elaborate marble tombs in Greek cemeteries today; they are like small shrines with an inner chamber for the deceased and an outer chamber with seats for the living, and they are the cheeriest places, often attracting bountiful picnics. Unas, a generation later, was already worried about his relationship with Osiris; but here there is not a single god, no judgement, no doubt—afterlife follows on from life as assuredly as day follows day, and without even an intervening night.

Now, returning to the pillared hall you turn left for the **chamber of Akhti-Hotep**, similarly though less finely decorated. A passageway leads out of the side of this and opening off it, on your left, is a chamber containing an anonymous mummy. The passageway leads back to the pillared hall and the entrance corridor.

Hairdresser and Estate Manager

The **mastaba of Ti** is to the north of the refreshment tent and you can follow the road that leads to the Serapeum part of the way there. The mastaba was discovered by Mariette in 1865 and has been well restored by the Egyptian Department of Antiquities. It originally stood above ground but is now entirely sunk in the sand. Its reliefs rival those in Ptah-Hotep's tomb chamber and exceed them in variety. Ti was a parvenu and royal hairdresser during the early V Dynasty; he was also overseer of several royal mortuary temples and pyramids and controller of royal ponds, farms and stock from which he evidently enriched himself. His wife was related to the royal family and his children bore the title 'royal descendant', to which Ti himself was not entitled. Ti's wife and eldest son were also entombed here, but some later would-be arriviste made off with the goods and disposed of the bodies.

In plan, the entrance is from the north, a two-pillared vestibule leading to a spacious open-pillared court at the centre of which a flight of stairs descends to a subterranean passage ending in an antechamber and the tomb chamber. A corridor leads out from the rear of the open court, passing a chamber on the right to arrive at the funerary chamber and the serdab.

Once through the open court, whose reliefs have been badly damaged by exposure, the walls of corridors and rooms are finely decorated with familiar scenes. The most interesting room, with the most beautiful reliefs, is Ti's **funerary chamber**. Through the slot in the far (south) wall you can see Ti (this is a cast of the original statue now in the Cairo Museum) staring vacantly northwards from his serdab, though lacking Zoser's look of adventure. Needless to say his hair, or rather his wig, is well done. Most enjoyable are the reliefs on the near (north) wall, all concerned with life in the marshes of the Delta. Look particularly at the central relief of Ti sailing through the marshes. This is a classic representation of a **hippopotamus hunt**; the hippopotamus, to the lower right, has seized a crocodile which is desperately trying to bite the hippo's leg. Ti is shown larger than his huntsmen who, from another boat, are harpooning the hippo. Below the boats are fine Nile fish of different species, identifiable as favoured catches in the river today. On the right, in a small boat with a curiously truncated stern, a fisherman is about to club a large schal fish over the head. Above Ti, among the papyrus clusters, birds are attacked in their nests by carnivorous animals, the reeds bending with their weight. In the register below is a line of elegant female bearers, their transparent coloured dresses surrendered to time, their nakedness and varied poses freshly pleasing.

This relief is unusual for having two layers of meaning. Literally it is a hunt in the marshes; but symbolically it is Ti against the forces of evil and chaos. The hippopotamus was particularly feared and hated in ancient Egypt, but Ti together with a helpful crocodile is killing it. Fish and birds represented chaos, but here again man and animals are subduing them.

The Serapeum: Tombs of the Apis Bulls

When I first penetrated into the sepulchre of the Apis, I was so overcome with astonishment that, though it is now five years ago, the feeling is still vivid in my mind. By some inexplicable accident one chamber of the Apis tombs, walled up in the thirtieth year of Ramses II, had escaped the general plunder of the monuments, and I was so fortunate as to find it untouched. Three thousand seven hundred years had had no effect in altering its primitive state. The finger mark of the Egyptian who set the last stone in the wall built up to cover the door was still visible in the mortar. Bare feet had left their traces on the sand strewn in a corner of this chamber of the dead; nothing had been disturbed in this burying-place where an embalmed ox had been resting for nearly forty centuries.

Auguste Mariette

The **Serapeum** is the strangest place at Saqqara. A temple once stood here amid the sands but what remain are the long underground galleries cut through the rock where the Apis bulls were buried. This was Mariette's great discovery in 1851 which began the serious excavation of Saqqara that has continued ever since.

Entry is to the west of the refreshment tent; you follow the road which first bends right towards Ti's mastaba and then turns left. At this second bend was Mariette's house, and immediately by the roadside, on your left and under the protective roof, is the surprising sight of several Greek statues arranged in a semicircle. These and their unlikely connection with bull burial requires some explanation.

The Legends

The huge tombs of these Apis bulls were previously known only from references to them by various writers of antiquity. For instance, Herodotus wrote: 'The Apis is the calf of a cow which is never afterwards able to have another. The Egyptian belief is that a flash of light descends upon the cow from heaven, and this causes her to receive Apis. The Apis-calf has distinctive marks; it is black, with a white diamond on its forehead, the image of an eagle on its back, the hairs on its tail double, and a scarab under its tongue.'

Apis thus miraculously conceived was considered to be an incarnation of Ptah, the god of Memphis. Worshipped as such during his lifetime within a special sanctuary in the Temple of Ptah, he was mummified after his death on those alabaster beds you can still see among the few surviving stones of Memphis. Then, identified with Osiris under the name Osiris-Apis, he was taken with great pomp to these underground galleries at the Serapeum and placed within a gigantic sarcophagus.

Sacred Bulls and Egyptian Nationalism

Sacred bull cults go back into the prehistory of Egypt, and during the I and II Dynasties a bull would wander across the field of the Heb-Sed race, symbolically fertilising the two lands. But animal cults enjoyed an astonishing popularity during the Late Egyptian Period as the old beliefs degenerated. Herodotus, attempting to demonstrate the madness of Cambyses, the Persian ruler of Egypt, records that 'the priests brought Apis and Cambyses, half mad as he was, drew his dagger, aimed a blow at its belly, but missed and struck its thigh. Then he laughed, and said to the priests: "Do you call that a god, you poor creatures? Are your gods flesh and blood? Do they feel the prick of steel? No doubt a god like that is good enough for the Egyptians; but you won't get away with trying to make a fool of me", and he had the priests whipped and forbade the cult, but when finally Apis died of his wounds he was buried by the priests without the knowledge of Cambyses.'

In this instance, at least, Cambyses sounds quite sane, but it is understandable that the once mighty priesthood should cling to some tangible shred of belief as the old order was being attacked by foreign rulers. The Ptolemies were more shrewd and flattered the priesthood, encouraged their cults, built temples and ruled Egypt for 300 years, the Serapeum in particular surviving as a weird testimony to their policy.

Mariette's Discoveries

The **galleries** of the Serapeum date from three periods, the earliest to the reign of Ramses II (XIX Dynasty), enlarged by his son Khaemwas; a second to the reign of Psammetichus I (XXVI Dynasty); and a main gallery to the Ptolemies. It was the Greek Ptolemies who encouraged an identity between Osiris and Dionysos, and Plutarch comments that 'as for what the priests openly do in the burial of the Apis when they transport its carcass on a raft, this in no way falls short of Bacchic revelry, for they wear fawn-skins and carry thyrsus-rods [a staff tipped with a pine cone, in short a phallus] and produce shouts and movements as do the ecstatic celebrants of the Dionysiac orgies'. (Recall the sarcophagus of the dwarf in Room 49 on the ground floor of the Cairo Museum.) It is from the Ptolemaic period that the semicircle of **Greek statues** of poets and philosophers dates. Homer is at the centre, Pindar plays the lyre at the far right, and at the far left is a base inscribed with the name of Plato. They must be turning over in their graves.

Mariette was led to the Serapeum by recalling a quotation from Strabo (24 BC): 'One finds at Memphis a temple to Serapis in such a sandy place that the wind heaps up sand dunes beneath which we saw sphinxes, some half-buried, some buried up to the head, from which one can suppose that the way to the temple could not be without danger if one were caught in a sudden wind-storm.' Mariette had found one such head at Saqqara, and removing the sand in the area found an entire avenue of sphinxes leading to the Greek statues and to the Serapeum galleries. The avenue has since sanded up again.

Saqqara can seem strange enough today. When Mariette was excavating here, he described the conditions in his house: 'Snakes slithered along the floor, tarantulas or scorpions swarmed in the wall crevices, large spider webs waved from the ceiling like flags. As soon as night fell, bats, attracted by the light, entered my cell through the cracks in the door and kept me awake with their spectral flights. Before going to sleep, I tucked the edges of my mosquito net beneath my mattress and put my trust in God and all the saints, while outside jackals, hyenas and wolves howled around the house.'

Today's Experience

Your own impression might be of a terrifying moronic force at work. You descend a ramp slipping under the formless desert surface and reach a corridor leading off to left and right. Down to the left it meets a transverse gallery and left into that, on the left, within a vault, is a massive pink granite **sarcophagus** with panels and across the top edge hieroglyphics—on the right an Apis bull is depicted with the characteristic black markings. The rest of this gallery is blocked off by a grate.

You now reverse direction, heading down a 150m gallery. On either side, in alternating succession, are more vaults, in all but one of which squats a monstrous black sarcophagus—bull-size. The finest sarcophagus of all is at the very end of this gallery, on the right, adorned with carved decoration and polished to a glassy lustre. You can climb down into its pit and stand on a step at the back to peer inside. Until a few years ago the Serapeum was lit only at lengthy intervals by dim yellow lights which in the murky darkness cast a greenish glow. At some places, the lights would have gone out and you had to walk through velvety blackness. In the silence and the dim light, the repetition of vaults and sarcophagi became like a bad dream from which you could not awake, and you just walked on, with literally no light at the end of the tunnel. It was macabre, and with your capillaries shot full with beer you achieved enough perspective to find it utterly incredible that the Ptolemies, whose gallery this is, could have perpetuated anything so repulsive and outlandish. The lighting has now been greatly 'improved', diluting the atmosphere of what was once the weirdest place in Egypt.

It was not here, but in the Ramessid gallery, now inaccessible, that Mariette found the one untouched Apis tomb, a mummified bull inside, and also the mummy of Khaemwas, who had been appointed by his father Ramses II High Priest of Ptah. And there he found those ancient **footprints**. You notice footprints in the sand in this Ptolemaic gallery too, of more recent visitors, and they bring to mind, as so often encounters with Egypt's pharaonic past do, our own voyages into the cosmos, those footprints left in the dust on the surface of the windless moon which may remain for thousands of years undisturbed.

Retracing your steps from the end of the main gallery, turn to the left and then to the right. An empty sarcophagus almost blocks the route. A little further on is its lid. It seems to have been abandoned before the interment of the bull, suggesting the cult was abruptly ended.

Other Animal Cults at Saqqara

This account of Saqqara has covered only the major points of interest to the layman. There is a search now going on for Imhotep's tomb, which is thought to be somewhere to the northeast of the Serapeum, and the mastaba of Ti. In this area have been found the Anubieion, sacred to Anubis, with a gallery for dogs; the galleries of the Bubasteion, sacred to Bastet, filled with mummified cats; the Temple of Thoth, its galleries piled with thousands of mummified ibises, baboons and falcons; and the Isieion, the Temple of Isis, with underground galleries containing the sarcophagi of the sacred cows that had given birth to the Apis bulls. It is possible that these stacks of smaller mummified creatures were brought over hundreds of years by pilgrims as offerings to a favoured god, or as supplication by those seeking a cure. It is because of these associations with healing cults that Imhotep's shrine and tomb might be here; he was later worshipped as the god of medicine, the Egyptian equivalent of Asclepios.

These cults continued into the Roman period and were only finally suppressed by the victory of Christianity over paganism, when the fashion changed from dogs, cats, birds and baboons to collecting bits of martyrs' bodies.

Pyramids Further South

Getting There

Dahshur, 6km south of Saqqara and until recently a military area and off-limits to foreign tourists, can now be freely visited. To get there you will need to take a taxi or you can make the long walk along the road from Badrashein or Memphis.

If driving to **Meidum**, 90km from Cairo and 55km from Saqqara, follow the road along the west bank of the Nile south towards El Wasta; the pyramid will appear on your right but you drive past it a bit until you come to a paved road signposted for the pyramid in English and Arabic. This heads off into the desert, at first passing south of the pyramid and then coming up to its northwest corner.

Access and Fees

Dahshur is *open 8am–5pm; adm LE10.* Meidum can be visited at any time; *adm free.*

Dahshur

The necropolis of Dahshur is 6km south of Saqqara. Of its four pyramids, two date from the Middle Kingdom and are so badly ruined they are likely to be of interest only to the specialist. The Bent and Red pyramids are the chief attraction. For a good distant view of them, stand on the southern ramparts of Zoser's funerary complex to see these great pyramids resting upon an endless plain confronting only the cosmos.

The pyramid age began with Zoser, but his was a pyramid that rose in steps. The first attempts at building true pyramids with smoothly sloping sides were made by Snofru, the first pharaoh of the IV Dynasty, while it was his son Cheops who at Giza built the greatest of all Egyptian pyramids. Later generations looked back admiringly on Snofru for the prosperity and power that he brought to Egypt. He was portrayed as a beneficent ruler, good-humoured and pleasure-loving, who spent idyllic hours in his royal barge being rowed across the palace lake by beautiful girls. But these were interludes in an exceptionally energetic 24-year reign marked by a far-seeing and vigorous foreign policy, campaigning against the Libyans and Nubians and in Sinai while greatly expanding trade with Lebanon, and the completion of not one but three massive pyramids, the Bent and Red at Dahshur and that at Meidum (for the story behind these, *see* pp.184–6).

The **Red Pyramid**, so named for the colour of its limestone, is the more northerly of Snofru's two pyramids at Dahshur. This was the third and final pyramid built by Snofru and also his largest; indeed it is the second largest pyramid ever built in Egypt, the Great Pyramid of Cheops only slightly exceeding it in volume. But Snofru's earlier ventures in pyramid-building led him in this case to play safe, so that the Red Pyramid, rising to a height of 104m at an angle of only 42.5°, looks squat compared to the bold outline of Cheop's Pyramid, which because of its steeper 52° angle rises to a height of 142m.

One and a half kilometres to the south is the aptly-named **Bent Pyramid**, whose sides rise evenly at 52° for part of the way but then bend to the flatter incline of 42.5°, so that instead of an intended height of 129m it is only 105m high. Nevertheless, this peculiarity makes it an impressive sight, as does its cladding of casing stones which has survived largely intact. Snofru seems to have gone on to build the Red Pyramid because he thought the Bent Pyramid was unstable, and indeed its two burial chambers show signs of having suffered some cracking under pressure, which lends some frisson to creeping about inside.

There are, uniquely, two entrances, one 33m up on the west face, the other 12m up on the north face, and it is by the latter that you gain access, making a steep descent through a passage 80m long but barely more than a metre high. This eventually reaches a short horizontal corridor amounting to a kind of vestibule with a high corbelled roof from which you climb by means of a ladder into the lower chamber, also corbelled, which is cut into the bedrock. From here a roughly hewn passage with a damaged roof leads to the upper chamber which was more directly reached by a steeply sloping corridor from the west entrance. In the western chamber are cedar beams, evidence of Snofru's trade with Lebanon, which presumably served as buttresses against lateral pressure on the walls, which show signs of cracking.

Where Snofru finally chose to be buried is uncertain, though Egyptologists think that in spite of his earlier misgivings about the stability of the Bent Pyramid, it was there that he was laid to rest. Its only certain occupants, however, were an owl, whose dismembered remains were found inside, and five bats whose wrapped skeletons had been placed in a wooden box. Neither the Red nor the Bent pyramids have revealed any sign of a royal burial, except that Snofru's name was found written in red ochre on a block lying beneath the floor of the Bent Pyramid's upper chamber.

Much further south, 55km from Saqqara and 90km from Cairo, is the **Meidum pyramid**, or what remains of it. This was the first attempt at a true pyramid (*see* p.154) and the lessons learnt from its monumental failure, if one accepts Mendelssohn's theory, led to the successful completion of those greatest pyramids of all at Giza. For that reason, but also for the spectacle of this abrupt tower on the desert's edge, the Meidum pyramid is as much worth visiting as any.

Where to Stay

For **camping** at a site between Giza and Saqqara, *see* p.169. For accommodation in Cairo, *see* pp.137–42, and in Giza, *see* p.169.

Luxor, Karnak, Thebes

The palm—an architectural tree. Everything in Egypt seems made for architecture—the planes of the fields, the vegetation, the human anatomy, the horizon lines.

Gustave Flaubert

The landscape all about Luxor is placid and horizontal, a broad plain on either side of the river cultivated mainly with sugar cane and maize. The desert to the east rises gently to the Arabian plateau, while to the west a low range of hills, the Theban Mountain, interpose themselves between the cultivation and the Libyan Desert. The Nile is majestic, at sundown an implacable lava flow. By day, feluccas seem to stride upon its surface like pond insects, and distant palms rise from the level stillness, distinct and exactly outlined in the clear air and brilliant light. For the ancient Egyptians, the richness and never-failing fertility of this landscape was a source of wonder. As capital of the New Kingdom Luxor was the focus of an architectural activity so grand, and still so well preserved, that it can lay just claim to being the world's greatest outdoor museum.

The name Luxor is loosely applied by travellers to include three distinct places: the town of Luxor, on the east bank of the Nile (676km south of Cairo), the village (suburb nowadays) of Karnak and its immense temple 4km north on the same bank, and on the west bank of the river opposite Luxor and Karnak the Theban necropolis. This chapter deals with each of these places in turn.

History

Where the houses are full of treasures, a city with a hundred gates.

Homer, *Iliad*

The name Luxor derives from the Arabic *al-qasr*, meaning palace (hence the Alcazar, the Moorish palace in Seville), and refers to the appearance of the town until the end of the 19th century when it lay largely within the remains of the palace-like Temple of Luxor. The ancient Egyptian name for the settlement was Weset, though it is best known by the Greek name Thebes.

At the height of its glory during the XVIII and XIX Dynasties, Thebes covered all the ground of Luxor and Karnak, and may have had a population as high as one million. During the Old Kingdom, however, when its dynasties resided at Memphis, Thebes was only one of four humble townships in the nome—with Tod and Armant to the south and Medamud to the north—each following the cult of falcon-headed Mont, a god of war. In the retreat to regional rule during the First Intermediate Period, Thebes emerged as the power binding Upper Egypt together. After a struggle it reunited the country under its administrative and religious authority, inaugurating the Middle Kingdom. Thebes repeated the pattern when, following the disintegration during the Second Intermediate Period and the Hyksos invasion of Lower Egypt, it liberated the country and also became the permanent residence of the pharaohs throughout the New Kingdom.

It is tempting to believe that apart from its prowess in war and its strategic position between the Delta and the cataracts, Thebes achieved ascendancy over the townships of its nome and eventually over all Egypt because of the special beauty of its situation. Certainly the great pharaohs of the New Kingdom responded, sometimes sensitively, sometimes grandiosely, to the architectural possibilities of the landscape.

Orientation

At Luxor the Nile flows north-northeast and the town and the temples in the area take the river as their axis, but to simplify matters it will be assumed here that the river flows north and that the temples therefore lie along one or the other of the cardinal axes of the compass. The **Temple of Luxor** is on the Nile, only the **corniche road**, **Sharia el Nil**, separating it from the river. The temple and the gardens lying along its east side are the focus of the town. All roads meet here. From the **station**, it is a 500m walk or carriage ride (the usual means of transport) west along **Sharia el Mahatta** to the gardens with the **Luxor Hotel** on the left. A bit further and you are on the corniche, the New and Old **Winter Palace hotels** immediately to the south, the **Mercure Luxor Hotel** north of the temple. The town proper, which extends on either side of Sharia el Mahatta, has little to recommend it apart from its market street, **Sharia el Souk**, running north off the western end of Sharia el Mahatta. There is an unappealing ribbon of new hotel development along the river to the south, its main drag **Sharia Khaled Ibn el Walid** which runs for 3km from the Novotel to the Sheraton.

Tour Schedule

The briefest possible tour of the area requires two days, one on either side of the Nile. Three or four days are required for a comprehensive impression, though still only an impression, of ancient Thebes and its necropolis. You must bear in mind that, outside the winter season, mid-afternoons get very hot (around 40°C) and you may want to limit your excursions to the early morning and the late afternoon.

On the **east bank** there is the enjoyment of carriage rides; on the **west bank** the choice is between donkey, camel, bicycle and car. Donkeys and camels are frankly a nuisance if you are serious about getting round the sites; a car is far more efficient and comfortable. But best of all for the sound of limb, and cheap, breezy and free of constraint, is a **bicycle**; if you hire it in Luxor you can use it on both sides of the river. **Karnak** and the **Temple of Luxor** can be visited on the same day; the latter is best seen in the late afternoon as it glows in the rays of the sinking sun, or at night when it is unsparingly and intelligently floodlit. Rising as early as possible, you should devote the whole of the second day to the **west bank**, and the third day too, if you have the time. A fourth day will not only allow you to revisit Karnak, and perhaps one or two temples or tomb clusters on the necropolis side, but will also give you greater leisure to **shop** in Luxor and visit the excellent **museum** there.

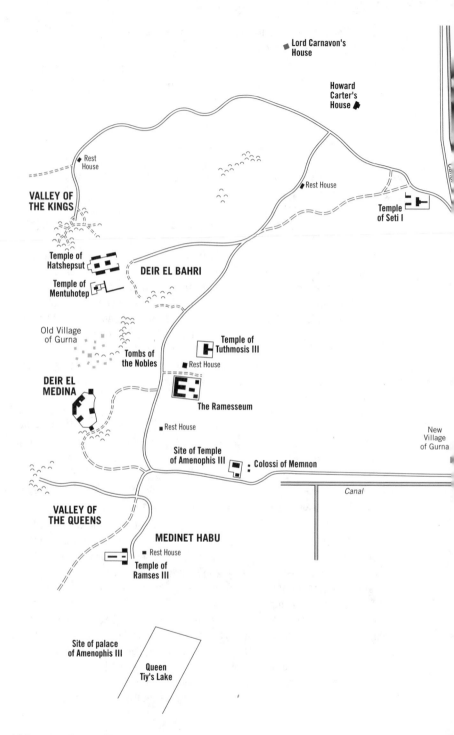

Lord Carnavon's House

Howard Carter's House

Rest House

VALLEY OF
THE KINGS

Rest House

Temple of Seti I

Temple of Hatshepsut

DEIR EL BAHRI

Temple of Mentuhotep

Old Village of Gurna

Temple of Tuthmosis III

Tombs of the Nobles

Rest House

DEIR EL MEDINA

The Ramesseum

Rest House

Site of Temple of Amenophis III

Colossi of Memnon

New Village of Gurna

Canal

VALLEY OF
THE QUEENS

MEDINET HABU

Rest House

Temple of Ramses III

Site of palace of Amenophis III

Queen Tiy's Lake

Luxor and the Theban Necropolis

KARNAK

Temple of Amun

Temple of Mut

to Luxor Airport

to Cairo

SHARIA EL MATAR

River Nile

SHARIA EL KARNAK

SHARIA AHMOS

Luxor Museum

CORNICHE

SHARIA EL NIL

SHARIA HATSHEPSUT

New Village f Gurna

Canal

Canal

People ferry

Railway Station

Temple of Luxor

Abu El Haggag Mosque

Tourist Office

Winter Palace Hotels

Egyptair

SHARIA SALAH AD-DIN

SHARIA TELEVISION

SHARIA KHALED

IBN EL WALID

LUXOR

to Aswan

to Aswan

See Luxor Centre Plan, p.197

maps and publications

For maps and guides covering Luxor specifically, try the Hachette bookshop in the Mercure Luxor Hotel, Aboudi in the Tourist Bazaar near the New Winter Palace Hotel, and A.A. Gaddis in the arcade in front of the Old Winter Palace Hotel. Jill Kamel's *Luxor* is the best guide to the area.

money

The National Bank of Egypt is just south of the Old Winter Palace, while the Bank of Alexandria is north along the corniche (Sharia el Nil) just past the Mercure hotel (*both open daily 8.30–2, 8.30–11 Fri, and 5–8; closed Sun*). American Express and Thomas Cook, both in the arcade in front of the Old Winter Palace, can change money and travellers' cheques (*open daily 8–8*). All 5-star hotels and most of the other better hotels have exchange facilities.

There are hole-in-the-wall banking machines (ATMs) at the south end of Sharia Khaled Ibn el Walid just outside the Gaddis Hotel, and another in the street just to the side of the Mercure Luxor Hotel.

post office

The main post office is on Sharia el Mahatta and there is a branch in the Tourist Bazaar next to the Winter Palace Hotel.

telephones

The central telephone office is on Sharia el Karnak north of Luxor temple (*open 24 hours*). There is a branch in the arcade by the entrance to the old Winter Palace Hotel (*open 8am–10pm*) and another at the railway station (*open 8am–8pm*).

email

Emails can be sent and received at the **Rainbow Internet Café** in the Officer's Club just north of the Luxor Museum (*open 9–2 and 6–midnight*).

visas

Visas can be extended at the Passport Office, © 380885, on Sharia Khaled Ibn el Walid, the street running south from the Novotel to the Sheraton, about halfway down on the left (east) side before you reach the Gaddis Hotel (*open daily 8–2, Fri 8–11*).

Getting There and Around

by air

Luxor airport, 5km northeast of town, is small and user-friendly. The terminal has been designed to look like a temple pylon. It handles direct scheduled and charter flights from Europe, and Egyptair domestic flights to Cairo and Aswan. The Egyptair office is in the arcade by the Old Winter Palace © 380580. The agents for British Airways are Eastmar, immediately south of the Old Winter Palace Hotel.

by balloon

Hot-air balloon flights over Luxor, Karnak and the Valley of the Kings are breath-taking. Most flights are in the early morning, with pick-up at 5am. Later morning and afternoon flights have a higher incidence of cancellation. There are two operators, both fully insured and CAA-approved. Balloons Over Egypt, ✆ 376515, who hold a franchise from Virgin, charge $250 per person, which includes a champagne break-fast or picnic in the desert. Hod-Hod Soliman, ✆ 370116, whose balloons are piloted by a Briton, charge $200 per person, which includes breakfast at the Mövenpick Hotel. Bookings for both companies can be made through travel agents or hotels, or by phoning the operators themselves.

cruises

For a Luxor–Aswan cruise, some of which take in Dendera and Abydos, you should already have made arrangements in Cairo or from abroad, though possibly Jolley's, Eastmar, Misr Travel, American Express or Thomas Cook could help you out (*see* p.65). For the Sheraton and Hilton cruises, contact their hotels in Luxor. Agents offer a day-cruise tour to Abydos and Dendera, which is recommended.

by felucca

A very pleasant time can be had by sailing about the Nile in a felucca, but for the time being it is not permitted to go beyond Luxor.

by ferry

Though a bridge now spans the Nile 7km south of Luxor, the quickest way to reach the West Bank and certainly the most agreeable is by what the locals call the **people ferry**, which departs from a jetty near the entrance to the Temple of Luxor. The fare is LE1; you pay going over, no charge for returning. The people ferry also carries bicy-cles. Additionally there are small motor launches which are found all along the corniche. These are aimed at tourists in a hurry and charge LE5 a head.

by train

The railway station is at the east end of Sharia Mahatta, 500m from the corniche. Trains link Luxor with Cairo to the north and Aswan to the south.

tours

Jolley's, Eastmar, Misr Travel, American Express and Thomas Cook all offer tours, though these are geared mostly to groups. You can often join a group tour by going to one of these agents the evening before and asking if there is space.

by service taxi

Another way of covering the distance between Luxor and Aswan, with the possibility of sightseeing along the way, is to take service taxis. These depart from the north end of town next to the bus station off Sharia el Karnak (*see* below). You can go from Luxor to Esna, Esna to Edfu, Edfu to Kom Ombo and Kom Ombo to Aswan, each leg costing about LE3.

by carriage

The most pleasant way to get about Luxor, and to Karnak, is by carriage (*calèche*). The rates are posted by law on the side of the carriages, though the driver will try to hide them. Check at the tourist office. Carriages cost LE3 for a journey within Luxor; LE10 for an hour's tour; LE15 to the museum, waiting and returning; and LE20 to the Karnak *son et lumière*.

by bus

The bus station is at the north end of town a couple of blocks back from the Luxor Museum, just east off Sharia el Karnak. Buses depart from here for Cairo and Aswan and points in between.

by bicycle

Bicycles can be hired for about LE5–10 per day from numerous places along Sharia el Mahatta. These tend to be single-speed only; for something better, rent a bike from the Hilton, Sheraton, Mercure Luxor or Windsor hotels, which will cost LE15 per day. In all cases go for a brief test ride first to make sure the machine is in working order. Bicycles can be taken across to the west bank aboard the people ferry.

Tourist Information

The **Tourist Office**, signposted as the Egyptian Tourist Authority, ✆ 372215, is at the Tourist Bazaar next to the New Winter Palace Hotel (*open daily 8–8*). There you can determine the official rates for transport on both sides of the Nile, the cost of taking the motor launch or the people ferry to the West Bank, and the up-to-date entry fees for all temples and tombs. You will then be fully armed against the touts. There is also a Tourist Office at the airport, ✆ 372306 (*open 8–8 in summer, 24 hours in winter*).

Misr Travel, **Thomas Cook** and **American Express**, all in the arcades by the Old Winter Palace, can also provide a variety of information and assistance.

In an **emergency**, telephone ✆ 123—but do not expect anything to happen. Better to seek help at your hotel.

For local festivities, *see* p.264.

The Temple of Luxor

Open daily 6am–9pm winter, 6am–10pm summer; adm LE20. A carriage to the temple costs about LE3.

Close to the more central hotels and to the landing stages for the Nile cruise boats, a visit to the Temple of Luxor can be casually arranged following a more rigorously organized morning. It is especially worth seeing in the evening when it is floodlit.

The temple is appealing: it is well preserved, its unity clearly stated, yet its plan has an intriguing irregularity. It was built largely under **Amenophis III** (XVIII Dynasty) on the site of an older sanctuary. He also built the Third Pylon at Karnak and began the Hypostyle Hall there, and erected an enormous mortuary temple on the west bank of which only the colossi

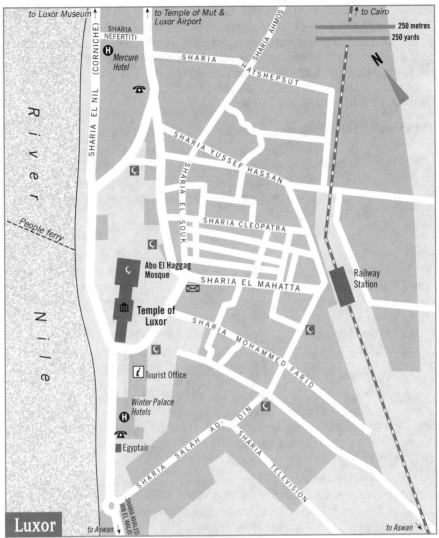

to Luxor Museum

to Temple of Mut &
Luxor Airport

to Cairo

250 metres
250 yards

N

River

Nile

People ferry

SHARIA NEFERTITI

SHARIA EL NIL (CORNICHE)

Mercure Hotel

SHARIA HATSHEPSUT

SHARIA AHMOS

SHARIA YUSSEF HASSAN

SHARIA EL SOUK

SHARIA CLEOPATRA

Abu El Haggag Mosque

SHARIA EL MAHATTA

Railway Station

Temple of Luxor

SHARIA MOHAMMED FARID

Tourist Office

Winter Palace Hotels

Egyptair

SHARIA SALAH AD-DIN

SHARIA TELEVISION

SHARIA KHALED IBN EL WALID

Luxor

to Aswan

to Aswan

of Memnon remain: he was the first pharaoh of the New Kingdom to go in for the gigantism that broadcasts the imperial pretensions of the period. He would have been delighted with the reaction of the French army in 1799: while in pursuit of the Mameluke Muradbey it rounded a bend in the Nile and came suddenly upon the temples of Karnak and Luxor. 'Without an order being given,' a lieutenant wrote, 'the men formed their ranks and presented arms, to the accompaniment of the drums and bands'.

Since 1885 when excavations began, the temple has been gradually cleared of the village once within it, the rubble blocking the pylon entrance and the kom to the north, which has revealed the **forecourt** and **avenue of sphinxes** leading to Karnak. It was from Karnak that Amun came during the annual Opet festival, but by water, amid a floating procession of great splendour to this harem of the South with his wife Mut and their son the moon god Khonsu. The forecourt wall is the work of Nectanebos I (XXX Dynasty), as are the sphinxes which are set at a lower level to the excavated remains of post-pharaonic houses on either side. In the northwest corner of the forecourt is the restored **Serapeum** dedicated by the Emperor Hadrian on 24 January AD 126, his birthday.

Ramses II's Additions to the Temple

The Pylon and Obelisks

> *The obelisk that is now in Paris was against the right-hand pylon. Perched on its pedestal, how bored it must be in the Place de la Concorde! How it must miss its Nile! What does it think as it watches all the cabs drive by, instead of the chariots it saw at its feet in the old days?*

Gustave Flaubert

Turn south to look at the **pylon**: this and the court behind it were additions by Ramses II (XIX Dynasty), the pylon a gigantic billboard advertising Ramses' dubious victory over the Hittites at Kadesh in Syria. The west (right) tower shows the Egyptian camp within a circle of shields and Ramses on his throne holding a council of war while beneath him two spies are being interrogated by beating. In the right light, or under floodlights, you can see that Ramses has been reversed on his throne, now facing east where he once faced west. (The floodlighting also attracts bats, which enjoy fluttering to rest upside-down within the deeper incisions of the drama.) The east (left) tower shows Kadesh on the left, surrounded by the waters of the Orontes, while to the right a heroically proportioned Ramses in his chariot is pursuing the broken enemy. In vertical lines below these scenes on both towers is the poem of Pentaur (*see* p.324 for partial translation). Comparison of this with Hittite sources, and taking into account the contemporary situation including the superior iron weaponry of the Hittites to the Egyptian bronze, suggests that the battle was less glorious for the Egyptians than Ramses made out.

The vertical grooves along the pylon façade were for supporting flagstaffs, the apertures above to receive the braces securing the staffs and to admit light and air to the interior. Except at the corners above the entrance passage, the cavetto cornices are missing. Originally the pylon stood 24m high; its width is 65m.

In front of the pylon were six **statues** of Ramses, two sitting, four standing. Only the two seated figures on either side of the entrance and the westernmost standing figure remain; they are all badly damaged. There were also two **obelisks** of exceptionally fine detail standing on plinths decorated with dog-headed baboons in relief. Mohammed Ali offered the pair, plus one at Alexandria, to France. It is said that the French desire for an obelisk was first expressed by Josephine to Napoleon before he embarked for Egypt: 'Goodbye! If you go to Thebes, do send me a little obelisk.' Napoleon left Egypt under circumstances that denied Josephine the pleasure. In celebration of the Bourbon restoration, Louis XVIII renewed the idea. In the event, the task proved so difficult and lengthy that Champollion's identification of the west obelisk as the finest in Egypt left the French satisfied with it alone, and in 1836 it

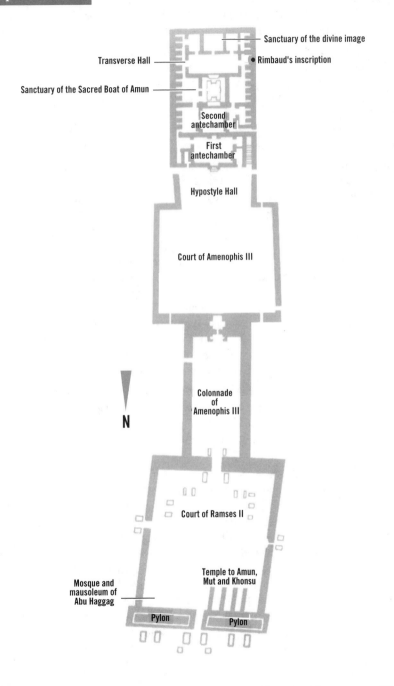

Sanctuary of the divine image

Rimbaud's inscription

Transverse Hall

Sanctuary of the Sacred Boat of Amun

Second antechamber

First antechamber

Hypostyle Hall

Court of Amenophis III

Colonnade of Amenophis III

N

Court of Ramses II

Mosque and mausoleum of Abu Haggag

Temple to Amun, Mut and Khonsu

Pylon

Pylon

was erected in the Place de la Concorde. As the obelisk was lowered at Luxor, Ramses' name was found engraved on the underside of the shaft; his titles, his achievements, his piety had already been carved on the four sides of each obelisk, but being a great usurper of other pharaohs' monuments, he knew well the value of this secret protestation of ownership.

Cocteau records that when the plinth of the obelisk was removed to Paris it 'was surrounded by the low reliefs of dog-faced baboons in erection. This was not thought to be proper and so the monkeys' organs have been cut off'. (These sculptures fairly represent the hamadryas baboon in nature. The male, sacred to the ancient Egyptians, wears an elaborate mantle of silky fur; but this reaches barely to the hips, leaving its bottom bare. Its large penis is driven exuberantly erect even by friendly interest, while its red hindquarters are resplendent at any time.)

The **entrance passage** through the pylon is decorated with carvings of the XXV Dynasty, a period when Egypt was ruled by Ethiopian or Cushite pharaohs, one of whom, Shabaka, is shown on the east (left) wall wearing the white crown of Upper Egypt, running a ritual race in the presence of an ithyphallic Amun-Re.

The Court of Ramses II

Belying the seemingly universal symmetry and regularity of Egyptian architecture, it is immediately obvious that this court does not lie on the same axis as the colonnade of Amenophis III. This in turn is out of line with the temple proper, but these are very slight divergences, while that of the court of Ramses II is striking. An explanation is found in the northwest corner of the court, a small **temple to Amun, Mut and Khonsu** built by Tuthmosis III and Hatshepsut 100 years before Amenophis, 200 years before Ramses. The granite columns are original, while the carvings were redone by Ramses II who integrated the temple into his court, aligning his court to suit.

Sitting above the northeast corner of the court, surviving the clearance of the old village within the temple, is the **mosque and mausoleum of Abu el Haggag**, a Sufi sheikh born in Baghdad, who spent the last 50 years of his life at Luxor, dying here in his nineties in 1243. The mosque, however, is only 19th-century, though the north minaret is 11th-century.

Ramses' court is entirely surrounded by a double colonnade of bud-capital papyrus columns, while the interior walls are adorned with reliefs. Especially interesting is the representation of the pylon façade at the west end of the south wall, complete with colossi, obelisks and fluttering banners. Approaching this, along the west wall, is a procession led by 17 of Ramses' sons (he fathered over 100 in his 90-odd years) and followed by priests and sacrificial oxen. The unnaturally long hooves indicate that the oxen have been fattened in their stalls for the occasion, while the model of an African's head between the horns of the fifth ox and the Asiatic head with long pointed beard between the horns of the sixth symbolizes the Egyptian triumph over Africa and Asia. The southern half of the court is further embellished with striding colossi of Ramses, and in an unexpected touch the slender figure of his beloved wife Nefertari between his legs, while the triumph motif is repeated round the bases of the black granite seated colossi on either side of the southern doorway: the shields and bound figures of vanquished Asiatics on the east base, Africans on the west.

Amenophis III's Temple

The Colonnade and Court

Passing between these last two guardians of Ramses' memory, you enter the imposing colonnade of Amenophis III. The 15.8m-high papyrus columns with calyx capitals bearing massive architraves contribute gently to the serene profile of the temple when viewed from the river. Originally, however, this columnar rhythm would have been lost behind flanking walls, the upper three-quarters of which have collapsed. The remaining courses bear fine and fascinating reliefs from the reign of Tutankhamun, a celebration of the re-establishment of the Amun orthodoxy, depicting the god with Mut and Khonsu accompanied by the pharaoh and priests on their voyage from Karnak to Luxor at the height of the inundation period. Crowds of common folk follow by land, and there are scenes of rejoicing, of musicians and dancers, and of sacrifice. The series begins at the northwest corner with the pharaoh sacrificing to the boats at Karnak, and continues with the water-borne procession and, at the southeast corner, the arrival at Luxor. Starting at the southeast corner, the procession returns 24 days later to Karnak.

The colonnade leads into the **court of Amenophis III**, once enclosed on the east, north and west by double rows of clustered papyrus columns with bud capitals, an ensemble that appeals through its harmony. The well-preserved east and west sides still carry their architraves. On the south side is the **Hypostyle Hall** with four rows of eight columns. On either side of its south wall are reliefs of the coronation of Amenophis by the gods. To the left of the central aisle, between the last two columns, is a **Roman altar** dedicated to Constantine.

The Temple

You now enter the temple proper. The first **antechamber**, which once had a roof supported by eight columns, bore reliefs on its walls of Amenophis. But in the 3rd or 4th century AD the walls were thickly whitewashed and covered with paintings. One view is that this became the chapel of a Roman imperial cult; others argue that it was a church. The only evidence are the paintings themselves, which must once have been very fine but are badly damaged and tantalisingly inconclusive. Those on the east wall are very faint; but on the south wall to the left of the arched niche there is a much clearer group of several figures. One figure, below the third from left, seems to be a woman. Also on the south wall, and on the north wall too, the reliefs of Amenophis worshipping Amun have been laid bare. The second antechamber is smaller, with four columns, and as the reliefs around the walls show—Amenophis driving calves to sacrifice, offering incense and sceptres to Amun—this was the offering chapel. Beyond that is the **sanctuary of the Sacred Boat of Amun**.

The sanctuary consists of a chapel open to north and south set within a chamber, whose walls are decorated with reliefs of Amenophis. The chapel was rebuilt by Alexander the Great and both its exterior and interior walls bear reliefs of him before Amun and other gods. A subsidiary room with three columns to the east of the sanctuary has badly damaged scenes of Amenophis' coronation, and on the north wall he is shown hunting in the marshes.

From this subsidiary room a doorway opens north onto the **Birth Room** with reliefs on the west wall referring to Amenophis' divine birth. At the left of the lowest register, Khnum is moulding the infant Amenophis and his ka on a potter's wheel. Moving from left to right across the middle register, Thoth foretells to Mutemuia, mother of Amenophis, the birth of her son; the pregnant Mutemuia is conducted by Isis and Khnum; her confinement; Isis presenting the infant to Amun; and Amun with the infant in his arms. The top register shows Amenophis and his ka nurtured by the gods and presented to Amun; to the far right, in the corner, Amenophis has become pharaoh.

The remaining rooms at the south end of the temple have suffered considerable damage and are without antique interest. The **transverse hall** with its 12 papyrus bud columns was an antechamber or hypostyle hall leading to the three southernmost chambers, the central one a sanctuary once containing the intriguingly described 'divine image of millions of years'. It was in this transverse hall that Cocteau noticed a more recent curiosity: 'Suddenly I was struck dumb. What could that be? High up, on top of the wall, Rimbaud had carved his name. He carved it, at the height of a man, and now that the temple is cleared, it shines forth like a sunflower. It blazes out, royal and sunlike, above suspicion, dreadful in its solitude.' Rimbaud gave up poetry by the time he was 21, in 1875; for the remaining 16 years of his life he travelled in the Far and Near East and into parts of Ethiopia where no European had been before, variously selling coffee, girls and guns—and making a mark for French culture at the Temple of Luxor.

The area outside the temple on the east serves as a storeyard for architectural fragments, pharaonic, Roman and Christian. The Christian friezes and fonts presumably came from the basilica which once stood outside Ramses' great pylon.

The temple is experienced most intensely at night when the floodlights throw the carvings into deeper relief and the black night rests like a roof on the brightness of the stone, enclosing you. On the dome of the mosque of Abu el Haggag, cursive green neon proclaims 'Allah'. Once a year at the saint's moulid a boat is carried in procession, as was Amun's 3,500 years before. (For his moulid and the Ramadan celebrations which take place in front of the mosque, *see* p.264.)

For a magnificent view over the Temple of Luxor, especially at sunset, you should go to the mosque on Sharia el Karnak that overlooks the courtyard and the Avenue of the Sphinxes (not the mosque of Abu el Haggag which sits atop part of the temple itself). By asking permission and afterwards offering baksheesh you can ascend its minaret.

The Mummification Museum

> *Down steps off the corniche halfway between the entrance to the Temple of Luxor and the Mercure Hotel. Open daily in winter 9–1 and 4–9, in summer to 10pm; adm LE20.*

If you ever wanted to know exactly how the brain was removed from the skull via the nostrils, this is the place. The tools of the trade are on display with full explanations of how they were used, including techniques for desiccating and wrapping the bodies. There are mummies of a XXI Dynasty official, a cat, a baboon, a ram and a crocodile, as well as artefacts necessary for a successful transition to eternity, and a number of painted coffins in which one would pass the time.

The Luxor Museum of Ancient Egyptian Art

Situated on the corniche to the north of the Mercure Luxor Hotel; open daily 9–1 and 4–9 in winter, 9–1 and 5–10 in summer; adm LE30; includes entrance to the new hall.

The presentation is superb, with some well-chosen objects lit to their best advantage. The exhibits include jewellery, furniture, pottery and stelae, almost all pharaonic though there are a few Graeco-Roman, Coptic and Mameluke pieces. Most outstanding in the general collection (quite apart from the Luxor Temple cache) are the **stone statues and busts**. The latter are most finely represented by granite and basalt works identified by the cartouches as Tuthmosis III, Amenophis II, Amenophis III (all XVIII Dynasty) and Sesostris III (XII Dynasty), any of which could stand in place of another for all they depict an individual (except for that of Sesostris with big ears). The craftsmanship is excellent, however, and the enjoyment of working with the graceful curves of crowns, necks and waists is clear. There is a marvellous alabaster statue of Sobek with a crocodile's head and man's body, and one of Amenophis III, usurped by Ramses II by altering the cartouche—which shows how little the figure itself served to identify.

A series of **scenes in sunk relief** on limestone blocks found within the Ninth Pylon at Karnak show Akhenaton and Nefertiti worshipping Aton, but also the most ordinary daily palace tasks. At least when Akhenaton attacked the Theban priesthood, he obliterated images of their god Amun; the post-Amarna counter-revolutionaries reverted to the traditional method of defeating a predecessor's bid for immortality. For example, exhibit 150 is a block showing Akhenaton worshipping Aton—so clearly understandable and evidence of his heresy—yet it is defaced only to the extent that his cartouche is gouged. Always the name, the sign, rather than the idea.

The **new hall** contains a cache of 22 magnificent New Kingdom statues, including those of Amenophis III, Tutankhamun, Ramses II and Nefertari, which was unearthed in 1989 at the Temple of Luxor, where they had been buried at the outset of the Roman occupation.

Karnak

Karnak by starlight is peace; not peace and joy, but peace—solemn peace. You feel like spirits revisiting your former world, strange and fallen to ruins.

Florence Nightingale, 1849

When Egypt stood at the height of empire, when Thebes ruled over Egypt and Amun was supreme over all, his temple here possessed 81,000 slaves and their families, 240,000 head of cattle, 83 ships, and from 65 cities and towns their vast annual tribute in gold, silver, copper and precious stones.

The Karnak site covers an enormous area, sufficient to accommodate 10 European cathedrals. The Hypostyle Hall alone is large enough to contain Notre Dame. At least two half-day visits are required to see the entire complex; if you can manage only one, then you will have to be content with walking through the main temple, that of Amun. Return at night for the *son et lumière*. The size and complexity of the site, the arrangement of its structures on both an east–west and north–south axis, the multiple extensions to several of these structures by successive pharaohs, and in some areas its ruinous state contribute to the lack of unity and proportion at Karnak. But this has probably always been so, even in its days of completeness. Karnak astounds, but does not awaken the sensibilities.

Getting There

Karnak is 4km north of the Temple of Luxor. You can of course walk or take a **taxi**, but it can be pleasant to take a **carriage** along the corniche to the First Pylon of the main temple at Karnak. When leaving ask the driver to return you to Luxor by the road which passes the Gateway of Euergetes. Somewhere deep beneath this present roadway of your return journey lies the old sacred way, lined with sphinxes that joined the temples of Karnak and Luxor, visible in newly excavated segments en route and at either end, where it leaves Euergetes' gateway, and where it enters the forecourt of the Temple of Luxor.

Son et Lumière Show

The *son et lumière* show lasts 90 minutes. There are three shows nightly: *6, 7.30 and 9 in winter, 6.30, 8 and 9.30 in summer; adm LE33 or LE5 when in Arabic.* The performances are in varying languages depending on the time and day of the week (check at your hotel or the Tourist Office): English, French, German, Italian, Spanish, Japanese and Arabic.

The best part is the walk deeper into the temple—the lights and voices lead you on and it hardly matters what is being said. The impression is magnificent and will enhance your daytime visit. In the Hypostyle Hall, take the opportunity to wander off alone to one side or the other, until you are deep among the faintly illuminated columns—that is the most enjoyable. But when you are stationary at the Sacred Lake, the vista does not change, and you are obliged to listen to the long and confused commentary, you experience a tedious anticlimax.

The Temples Complex

The Karnak temples complex is open daily 6am–5.30pm in winter, 6–6 in summer; adm LE20. The Open Air Museum is LE10 extra. Both tickets must be bought at the kiosk outside. There are toilets by the son et lumière *grandstand at the far end of the Sacred Lake.*

Apart from its size, Karnak represents a vastness of historical time. The main Temple of Amun, from the foundations of the original Middle Kingdom temple to the First Pylon, built (probably) during the XXV Dynasty, saw construction over 1,300 years. Comprehension of the site requires a brief historical review.

'Thebes, Karnak' by David Roberts, 1838

Thirteen Centuries in Stone

Although the war god Mont, associated with Thebes during the Old Kingdom, continued to be worshipped at Karnak, Amun achieved pre-eminence by the beginning of the Middle Kingdom and was honoured during the XII Dynasty by a series of temples facing west, the principal orientation throughout subsequent periods. All that remains of these are the alabaster foundations of what was to become the most venerable part of the extended Temple of Amun, and limestone blocks belonging to the White Chapel of Sesostris I, recovered from the foundations of the Third Pylon and re-erected in the Open Air Museum to the north of the Great Court.

With the expulsion of the Hyksos from Egypt and the elevation of Amun to victorious national god, the early pharaohs of the XVIII Dynasty set about turning Karnak into the principal sanctuary of their kingdom. Amenophis I and his son Tuthmosis I built chapels around the Middle Kingdom temple, while in front of it (to the west) the latter built the Fourth and Fifth Pylons and erected a pair of obelisks. Hatshepsut added two further obelisks between those of her father, chambers with carved decorations in front of the original temple, and initiated the north–south axis of the complex by building south. Her nephew Tuthmosis III continued building along the north–south axis with the Seventh and Eighth Pylons, and constructed the Festival Hall behind (to the east of) the Middle Kingdom temple.

In the century that passed between the Asian conquests of Tuthmosis III and the reign of Amenophis III, artistic and architectural restraint gave way to an overblown imperial style, expressed at Karnak by the Third Pylon built by Amenophis and his start on the great Hypostyle Hall. Empire introduced foreign influences and new wealth to the country, required an enlarged bureaucracy and upset the status quo. Amun, who had lent his sword to pharaoh's victories, saw the coffers of his priesthood and of the old aristocracy from which it was drawn swell with tribute, and so their power grew. But another class, which owed its very existence to empire, grew up around the pharaoh. Tuthmosis IV married an Asian princess, and her son Amenophis III married Tiy, an Egyptian commoner. Tiy was given unusual artistic prominence alongside her husband, and her parents, Yuya and Tuyu, were buried in splendour in the Valley of the Kings. Pharaoh and temple no longer represented identical interests. Before decamping to Amarna with his court of parvenus, Amenophis IV (Akhenaton as he became) did some building at the east of Karnak, where several of his statues now in the Cairo Museum were found, while some blocks now in the Luxor Museum were reused in the foundations of later pylons and the Hypostyle Hall.

But the Amarna revolution did not survive the death of Akhenaton, and the reign of Tutankhamun marked the beginning of the counter-revolution which proceeded with a vengeance. The power of Amun was reaffirmed, and, as though to sweep away all memory of heresy, internal conflict and the diminution of empire associated with the last pharaohs of the XVIII Dynasty, Seti I of the XIX Dynasty declared his reign the era of the repeating of births, literally a renaissance. Both he and his son Ramses II outdid all that had gone before, both in architecture and in military propaganda, to make good any deficiencies in this assertion. Between them they completed the Hypostyle Hall. It remained only for later dynasties to build the Great Court and the First Pylon for Karnak to assume the form it has today. The Ptolemies embellished, and the Copts cut crosses in stones.

Amun dominates Egypt

The XIX Dynasty made its peace with Amun, but the cost in sacrificed wealth was greater than could be borne for long without the pharaoh becoming a mere creature of the priesthood. The Hypostyle Hall, the Ramesseum and Abu Simbel may all have glorified Ramses II, but only through Amun, who long survived that long-lived pharaoh. By the time Ramses IV (XX Dynasty) came to the throne, 200 years after Akhenaton's resistance and only 60 years after the death of Ramses II, the Temple of Amun owned at least seven per cent of the population of Egypt and nine per cent of the land, with some estimates trebling those percentages, while the family of the high priest of Amun directly controlled the collection of pharaoh's taxes and management of pharaoh's lands. Pharaoh had become no more than an instrument of a ruling oligarchy, and Karnak was its juggernaut.

Amun's Temple

You approach the maw of the beast along a short **processional way** (1) lined with ram-headed sphinxes with figures of Ramses II in mummy wrappings between their forelegs. This exactly expresses the new enveloping relationship between god and pharaoh, for the ram was identified with Amun. A now filled-in canal once linked the temple with the Nile, giving egress during the Opet festival for gods, priests and pharaoh aboard their boats.

The First Pylon, 113m wide and 43m high, is the largest at Karnak and nearly twice the size of the entrance pylon at the Temple of Luxor. It was probably built by Taharka during the XXV (Ethiopian) Dynasty, a trumpeting echo of XIX Dynasty bombast, but left unfinished, the south tower higher than the north and neither bearing any decoration.

The north (left) tower can be climbed for magnificent views over Karnak and the surrounding countryside.

The Great Court

The **Great Court** (2) was built by the rulers of the XXII Dynasty but encloses earlier structures. Columns with papyrus bud capitals line the north and south sides of the court, while a tall doorway in the southeast corner leads to the south end of the **Second Pylon** on which is cut a scene commemorating the victory of Sheshonk I (Shishak of the Bible) over Rehoboam, son of Solomon. The pylon itself was built by Horemheb, an XVIII Dynasty general who became military dictator and finally last pharaoh of the dynasty he had served. Like the Ninth and Tenth Pylons, also built by Horemheb, the Second Pylon made use of blocks that had once formed temples to Akhenaton's god, Aton. Continuing the palimpsest of politics, Ramses I and II cut their names on the pylon over that of Horemheb, and Ramses II installed two colossal figures of himself in pink granite on either side of the pylon entrance. Of the one on the left hardly anything remains; nor does that sector of the avenue of rams which once ran through the area that became the court, to continue beyond the First Pylon towards the Nile. Instead, at the centre of the court Taharka (XXV Dynasty) built a **kiosk** (3) with 10 enormous columns 21m high with papyrus calyx capitals, only one still standing. In the northwest quadrant of the court is the **Temple of Seti II** (4), a simple arrangement of three chapels facing south, the one at the centre to hold the sacred boat of Amun, those to the left

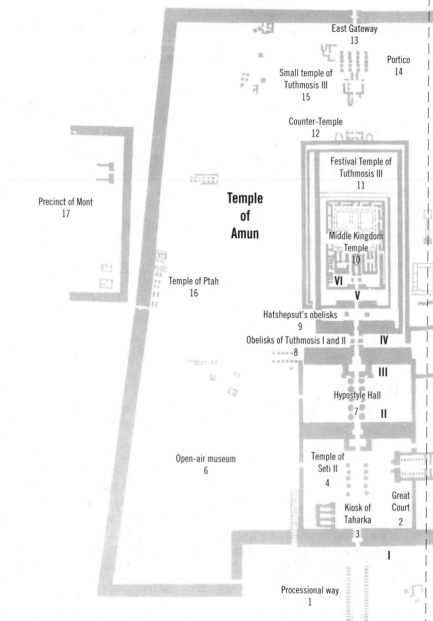

Precinct of Mont
17

Temple
of
Amun

Temple of Ptah
16

East Gateway
13

Portico
14

Small temple of
Tuthmosis III
15

Counter-Temple
12

Festival Temple of
Tuthmosis III
11

Middle Kingdom
Temple
10

VI

V

Hatshepsut's obelisks
9

Obelisks of Tuthmosis I and II
8

IV

III

Hypostyle Hall
7

II

Open-air museum
6

Temple of
Seti II
4

Kiosk of
Taharka
3

Great
Court
2

I

Processional way
1

Roman numerals I, II etc. indicate pylons

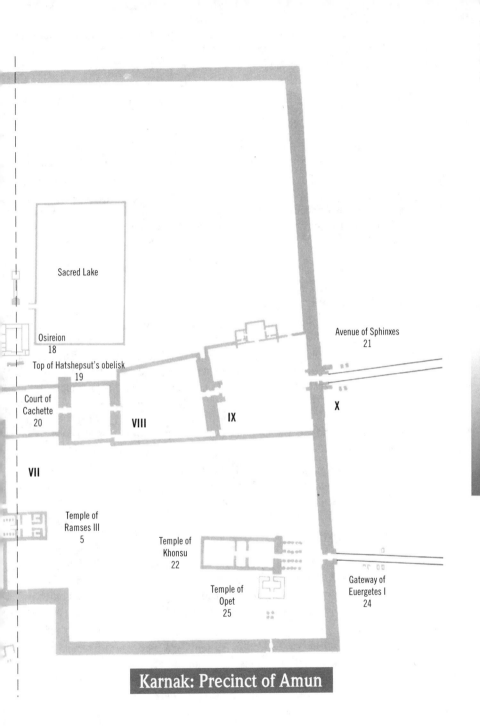

Karnak: Precinct of Amun

and right to hold the boats of Mut and Khonsu, during preparations for the Opet festival. The **Temple of Ramses III** (5) intersecting the south wall of the court similarly served as a station chapel during processions and is a fine example of a simple pharaonic temple. Its pylon, facing north, is decorated with the obligatory triumphal scenes on the outside and with jubilee scenes, assuring the pharaoh a long life, on the inside. An open court leads to a pronaos of four columns and then to a hypostyle hall of eight columns beyond which are the three boat chapels, Amun's at the centre.

A doorway on the north side of the Court leads to an outside staircase at the north end of the First Pylon for views from the top. Also through this doorway you come to the **Open Air Museum** (6) where statues, blocks and architectural fragments from around the site were once gathered for private study but are now on public display (*additional adm*). The finest thing here is the **alabaster shrine**, reconstructed in the 1940s from blocks found reused in the Third Pylon. It dates from the reigns of Amenophis I and Tuthmosis I (XVIII Dynasty), and apart from the pleasing gleam of the alabaster itself it is notable for the very fine style of the hieroglyphics and portraits of Amenophis, and for the oldest complete representation of the sacred ark of Amun inside.

Through the Hypostyle Hall

Passing through the Second Pylon, you enter the **Hypostyle Hall** (7), certainly one of the most spectacular sights in Egypt. It is the height and massiveness of the columns that is over-whelming rather than spaciousness or even rhythm or repetition of form, for on either side of the central aisle the columns are packed tightly together in overgrown forests of stone. The eye is permitted no perspective and is incapable of taking in more than a glimpse of the whole at any one moment. It is best to come early in the morning or late in the afternoon when the effect of the columns is heightened by the black diagonals of their shadows. Like ants, tourists wander round the column bases where priests and pharaohs once wandered, and the idiot in us all is enthralled.

The columns are in fact composed of semi-drums, the 12 along the central aisle (probably originally 14) rising to 23m and with a girth of 15m. It requires six men with outstretched arms to span one of these columns. As with the papyrus columns forming the colonnade of Amenophis III at the Temple of Luxor, these also have calyx capitals and were probably erected as a processional way. But Seti I and Ramses II elaborated on the plan by adding a further 122 columns with bud capitals, creating extensive wings on either side. The entire hall was roofed over and the 10m difference in height between the central and wing columns was accounted for by raising stone lattice windows from the architraves of the wing columns closest to the nave, providing lateral support for the higher central roof otherwise resting on the taller columns. Several of these windows, in a better or worse state of preservation, remain in place.

The central columns are richly painted and cut in sunk relief with standard temple themes, most often pharaoh making various offerings to Amun and other Theban gods. These cult scenes, with recurrent images of Amun in a state of erection (ithyphallic), are continued on the phallus-like columns of the wings, those in the north wing executed in bas-relief during the reign of Seti I, those in the south wing in the sunk relief preferred by Ramses II. The inside walls of the Hypostyle Hall are similarly decorated, but the outside walls proclaim the military exploits of Seti I in Palestine and Libya (north wall) and of Ramses II against the Hittites (south wall).

Of some romance in the study of ancient history is a stele standing upright against the west wall of the **Court of the Cachette** (20) which runs into the south wall of the Hypostyle Hall: it records a treaty between Ramses II and the Hittite king. Not only is it one of the earliest codifications of international relations, but its cuneiform version (now in the Museum of the Ancient Orient, Istanbul) was found inscribed on clay tablets at the Hittite capital, Hattuşaş, east of Ankara in Turkey. When independently translated, it served to confirm the accuracy of the labours of philologists in the two languages. A large votive pit in the court of the Cachette (20) was excavated early this century and found to contain several thousand bronze statues and 800 in stone. The best are on display in Cairo's Egyptian Antiquities Museum.

The intimate relationship between the structure of the Temple of Amun and the development of the Egyptian state has already been outlined (*see* p.206). It is ironic that the great columns of the Hypostyle Hall stood on bases formed of reused blocks from the time of Akhenaton (since removed and replaced mostly by concrete) and that these in turn stood on no firmer foundation than sand. Pretension was careless of the future, though more than a century of archaeological engineering has made good the past. Yet though grandiosity so suited the pharaohs of the XIX Dynasty, it is arguable that it was dictated by the temple itself. It was a canon of Egyptian temple architecture that, as you approached the innermost sanctuary, perspective should narrow, that pylons and columns should get smaller, ceilings lower, and that even the temple platform should rise so that you walked upwards towards the sanctuary as walls and ceilings funnelled in around you. Once Amenophis III decided to build his Third Pylon, it had to be larger than the one before, and the Hypostyle Hall, the Second Pylon and finally the First Pylon had to grow more massive still.

The Oldest Part of the Temple

A constricted court lies between the Third Pylon of Amenophis III and the Fourth Pylon of Tuthmosis I, a narrow gap of space and time between traditional and imperial Egypt. When the Fourth Pylon still marked the entrance to the temple, two pairs of **obelisks** (8) were erected before it by Tuthmosis I and Tuthmosis III. Only one obelisk survives. Of the pink granite pair raised by Tuthmosis I, originally tipped with electrum (a natural alloy of gold and silver), one fell as recently as the 18th century, some of its parts lying nearby, and the other leans a little but is still stable. Beyond the Fourth Pylon the outline of the temple becomes difficult to follow. The successive pylons are closely set, and the buildings have undergone repeated alterations and suffered extensive damage. But many beautiful details reward your exploration, and the absence of both overwhelming architecture and overwhelmed tourists encourages tranquil reflection.

Hatshepsut and Tuthmosis

The numerous columns in the open space behind the Fourth Pylon suggest that this, at least in part, was a hypostyle hall. It was built by Tuthmosis III and may have been part of his extraordinary attempt to disguise the existence of Hatshepsut's two magnificent **obelisks** (9). The lower shaft of one of these remains on its base, the upper shaft lying near the northwest corner of the Sacred Lake where you can closely examine its inscriptions. The second obelisk is *in situ*, the tallest completed obelisk in Egypt and of ancient obelisks second in height only to the Lateran obelisk in Rome. It stands 29.5m high and was covered in electrum not only at the pyramidion but also down half its shaft, so that as its inscription tells, 'Hatshepsut made as her monument for her father Amun two great obelisks of enduring granite from the south, their upper parts, being of electrum of the best of all lands, seen on the two sides of the river. Their rays flood the two lands when the sun-disc rises between them at its appearance on the horizon of heaven.' Stepmother to Tuthmosis III and originally regent to the young pharaoh, Hatshepsut soon proclaimed herself pharaoh and relegated Tuthmosis to the shadows for the remainder of her life. He later showed his resentment by chopping out her name wherever he found it, and here at Karnak went to the absurd length of building a now removed sandstone structure around her obelisks to a height of 25m.

The Fifth Pylon was also built by Tuthmosis I and leads almost immediately to the badly ruined Sixth Pylon, the smallest of all, built by Tuthmosis II. In the court beyond it he erected two tall pink granite pillars. Carved in high relief on their north and south sides are three lilies (south pillar) and three papyrus flowers (north pillar), the heraldic plants of Upper and Lower Egypt, beautifully stylized. At the north end of the court are two colossal sandstone statues of Amun and his 'grammatical consort' Amonet in the likeness of Tutankhamun. Further along the main axis of the temple, on the spot where Hatshepsut's Red Chapel once stood (its quartzite blocks engraved with scenes of the procession of the sacred boats are in the Open Air Museum), is the granite **sanctuary of the Sacred Boats** built by the half-witted half-brother of Alexander the Great. The interior decorations in bas-relief and the exterior ones in sunk relief are finely worked and vividly coloured in yellow, red and blue. High though the standard is, however, its mock-traditional Egyptian terms were adopted by the Ptolemies for political expedience and are sadly inferior to the terms governing the greatest period of Greek art only 100 years before.

Walls and Heroes

On the north side of the sanctuary, where there was much rebuilding, a **wall erected by Hatshepsut** was found concealed behind a later wall of Tuthmosis III, thus preserving the original freshness of its colouring. The wall has now been removed to a nearby room, and shows Amun, his flesh painted red and with one foot in front of the other, and also Amun in the guise of ithyphallic Min, a harvest god often amalgamated with Amun, his flesh painted black. The wall of Tuthmosis, known as the **Wall of Records**, was erected after the battle of Megiddo (Armageddon) in northern Palestine, fought in April 1479 BC. In *A History of Egypt*, James Henry Breasted wrote of Tuthmosis that 'he was the first to build an empire in any real sense; he was the first world-hero. He made not only a worldwide impression upon his age, but an impression of a new order.' Political history, in so far as it tells the story of territorial imperialism, began that April day when Tuthmosis, instead of destroying his enemies, organized the vanquished into agencies of tribute and annually recorded on this wall the share that was due to Amun.

Temples

The open space beyond the sanctuary marks the site of the original **Middle Kingdom Temple** (10), its plan suggested by the remaining alabaster foundation stones.

To the east of the original temple is the **Festival Temple of Tuthmosis III** (11), and running north–south within it the **Festival Hall** of many columns and pillars where Tuthmosis celebrated his jubilees, those reinvigorations of temporal power and divine spirit. The pillars form a rectangular cloister around a central and taller colonnade. The two rows of ten columns are unique in Egypt, affecting the form of tent poles or upturned tree trunks (as in Minoan Crete), broader above than below. The capitals, like bells or inverted calyxes, are incised and painted in patterns of overlapping leaves or of vertical stripes. The architectural suggestion is of an outdoor tent or, as echoed in stone at the Heb-Sed Court at Saqqara, of a temporary timbered building. Early in the Christian era the hall was converted into a church, and the occasional haloed saint may be discerned on its columns.

A chamber at the southwest corner of the hall contained, until taken to the Louvre, the Table of Karnak, a list of 57 predecessors of Tuthmosis. It is probable that statues of ancient pharaohs carried in procession were also kept here. From the northwest corner of the hall, an antechamber leads into a corridor lined with fine reliefs of Tuthmosis in the presence of Amun. Without the hall but in the northeast area of the Festival Temple is a small room with four papyrus bundle columns with bud capitals still supporting the architraves, though the roof is gone. This is popularly known as the **Botanic Garden** for its bas-reliefs of plants and animals seen in and perhaps brought from Syria by Tuthmosis.

Towards the East Enclosure Wall

A footbridge leads east across the remains of enclosure walls, and against this wall, on the axis of the main temple, is a **counter-temple** (12) facing east. Beyond this is the **east gateway** (13) to the Karnak complex, set in an outer wall of mud brick and built by Nectanebos I (XXX Dynasty). From the avenue of rams before the First Pylon to this gateway, it is 500m. Before exploring the breadth of the complex, have a look at the two structures standing between the counter-temple and the east gateway. The one to the east is a **ruined portico** (14) built by the same Taharka who built the kiosk in the Great Court; he placed similar structures at the north and south ends of the site, so covering the four cardinal points. Adjacent to this to the west is a small **temple** (15) built by Tuthmosis III. On the centre line of this temple is a large square base on which once stood the world's largest obelisk, the Lateran obelisk in Rome.

The Lateran Obelisk

It was a considerable achievement for the French to get the 22.5m-high obelisk of Ramses II from the Temple of Luxor to the Place de la Concorde in the 1830s, yet the giant 32.3m obelisk that stood in this small temple at Karnak was removed by order of the Emperor Constantine in the 4th century AD. It was consigned originally to Constantinople but its course was changed upon the emperor's death and it was delivered to Rome instead and erected in the Circus Maximus in AD 357. It fell or more probably was toppled some centuries later, but in 1588 was re-erected in the Piazza San Giovanni in Laterano.

Hieroglyphics on its shaft state that Tuthmosis III 'made as his monument for his father Amun-Re, Lord of the Thrones of the Two Lands, the setting up for him of a single obelisk in the Upper Court of the Temple in the neighbourhood of Karnak, on the very first occasion of setting up a single obelisk in Thebes.' It is stressed that the erection of a single obelisk was unusual, and it is probable that the Lateran obelisk comes from the same quarry of pink granite as that in which the great unfinished obelisk at Aswan still lies (*see* p.299), and that the unfinished obelisk, until faults in the stone were discovered, was intended to complete the pair.

The North Complex Area

The Temple of Ptah and the Precinct of Mont at the north end of the Karnak complex are reached by a winding path that leads from the north wall of the Great Court of the Temple of Amun. The ground is overgrown and barely excavated.

Against the north enclosure wall and shaded by palms, the **Temple of Ptah** (16) is approached through an east–west series of five doorways. If the inner doorway is locked, call to what looks like a sentry tower atop the mud brick wall. Shout. The keeper is probably asleep and will have to put on his galabiyya before coming down to let you in. Each of the doorways is carved with scenes and texts of the Ptolemaic period. The fifth doorway leads into a columned vestibule; to the rear is a small pylon marking the entrance to the temple proper. Beyond the antechamber are three chapels dating from the reign of Tuthmosis III; unusually, the cult statue of Ptah (with head missing) is still in the middle chapel. In the chapel to the right is the startling apparition of Sekhmet, her bare-breasted body surmounted by the head of a lioness. The keeper will close the doors to enhance the eerie effect of the single shaft of sunlight from an aperture in the roof casting a greenish glow within.

A gateway, also often locked, leads through the enclosure wall to the **Precinct of Mont**, god of war (17), its structures largely dilapidated and only of specialist interest. The main temple, totally ruined, was built by Amenophis III.

The South Complex Area

Exploration of the south end of the Karnak complex can begin at the **Sacred Lake**, restored and cemented. A grandstand at its east end is where visitors sit for the culmination of the *son et lumière*. Near the northwest corner is a giant scarab dedicated by Amenophis III to Atum, the god of the rising sun. Also here is the base with underground chambers of an **Osireion** (18) built by Taharka, and the broken-off top of Hatshepsut's other **obelisk** (19). On the pyramidion a kneeling Hatshepsut is being blessed by Amun; his figure was recut by Seti I in the gouge caused by Akhenaton's attempt to obliterate the god of his priestly opponents.

Pylons along the Processional Way

At the south ends of the Third and Fourth Pylons of the Temple of Amun begins the second (north–south) axis of the Karnak complex, a **processional way** which consists of a series of open courts bounded by walls along their east and west sides and separated from each other by pylons. The Seventh and Eighth Pylons led originally to a Middle Kingdom temple and a temple of Amenophis I, which both stood in what is now the court of the Cachette.

The temples were taken down by Tuthmosis III, although not before he had erected the Seventh Pylon.

Considerable restoration work is being carried out along the north–south axis and the pylons may be closed off to the public. Nevertheless, the keepers will not hesitate to show you around for some baksheesh, and will lead you up the inner stairways to the tops of the pylons, or encourage you to follow them as they leap like goats across deep gaps in the towers and walls.

Seven statues of Middle Kingdom pharaohs stand or sit before the north face of the Seventh Pylon, while on its south side are the remains of two colossi of Tuthmosis III. On the outside of the east wall between this and the Eighth Pylon is an interesting **relief of the high priest** of Amenophis, his arms raised as though adoring Ramses IX (XX Dynasty), who extends his palm in a reciprocal gesture. The very presence of the high priest, adoring or not, is unusual, but it is revealing that the priest is as large as the pharaoh and is even the focus of the composition. The relief is a vivid illustration of how much priestly power and arrogance had grown within a century after the reign of the great Ramses II.

The Eighth Pylon was built by Hatshepsut and, though the oldest part of the north–south axis, is well preserved. On its south side a relief shows Amenophis II slaughtering his enemies, while of the original six colossi on this side of the pylon, four remain, the figure of Amenophis I, on the left, the most complete.

The Ninth and Tenth Pylons were built by Horemheb in part with blocks from buildings erected by Akhenaton in honour of Aton. In front of the north side of the west tower is a stele erected by Horemheb proclaiming the restoration of the Amun orthodoxy. On the east side of the court between the Ninth and Tenth Pylons is a small temple built by Amenophis II, probably for his jubilee, with a graceful portico of square pillars. The fine bas-reliefs inside the hall, some of their colouring well preserved, show Amenophis before various deities. On the interior wall of the court between this temple and the Tenth Pylon, Horemheb is shown in relief leading captives from Punt bearing gifts for the Theban triad, and to the right of this he appears with fettered Syrian captives. Both claims of foreign triumph are almost certainly false, at best mere conventions, for Horemheb is known to have spent most of his energies imposing law, order and the old religion on post-Amarna Egypt, and there is no evidence at all that he led his armies abroad.

From the Tenth Pylon an **avenue of sphinxes** (21) runs for several hundred metres to the **Precinct of Mut**, still not entirely excavated and all the more picturesque for its ruins rising from the overgrown scrub. Consort of Amun and originally a vulture goddess, Mut was depicted during the New Kingdom with the skin of a vulture on her wig. Approached through a propylaeum cut with Ptolemaic cartouches, her badly ruined temple, built by Amenophis III, consists of two courts, a hypostyle hall and sanctuary. All around it, rising from the scrub, are figures of Sekhmet, the lion goddess, beautifully worked and with care taken to use the pink veins in the bluish granite to highlight certain features such as the ankh sign or the goddess's breasts. A sacred lake enwraps the temple and across it, to the west, is a temple of Ramses III. Another temple, of Amenophis III, is in the northeast corner of the precinct.

The Temples of Khonsu and Opet

Still within the main Karnak enclosure, in the southwest corner, is the **Temple of Khonsu** (22), the moon-god son of Mut and Amun. It faces south towards the Gateway of Euergetes and so towards the avenue of rams which disappears beneath village houses before emerging again in front of the entrance pylon of the Temple of Luxor. For the most part the Temple of Khonsu is in a good state of preservation; its simplicity and clarity of layout make it a classic of New Kingdom architecture. It was started by Ramses III, though possibly completed and certainly almost entirely decorated by his successors down to Herihor (XXI Dynasty), who like Horemheb rose from the army to seize power as pharaoh, and went one better by making himself high priest of Amun as well. The pylon of the temple is small but well proportioned, and decorated with a variety of religious scenes. On the rear wall of the first court, to the right, is a carving of the temple façade, banners flying. To the left is Herihor performing rites before the boats of the Theban triad. Beyond this is a small transverse hypostyle hall leading to the dilapidated sanctuary. Walking through its centre chapel, once containing the sacred boat of Khonsu, you come to a small hall of four columns with reliefs of Ramses IV, and also, on either side of the entrance, Augustus. From the southeast corner of the sanctuary a staircase leads up to the roof, from which there are good views of the ruins.

Immediately to the west is the smaller **Temple of Opet** (23), a hippopotamus goddess and mother of Osiris. It was left unfinished by Euergetes II, though otherwise finely decorated throughout the Ptolemaic period and into the reign of Augustus.

You can leave the Karnak site through the **Gateway of Euergetes I** (24), its concave cornice adorned with a winged sun disc.

The Necropolis of Thebes

During the New Kingdom, when Thebes was the opulent capital of Egypt, a vast necropolis was founded across the river, on the west bank of the Nile. A **tour** of the necropolis involves following a north–south arc, starting at either end. If you are feeling adventurous and want to follow the path from the Valley of the Kings to Deir el Bahri for its marvellous views, you should start at the north, visiting first the Temple of Seti I, continuing to the Valley of the Kings, Deir el Bahri, the Tombs of the Nobles, the Ramesseum, Deir el Medina, the Valley of the Queens, Medinet Habu and back to the river via the Colossi of Memnon. This guide describes the tour in that order.

At least two days are required to complete this tour, but if you have only one day you will have to pick among the highlights: the Valley of the Kings (2 hours), Deir el Bahri (30 minutes), the Tombs of the Nobles (30 minutes–1 hour) and either the Ramesseum (30 minutes) or Medinet Habu (30 minutes)—and if you are keen and can get a ticket, Nefertari's tomb in the Valley of the Queens (you are limited to 10 minutes in the tomb itself). If you have a second day, visit those sites you missed the first time round.

Getting There and Around

Because of the intense heat of the afternoon, it is usual to take a **ferry** across to the west bank of the Nile very early in the morning and to complete your explorations by about 1pm. However, if you do not mind the heat, stay until the tombs close when there are fewer fellow tourists (especially fewer tour groups, coachloads of whom now pound over the new bridge 7km upriver from Luxor).

The long incline to the Valley of the Kings is best done by **car** followed by a walk over the escarpment and down to Deir el Bahri, the Temple of Hatshepsut; the driver will leave you at the Valley of the Kings and collect you later at Hatshepsut's temple. The rest of the west bank should be covered by **bicycle** if you are up to it; it gives you more time and frees you from the impatient harassment of a driver. Distances can be long and **donkeys** are recommended only for those seeking the perversely picturesque. If you are exploring the necropolis by donkey or taxi, always agree clearly on the price beforehand and do not pay a single piastre until the boy or driver has fulfilled his side of the bargain.

Note that before even crossing over to the west bank you should go to the Tourist Office in Luxor (*see* p.196) and arm yourself with the official rates for taxis, etc.

Aboudi and his Guidebook

In the bad old days when donkeys were the only means of getting about the west bank, there was a wonderful Cook's dragoman called Mohammed Aboudi, who later opened a shop in Luxor and published a near-to-useless and vastly entertaining guide. Alas, neither is extant. But for a while Aboudi was private secretary to Cole Porter in both Europe and Egypt, and it was perhaps this connection which encouraged Aboudi to leaven his guide book with his own poetry. It deserves what further lease on life this present guide can offer it. A sample:

> *O East is East and West is West in Luxor or in London town;*
> *But Aboudi, our faithful Aboudi, will never let us down.*
> *Through all the plagues of Egypt, donkey-boys, the flies, the sand,*
> *This trusty modern Moses leads us towards the Promised Land.*
> *Weird tales of long dead ages come tripping from his tongue,*
> *With him through tombs and temples we pass in wondering throng.*
> *And when foot and brain are weary with the sights we've come to see,*
> *He calls our patient donkeys up to bear us home to tea.*
> *Surely in future ages the tourists all will stand,*
> *An unabridged edition of Rosetta in each hand,*
> *And read the hieroglyphics which proclaim how Pharaoh's Cook,*
> *By his henchman, great Aboudi, mighty hosts through Egypt took!*
> *There's one thing more, if you can stick it:*
> *The law of this land is very intricate.*
> *At each temple gate is an Arab picket,*
> *So please don't forget your little ticket;*
> *And galloping donkeys is not allowed!*

by taxi

Taxis should display in their windows the list of officially determined fares; if the list is not evident, ask to see it. At present, the fare for a half-day (4 hours) is LE50; proportionately more per additional hour. This is regardless of the number of people carried, which depending on the car can be from four to seven. For this price the taxi is exclusively yours throughout. If during winter there is a lot of business, the driver may ask that he be free to zoom off when you do not need him; if you agree then a discount is in order.

For odd journeys, you can try your luck by hiring a taxi to the Valley of the Kings and walking over the ridge to Deir el Bahri, and then catching a taxi on from there to somewhere else.

by pick-up

A recent innovation, and a variation on taking a taxi, is the use of small pick-up trucks or vans with flat backs and bench seats arranged along each side. They are as roadworthy as taxis, much cheaper and more fun. You can usually flag one down to take you from one site to another or to ride between the ferry landing and the ticket office, each leg costing LE1–2.

by bicycle

Bicycles, hired for LE5–10 per day in Luxor or on the west bank, are the best way to get around—if you are fit. As you pedal along past tombs and temples you are surprisingly cool and sweatless in the dry air (though beware of sunstroke); the instant you stop the sweat pours off you in buckets. Bring water.

The one disadvantage of using a bicycle (apart from heart attacks and sunstroke) is not being able to walk from the Valley of the Kings to Deir el Bahri—this is highly recommended (*see* p.236).

Bicycles can be hired at a number of places on the west bank. The most useful is about 400m along the main road from the people ferry landing stage where a sign on the left says 'Ask for Mohammed'. Mohammed, as well as renting bicycles, is also an excellent bicycle mechanic. There are many places dotted about the west bank that will mend punctures and do general running repairs. If you have a problem or get too tired, you can always flag down a taxi and put your bike in the back.

by donkey

Donkeys cost LE20–30 per person for the whole day, to all the sites, which in practice when there are several of you makes them no cheaper than a taxi. They are uncomfortable and, unless you are possessed by some masochistic nostalgia for pre-internal-combustion-engine forms of transport, should be avoided. Donkey boys can be bastards: they have a habit of agreeing to a price, then increasing it as you trot along, and tossing you off the donkey if you do not give in.

by horse and camel

Though not for hire to visit the sites, it is enjoyable, especially if you are staying on the west bank and have the time, to go riding along farm tracks and the edge of the desert. The best riding is early in the morning and during the late afternoon. Camel drivers wait amid the scrum at the people's ferry landing, while Arab horses can be hired from the stables on the left of the road leading away from the landing, just before the point where it is joined by the road from the old Nile-side ticket office.

crossing the Nile

The recent construction of a bridge (no toll) 7km south of Luxor is already having an unfortunate effect on the west bank. Ferries were the only way across in the past, and this preserved something of its traditional character and tranquillity. Now that unlimited numbers of tourist coaches can pound across the bridge, the west bank is becoming increasingly developed and commercialized. The independent traveller can join the rat-run, hiring a taxi in Luxor to take him over the bridge and round the west bank sites, but it is a dull thing to do and will prove more expensive than hiring a taxi on the other side.

Motor launches to the West Bank leave from all along the Luxor corniche. The fare is LE5 and they do not carry bicycles. There are also the frequent people ferries (as the locals call them, carefully distinguishing themselves from mere tourists) which depart from near the Temple of Luxor. These will carry bicycles. The fare is LE1 on the way over; there is no charge for the return journey. Both the launches and the ferries will land you smack amid a hive of taxi drivers and donkey boys. You negotiate a price (having first checked the official rates at the Tourist Office in Luxor), travel to the kiosk by Medinet Habu to buy your tickets, and you're off.

A Warning

The mystery of a Canadian woman's disappearance two years ago at Luxor was unravelled this week when police located her remains in an archaeological ditch. Before dying she had scribbled on a postcard that she fell inside the labyrinth after losing her way, and she was preparing herself for death from thirst and hunger. The police located her skeleton this week, her clothes still on, in a distant area behind the pharaonic temples where archaeological digs were underway.

newspaper report

While not wishing to inhibit the curiosity of travellers, it is worth mentioning that care should be taken at excavations and you should not get off the beaten track if exploring on your own.

Access and Fees

With the exception of Nefertari's tomb (see below and pp.248–50), sites on the west bank are open 7–5 in winter, 6–6 in summer, with no lunchtime closure. The ticket kiosk opens at 6am all year and closes at 4pm in winter, 5pm in summer. Tickets are valid on the day of purchase only.

It is often said that you should start early to avoid the crowds. But the crowds all have the same idea, giving you good reason to start late.

Tickets are required for almost all sites and must be purchased in advance at the ticket kiosk between the Colossi of Memnon and Medinet Habu (though you may be told that tickets for Tutankhamun's tomb must be bought at the Valley of the Kings, where in any case you can buy additional tickets if you want to see more than three tombs). Tickets are sold for specific sites and normally can only be used for that site (though sometimes you can haggle your way in to a site with a different but same-price ticket). As the opening times for the various sites can change from time to time, you should check at the ticket kiosk where the information is clearly displayed. Only 150 people per day are admitted to Nefertari's tomb in the Valley of the Queens, so to be sure of gaining entrance you should be at the kiosk when it opens at 6am: tickets go quickly, often by 6.30am, though it is worth enquiring later (*see* p.250).

As tickets are valid on the day of purchase only, you should ration yourself to what your time and energy will allow: it is easy to be over-ambitious, especially given the heat and more especially if you are intending to walk over the mountain path between the Valley of the Kings and Deir el Bahri. You could either make a selection from the highlights (the Valley of the Kings, Deir el Bahri, the Tombs of the Nobles, the Ramesseum or Medinet Habu, and Nefertari's tomb in the Valley of the Queens) or you could first buy tickets for a selection of sites in the northern part of the necropolis and then return to the kiosk to buy tickets for those in the southern part (remembering, however, that if you want to visit the tomb of Nefertari, you will need to buy that ticket first thing in the morning).

Tickets are generally LE12 per site, but there are exceptions. The Valley of the Kings is LE20 for three tombs (a further LE20 must be paid for each additional set of three tombs you wish to visit); Tutankhamun's tomb is charged separately at LE40. Nefertari's tomb in the Valley of the Queens is LE100. Some sites are covered by several tickets, e.g. it costs LE12 to visit each group of two or three tombs at the Tombs of the Nobles. There is no charge for seeing the Colossi of Memnon, nor for wandering around Deir el Medina (the Workmen's Village), though LE12 is payable to enter the tombs there.

Photography

To take photographs or use a video camera inside the tombs you must obtain a permit from the ticket kiosk, valid on the day of purchase only. For a normal camera the cost is LE10 per tomb; an additional LE50 is charged for use of a tripod. No flash photography is permitted, so use at least 400 ASA film. Use of a video camera is LE400; this covers all tombs except those at the Valley of the Kings where video cameras are not permitted (they can be left at the entrance). Neither photography nor video recording is permitted in the tomb of Tutankhamun.

Toilets

Toilets are found at the Valley of the Kings, at the Hatshepsut Restaurant opposite Deir el Bahri, near the Ramesseum and at the Marsam Hotel at the intersection for Medinet Habu beyond the Colossi of Memnon. There are also 'mobile' toilets in the car parks at most sites.

Soft **drinks** and mineral water are sold at the major sites; there is a juice bar opposite Mohammed's bike hire about 400m along the main road from the landing stage for the people ferry, another further along just past the crossroads near New Gurna, and another near the mortuary temple of Seti I, opposite the new hospital.

Meals can be had at the **Tutankhamun** and **African** restaurants by the people's ferry landing, both serving good Egyptian food; the **Ali Baba** opposite the Colossi of Memnon which offers an inexpensive three-course Egyptian meal as well as pasta, pizza and sandwiches; at either of the two **café-restaurants** on the corner opposite the temple at Medinet Habu (avoid eating at the Habu Hotel, a lovely place to stay but offering terrible meals); and at the new three-star **Hatshepsut Restaurant** opposite Deir el Bahri—identified also by signs mysteriously reading No Galag, the place turning out to be run by Sayed No Galag. Open all day and evening, this is a white domed building covered with Hajj-style paintings and has both a first floor air-conditioned restaurant and a rooftop restaurant and bar.

Pharmacies and Hospital

There is a pharmacy opposite Mohammed's bicycle place, about 400m along the main road running west from the people ferry landing stage. There are two good pharmacies near the mortuary temple of Seti I; the hospital is also close by.

To the Necropolis

From the west bank landing stages the road runs to the new village of Gurna and continues on past the Colossi of Memnon towards the Theban Mountain. At the village another road runs north towards the Temple of Seti I.

The New and Old Villages of Gurna

The work of an architect who designs, say, an apartment house in the poor quarters of Cairo for some stingy speculator, in which he incorporates various features of modern design copied from fashionable European work, will filter down, over a period of years, through the cheap suburbs and into the village where it will slowly poison the genuine tradition.

Hassan Fathy, *Architecture for the Poor*

New Gurna was built in the late 1940s by the Egyptian architect Hassan Fathy. Employing the almost forgotten art of forming vaults and domes in mud brick without the use of timber centring, his aim was to reintroduce 'a way of building that was a natural growth in the landscape, as much a part of it as the palm tree.' He died in 1989, disappointed in his hope that traditional methods could solve urgent housing needs in the Third World, avoiding extravagant and climatically unsuitable Western technology. In his famous testament, *Architecture for the Poor*, he objected to the bastardization of Arab architecture as applied to recent hotel design and the interior decoration of restaurants and nightclubs.

Though the project was commissioned by the government, bureaucratic red tape and the erratic provision of funds ensured that new Gurna was never entirely finished. Nor has it ever been entirely occupied, though the houses all have plumbing, and a theatre and recreation centre were provided. One reason for this lies in Luxor's oldest profession. Over the past 3,000 years or more, easy access to the Theban tombs has provided villagers on the west bank with an extra source of income. It was partly to check this that the new village was built, and for this same reason that new Gurna has been so much resented. However, a locally-based group plans to restore new Gurna and bring it back to life. The intention is for Hassan Fathy's house, next to the theatre and at present uninhabited, to become a museum and a study centre dedicated to his work, while the khan is meant to provide workshops and become a showcase for traditional crafts.

Meanwhile the Ministry of Antiquities has recently renewed attempts to move the inhabitants out of the string of hamlets that make up the village of **old Gurna** (properly Sheikh Abd el Gurna) at the foot of the Theban Mountain. Modern housing estates are under construction to the north, just past the turning to the Valley of the Kings. But the villagers are offering strong resistance, objecting to leaving the houses in which they have lived for generations and having to move away from the land they farm close by. They object also to losing the income they gain by hustling visitors to the tombs over which many of their houses have been built. For the time being, Sheikh Abd el Gurna has not been entirely abandoned, nor, go the rumours, have its inhabitants entirely abandoned tomb-robbing.

Historical Background

A Case of Looting in Pharaonic Times

> *And we made the gold which we had found on these two gods—from their mummies, amulets, ornaments and coffins—into eight shares. And two kilos of gold fell to each of us.*

> A XX Dynasty tomb robber

Under the powerful pharaohs of the XVIII and XIX Dynasties local officials were closely supervized and tomb looting kept in check. But under the weaker rulers of the XX Dynasty, tombs were robbed. A picture of surprising detail can be built up from surviving papyri of the necropolis workers enduring food shortages and late payment of wages, of riots, pay disputes and strikes. There are also documented accounts of bribery and collusion among workers, priests and officials. One papyrus describes a major Theban law case during the reign of Ramses IX (XX Dynasty) in which the mayor of Thebes brought to the vizier's attention stories of tomb robbing at the necropolis. The matter was investigated by the chief of the necropolis police and the stories denied; the vizier then ensured that the mayor of Thebes was disgraced for making malicious and politically inspired accusations. Some years later, however as the tomb robbings continued, the case was reopened and it became clear that both the vizier and the chief of police were up to their eyeballs in corruption. Examined by birch and screw, the stonemason Amun-pa-nefer admitted tunnelling into a royal tomb and stripping the pharaoh and his queen of gold, silver and precious stones.

Amun-pa-nefer then described the chain of corruption: 'We then crossed over to Thebes. And after some days, the agents of Thebes heard that we had been stealing in the west, so they arrested me and imprisoned me at the mayor of Thebes' place. So I took the two kilos of gold that had fallen to me as my share, and gave them to Kha-em-Opet, the District Clerk of the harbour of Thebes. He let me go, and I joined my companions, and they made up for me another share. And I, as well as the other robbers who are with me, have continued to this day in the practice of robbing the tombs of the nobles and people of the land who rest in the west of Thebes. And a large number of the men of the land rob them also.' Presumably the bribe was shared out among other officials higher up the ladder, though no share fell to the mayor of Thebes who was either an honest man or complained because he was being cut out of the action.

Iron Age Economic Crisis

The case has its anecdotal interest, but it throws light too on the causes underlying the enfeeblement of the New Kingdom from the XX Dynasty. In describing Karnak it was mentioned how an ever greater proportion of the nation's wealth went to the priesthood; much gold and silver was also literally buried underground in the tombs, taken out of circulation. Yet it was precisely at this time that the world was shifting from the Bronze Age to the Iron Age, and while Egypt had copper mines, she had no iron—the essential metal for weapon superiority. Under the Egyptian Empire, iron could be expropriated abroad; as the rule of the pharaohs weakened and the empire shrank, Egypt was forced to buy iron abroad, making payment in gold and silver. The value of these precious metals rose during the period 1150 to 1110 BC (Ramses V–Ramses X, approximately). Food shortages and wage delays followed; the necropolis workers struck and many of them turned to tomb robbing. The bonanza of precious metals and stones they clawed back from the tombs and put into circulation, however corrupt the channels might have been, soon relieved the situation. By that time the Empire was finished, the moral authority of the administration had been sapped, and power fell to Herihor, a general who became military dictator, assumed the high priesthood of Amun and made himself pharaoh. His power extended only over Upper Egypt however; Lower Egypt was ruled by merchant princes at Tanis and the country was never long united again.

Modern Tomb Robbing

The fuel they use for the locomotive is composed of mummies three thousand years old, purchased by the ton or by the graveyard for that purpose... Sometimes one hears the profane engineer call out pettishly, 'Damn these plebeians, they don't burn worth a cent—pass out a king.'

Mark Twain, *The Innocents Abroad*

There are at least 900 tombs built into the rock. The authorities say all have been checked and locked. But there are constant rumours of secret finds beneath the houses and even the wall paintings in known tombs are occasionally removed. The modern heyday for tomb robbers was during the late 19th century with the explosion in Europe and America of archaeological and tourist interest in ancient Egypt. Luxor saw a roaring trade in tablets, statuettes and scarabs, both real and faked—home-made scarabs were fed to turkeys to 'acquire by the simple process of digestion a degree of venerableness that is really charming', wrote one visitor. Mummies were dragged out of their tombs and unrolled, stripped of their valuables, broken up and left to crumble in the sands. In earlier centuries, mummy cases were chopped up for firewood, and from at least the 13th century to the 19th century 'mummy' was highly regarded in Europe for its medicinal properties, the export demand sometimes proving so great that Egyptians often substituted modern corpses.

Not that the humble quest for loot has always been without its larger benefits, or that even the poorest Egyptians have not sometimes shown respect for the objects of their peculations. In an effort to save their royal masters from contemporary tomb robbers, priests in the XXI Dynasty removed the mummies from their tombs in the Valley of the Kings and stacked them, 30 in a shaft, in a nearby rocky cleft. In 1875, Abdel Rasul, sheikh of Gurna, found the cache and kept it secret for six years, selling off bits and pieces as he needed money. Archaeologists traced these clues to their source, and the mummies are those on display in the Mummy Room of the Egyptian Antiquities Museum in Cairo. As these long-dead pharaohs sailed down the Nile by steamer, fellahin lined the banks at village after village, the women ululating in lament, the men firing their rifles in homage.

Temple of Seti I

Even more than Karnak, the tombs and mortuary temples of the Theban necropolis tell of the rise and fall of the New Kingdom and the Egyptian Empire.

The Mortuary Temple of Seti I (XIX Dynasty) lies off the road to the Valley of the Kings and is usually bypassed by tourists in haste. This in itself should recommend it; also that the works of Seti's reign—famously his temple at Abydos—are among the finest and most restrained of the New Kingdom. The temple was founded in honour of Amun but was also devoted to the worship of Seti's father, Ramses I. The first two pylons and courts have been destroyed; what remains is the temple proper and a tour of it is made both at ground level and, the better to see certain reliefs, by leaping goat-like after the resident guide from architrave to broken architrave.

A colonnade facing east towards the Nile admits you, through a central door, to a **hypostyle hall** with six columns decorated with reliefs of Seti and Ramses II making offerings to divinities. On either side of the hall are small **chapels** with very fine reliefs of Seti, his ka, his sacred boat, Thoth and Osiris, as he offers sacrifices and performs ceremonies en route to the afterlife. The **sanctuary**, once containing Amun's sacred boat, lies beyond. Reliefs show Seti offering incense before the boat. To the left (south) of the hypostyle hall is the **chapel of Ramses I**. On the side walls of the central chamber, Seti is again depicted offering incense to Amun's boat, and anoints a statue of Ramses I with his finger. The chambers on either side were given inferior reliefs by Ramses II. The right (north) side of the temple is in a state of ruin; a larger hall, dedicated to Re-Herakhte, was built by Ramses II and decorated with crude reliefs.

The obsessive appropriations of Ramses II and their inferior quality stand out among the works of Seti I who consciously sought a renaissance in taste and values. But then Seti's own reliefs suffer from the New Kingdom preoccupation with gaining access to the afterlife: they are reassuring encounters with the gods at death, but do not concern themselves with the quality of life. If not yet in empire, certainly in spirit Egypt was in retreat.

To the Valley of the Kings

The flat alluvium suddenly quits and it is utter desert to the Valley of the Kings. Set amid trees on a hill where the road from Seti's temple is joined by the road from Deir el Bahri is the house where Howard Carter lived during his search for the tomb of Tutankhamun. Above it, on the barren summit of the hill, is Lord Carnarvon's house. The road climbs towards the oven of white sand and sun that is **Biban el Muluk**—the 'Gates of the Kings'. Unblinking tomb entrances stare vacantly from the close valley walls. Each ramp is cut and swept, each doorway numbered in order of discovery. It's the most exclusive suburb in the world, where the mightiest dead once lay in silent, motionless expectation of awakening. Anxious priests, covetous archaeologists, and robbers caring more for life than life after, carried them away. Anubis and Osiris remain, paintings on the wall.

Burials at the Valley of the Kings date from the XVIII to the XX Dynasties, with Tuthmosis I being the first to select the site. Though the pharaohs and, rarely, certain exalted but non-royal personages were entombed here, offerings to the dead were made at the mortuary temples built on the plain. The tombs therefore were entirely private receptacles for the sarcophagus, and their decoration concentrated exclusively on the formulae efficacious in transferring the deceased from this world into the next. The tombs and their decorations can be impressive, and their contents of course were staggering, but they do not speak of life, of humanity, or even of personal death and resurrection—they are monuments of state and of ideology, and less vivid, less revealing than the tombs of the lesser dead elsewhere in the Theban necropolis.

Tomb Construction and Decoration

Each of the tombs follows a similar pattern of construction and decoration. Three corridors lead to an antechamber giving onto the main hall with its sunken floor for receiving the sarcophagus. The tombs were cut into the soft limestone by two teams of 25 men working alternating ten-day shifts. They normally lived at Deir el Medina but when on shift stayed in huts within the valley. Construction of a tomb began at the beginning of a reign and never took more than six years to complete. Once the interior surfaces were prepared, the designs and inscriptions were sketched in black; the designs filled in, the hieroglyphics outlined in red; the decorations carved and finally painted. In some tombs, notably that of Horemheb (57), these various stages of decoration are evident.

The dead pharaoh, absorbed in the sun god, sailed through the underworld at night in a boat, avoiding enemies and dangers along the way. This is the recurrent theme of the decorations, the inscriptions being extensive quotations from the Amduat or Book of the Underworld and the Book of the Gates which provide instructions for charting the course; the Book of Day and Night is also sometimes employed. Pictorially, there are three registers, the middle one showing the river of passage, the top and bottom registers depicting the shores with their inhabitants of deities and demons. The registers are divided into 12 sections for the 12 hours of the night. After this nocturnal voyage the naked body of the goddess Nut gives birth each morning to the sun. This is beautifully represented on the ceiling of the sarcophagus hall of the tomb of Ramses VI.

The Tombs of the Pharaohs

In all, 62 tombs are known in the Valley of the Kings. A few of these were known and visited by tourists in Ptolemaic times as indicated by Diodorus and Strabo and occasional Greek and Latin graffiti. Most are of little interest except to scholars and are closed to the public. Only tombs 2, 6, 8, 9, 11, 16, 17, 34, 35, 57 and 62 have electric lighting, and most visitors will be content to see those of **Tutankhamun** (62), **Ramses VI** (9), **Seti I** (17), **Ramses IV** (2) and **Tuthmosis III** (34), and then possibly the tombs of **Amenophis II** (35) and **Horemheb** (57). Not all of these will necessarily be open when you visit. Those of Seti I and Horemheb were closed for restoration at the time of writing. There are plans to substitute replicas for Tutankhamun's tomb and others. The identity of all 62 tombs is given on the accompanying map, but only those electrically lit are described below.

Tomb 2: Ramses IV (XX Dynasty)

Only electrified and therefore made more accessible to the public in 1983, the bright and excellent lighting of this tomb contributes towards a favourable impression, for though the decorations are third-rate the overall effect is entirely enjoyable. There is much Ptolemaic and Coptic graffiti throughout, particularly by the entrance—on the right, two haloed saints raise their arms in prayer. Robbed in antiquity, Ramses' body never found, the tomb has long been open to the curious. Steps and then three high white corridors descend gently in a straight line to the sarcophagus chamber. The ceiling here is decorated with the goddess Nut in duplicate. The huge sarcophagus of pink granite is covered with texts and magical scenes, while Isis and Nephthys on the lid were meant to protect the hijacked body—the empty sarcophagus has been retrieved from the tomb of Amenophis II where the priests had hidden it. Throughout the chambers and corridors of the tomb, against all the whiteness, are small patterns of red, blue, yellow and some green pastels which are pleasing, despite the poor carving and line and the sloppy application of colour. Indeed this slapdash effect has a quality of gaieté, as though the whole affair was a French reproduction.

Tomb 6: Ramses IX (XX Dynasty)

A flight of steps on either side of an inclined plane leads you down to the tomb door, its lintel decorated with the solar disc, the pharaoh worshipping it on both sides. Behind him stands

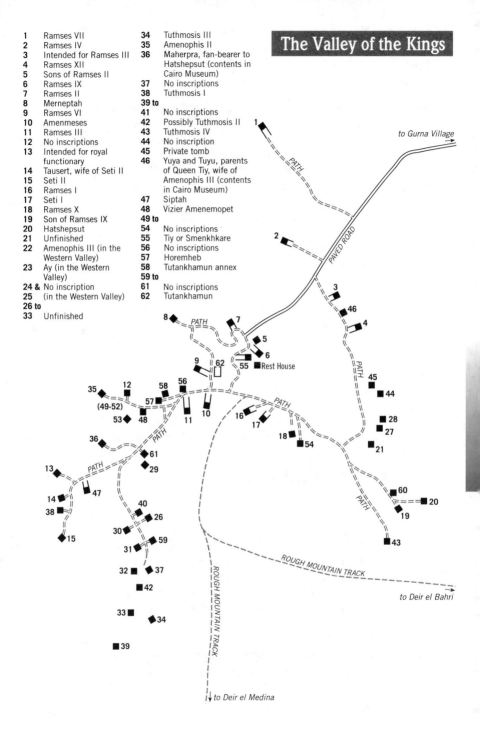

1 Ramses VII
2 Ramses IV
3 Intended for Ramses III
4 Ramses XII
5 Sons of Ramses II
6 Ramses IX
7 Ramses II
8 Merneptah
9 Ramses VI
10 Amenmeses
11 Ramses III
12 No inscriptions
13 Intended for royal functionary
14 Tausert, wife of Seti II
15 Seti II
16 Ramses I
17 Seti I
18 Ramses X
19 Son of Ramses IX
20 Hatshepsut
21 Unfinished
22 Amenophis III (in the Western Valley)
23 Ay (in the Western Valley)
24 & No inscription
25 (in the Western Valley)
26 to
33 Unfinished

34 Tuthmosis III
35 Amenophis II
36 Maherpra, fan-bearer to Hatshepsut (contents in Cairo Museum)
37 No inscriptions
38 Tuthmosis I
39 to
41 No inscriptions
42 Possibly Tuthmosis II
43 Tuthmosis IV
44 No inscription
45 Private tomb
46 Yuya and Tuyu, parents of Queen Tiy, wife of Amenophis III (contents in Cairo Museum)
47 Siptah
48 Vizier Amenemopet
49 to
54 No inscriptions
55 Tiy or Smenkhkare
56 No inscriptions
57 Horemheb
58 Tutankhamun annex
59 to
61 No inscriptions
62 Tutankhamun

The Valley of the Kings

to Gurna Village

PATH

PAVED ROAD

PATH

PATH

Rest House

(49-52)

to Deir el Bahri

ROUGH MOUNTAIN TRACK

to Deir el Medina

Isis (left) and Nephthys (right). The tomb is of near-model design: three corridors, an antechamber, but then a pillared hall and short passage before the final sarcophagus chamber. The decorations are similar to those in Tomb 9.

Tomb 8: Merneptah (XIX Dynasty)

Merneptah, the possible pharaoh of the Exodus, was the son of Ramses II by his secondary wife Istnofret. His tomb, which descends steeply through corridor steps, is typical of XVIII and XIX Dynasty tombs; those of the XX Dynasty are shallower. Over the entrance, Isis and Nephthys worship the sun disc, while the entrance corridors are decorated with scenes from the Book of the Gates and other texts. In the small antechamber is the huge granite lid of the outer sarcophagus; a further flight of steps leads down to a pillared hall with a barrelled roof containing the pink granite lid of the inner sarcophagus. Carved on the lid is the recumbent figure of Merneptah as Osiris, and on the underside is the goddess Nut.

Tomb 9: Ramses VI (XX Dynasty)

Though decorated in sunk relief with workmanship inferior to that of the previous dynasty, the colouring remains fresh. The tomb was originally constructed for Ramses V and ended with Chamber E. On the left walls of this part of the tomb is the complete text of the Book of the Gates with a summary of the creation of the world on the left part of the rear wall of E. Another text, the Book of Caverns, decorates the right walls, while the ceilings of C, D and E are decorated with the Book of Day and Night. Corridors F and G show the hours from the Amduat on their walls. In Chamber H are portions of the Book of the Dead; on the left wall is the negative confession. The admission of any transgression would have prevented entry into the afterlife, and so the 'confession' was a series of denials ('I have not done this or that'). The pillared Chamber I contains fragments of the great granite sarcophagus. Its vaulted ceiling is splendidly painted with the Book of Day and Night, the sky goddess Nut appearing twice, back to back, framing the Book of Day on the entrance side, and on the far side the Book of Night.

Tomb 11: Ramses III (XX Dynasty)

One of the largest tombs in the valley, the second half is in ruins and not illuminated. Once again the decorations are inferior sunk relief, but they are exceptionally varied and remain freshly coloured. This is sometimes called the 'Harpers' Tomb' after the two harpers playing to divinities in the last of four small chambers opening off the left-hand side of the second corridor. This tomb is unique in having ten side-chambers off its entrance corridors; where these occur in tombs, they were for receiving tomb furniture. Beyond these the tomb turns to the right and then to the left and the third chamber along is a sloping passage with side galleries and four pillars: the perspective through here to the rooms beyond is impressive.

Tomb 16: Ramses I (XIX Dynasty)

Though founder of his dynasty, Ramses I reigned for only a year or two and was interred in a simple tomb. A sloping corridor and steep flight of steps leads to a single almost square chamber containing the open sarcophagus. The decoration—painted, not carved—is brilliantly coloured on grey ground. The pharaoh is variously shown with Maat, Ptah, Osiris,

The 'Harpers' Tomb' of Ramses III

Anubis and other deities, and portions of the Book of Gates are depicted (on the left wall, notice the 12 goddesses representing the hours of the night).

Tomb 17: Seti I (XIX Dynasty)

At 100m, this is the longest tomb in the valley. Its **reliefs** are wonderfully preserved and so beautifully executed that they rival the famous decorations in Seti's temple at Abydos. Beneath a ceiling painted with vultures flying towards the back of the tomb, the walls of Corridor A are decorated on the left with Seti before the falcon-headed Re-Herakhte, god of the morning sun. The sun in other forms, as disc, scarab and ram-headed god, follows, and the text of the Sun Litany continues on the right wall. This and other texts continue in Corridor B, with staircase. On the upper part of the recess in the left wall are represented 37 forms of the sun god. Corridor C is decorated with the fourth (right) and fifth (left) hours of the night from the Amduat. In Chamber D Seti is shown on four walls in the presence of various deities. Chambers E and F show Seti on each side of the square pillars with a deity. The wall decorations are various hours from the Book of the Gates.

The pattern of construction and decoration of the tomb so far is now in a general sense repeated, with G, H and I corresponding to B, C and D. Corridors G and H are decorated

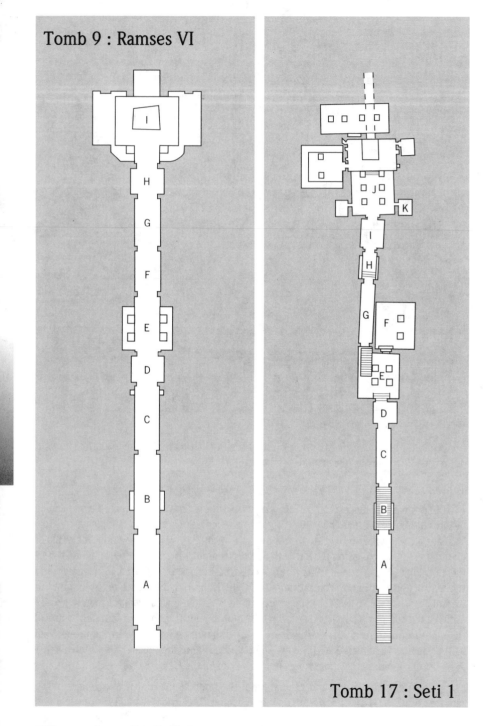

Tomb 9 : Ramses VI

Tomb 17 : Seti 1

with the **Ritual of the Opening of the Mouth** which ensured that the mummy's organs were functioning, particularly to permit eating and drinking. The decorations in Chamber I are similar to those in D. Chamber J is in two parts, the first a pillared hall with hours from the Book of the Gates on the walls, the second with the Amduat on the walls and astronomical figures on the vaulted ceiling. The northern constellation here was intended to permit Seti to orient himself with the sun. The sarcophagus (now in the Sir John Soane Museum, London) rested in the depression in this second part; a passage behind runs for 46m, apparently to nowhere. A side room, K, to the right, is known as the **Chamber of the Cow** for its representation of the sky goddess Nut in the form of a cow. The texts here recount the myth of the destruction of mankind, the Egyptian equivalent of the Mesopotamian and biblical story of the Flood.

Tomb 34: Tuthmosis III (XVIII Dynasty)

At the far end of the rising valley and requiring a steep climb up metal steps to reach the entrance, and then a steep descent within, this tomb is unusual for the rounded shape of the **sarcophagus chamber**. A pit (A) that you now cross by footbridge in one of the approach corridors was probably meant to deter tomb robbers, though later the priests removed Tuthmosis' mummy to a rocky cleft (*see* p.224) for safekeeping; it is now in the Cairo Museum, though the red granite sarcophagus remains *in situ*.

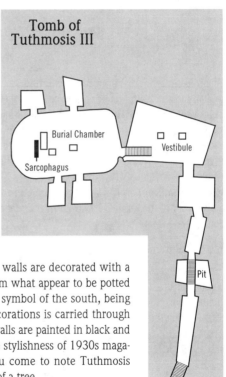

The tomb is worth visiting for its unusual paintings. In the room (B) preceding the sarcophagus chamber the walls are decorated with a repeating pattern of stars, and below them what appear to be potted plants. They *are* potted plants: papyrus, symbol of the south, being grown in pots. The spareness of the decorations is carried through into the sarcophagus chamber (C). The walls are painted in black and red only; the black stick-figures have the stylishness of 1930s magazine illustrations. On the first pillar you come to note Tuthmosis being suckled by his mother in the form of a tree.

Tomb 35: Amenophis II (XVIII Dynasty)

This tomb is unadorned except for the sarcophagus chamber, approached by a long corridor and steep flight of steps. A shaft at A is crossed by a modern gangway leading to Chamber B with unfinished walls. The walls of the Sarcophagus Chamber C are painted yellow in imitation of papyrus and bear the complete text of the Amduat as though inscribed on a continuous scroll. The blue ceiling is painted with yellow stars. The tomb was not discovered

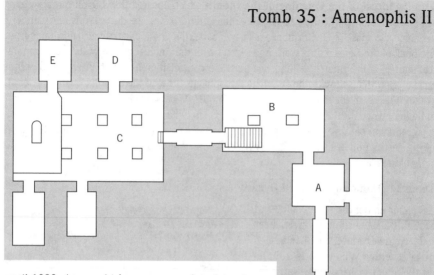

until 1898. Amenophis' mummy was found *in situ*, a floral garland still round its neck, and only in 1934 was it removed to the Cairo Museum. The quartzite sarcophagus was left in the tomb. Three mummies were found in side room D, and nine royal mummies, hidden there by priests, were found in room E. These last included Tuthmosis IV, Amenophis III and Seti II, now all in the Egyptian Museum in Cairo. It is to the late discovery of the tomb that the survival and identification of these mummies is owed.

Tomb 57: Horemheb (XVIII Dynasty)

The plan is almost identical to that of Tomb 17 (Seti I) and some of the decorations are finely executed. The principal interest, however, is in the partially finished work, showing the various stages of decoration.

Tomb 62: Tutankhamun (XVIII Dynasty)

Gold—everywhere the glint of gold.

Howard Carter

This most famous of Egyptian tombs is neither large nor impressively decorated. It bears all the marks of hasty burial following the early death of Tutankhamun while in his late teens. Even its fabulous contents, seen by millions of people around the world, cannot have compared to the funerary treasures of far greater pharaohs entombed in the valley. The relative lack of importance of a briefly reigning pharaoh caught up in the Amun priesthood's counter-revolution probably assisted in the long secrecy of the tomb's existence and where-abouts. Also, nearly above it was the entrance to the grander tomb of Ramses VI (Tomb 9), the debris from which early on covered the entrance to the young pharaoh's tomb.

Discovery and Curse

The tomb was discovered on 4 November 1922 by Howard Carter and opened by him and his patron Lord Carnarvon on 26 November. In *The Tomb of Tutankhamen* (his spelling), Carter described his famous landfall on that ancient world: 'At first I could see nothing, the hot air escaping from the chamber causing the candle flames to flicker, but presently, as my eyes grew accustomed to the light, details of the room within emerged slowly from the mist, strange animals, statues and gold—everywhere the glint of gold. For the moment—an eternity it must have seemed to the others standing by—I was struck dumb with amazement, and when Lord Carnarvon, unable to stand the suspense any longer, enquired anxiously, "Can you see anything?" it was all I could do to get out the words, "Yes, wonderful things."'

The popular fantasy of 'the curse of Tutankhamun' began the following April when Carnarvon died of septicaemia caused by an insect bite. The origins of the curse lay not in the tomb, however, but in newspaper offices around the world. Carnarvon had granted *The Times* exclusive coverage of the tomb story, including photographs, leaving other newspapers resentful and empty-handed. As newspapers will, they simply invented a story of their own, and despite the fact that even 10 years later only one of the five people present at the tomb's opening, and only two of the 22 who witnessed the opening of the sarcophagus, had died, the story ran and ran. Whenever he was asked about the 'curse', Carter's own irritable reply was 'tommy-rot'.

The autopsy performed on Tutankhamun in 1926 showed a young man, no more than 19 years of age, who had suffered a cheek wound—in the same place, as it happens, where Carnarvon suffered his insect bite. But the likely cause of death did not become clear until his torso was X-rayed for the first time, in 1968, showing that his chest had been crushed. One suggestion was that Tutankhamun might have fallen from his hunting chariot and got caught up by his reins beneath its wheels. No mystery surrounds Carter's death at 65 of Hodgkin's disease and cardiac failure. He lies obscurely in grave 45, block 12, of Putney Vale Cemetery, London. His headstone reads simply: 'Howard Carter, Archaeologist and Egyptologist, born May 9, 1874, died March 2, 1939.'

The Chambers and Tomb

The door at the bottom of the entrance stairway A was found walled up and sealed with the royal seal. The entrance corridor B was found filled with stone debris through which a tunnel had been dug soon after interment in an unsuccessful attempt to rob the tomb. The undecorated Chambers C, D (now walled up) and F contained most of the funerary objects now on display at the Cairo Museum. Chamber E, originally walled off from C and at a lower level, contained the four gilded wooden shrines, one inside the other, within which lay the rectangular stone sarcophagus, then three mummiform coffins, the innermost of solid gold, and then finally the mummy of Tutankhamun himself. The wall has now been replaced by a railing beyond which visitors cannot venture.

From here you can view what remains in the tomb. The sarcophagus turned out to be a second-hand retread: a 1993 study revealed that it had been intended for Tutankhamun's predecessor, Smenkhkere—the wings of the figures at the four corners were carved later to obscure the original inscriptions. The largest of the mummiform coffins within the sarcophagus remains, and, unseen within that, the mummy of Tutankhamun. (Minus, as it happens, his penis—photographs taken in 1926, before the body was reinterred, show it *in situ*, but when the remains of Tutankhamun were examined again in 1968 the penis was missing, perhaps having found its way onto somebody's mantelpiece.) This chamber was the only

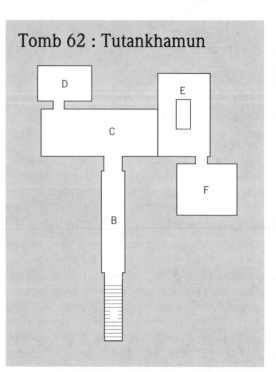

Tomb 62 : Tutankhamun

one decorated, its paintings betraying signs of haste. (The paintings have been suffering damage, perhaps from visitors' humid exhalations.) On the right wall, the coffin is transported on a sledge. To the rear from right to left, Ay, the young king's successor, performs the rite of the opening of the mouth (note a suggestion of the Amarna style); Tutankhamun sacrifices to Nut; the young pharaoh, this time with his ka, comes before Osiris. On the left wall is the sun god's boat, while on the all-but-impossible-to-see entrance wall Tutankhamun, accompanied by Anubis and Isis, receives life from the goddess of the west.

The Plight of Tut's Widow

Perhaps among the last people to have left this tomb before Carter entered it 3,300 years later was Tutankhamun's young widow, Ankhesenamun, and to her attaches a romantic tale. Like her husband, she had only recently changed her name—he from Tutankhaton, she from Ankhesenpaaton, as both had been raised at Amarna during the Aton cult of Akhenaton (indeed she was Akhenaton's daughter by Nefertiti and he may have been Akhenaton's son by a lesser wife). The story, as Carter unfolds it, goes that Ankhesenamun found herself faced with the political ambitions and, possibly, the nuptial intentions of her grandfather Ay, retainer to her late husband and power behind the throne. 'I have no son, and my husband is dead,' Ankhesenamun is said to have written to the Hittite king. 'Send me a son of yours and I will make him king.' In reply, Suppiluliumas, far off in the Hittite capital of Hattuşaş, east of present-day Ankara in Turkey, sent one of his sons to be Ankhesenamun's husband and rule as pharaoh. But, as a later Hittite text tells us, 'they killed him as they were conducting him to Egypt', while Ay, beneficiary of two deaths, hastily installed Tutankhamun in this small tomb. As Horus buried Osiris, so he who buried the pharaoh became pharaoh in turn, though whether Ay also married his own granddaughter is disputed by scholars.

A different scenario is put forward by some scholars, who say that the letter-writer was not Tutankhamun's widow but Nefertiti after Akhenaton's death, and that the villain of the piece was Smenkhkere—although yet other scholars say Smenkhkere may have been none other than Nefertiti herself, making an attempt to rule in masculine guise after her husband's death, as had Hatshepsut. Possibly it is better just to stick to reading Agatha Christie.

At any rate, *somebody* wrote a letter to Suppiluliumas, whose son was killed on his way to Egypt—and that in itself is one of those fascinating might-have-beens of history. For instead of an alliance between the two superpowers of the day, the murder of the Hittite prince contributed to nearly a century of enmity that encompassed the later battle of Kadesh fought between Ramses II and Suppiluliumas' grandson Muwatallis and found its reconciliation only in the marriage of Ramses II to a Hittite princess.

Surprise Discovery of Massive Tomb for Ramses II's Sons

Recent archaeological work at Tomb 5 shows that surprises may still lie in store at the Valley of the Kings. The entrance to the tomb was discovered in the 19th century, but inquisitive Egyptologists, including Howard Carter early in the 20th century, were prevented by flood-borne debris from exploring more than the front three chambers—what lay beyond was entirely unknown.

Then in 1995 a team from the American University in Cairo penetrated beyond the debris, finding a T-shaped arrangement of galleries. The stem of the T is a corridor leading past 20 chambers to a statue of Osiris from where the arms of the T are lined with more chambers, each arm ending at stairs that perhaps lead to yet further rooms. In all, 67 chambers have now been discovered, making this the biggest rock-cut tomb ever found in Egypt.

Tomb 5 was looted in ancient times, but the various finds, including fragments of sarcophagi and mummies, inscribed stone vessels, pottery and jewellery, prove that this was the burial place for many of Ramses II's sons. Fifty-two of his sons are known by name (he had over 100, and another hundred or so daughters, variously by his chief queen Nefertari, his associate chief queen Istnofret, and an extensive harem) but the burial places of only three sons have been identified: Tomb 8 in the Valley of the Kings is that of Merneptah, his son by Istnofret and his ultimate successor; a chamber in Tomb 5 is where Amen-hir-khopshef, Ramses' first-born son by Nefertari and intended heir, was interred; and a tomb thought to be that of Khaemwas was found in 1993 at Saqqara. It is now thought that Ramses' remaining 49 sons may also have been buried in Tomb 5.

Egyptologists have been taken aback by this unexpected discovery and are now asking themselves what else lies hidden within the tomb and indeed elsewhere in the Valley of the Kings.

You can leave the Valley of the Kings by the road you came, that same ancient road along which the bodies of the pharaohs were drawn here on sledges. Or you can leave on foot, climbing the path to the right of Tomb 16, opposite the resthouse. As it gains the ridge, there is usually a donkey boy waiting but the donkeys should be declined. Almost certainly, a guide will fasten himself on you in hope of baksheesh. He can be useful for those who are not footsure, but otherwise he is not necessary. On the ridge, the path divides. One heads south, rising slowly over the mountain; the other runs to the left, level along the ridge. The first leads to Deir el Medina and is the same path the workmen used when returning home from their shift at the tombs. There are sweeping views of the Nile valley, magnificent in the afternoon with the sun in the west. The second path soon creeps high along the edge of the amphitheatre of Deir el Bahri and offers changing angles and elevations of Hatshepsut's temple, and views towards the Nile. You continue along round the north flank of Deir el Bahri and then pick your way down, to be met by your driver after visiting the temple. Both walks are highly recommended, but the second (about 30 minutes) is a must for a full appreciation of Hatshepsut's architectural achievement.

Hatshepsut's Mortuary Temple

The Mortuary Temple of Hatshepsut at Deir el Bahri is the finest building in Egypt. Elegant, revolutionary, it satisfies and provokes in whole and in detail. Along with the Parthenon, the Taj Mahal, the interiors of Chartres and Hagia Sophia, it is one of the great buildings of the world. Not that the temple has received its fullest due: though far older than the others, it was unknown in modern times until Mariette made preliminary excavations in the third quarter of the 19th century. The temple was only entirely cleared in 1894–6 and since then has undergone sporadic restoration, still in progress today.

Hatshepsut's Reign

Interpretation of the events following the death of Tuthmosis I (XVIII Dynasty) is marked by controversy among archaeologists which mimics, even if it does not rival, the original dynastic struggle played out between Hatshepsut, his daughter, and Tuthmosis III, his grandson. By any interpretation, Hatshepsut emerges as one of the most formidable figures in Egyptian history, only the third woman to rule as queen, the first to rule as king. In the ruthlessness and romance the story implies, and the high policy at stake, parallels between the reigns of Hatshepsut and Elizabeth I easily suggest themselves to the imagination.

Hatshepsut married her father's son and successor, Tuthmosis II, and during the lifetime of her husband her full titles were 'pharaoh's daughter, pharaoh's sister, god's wife and pharaoh's great wife'. But Tuthmosis II died before Hatshepsut could bear him a child, and it was one of her husband's secondary wives who became 'pharaoh's mother' to Tuthmosis III. But for her gender, Hatshepsut's claim to the throne through her father was at least as good as Tuthmosis III's and through her mother she was descended from the Ahmose family who had thrown the Hyksos out of Egypt. But, as Tuthmosis was later to advertise, his future as pharaoh was proclaimed by no less a god than Amun who, while Tuthmosis I was sacrificing at Karnak, stood the young prince in the place usually occupied by the sovereign. This conveniently has Tuthmosis III designated heir in the lifetime of his own father, but betrays the more pedestrian likelihood that the priests of Amun eventually sided with the army in its support of Tuthmosis and his imperial designs against Hatshepsut and her party in the civil service who preferred a peaceful domestic policy.

Tuthmosis III, when finally he became sole pharaoh well into his manhood, launched Egypt upon her period of conquest abroad and bloated magnificence at home, so often celebrated in stone at Thebes. Yet, as powerful a pharaoh and warrior as he was to become, Tuthmosis was no match for Hatshepsut in her prime. In the first few years following her husband's death, Hatshepsut reigned as widow-queen, but she soon took the momentous step of assuming the title of pharaoh, co-reigning with but entirely overshadowing her stepson. She went so far as to pose and dress as a man—at least on reliefs—and to wear the pharaonic beard. In this way she ruled for about 20 years.

Elizabeth I had her Essex; Hatshepsut had her **Senmut**, a man of modest birth who rose to occupy a score of high offices, including steward of Amun, probably giving him control over the vast wealth of the Karnak temple, and minister of public works, with the suggestion that he was the architect at Deir el Bahri. As such favourites often do, Senmut overstepped the mark. He used his royal mistress's temple for his own purposes, introducing reliefs of himself in niches that would be concealed behind opening doors and, though he built himself a tomb at Gurna, planned secretly to be buried within the great court at Deir el Bahri. Most of his reliefs were hacked out and his sarcophagus smashed, yet in his secret tomb the name of Hatshepsut was left untouched, suggesting the destruction was wrought not by Tuthmosis III, who in malice destroyed so much that was Hatshepsut's, but by Hatshepsut herself in rage at this attempt to extend familiarity into the eternal. The last record of Senmut comes from about five years before the end of his mistress's reign. In those last years she was alone.

How Hatshepsut's reign ended is not known. Perhaps she fell victim to a coup d'état, or merely died a natural death. In any case her inward-looking peace policy was suddenly eclipsed and Tuthmosis III, obliterating her name and her image wherever he found them, within 75 days of her death was leading his army into Palestine (*see* p.212).

The Conception of Hatshepsut's Temple

Into the rugged eastern flank of the Theban Mountain nature has cut an immense amphitheatre facing Thebes. Its sheer golden walls embrace the site like the wings of some mighty hovering solar disc. Just off centre, to the left and rising from the cliffline, is a pyramidal peak. A magnificent backdrop, it invites a performance, and would condemn any but the most brilliant to insignificance before it. The Middle Kingdom pharaoh Mentuhotep II (XI Dynasty) built a temple here; you can see its ruins to the south of Hatshepsut's. What impression it made cannot fairly be judged from its remains. Like Hatshepsut's temple, it rose in terraces but then was surmounted by a pyramid, a Memphite legacy perhaps. Mentuhotep II and III were both entombed here. But a pyramidal structure set against the pyramidal peak seems superfluous, and any structure vying with the cliffs for height can only have been overwhelmed.

Mentuhotep's temple was already in ruins when 500 years later Hatshepsut was drawn to the holy site. (Whether out of convenience or some similar feeling of awe, Hatshepsut's temple was taken over by early Christians as a monastery and called Deir el Bahri, the Northern Monastery.) She was obviously influenced by the earlier temple, and in all probability would have replicated it on a larger scale: the foundations suggest a pyramid was intended. One purpose of a pyramid is to protect the tomb, but her father Tuthmosis I had abandoned this idea for the greater security of discreet entombment in the Valley of the Kings. It remained necessary therefore to build only a mortuary temple at which the appropriate ceremonies would be performed. At some point Hatshepsut decided to build wide instead of high.

If it is true that circumstances dictated this decision, or suggested that the alternative was now pointless, it is no less true that the new form was seized upon with conviction and executed with genius. The terraces of Hatshepsut's temple emphasize the stratification of the cliff behind and the line between rock and sky. At the same time, the bold rhythm of the pillared colonnades, vertical shafts of light-reflecting stone framing and contrasting with the shadowed ambulatories, reflect the dark gashes of gullies and fissures in the cliff face itself. Even the peak seems brought into the conception: a pyramid offered by nature. The temple mediates between the wildness of the mountain and the cultivation of the valley. The power and contradiction of the landscape is gripped and tamed with a confidence and elegance that is breathtaking, and then played throughout the structure so that as you walk round the temple you feel it, never too much, but to a measure that insists on the spiritual nature of man.

A Tour of Hatshepsut's Temple

The Lower Terrace

The main temple complex may originally have been preceded by a valley temple near the Nile; if so, it has been lost beneath the tilled alluvium. From this temple ran a promenade lined with sphinxes to the Lower Terrace, a zone of transition between the profane and the sacred. This was a garden with myrrh trees and fountains, as though a foretaste of that life which endures in the desert of the other world. (The stumps of some trees are visible on the Lower and Middle Terraces.) A pair of lions (the left-hand one survives) stood at the bottom of the ramp leading up to the Middle Terrace and another pair (the right-hand one survives) stood at the top. These were at once guardians of the temple and witnesses to the rising sun, proof of rebirth. Colonnades are on either side of the ramp, to the north and to the south. On their pillars are simple devices stating a variation of Hatshepsut's name surmounted by the solar falcon wearing the double crown. Within the colonnades, the retaining walls of the Middle Terrace are decorated with vividly coloured reliefs.

Not all of the original courses have survived and, where they have, the decorations have suffered deliberate defacement, first by Tuthmosis III, later by Akhenaton. Representations of Amun were restored at the counter-revolution, but Hatshepsut remains obliterated; the pharaoh seen is Tuthmosis III, who, as co-ruler, had been included in the original decorations. The carvings within the North Colonnade depict an idealized country life,

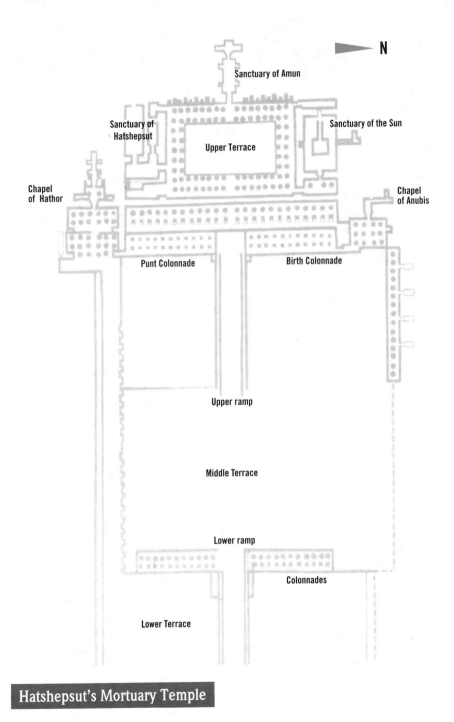

Hatshepsut's Mortuary Temple

continuing the theme established by the gardens of the Lower Terrace. Of the greatest delicacy are the scenes (right) of water birds being caught in nets. The reliefs within the South Colonnade depict the transport down the Nile of two obelisks cut at Aswan at Hatshepsut's order. At the far ends of the colonnades stood large Osiris statues of Hatshepsut (the north one imperfectly restored).

The Middle Terrace

The lower ramp leads up to the Middle Terrace. At its centre rises a second ramp to the Upper Terrace. Again, at the rear of the Middle Terrace and on either side of the second ramp are colonnades and at their furthest ends, pressing against the rock of the cliff face, are the chapels of Anubis (north) and Hathor (south). Along the north side of the terrace is an unfinished colonnade.

The north and south colonnades of the Middle Terrace have double rows of square pillars, simple but well-proportioned and achieving a modest grace. On the walls of the **Birth Colonnade** (north) are reliefs depicting Hatshepsut's divine parentage: Amun has assumed the form of her father who sits facing Ahmosis, her mother, on a couch. The couple gaze at one another, their knees touching in a scene at once conventional and reserved and yet sensitively conveying their ardour. Queen Ahmosis is led to the birth chamber, accompanied by strange deities, a smile of suffering and delight playing on her lips. The child, conventionally shown as a boy, is fashioned by Khnum on his potter's wheel, as is its ka. Just as Tuthmosis III justified his claim to the throne with the story of Amun's selection of him at the Temple of Karnak, so these reliefs serve the same purpose for Hatshepsut. Not that we should think that either pharaoh was simply cynical; overriding the political propaganda was probably a sincere belief in their divine birth, and these reliefs' delicacy and feeling suggest that this belief was honestly integrated in Hatshepsut's character, sustaining her in her rule. On the lateral faces of the pillars, Tuthmosis is shown with Amun; on front and back it is Hatshepsut (defaced) with Amun.

The façade of the **chapel of Anubis** continues the line of the colonnade, but with columns (fluted, with simple capitals, like Doric columns). From a distance, the columns are indistinguishable from the pillars, but stand in the northwest corner of the terrace and look along the façades towards the ramp: that almost unnoticed variation creates a subtle yet entirely harmonious contrast. There is a touch of Greece here, and in the discreet widening of the distance between the central columns as if inviting the visitor into the sanctuary within. The walls of the hall are brilliantly coloured and show the co-rulers (Hatshepsut hacked out), Anubis, protector of the dead, and, facing each other at either end, the falcon-headed sun god (north wall) and his wife Hathor (south wall). Cut into the rock in a series of right angles are several chambers with vaulted roofs of brick, though lacking the wedge-shaped keystones of true weight-bearing vaults which do not appear in Egypt until the 8th century BC (and which were not universalized until taken up by the Romans).

On the south side of the ramp is the **Punt Colonnade**, named after the decorations on its rear wall of the expedition to the land of Punt (probably the coastal region of the modern Somali Republic) instigated by Hatshepsut. Amun had told her: 'It is a glorious region of god's land, it is indeed my place of delight; I have made it for myself in order to divert my heart.' Hatshepsut's ancestors had often sent expeditions there to procure the precious myrrh necessary for the incense in temple services, but now, as she recorded, Amun desired her 'to establish a Punt in his house'. So the purpose of the expedition was to obtain for the first time living myrrh trees and to plant the terraces of this temple dedicated to Amun with them.

The walls illustrate and relate the story. After presumably crossing the desert to a Red Sea port, the expedition sailed southwards in five ships. The Egyptians are shown being greeted on the shore by the chief of Punt and his extraordinarily corpulent wife—a rare instance of humorous caricature, the rolls of fat from her body reaching right down to her ankles. In exchange for gifts, the beached ships are laden 'very heavily with marvels of the country of Punt; all goodly fragrant woods of god's land, heaps of myrrh resin, of fresh myrrh trees, with ebony and pure ivory, with green gold of Emu, with cinnamon wood, with incense, eye cosmetic, with baboons, monkeys, dogs, with skins of the southern panther, with natives and their children. Never was the like of this brought for any pharaoh who has been since the beginning.' Back at Thebes, Tuthmosis III and Hatshepsut are shown offering incense to Amun's sacred boat, his offering paltry compared to hers. Tuthmosis' portrait, however, is beautifully carved, his individuality realized in a way lacking in the idealized representations on the pillars. He had Hatshepsut defaced here too.

At the far south end of the colonnade it is the **chapel of Hathor** that continues the façade. This time there are pillars, not columns; they differ from the rest in having the cow-eared head of Hathor serve laterally as capitals, unnoticeable from any distance. Beyond the pillared chambers, the second decorated with a procession of boats along the Nile, is the **sanctuary of Hathor** with a vaulted roof. After all the hacking out of Hatshepsut's figure you yearn to see one intact and here, in the furthest recess of the sanctuary, that desire is satisfied. Either because the room was sealed or because at least here in Hathor's sanctuary Tuthmosis respected Hatshepsut's right to some modest remembrance, she survives, albeit in stylized and masculine form. She meets Amun, she suckles regenerating milk from Hathor, and above a recess in the left wall she and Tuthmosis III are shown kneeling, she to the left with an offering of milk, he to the right with wine. Also within this chamber, in a little alcove on the right and towards the floor, is a portrait of Senmut, Hatshepsut's favourite.

The Upper Terrace

The second ramp leads to the Upper Terrace, badly ruined and currently being restored (it may be closed). A portico of Osiris pillars stood a short distance from the edge; their restoration is well under way. On what remains of the rear wall are reliefs of boats accompanied along the Nile banks by a festive procession of soldiers, and of the Festival of the Valley during which Amun visited the necropolis.

Passing through the last wall against the cliffs is a granite doorway leading into the **sanctuary of Amun** hewn out of the rock. The walls are decorated as elsewhere in the temple but are blackened with smoke. In Ptolemaic times the sanctuary was cut deeper and was dedicated to the healing cults of Imhotep, counsellor to Zoser, and Amenhotep, son of Hapu, counsellor to Amenophis III.

At the left (south) end of the Upper Terrace is the **sanctuary of Hatshepsut**. The reliefs are of high quality and show processions of priests and offering-bearers. At the right (north) end of the terrace is the **sanctuary of the Sun**, an open court with an altar in the centre. A flight of steps on its west side permitted a priest to mount the altar, gaining a magnificent view of the valley and river below and the rugged horizon to the east, to await the rising of the sun.

The Noble Tombs

Over 400 private tombs have been discovered at the Theban necropolis, dating from the Old Kingdom to the Ptolemaic period. These include the workmen's tombs at Deir el Medina (*see* p.248), and the tombs of the nobles (in fact nobles, priests and officials) found in clusters from near the Temple of Seti I at the north end of the necropolis to Medinet Habu at the south end. The noble tombs are interesting because they often give a vivid picture of contemporary life instead of the impersonal ritual decorations of the royal tombs. The artists have been more free to express themselves and the sensitivity of their work has been greater. The limestone on this side of the mountain is of poor quality, generally not suited to cutting reliefs; usually the decorations are paintings on stucco walls of white, grey or yellow ground. The tombs are, strictly, mortuary chapels; a filled-in shaft led to a deeper chamber containing the sarcophagus.

Seven of the most outstanding tombs of the nobles are described here, all XVIII Dynasty, all near the old village of **Gurna** (Sheikh Abd el-Gurna). They are signposted from the Ramesseum and fall into three groups (*ticket for each group*): Rekhmire (100) and Sennufer (96); Menna (69) and Nakht (52); and Ramose (55), Userhat (56) and Khaemhat (57).

To visit all seven tombs would take two hours or so. For a good sample of differing types of tomb, you should visit **Rekhmire** (100), **Sennufer** (96), **Nakht** (52) and **Ramose** (55).

Tomb 100: Rekhmire

Rekhmire was vizier under Tuthmosis III and Amenophis II, and the decorations therefore concentrate on foreign policy, and matters of justice and taxation. The tomb is cruciform, i.e. a transverse chamber extending far to left and right, and a long corridor leading straight ahead, its ceiling steadily rising to 5.5m at the far end where there is a false door.

In the **left arm of transverse chamber**, on the far left wall, Rekhmire is shown being installed as vizier; on the far right wall tribute is brought to Egypt. This is delightful: from the top register the tribute is shown from Punt, Crete and the Aegean, Nubia, Syria and Cush (on the western shore of the Red Sea), including a wonderful procession of African beasts, among them a giraffe, and precious goods, including elephants' tusks.

In the **right arm of transverse chamber**: on the left wall there are scenes of hunting, fowling and the treading of grapes; on the near right wall are shown taxes and offerings; on the far wall are Rekhmire's ancestors.

On the near left of the **corridor** Rekhmire is shown inspecting the workshops of Amun; centre left, the voyage to Abydos (*see* pp.272–5); right wall, the afterworld, with trees and lake, and a funerary feast.

Tomb 96: Sennufer

Up the hill from Rekhmire's tomb. **Sennufer** was mayor of Thebes and overseer of the gardens of Amun during the reign of Amenophis II. It is likely that he was also chief vintner, and you wonder whether his tomb is not his last laugh on that theme. You go down steep steps to an antechamber, the highly irregular surface of its ceiling seeming to give deliberate relief to a painted arbour with vines and grapes. But when you step into the chamber beyond, you see that everything—ceiling, walls, pillars—wobbles before your eyes as though you were drunk. It is possible that the rock here was difficult to cut. It is also possible that Sennufer said what the hell. In either case the effect is extremely pleasing. The walls in both chambers are painted with religious scenes, Sennufer repeatedly depicted with his daughter, his sister and his wife.

Tomb 69: Menna

This and 52 are across the road from one another. **Menna** was an estate inspector under a mid-XVIII Dynasty pharaoh, and so the decorations emphasize country life. The paintings are finely executed and excellently preserved. In the **entrance passage**, Menna, his wife and daughter are shown worshipping the sun. In the left wing of the **first chamber** are a variety of rural scenes, while the right wing depicts various ceremonies, with the dead man and his wife receiving offerings, Anubis facing Osiris, Re and Hathor. A lively hunting and fishing scene occupies the centre of the right-hand wall of the **second chamber**, though generally mourning and burial scenes are depicted.

Tomb 52: Nakht

Across the road from 69. **Nakht** was a scribe and astronomer of Amun in the middle of the XVIII Dynasty. A short passage leads to a transverse **first chamber**, the only decorated part of the tomb. The paintings are well preserved and brilliantly coloured, and like those of Menna depict country life: the supervising of field labours by Nakht; the deceased and his wife banqueting and making offerings. Nakht is frequently defaced, his eyes gouged, even the upper part of his body destroyed; also the name of Amun is everywhere obliterated—acts committed, presumably, during Akhenaton's reign. The chamber beyond, as was the custom, contained a statue of the dead man with his wife: it was shipped to America but the boat sank. A shaft here runs down to the sarcophagus chamber.

Tomb 55

To the south of 69 and 52; to the east of 100. A relatively grandiose structure with wall carvings, the unfinished tomb of **Ramose** is one of the most fascinating in the necropolis. Ramose was governor of Thebes and vizier in the early years of Amenophis IV's reign and took pains to honour himself with two hypostyle chambers (only the first is open) decorated in the most exquisite classical Egyptian style.

From an open court you enter the **first chamber** and follow the decorations from the near wall of the right wing: classical reliefs show Ramose and his wife in several offering ceremonies. These scenes are continued along the near wall of the left wing. The groups of seated figures are friends or relatives of the dead man. Continuing clockwise, the south wall

Noble Tomb 55 : Ramose

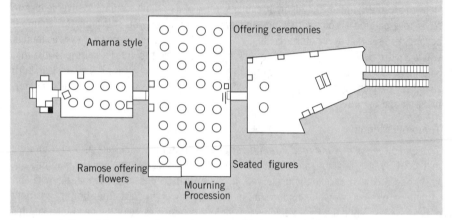

Amarna style

Offering ceremonies

Ramose offering flowers

Mourning Procession

Seated figures

bears a painting of the procession to the tomb with bearers of offerings, mourning women and priests; to the right, the dead man and his wife worshipping Osiris; and below, four representations of the dead man before his tomb. The west wall in the left wing resumes the reliefs and shows Ramose four times offering flowers to Amenophis IV seated under a canopy with the goddess Maat. At the very south (left) end of this wall you can see that prior to cutting the relief the figures were drawn in black outline over a red grid, suggesting the usual artist's concern to transfer the scene in the same detail and proportions as it appeared on the (perhaps smaller) original sketch.

Passing across the closed entrance to the second chamber you come to the north end of the west wall where suddenly the style changes from the classical to the Amarnan. The explana-tion is that while Ramose was working on his tomb Amenophis IV had become Akhenaton, introducing both Aton and a new art. Ramose never did finish his tomb here because he followed Akhenaton to Amarna. This wall shows Akhenaton and Nefertiti at their palace window under the rays of Aton, receiving homage from Ramose. In sketch form you can see Ramose receiving a decoration (a gold collar, as at Ay's tomb at Amarna) and acclaimed by courtiers and representatives from Nubia, Libya and Asia, and also Ramose receiving bouquets in the temple. It is interesting to compare these new-style portraits of Ramose to his classical portrait at the north side of the east wall. Significantly, not only are Akhenaton and Nefertiti depicted with elongated heads, but now so is Ramose (though not quite so much)— in some measure countering the argument that Akhenaton and his family were portrayed in this way because they were afflicted by some deforming disease or gene.

Tomb 56: Userhat

Immediately south of Ramose's tomb. **Userhat** was a royal scribe and tutor during the reign of Amenophis II. The walls and ceiling are finely painted, and there are some interesting scenes of barbers cutting hair and of Userhat hunting gazelle from a chariot, and fowling and fishing in the marshes. The tomb was later used by Coptic hermits who here and there added their own curious creatures and crosses.

Tomb 57: Khaemhat

Adjacent to 56. **Khaemhat** was a royal scribe and inspector of granaries in Upper and Lower Egypt under Amenophis III. His is another carved tomb, as fine and even firmer in style than that of Ramose. In the entrance court, to the right of the doorway, are reliefs showing the complete set of instruments employed in the Opening of the Mouth ceremony, while to the left is Khaemhat adoring Re. The first chamber presents scenes of country life and, particularly, aspects of Khaemhat's official life: unloading of boats, an amusing market scene, cattle herds, the harvest. The second chamber shows the funeral procession and ceremonies in honour of Osiris. The chapel beyond contains several statues with finely modelled heads; in the left wing, on the right-hand wall, the dead man in the act of worship; in the right wing, on the right-hand wall, the cast of a portrait of Khaemhat.

A coffin was traditionally carried through a banquet, giving the lie to an unending feast of life. Macabre though it might seem to us, to the Egyptians it must have carried with it some promise against time: 'You live again, you live again for ever, here you are young once more for ever'—the final benediction of the priests as the desiccated mummies of these titled dead were interred in their tombs.

The Ramesseum

The Ramesseum, the mortuary temple of Ramses II, is part of a still larger rectangular complex enclosed by its original brick wall. The area was filled with vaulted brick storehouses, now entirely ruined, which were once invaded, as is known from an extant papyrus, by desperate tomb workers who had not been paid for two months: 'We have reached this place because of hunger, because of thirst, without clothing, without oil, without fish, without vegetables! Tell pharaoh, our good lord, about it, and tell the vizier, our superior. Act so that we may live!' So that the great Ramses should live for ever this grandiose temple was built, and enough of its stones remain piled atop one another to remind us of *his* hunger.

The 1st century BC Greek historian Diodorus was impressed. Coming upon the granite colossus of Ramses he fancifully interpreted its inscription, corrupting the pharaoh's praenomen, User-maat-Re, as he went: 'I am Ozymandias, king of kings. If any would know how great I am, and where I lie, let him excel me in any of my works.' To which Shelley offered time's reply:

> *I met a traveller from an antique land*
> *Who said: Two vast and trunkless legs of stone*
> *Stand in the desert. Near them, on the sand,*
> *Half sunk, a shattered visage lies, whose frown,*
> *And wrinkled lip and sneer of cold command,*
> *Tell that its sculptor well those passions read*
> *Which yet survive, stamped on these lifeless things,*
> *The hand that mocked them, and the heart that fed;*

And on the pedestal these words appear:
'My name is Ozymandias, king of kings:
Look on my works, ye Mighty, and despair!'
Nothing beside remains. Round the decay
Of that colossal wreck, boundless and bare,
The lone and level sands stretch far away.

Pylons and Courts

You approach the temple at its north flank, so to reach the **First Pylon**, measuring 67m across, you must turn left through the ruined First Court. The outer wall of the pylon is as intelligible as a quarry face, but on the pylon wall facing the court there are excellently carved reliefs, albeit of Ramses' all too familiar exploits against the Hittites (*see* p.198). It is possible to enter the First Pylon from the north: an ascending passage emerges at the top amid a heap of fallen stones, and by clambering over these (it is best to have someone with you for assistance) you can gain a towering view over the First Court. A double colonnade on the south side of the court formed the façade of the royal palace, of which little remains. A colonnade of Osiris pillars runs along the north side of the court, their folded arms a reminder of Ramses' mummy in the Egyptian Museum at Cairo, where he seem to be uncrossing his arms as though reaching out to life. At the far (west) end a flight of steps leads to the Second Court; on the left, as you ascend, is the fallen **Ozymandias**. Weighing more than 900,000kg and once standing at 17.5m, this was one of the largest free-standing statues in Egypt, surpassed by the Colossi of Memnon only by virtue of their pedestals. The index finger alone is 1m long. A nearby stand of trees gives the spot an Arcadian touch, and it is pleasant to linger here, though the trees may soon be cut down as their roots are said to be causing structural damage.

The Ramesseum as depicted in Description de l'Egypte 1809–28

The inner surface of the north tower of the **Second Pylon** is decorated, again, with the Battle of Kadesh, though the top register more peacefully portrays the festival of the harvest god Min. The front and back of the **Second Court** is lined with Osiris pillars, and where three stairways rise to the west portico, another granite colossus, not quite so large as the first, lies in fragments, the head in good condition with only the nose smashed. On a nearby throne, next to the name of Ramses, Belzoni carved his name. An Italian artist and one-time seminarian, in the early years of the 19th century Belzoni appeared on the stage of Sadler's Wells and elsewhere in England with his famous human-pyramid act, 'bearing on his colossal frame, not fewer, if we mistake not, than 20 or 22 persons'. He later turned serious explorer and succeeded in removing from the Ramesseum the giant bust of Ramses II now in the British Museum.

The Portico and Great Hypostyle Hall

On the rear wall of the **portico** (reached by stairways at the rear of the Second Court) between the central and left-hand doorways, are three rows of reliefs. The bottom register shows 11 of Ramses' sons; the middle shows Ramses with Atum (a Heliopolitan sun god) and falcon-headed Mont who holds the hieroglyph for 'life' to the pharaoh's nose, while to the right Ramses kneels before the Theban triad and Thoth inscribes the pharaoh's name on a palm branch; the top shows Ramses sacrificing to Ptah, and to the right offering incense to an ithyphallic Min. Against the outside north wall of the portico and the Great Hypostyle Hall are the scant remains of an earlier temple of Seti I, its alignment probably accounting for the overall alignment of the Ramesseum which accordingly skews to the south instead of fitting squarely within the rectangular walls of the complex.

The **Great Hypostyle Hall** had 48 columns, of which only 29 still stand. It was similar to the one at Karnak (to which Ramses II made a major contribution), a higher ceiling over the central aisle allowing illumination through windows set upon the architraves of the adjoining row of shorter columns. The First Small Hypostyle Hall of eight papyrus bud columns still retains its ceiling, decorated with astronomical signs. Only four out of eight columns survive in the Second Small Hypostyle Hall, while of the shrine beyond nothing remains.

Here, as elsewhere beneath the glaring sun of Egypt, the columns, the reliefs, the sculptures are streaked with white. Ramses boasted and Shelley cut him down to size; and Flaubert dispassionately observed: 'Birdshit is Nature's protest in Egypt; she decorates monuments with it instead of with lichen or moss.'

The Workmen's Village at Deir el Medina

From the Valley of the Kings a mountain path leads down to Deir el Bahri, or if you continue along the crest southwards it brings you to the village of the ancient tomb workers, Deir el Medina. This is more usually reached by road, travelling 700m or so west from the Ramesseum. There are rows of humble **houses**, 70 in all, mud brick walls rising on stone foundations along straight and narrow alleys. They had a second storey or at least a living area on the roof, reached by stairs. Some have simple wall decorations inside.

The men who worked at the Valley of the Kings (which they called the Place of Truth) were not mere labourers but artisans and freemen whose food was delivered to the village by serfs, and whose houses were swept by slaves. They fashioned their own **tombs**, and decorated them not so much with scenes of the everyday as did the nobles but with the afterlife, borrowing from their experience in the pharaonic tombs. Over their tomb entrance they would construct a man-size pyramid.

Several of the tombs, which like the village date from the XVIII to XX Dynasties, can be visited. A favourite is **Tomb 1 of Sennedjem** (contents in Cairo's Egyptian Museum), a vaulted chamber down steep steps, with reliefs and paintings on religious themes, including a fine funeral feast and, in the passage that opens onto the final chamber, a nicely observed cameo of a cat killing a snake under the sacred tree. Also worth visiting is **Tomb 3 of Peshedu** (in the burial chamber note Peshedu praying beneath the tree of regeneration) and **Tomb 217 of Ipy** (unusual for its scenes of everyday life).

Deir el Medina means the monastery of the town, for the workmen's village and the small **Ptolemaic temple** just north of it were occupied by monks during the early years of Christianity. Dedicated to Maat and to Hathor whose head adorns the pillars between the outer court and pronaos, this elegant temple is worth a look if you have the time, though there are other, more considerable, Ptolemaic temples at Edfu, Kom Ombo and beyond Aswan at Philae.

The Valley of the Queens

Beyond, in the Valley of the Queens, Biban el Harem, there are over 70 tombs of queens, princes and princesses, some from the XVIII Dynasty though mostly from XIX and XX. These dead, however, were not gods and so their tombs were not built on the same scale as those of the pharaohs. Nor did the friable limestone at this end of the Theban Mountain permit much carved decoration; the tombs are more often only painted, though many were left unfinished and have merely the appearance of caves. An exception is the recently opened tomb of Nefertari (*see* below).

Tombs 43, 44 and 55 belong to sons of Ramses III. A smallpox epidemic towards the end of Ramses' reign killed several of his sons, and in **Tomb 55 of Prince Amun-herkhopshef** in the hall at the bottom of the entrance steps it falls to the father to introduce his son to the gods. The sarcophagus chamber at the end of the corridor contains a mummiform sarcophagus and, in the far right corner, in a glass case, a six-month-old foetus. It is perhaps the latter that makes this tomb so popular, though its real interest is the well-preserved colours of the paintings, and you can have the benefit of this with fewer tour groups getting in the way by visiting **Tomb 44 of Prince Khaemweset. Tomb 52 of Queen Titi**, wife of one of the Ramessid pharaohs, is one of the few queens' tombs that can be visited without special permission, but the rooms are small and low, and the painting faded.

The outstanding tomb in the Valley of the Queens is **Tomb 66 of Nefertari**, wife of Ramses II, which had suffered greatly from salt deposits and from its discovery in 1904 could be visited only by special permission. Following painstaking restoration work it was opened to the general public in 1995:

A reconstruction of the temple at Deir el Medina from Description de l'Egypte, 1809–28

even so, only 150 visitors are permitted per day and each may spend no more than 10 minutes in the tomb. Tickets are often sold out by 6.30am (*see* p.220); the day's visits are staggered throughout the opening hours (*summer 7.30–noon and 1–5, winter 8.30–noon and 1–4; adm LE100*).

Nefertari, the Beautiful Lady

No other woman of ancient Egypt has been so honoured by monuments as Nefertari, the wife and chief queen of Ramses II, yet her life is veiled in mystery. Ramses was still heir-apparent, his father Seti I still on the throne, when he married Nefertari, the girl who was to share the first 24 years of his 66-year reign, those daring, dangerous and glorious years when he took to the field against the Libyans, the Nubians and most famously the Hittites at Kadesh. We see her in the third year of his reign in the first court of the temple of Luxor, the graceful high-breasted figure standing between Ramses' striding legs; she is at Abydos, Karnak and the Ramesseum also, but she is most celebrated at Abu Simbel. There at the temple of Hathor, completed in the 24th year of Ramses' reign, Nefertari appears as often as her husband, who dedicated the temple to her, 'Nefertari for whose sake the very sun does shine' (*see* p.325).

It was a poignant dedication, for it is the last we hear of Nefertari. She was then in her mid-40s and had borne Ramses seven or eight children, and it was one of these, their eldest daughter Meryetamun, who stood by her father at the dedicatory rites at Abu Simbel. If Nefertari made the long river voyage into Nubia, perhaps she was ill and unable to leave the royal barge to attend the ceremonies herself. At any rate she very soon after was brought to this tomb in the Valley of the Queens.

Looted already in ancient times, when the tomb was discovered in 1904 neither her treasure nor her body was found. What remained were the carvings of Nefertari, delicately modelled in low relief and beautifully painted, but even then suffering from water containing sodium chloride (table salt) seeping through the limestone walls. Once exposed to the dry air, the solution formed crystals between the walls and the surface plaster, reducing sections of murals to thousands of pieces scattered about the floor. In 1985 the source of the seepage was identified and technology used by space scientists, geologists and biologists was prescribed to prevent any further penetration. Then starting in 1989 and taking six years, each of the thousands of dislodged pieces of mural were dusted and cleaned, revealing their vivid original colours, and by referring to photographs taken at the time of the tomb's discovery were refixed in place using paper-thin slivers of Japanese mulberry bark.

The result is a startling freshness of colour, as brilliant as it was on the day Ramses laid his queen to rest, all other tombs seeming dim by comparison. Here indeed is Nefertari, whose name means Beautiful Lady, elegant, gracious, charming and luminous, 'for whose sake the very sun does shine'.

Entering Tomb 66 of Nefertari, you go down a staircase leading to a hall, on the outer lintel of which are Nefertari's titles with a winged sun disc between Isis and Nephthys. Stepping into the hall you see on the left near wall inscriptions from the Book of the Gates and on the right near wall Nefertari before Osiris. The left side wall is blank, having been too much damaged to restore. On the projection to the near right are Anubis and Neith, while on the projection to the far right are Selket and Osiris. Here in this hall and throughout the tomb the ceilings are painted deep blue and scattered with gold stars. Above the door on the opposite side of the hall are the sons of Horus and again the queen's titles. From here runs a staired corridor; on the upper parts of its walls, to left and right, Nefertari is shown making offerings to various deities, while along the lower parts of the walls are Isis and Nephthys kneeling in mourning. You come now to the large pillared burial chamber containing Nefertari's sarcophagus, at the entrance to which the queen is shown making offerings to Osiris and Atum. Within the chamber the walls on the left-hand side are inscribed with the Book of the Gates, while the walls on the right-hand side show Nefertari adoring the Book of the Gates. On the pillars are symbols of Isis and Osiris. In the small chamber opposite are Isis and Selket, and Nefertari's cartouche between two uraeuses.

Mortuary Temple of Ramses III at Medinet Habu

> *I caused the woman of Egypt to walk freely wheresoever she would unmolested by others upon the road. I caused to sit idle the soldiers and the chariotry in my time, and the Sherden and the Kehek [Sardinian and Libyan prisoners, or their children, who were recruited to the royal bodyguard] in their villages to lie at night full length without any dread.*

Ramses III

Though built by Ramses III of the XX Dynasty, the temple complex of Medinet Habu is in the great building tradition of the XIX Dynasty pharaohs, with many points of similarity with the Ramesseum, though better preserved. Not long after the reign of Ramses III, the power of the pharaohs declined and Egypt herself became divided once more. Medinet Habu is the last major architectural work of the pharaonic period. Though Egypt was threatened by foreign invaders early in Ramses' reign and a palace conspiracy against him and the succession of his son was uncovered, the greater part of his 30-odd years of rule seems to have passed in peace, as recorded in the quote above which was probably part of the palace archives.

Ramses at Work and Play

In nomen and praenomen, Ramses III imitated his great predecessor of the XIX Dynasty, and the designers of Medinet Habu freely borrowed from the Ramesseum. They sometimes cut reliefs celebrating triumphs by Ramses III over Asian foes who had either long since perished on the field of history, or who since the reign of Ramses II lay beyond the enfeebled might of Egypt. This motif is echoed in the lofty **gatehouse**, a unique feature in Egyptian architecture, through which you enter the site. It was meant to resemble one of those Syrian fortresses with which the Egyptian armies had met so often in their Asiatic campaigns, but here the purpose was not military, the **upper storeys** serving as a resort where the pharaoh could

Medinet Habu

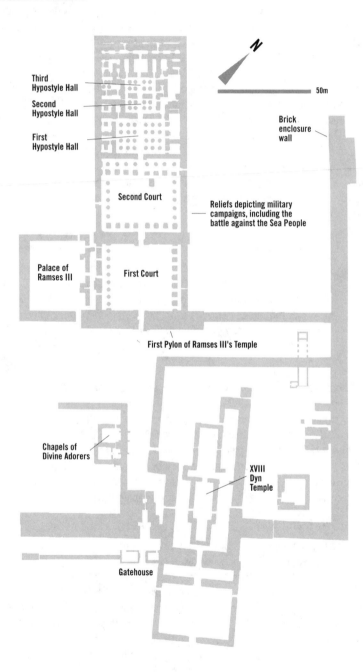

Third Hypostyle Hall

Second Hypostyle Hall

First Hypostyle Hall

Brick enclosure wall

50m

N

Second Court

Reliefs depicting military campaigns, including the battle against the Sea People

Palace of Ramses III

First Court

First Pylon of Ramses III's Temple

Chapels of Divine Adorers

XVIII Dyn Temple

Gatehouse

amuse himself with the women of the harem. The carved heads of captured prisoners enlivened the view from the east window above, reached now by a staircase on the south (*if this is closed, offer baksheesh*). Scenes inside the top apartment show Ramses waited on by harem girls, their bodies denuded of even the transparent dresses once suggested by a light wash of paint. To the left of the west window the pharaoh is stroking one of the girls under her chin.

The Primeval Hill

To the north (right) of this gateway is an earlier **XVIII Dynasty temple** built and partly decorated by Hatshepsut. Her image and name were obliterated, as elsewhere, by Tuthmosis III; Akhenaton scratched out all reference to Amun but Horemheb and Seti I replaced them; and Ramses III then decorated the north and south walls to suit his own purposes. This temple stood on one of the most sacred spots in Egypt, the primeval hill which first rose clear of the receding waters of Chaos. An inscription identifies it as the burial place of the four primal pairs—Ocean and Matter, the Illimitable and the Boundless, Darkness and Obscurity, and the Hidden and Concealed ones—who preceded even the creator god, Re-Atum. While preserving this older temple, Ramses III levelled the ground behind to build his own mortuary temple dedicated to 'Amun united with Eternity', and a palace and other structures, set within gardens, surrounded by walls, and linked to the Nile by a canal.

Chapels and Campaigns

Through the gateway and to the south (left) are the mortuary **chapels** of the Divine Adorers, princesses who were the chief priestesses of Amun at Thebes. The chapels are late additions, dating from the XXIII to XXVI Dynasties.

Straight ahead (to the west) is the **First Pylon** of Ramses' mortuary temple. The pylon would have almost the same dimensions as that at the Temple of Luxor except that it has lost its cornice. A stairway at the north end leads to the top for an excellent view across the temple towards the Theban Mountain. The pylons, columns and chambers are smaller as you gaze westwards and the platforms at each stage of the temple are higher: an architectural funnel pointing towards the final sanctuary, as at Karnak, and with Egyptian temples generally. The reliefs on the pylon towers depict campaigns against the Nubians and Syrians, campaigns never fought by Ramses III and probably copied from the Ramesseum.

Battle with the Sea Peoples

> A net was prepared for them to ensnare them, those who entered into the river-mouths being confined and fallen within it, pinioned in their places, butchered and their corpses hacked up.
>
> Inscription on relief

In the eighth year of his reign, Ramses III was in desperate struggle with the Sea Peoples, a coalition of northerners including Sardinians, Cretans, Philistines and others, not all of whom have been identified. By sea and by ox-carts carrying their women and children overland, these peoples were bent on permanent settlement in the rich Delta pasturelands. One group,

The only Egyptian relief portraying a sea battle, that of Ramses fighting the Sea Peoples

whom the Egyptians called the Danu, the Danaoi of the Iliad, here emerged into history for the first time. The invasion is recorded in dramatic detail by reliefs along the outer north wall of the mortuary temple (walk round to it before passing through the pylon) and should not be missed. It is the only Egyptian relief portraying a sea battle. In a single sweeping picture the artist has combined the various phases of the engagement: the Egyptians stand on their decks in steady order; an opposing vessel is held fast with grappling irons, the enemy in confusion, many of them falling into the water; while from the shore Ramses standing upon the heads of captives joins with his archers in shooting volleys of arrows at the invaders. In places, deep grooves have been cut into the wall by ancient visitors seeking to obtain stone dust from this sacred place for use in magical charms.

Proceeding Through the Temple

The **First Court** was the scene of ceremonies and entertainments which would have included sword fights and wrestling. The east wall celebrates Ramses' victory in his eleventh year against the Libyans: trophies of enemy hands and genitals are counted by scribes, and soldiers are rewarded for their valour. The pharaoh himself might have distributed rewards from the window in the south wall, decorated on either side with reliefs of prisoners' heads. This was the façade of the **royal palace**; its central hall surrounded by six columns was for holding audiences, while the private apartments were on the south side.

The mortuary temple continued in use for only 200 years, though the smaller temple of Hatshepsut remained a place of worship throughout Ptolemaic times. In the Ptolemaic and Roman periods the First Court was filled with houses and a monastery, the **Second Court** with the principal church of what was now a town of some size.

Early Christian Church

Traces of the church can still be seen, for example the base of an octagonal font on the south side. Osiris figures against the pillars along the east and west sides were removed in building the church, and the central pillar on the north side was taken down to make way for the apse. A few of the **Osiris figures** remain at the north end. Along the west colonnade, which is also the façade of the temple proper, the colours on the **reliefs** are especially bright. In the central register on either side of the doorway, Ramses is shown variously with Atum and Mont entering the temple; being crowned in the presence of the Theban triad; and being purified before receiving the emblems of his rank from the gods of Heliopolis. In the lower register on either side, Ramses' name is written in alternation with figures of his sons. None of their names, however, is inscribed as there appears to have been some uncertainty over the succession. On the architrave over the doorway is a brightly painted winged solar disc.

Hypostyle Hall

Beyond is the **First Hypostyle Hall**, roofless now but once with a raised ceiling over the central aisle as at the Ramesseum and Karnak. To the right are a series of sanctuaries, the first for the cult of the living pharaoh. To the left are treasure chambers, still with their original roofs. The central chamber of these shows the weighing of gold on its south wall, sacks of gold on the west wall, and precious stones on the east wall. Off to the left of the **Second Hypostyle Hall** is the funerary chamber of Ramses III with Thoth represented on the south wall inscribing the pharaoh's name on the sacred tree of Heliopolis.

In the **Third Hypostyle Hall**, on either side of the central aisle, are statues of Ramses with Maat and with Thoth. At the west end of this hall are three sanctuaries: to the right, that of Mut; to the left, Khonsu; between them, the sanctuary of Amun, once finished with electrum, its doorway of gold, the doors themselves of copper inlaid with precious stones. The granite pedestal, now to one side of the sanctuary but originally at its centre, supported Amun's sacred boat.

Back through the temple to the First Pylon, turn to the right to view the reliefs along the outer south wall. Above, Ramses is shown hunting various desert animals; below, most vividly, he is shown impaling with his hunting spear writhing bulls in a marsh.

The Works of Amenophis III

The remaining sights on the west bank of the Nile are associated with Amenophis III (XVIII Dynasty) who ruled over Egypt at the height of her prosperity. He was the first to display the penchant for the grandiose, and though it later served pharaonic bombast, in the works of Amenophis there is always a more tolerable touch of grandeur and opulence. It is unlikely that he was ever personally engaged in any military exploits, though some inscriptions make this claim by way of convention; rather he comes across as a man who enjoyed life to the full, and had the means to enjoy it more fully than any other man of his times. A smile of contentment plays upon his lips as he sits with Queen Tiy in the colossal group at the Cairo Museum; a stele found at Amarna and now at the British Museum shows him in later years, his weary frame and jaded expression suggesting that he had known pleasures beyond even his ability to enjoy them.

The House of Joy

Though the ancient Egyptians built their temples of stone, their homes and even their royal palaces were built merely of mud brick and so have barely survived the millennia. **Amenophis' palace** lies about 1km south of Medinet Habu. Though much of it is ruined and it is rarely visited, it is one of the few royal residences in Egypt of which substantial portions remain. The palace contained living and state apartments for Amenophis, a separate residence for Tiy, a large festal hall built for the pharaoh's jubilee and quarters for courtiers and for the harem. When it was excavated, traces of plastered walls were found, bearing lovely paintings of birds and water plants prefiguring the art of Akhenaton. These have now disappeared.

Though Tiy clearly enjoyed her husband's love and confidence, and was often represented as his equal in size, Amenophis did not deny himself the delights of an extensive harem. The dowry of a Hittite princess whom Amenophis married as a secondary queen included 317 damsels for most of the other nights of the year. Another text shows that having already married the sister of a Babylonian king, he was now clamouring for the king's daughter as well; in his old age Amenophis is known to have married one of his own daughters by Tiy. Little wonder he called his palace the House of Joy.

To the east of his palace Amenophis shared his bounty by digging for Tiy an enormous **lake**, 370m broad by 1,940m in length, whereon the imperial couple might sail in the royal barge named Aton Gleams—suggesting that in spite of his indulgence Amenophis played some role, insensible though he might have been of the effect, in raising his son Akhenaton to worship Aton and bringing religious revolution to Egypt. Amenophis claimed, improbably, that the lake was dug in 15 days, though signs of haste are apparent in the mounds of excavated earth still lying along its western boundary.

The Colossi of Memnon

Amenophis also built a **mortuary temple** which has now vanished beneath ploughed fields between the Ramesseum and Medinet Habu. Responsibility for its destruction lies principally with Merneptah, possible pharaoh of the Exodus, who used it as a quarry for building his own temple immediately to the north. All that remains are the two famous **Colossi of Memnon** that once guarded its outer gates. The Colossi are along the road leading back to the new village of Gurna and are visible from some distance. They are in fact gigantic statues of the enthroned Amenophis himself, rising 19.5m from the plain. At one time they wore the royal crown and were even higher. Both are damaged and are lacking their faces; the one on the right (north) broke at the waist during an earthquake in AD 27 and was later crudely repaired, the top having been sawn into blocks. Cocteau described them as victims of rainless thunderstorms: 'Crucified, sitting against great crosses; the lightning has left nothing untouched except their legs.'

If it was lightning that crucified them, it was Greek and Roman tourists who cut graffiti into the legs of the figure on the right. The inscriptions reach as high as a man can stretch and were usually cut by visiting notables, including eight Roman governors. The Colossi had early on been accorded the wonder due to the divine, perhaps because of their imposing size, perhaps because Amenophis was recognized as both pharaoh and god. But by Ptolemaic times all memory of Amenophis III was forgotten, and the Greeks decided the statues were of Memnon, son of Tithonus, a legendary king of Egypt, and Eos, the Dawn, who went to fight in defence of Troy and was slain by Achilles.

The **north colossus**, with its diminutive figures of Amenophis' mother Mutemuia on the left and Queen Tiy on the right, eventually attracted much curiosity, for after it was shattered by the earthquake it would sometimes emit a musical note as the sun rose over the eastern mountains. The Emperor Hadrian came in AD 130 with his wife and a large retinue, and camped for several nights at its feet to hear the phenomenon. He was at last rewarded with three performances on a single morning and was declared to have been exceptionally favoured by the gods. The association with Memnon was expanded to account for the sound: fallen at Troy, he now greeted his mother Eos with a sweet and plaintive sound when she appeared at dawn, and she in turn wept tears of dew upon her beloved child. Nowadays it is thought that the rapid change in temperature as the sun rose caused splittings off of quartzite particles which resonated within the fractures. Certainly, once the colossus was repaired in AD 199, it cried out no more.

The colossi of Memnon, from Description de l'Egypte, 1809–28

The principal market street in Luxor is **Sharia el Souk**, which begins north off Sharia el Mahatta as Sharia el Birka. Galabiyyas and spices can be purchased here.

Along the front of the Old Winter Palace are **arcades** of agencies and shops selling the usual souvenirs, among them A.A. Gaddis, with a good range of books, prints and old photographs. Decent replicas of antiquities are on sale here.

Immediately north of the New Winter Palace is the **Tourist Bazaar**. Here you will find Aboudi's shop, run by the successors of that wonderful dragoman-cum-poetaster (mentioned on p.217), which sells books (but alas not his guide), clothing, jewellery and souvenirs.

There is a Hachette **bookshop** in the Mercure Luxor, where you will also find a range of jewellers and bright boutiques, and there is the new and fashionable On Safari boutique in Midan el Mahatta, opposite the railway station.

If you are shopping for **souvenirs** there are any number of touts on both sides of the river who will importune you *ad nauseam* with pharaonic relics such as scarabs, mummified ibises, their grandmother's big toe and God knows what else. None of it is genuine, and you should offer no more than one-tenth the asking price: it will be accepted with alacrity.

For an interesting selection of **alabaster** bowls and figurines, there are workshops on the **west bank** (by the Abul Kassem Hotel and elsewhere) where you can watch these things being made (it can take five days to make an alabaster bowl)—the prices are, yes, one-tenth of those asked by the hawkers at the landing stage. The people here are continuing in the line of their ancient forefathers, churning out artefacts which are in a sense no less authentic. You can imagine pharaonic craftsmen working with a bit more belief, perhaps, but no less a mercenary spirit.

Luxor and Karnak © (095)   **Where to Stay**

Places to stay on the east bank, that is Luxor and Karnak, are listed below. A separate listing follows for places on the west bank.

During Luxor's high season (October–May) it is not advisable to show up expecting to get a room at the hotel of your choice, so it is wise to reserve in advance.

Luxor offers various luxury hotels, mostly built in the last 15 years. Each is 'luxurious' in the sense of costing an arm and a leg and having the requisite quantity of restaurants, coffee shops, swimming pools and tennis courts, and being self-contained in their own gardens. Courtesy buses, even boats, take you into town. You might just feel, though, that for all the service and quality, you are staying at a dormitory suburb.

Many of the newer places from *luxury* to *inexpensive* are aimed at the package tour market, and they can suddenly fill up when a group arrives. Standards however are at least decent throughout the range, and rooms are usually air-conditioned.

Nevertheless you should check your room before accepting; standards can vary greatly within a hotel. Note also that many places are upgrading themselves, so that some of the more inexpensive hotels mentioned here might suddenly leap in price because a swimming pool or bathrooms have been added.

luxury

★★★★★**The Old Winter Palace**, now part of the Sofitel group, on Sharia el Nil, ✆ 380422, ✉ 374087, just south of the Temple of Luxor, is the place to stay for atmosphere. Make sure, however, that it is the Old and not the New Winter Palace, which has been tacked on alongside. The Old Winter Palace dates back to the heyday of leisured travel earlier this century and retains that atmosphere. It has been refurbished and equipped with the usual modern in-room facilities. At the rear, the rooms overlook a well-planted garden, where there is a swimming pool, bar and outdoor restaurant, while the Nile-side rooms offer beautiful views across the river and towards the Theban Mountain.

★★★★★**The New Winter Palace**, ✆ 380422, ✉ 374087, adjoining the Old, is unimaginatively modern if luxurious. There is a bank and shops at both hotels, while the arcades on either side of the drive leading up to the Old Winter Palace are lined with more shops and agencies.

★★★★★**The Luxor Sheraton**, PO Box 43, El-Awameya, Luxor, ✆ 374463, ✉ 374941, is some distance along the new tourist strip south of the Winter Palace. It offers its own 'bazaars'; the rooms are set in chalets in its large grounds. There are the expected restaurants (one Italian), air-conditioned en site rooms; it has its own marina from which felucca trips can be arranged and also offers yacht trips up to Dendera.

★★★★★**The Luxor Hilton**, New Karnak, ✆ 374933, ✉ 376571, is set in Karnak village on the east bank of the Nile. It offers three restaurants, one Italian, and can arrange felucca lunches or Japanese food on request. Lots of sports and activities, from horse-riding to speedball and giant chess.

The Mövenpick Jolie Ville Resort (unrated), ✆ 374855, ✉ 374936, is 5km south of town in a peaceful and luxuriant setting on Crocodile Island; a shuttle bus and boat service connects you to downtown Luxor. Aside from jogging track, hairdresser, etc. the hotel also offers a 'folklore attraction package' with sunset sailing, traditional food and a folklore show of 'Arabian delights'.

expensive

★★★★★**The Isis**, overlooking the Nile on the nasty new tourist strip immediately south of the Winter Palace, ✆ 373366, ✉ 372923, is cheaper than the other modern five-star hotels and has the same range of facilities.

★★★★**The Luxor Wena** (once called simply the Luxor), facing the Temple of Luxor, ✆ 380018, ✉ 380017, is another survivor from the good old days. Dating back to the 19th century, this is the oldest of Luxor's old hotels, and though refurbished in 1989 it still retains an old-world feel. It is built in Moorish style with ablaq arches and columns along the verandah (where a thermometer mounted on an old enamel plaque advertises '*Encres Stephens: Pour toutes les températures*', the gauge reading *glacé 0°C, tempéré 12°C, chaleur humaine 37°C, Sénégal 47°C*). The hotel is set back in its gardens from the Nile and so lacks river views, and indeed the front gardens themselves, once private and secluded, where you could enjoy late afternoon tea and evening drinks, seem to have been squatted upon by several ramshackle popular cafés—in short the *tone* is not what it was. Behind the hotel, however, is another garden, lovely and with swimming pool, bar and restaurant, and this the guests have entirely to themselves. The rooms have all the requisite modern facilities and are large and have balconies.

★★★★**The Akhetaton Village**, ✆ 380850, ✇ 380879, next door to the Isis, is a Club Med resort hotel, with disco, pool and fairly simple rooms.

★★★★**The Mercure Luxor** is on Sharia el Nil between the Temple of Luxor and the museum, ✆ 380944, ✇ 374912. This is a modern hotel in which the architect clearly attempted to re-create the claustrophobia of a pharaonic tomb—and succeeded. You will not actually bang your head on the lobby ceiling, and perhaps because the area is crammed with shops and a 24-hour café there is a sense of life and busyness here. The bars and restaurants are good, there is entertainment (disco, belly dancing) and a pool. In the main building, all rooms have Nile-side balconies; in the annexe behind, all rooms look at other rooms.

★★★★**The Novotel**, on the hotel strip 500m south of the Temple of Luxor, ✆ 380925, ✇ 380972, has a pool, indoor and outdoor dining, and well-equipped rooms, some overlooking the Nile.

moderate

★★★**The Emilio**, Sharia Yussef Hassan, ✆ 373570, ✇ 374884, is on the corner of Sharia el Karnak, back from the corniche and just north of the Temple of Luxor. Rooms are comfortably furnished and include video TV; some have balconies with views over the temple, and there is a shaded roof terrace restaurant. This is a popular place, so book ahead.

★★★**The Philippe**, Sharia Nefertiti, off the corniche north of the Mercure Luxor, ✆ 372284, ✇ 380050, is a newish hotel, clean and friendly, with a good reputation—try to book ahead. There is a downstairs restaurant and bar and a rooftop garden. All rooms are air-conditioned; those to the front, with a glancing view of the Nile, have small balconies.

★★★**The New Windsor**, ✆ 374306, ✇ 373447, in a small street running north off Sharia Nefertiti, has comfortable rooms, air conditioning, TV and restaurant.

★★★**Pharaon**, ✆ 374924, ✇ 376477, is a new hotel out at Karnak on the Nile near the Temple of Amun. Rooms come with air conditioning and colour TV and have either bath or shower; many have balconies with views of the Nile, and there is a poolside bar and a disco.

inexpensive

★★**The Horus**, Sharia el Karnak, ✆ 372165, ✇ 373447, is a few metres north off Sharia el Mahatta as it reaches the Temple of Luxor. The hotel overlooks the temple but also the Abu el Haggag Mosque, so you will benefit from the dawn call to prayer which announces that 'it is better to pray than to sleep', and the four calls to prayer that follow throughout the day. Gaudy from the outside, simple and decent within, the Horus is a refurbished old-style hotel offering a range of rooms and prices, including air conditioning and bathrooms, so you should ask to be shown a few first. The hotel has laundry service, a currency exchange desk, a bar and restaurant.

The Mina Palace, Sharia el Nil, ✆/✇ 372074, is on the corniche immediately north of the Temple of Luxor, with most of its balconied rooms overlooking the Nile, those on the south corner with a second balcony overlooking the temple as well.

The St Catherine, Sharia Yussef Hassan, ✆/✇ 372684, is near the souk area north of Sharia el Mahatta and offers somewhat worn but comfortable rooms.

The Golden Palace Hotel, Sharia Television, ✆ 382972, ✇ 382974, is a sprucer place with clean air-conditioned rooms, with TV and fridge; there's also a pool.

*The Santa Maria**, Sharia Television, ✆/✇ 380430, provides excellent facilities for the price, but against that you have to put up with being in an unpleasant part of town. The comfortable if somewhat run-down rooms have air conditioning and bathrooms; there is also a bar and restaurant.

cheap

Most of Luxor's cheap hotels and pensions are clustered in three areas, near the railway station (Sharia el Mahatta), on and in the streets off Television Street (Sharia Television) in the south of town, and along Sharia Yussef Hassan near the souk. Standards, even from room to room within a place, vary considerably, so look at several rooms before accepting. Some might insist on half-board, especially during the winter season. And some may have upgraded themselves by adding facilities, lifting them out of the cheapest price bracket by the time you get there. If the places listed below do not suit, or are full up, have a look at the places nearby.

The Ramoza, Sharia el Mahatta, ✆ 372270, ✇ 381670, with clean, air-conditioned rooms and private showers, is a convenient and popular place just 100m west of the railway station.

*El Moustafa**, Television Street, ✆/✇ 374721, is a shining new place with air conditioning and private bathrooms.

*Happy Land**, Sharia el Kamrr, off Television Street, ✆ 371828, is small and quiet, its rooms clean, all with fans, most with private baths. A friendly place.

*The Anglo Hotel**, ✆ 381679, just south of the station, is a clean and friendly place, recently improved by the addition of new rooms equipped with air-conditioning and private bathrooms.

*The Pyramids**, Sharia Yussef Hassan, north of Sharia el Mahatta, ✆ 373243, has large comfortable rooms; air conditioning, TV and private bath are extra. There is a bar and restaurant with good food.

★**The Venus**, Sharia Yussef Hassan, ✆ 382625, a favourite with backpackers, is perhaps the best centrally located cheap place to stay with lively views over the souk. The rooms are clean, simple and have fans; most have private baths, some are air-conditioned. Meals are cheap and good, beer is served in the bar, and the atmosphere is liberal and friendly.

★**The Sphinx**, Sharia Yussef Hassan, ✆ 373243, is a simple place with clean if musty rooms, fans and shared bathrooms, though some rooms have air conditioning. It also has a rooftop restaurant.

Where to Stay on the West Bank

Accommodation on the West Bank is generally of a more basic standard than at Luxor or Karnak, but there is tranquillity and the sense of being close to rural Egypt (though this is rapidly changing, especially since the construction of the bridge upstream), and for those serious about exploring the sites there is considerable convenience too.

inexpensive

★★**Gezira**, ✆/🖪 310034, is a new small hotel near the people ferry landing with a roof garden restaurant giving good views over the Nile.

★★**Amun el Gezierat**, ✆ 310912, a few hundred metres up from the people ferry landing stage behind the horse hire stables, is a pleasant small hotel set in a garden.

★★**Pharaohs**, ✆/🖪 310702, near the entrance to Medinet Habu, is an older hotel, more like a villa set in gardens, with comfortable rooms, some with air conditioning and private bathrooms.

cheap

The Habu, ✆ 372477, near the entrance to Medinet Habu, built in traditional village style, offers insulation against extremes of temperature. Rooms have fans, and there are shared bathrooms. The situation is lovely, but the place is filthy.

The Mersam Hotel, ✆ 382403, behind the Colossi of Memnon on the road running towards the Ramesseum, is a rustic place amid lush fields. Run by an Austrian woman, the rooms (doubles and triples only) are clean and are cooled by fans, and there are shared hot-water bathrooms. An extension should soon provide rooms with private baths.

Abul Kassem, ✆ 310319, east of Seti I's mortuary temple, has large carpeted rooms, airy and equipped with fans and showers. The best are on the top floor. There is a restaurant next door, and you can hire both bicycles and donkeys.

youth hostel and camping

You will not save much by staying at a hostel or campsite, nor are they conveniently situated—all are in the north of town and something of a lonely exile. The Rezeiky Camp at least has a swimming pool, but otherwise these places will only suit those with a passion for tents and curfews.

There is a **YMCA** campsite, ☎ 372425, along Sharia el Karnak about halfway to Karnak. Used chiefly by Egyptian families and so-called adventure tour groups, the site is guarded 24 hours. The **Youth Hostel**, ☎ 372139, is on a side road opposite the YMCA campsite on Sharia el Karnak. Membership is not obligatory but makes your stay still cheaper. There are dorms with bunks and also family rooms with double beds and private baths. It fills up quickly with Egyptian students in winter. Lockout is from 10am to 2pm, and curfew is at 11pm.

The **Rezeiky Camp**, ☎ 381334, 🖷 381400, is another couple of hundred metres farther north along Sharia el Karnak and has a swimming pool, bar and restaurant. You can pitch your tent in the partly shaded grounds, seek a roof over your head in one of their grotty cabins with shared toilets and showers, or shell out for a room with bath. You may also be able to sleep out or pitch a tent at some of the west bank hotels (*see* above).

Eating Out

There is a certain earnestness about Luxor: so many antiquities lying on either side of the river, requiring early risings to see them before the day grows too hot. Accordingly, visitors go to bed early and there is not a great deal of choice, nor are the standards particularly high for eating out.

The **expensive** eateries are in the top hotels (listed above); the finest is the **1886 restaurant** in the Old Winter Palace Hotel, a superb experience and not necessarily all that pricy. A selection of less expensive options follows.

moderate

Atop the Tourist Bazaar building next to the New Winter Palace is the **Marhaba Restaurant**, with beautiful views. The place is air-conditioned in summer, the menu is Egyptian, and beer is served. Also for a meal with a Nile view, try the **Emilio Hotel**'s rooftop terrace with bar, open 24 hours, on Sharia Yussef Hassan. A good light meal can be had at the **Mercure Luxor** hotel's 24-hour lobby café.

The rear garden of the **Luxor Hotel** is a very pleasant place to while away the late afternoon or evening with a drink or other light refreshment. The **Old Winter Palace**'s lovely garden terrace offers light refreshments until 5pm. The Isis Hotel's **Lotus Restaurant** does a buffet breakfast, lunch and dinner where you can stuff yourself for a reasonable fixed price.

For a buffet dinner with drinks and folkloric show, try the **Mövenpick Jolie Ville's Fellah Tent**, reached from Crocodile Island by felucca, every Thursday and Friday from 5pm to 9pm. The **Karnak Hilton** does felucca lunches daily, floating up and down the Nile; minimum two people, maximum ten. A beautiful new Nileside restaurant has just opened along the corniche near Karnak.

inexpensive

The **Amun** and the adjacent **El Hussein** restaurants, just north of the Abu el Haggag Mosque, offer simple Egyptian dishes served at tables both indoors and outdoors, but no alcohol. Beyond these, about a block north and off to the right (east), is a narrow street with several agreeable local cafés, among them the **Oum Kalsoum**, where tric trac is played. The **King's Head Pub** is about two-thirds of the way along Sharia Khaled Ibn el Walid (the street running parallel to the river from the Novotel south to the Sheraton); the pub sign, a head of Akhenaton, hangs from the building, and the pub itself is on the second floor above a carpet bazaar. Good food, good bar, excellent service, jazz and reggae music, a pool table and a wide selection of newspapers and magazines to read. *Open all day and most of the night.*

Sport and Entertainment

swimming

The **swimming pools** at the five- and four-star hotels are usually available to non-guests for a fee.

discos

The five-star and some lesser hotels have oriental **floorshows** and **discos**, but they are not late-night raves. The discos usually have a mixed couples only policy.

moulid and Ramadan celebrations

For the **moulid** of Abu el Haggag (the biggest in Upper Egypt), on the 14th of the Muslim month of Shaaban, and throughout **Ramadan**, the mosque of Abu el Haggag is the focus of the nightly festivities. Hundreds of men gather in the gardens, some off to the sides playing cards, gambling, smoking hashish, many more listening raptly or dancing wildly to the drums, tambourines, ouds and violins, and to the teasing, climaxing, repeating passages of the imam's songs. They are religious songs, but passionate, or occasionally playful: a boy and girl are walking down a street hand in hand, they enter a house, they 'go to God together'. The audience laughs and shouts, but the lyrics are always secondary, and it is the narcotic beat and wailing of the music and the imam's exquisite phrasing that draws cries from the crowd. The imam twirls and sings, his eyes closed, his head shaking violently from side to side. A policeman in baggy khakis embraces him, rushes into the crowd to collect fistfuls of paper money and presses it into the imam's hands. Two or three dozen men begin to dance, arranging themselves in facing rows. First half-whirls, to the right, to the left, then hopping up and down, now jackknifing, eyes closed, bodies sweating, shouting, whirling, hopping and jackknifing in unison, beyond exhaustion. An onlooker intervenes to ask a young boy, an old man, to rest. But they all dance until they can barely stand, can merely twitch, or until they collapse.

On the west bank the moulid of Abu Kumsan starts ten days before Ramadan and runs for three action-packed days and nights with horse-racing, stick-dancing, market stalls, entertainments, a funfair and prayer meetings. It takes place to the west of the mortuary temple of Seti I.

A River Journey

It is godly to cruise the Nile through Egypt. Before the roads and the railways there was only this river, and as the pharaohs and *hoi polloi* sailed upon it and watched their world unroll it cannot have failed to make a special impression on them all. The echoing silence of the deserts spoke of the void beyond the grave. But here along the river was the rhythm of bright green fields perpetually tender, small brown figures absorbed in their patches, fishermen like spiky water insects poling through the reeds. A flap of egret wings as you glide by, distant, breeze-blown, upon the artery of life itself. It is like the most beautiful murals in the ancient tombs, too sweet not to carry into eternity.

Like a string of citadels extending Alexandrian power towards Nubia, the Ptolemies built temples along the Nile between Luxor and Aswan at Esna, Edfu and Kom Ombo. Cruise boats ply this stretch of the river south of Luxor throughout the year, and some also include in their voyage the Ptolemaic temple of Dendera and the New Kingdom temple of Abydos, both of which are north of Luxor. Apart from being an agreeable way to visit these ancient sites, a cruise is also the best way to enjoy the lush valley scenery en route. The experience can be improved, for the more adventurous, by hiring a felucca and entrusting yourself to the power of the current and the winds.

The Nile North of Luxor

The two outstanding sites to the north of Luxor are the Ptolemaic temple of Hathor at Dendera (64km from Luxor) and the ancient shrine of Osiris at Abydos (200km from Luxor) where Seti I built his mortary temple.

Getting There and Around

Bear in mind that, owing to **security concerns**, your freedom of travel between Luxor, Dendera and Abydos will almost certainly be restricted. If coming by private taxi you will most probably have to join an absurd convoy, while if you manage to come by other means the police will place you under escort.

The most convenient base for visiting Dendera and Abydos is **Luxor**, or you can travel via **Qena** on the east bank of the Nile, which is served by trains, buses and service taxis from Luxor.

Dendera is on the west bank of the Nile, 4km from Qena, where you can catch a **service taxi** for LE2 or hire a **carriage** or **private taxi** for LE15 (round trip).

If travelling direct to **Abydos** from Luxor, you can hire a **private taxi** for the round trip: first check at the Tourist Police/Ministry of Tourism office at Luxor for what the rate should be, then go to one of the travel agencies, or bargain for yourself outside one of the hotels. For an early start, make arrangements the evening before. Or take a **service taxi** from Luxor (about LE15).

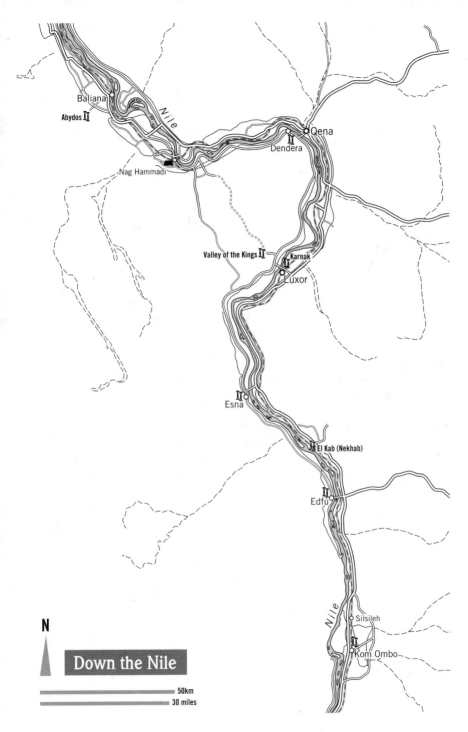

Travel agencies in Luxor operate standard **tours**, and some of the **boats** cruising between Luxor and Aswan also come downriver to Dendera and Abydos. Until the security situation improves, these boats will dock within a specially guarded zone at Qena from where passengers are taken to the site under armed guard.

You might be able to travel by **train** or **bus**, but as these can be slow and with awkward connections, you will waste much time and most likely will be unable to visit Abydos and Dendera on the same day. Abydos is 10km from Baliana, which is on the railway line midway between Sohag and Qena. Baliana is also served by buses and service taxis, and from there you can make the final leg of your journey by taking a service taxi (LE2) or minibus (LE1) out to the temple, almost certainly with a police escort for which a charge of about LE5 is made.

Dendera

The Worship of Hathor

The primitive roots of Egyptian religion—an animal fetishism that it never quite escaped and to which it retreated at the end, as seen at Saqqara—are illustrated in Hathor, the cow goddess of joy and sexual love, identified by the Greeks with Aphrodite, despite her bovine features. One thinks of the Dinka and other Nilotic tribes of the southern Sudan, whose entire culture is based on cattle. The cow to them is the epitome of beauty; it is tended for its milk and aesthetic satisfaction, never used for its meat unless it dies. The Dinka have contempt for agriculture, the nomad's disdain for those tied to the land. Perhaps it was so with the pre-dynastic Egyptians as their grasslands were swallowed by the desert and they were forced to labour for their existence along the Nile—a yearning for a stolen way of life expressed through Hathor, called also the lady of the sky, one of the most ancient and revered of their gods. At any rate, the worship of Hathor at Dendera went back to the earliest times.

History

Cheops built, or rather rebuilt, here, as did numerous pharaohs throughout the Old, Middle and New Kingdoms. By Ptolemaic times the ancient cosmology had become much simplified. Deities, concepts and aspects were often assimilated to the dramatis personae of the **Osiris myth**. Through the incestuous working of mythology the fertility goddess Hat-Hor, literally castle of Horus, first suckled the son of Osiris and then lay with him at Edfu in culmination of a great pageant issuing each year from Dendera. As it was important that each pharaoh should trace his ancestry back to Horus (*see* pp.304–5), it was especially necessary that the foreign Ptolemies should stress their links with the Osirid trinity and with the wet-nurse and bedmate of Horus. The Temple of Hathor at Dendera was part of this Ptolemaic assertion, and the Romans too found it expedient to contribute stones to the story.

Cosmological simplification and single-mindedness of political purpose—and perhaps a Greek concern for harmony—gave unity to Ptolemaic temples in contrast to the sprawling accretions of earlier dynasties. The old motifs in architecture and decorations were retained

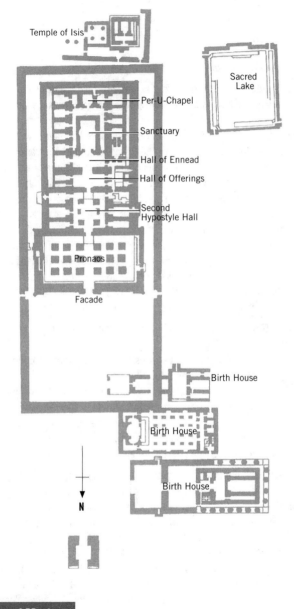

Temple of Isis

Sacred Lake

Per-U-Chapel

Sanctuary

Hall of Ennead

Hall of Offerings

Second Hypostyle Hall

Pronaos

Facade

Birth House

Birth House

Birth House

N

The Temple of Hathor

to gratify the priesthood in exchange for their absorption into the machinery of Alexandrian rule, and perhaps to impress the populace—though not to include them, as the abstruseness of Ptolemaic inscriptions makes clear. Non-pharaonic nationalism was shut out, though it intruded in the protesting defacings of later centuries.

The Dendera Site

Open daily 6–6 summer, 7–5 winter; adm LE20.

The temple **façade** is a pylon in outline, relieved by six Hathor-headed columns rising from a screen. A winged disc hovers at the centre of the huge cavetto cornice, an inscription above it, in Greek, from the reign of Tiberius—the façade and pronaos are Roman works. A central doorway admits you to the **pronaos**, a great hypostyle hall, again with Hathoric columns. Its ceiling decorations include the signs of the Egyptian zodiac, the various deities traversing the heavens in their sacred boats amid bursts of stars. The columns bear reliefs of the ankh and sceptre in alternation—life and prosperity. The grooves at the column bases were made by the insistent fingers of the faithful. The divinity reliefs on the columns were once covered with gold, and it is possible that even the floor bore a veneer of gold and silver. The successive chambers become smaller, lower, darker. The second hypostyle hall of six columns is decorated with scenes concerning the temple foundation rites, such as turning the first spadeful of earth and laying the first stone. This was the **Hall of Appearances** where Hathor consorted joyfully with the gods and goddesses of her court before voyaging to Edfu. Beyond this is the temple proper, the sanctuary at its centre surrounded by a corridor lined with chapels. But first you pass through the Hall of Offerings and the Hall of the Ennead.

The **Hall of Offerings** marks the scene of the daily cult ritual in which offerings were laid out before the sanctuary. From here the divine images were carried in New Year processions up the staircases and onto the roof, to a kiosk where they made contact with the rays of Re— a spiritual emergence from darkness into light. The processions are depicted ascending and descending on both the east and west stairway walls. (*See* below for a description of the roof.) The **Hall of the Ennead**, immediately before the sanctuary, contained statues of Hathor's nine consorts, these being the primal elements or deities following on the creation (among them air, moisture, earth and sky) as opposed to the pre-creation forces (*see* p.253) —that is, the elements of cosmic order rather than the elements of cosmic disorder.

The **sanctuary** itself would normally be bolted and in complete darkness. It was opened and illuminated by torchlight to permit the pharaoh to adore the goddess, and for her consorts to dine in communion with her. These rituals are depicted on the inner walls: on the right, the top pictorial register shows, from right to left, the pharaoh opening the door after repeating four times 'I am pure' (frames 1 and 2), meeting Hathor (frame 3) and offering libations (frame 4); the same sequence is on the left wall. The surrounding chapels each had their different ritual and ceremonial functions. Most interesting are the three chapels immediately behind the sanctuary: at the centre the Per-Ur, to its left the Per-Nu, and to its right the Per-Neser. The **Per-Ur Chapel** was the starting point for the New Year procession and its decorations include the pharaoh offering Hathor a drink of intoxicating liquor, as she was the goddess of joy. From the **Per-Nu Chapel**, Hathor embarked on her annual voyage to Edfu and congress with Horus. In the **Per-Neser Chapel** the goddess is represented in her terrible aspect, for example as a lioness goddess (by Ptolemaic times Hathor had assimilated the lioness goddess Sekhmet and the cat goddess Bastet, reflecting the terrible and gentle aspects of her nature). In the corridor outside the Per-Nu Chapel you can descend steps to the 32 treasure **crypts** beneath the temple.

To reach the roof you follow the west corridor back to the Hall of Offerings, pausing first about halfway along the length of the sanctuary to look at the **New Year Chapel** where rituals were performed preparatory to Hathor's communion with the sun. On the ceiling is a magnificent relief of Nut the sky goddess giving birth to the sun, whose rays illuminate Hathor. The stairway, decorated with reliefs of the New Year processions, ascends to an elegant stone kiosk which was covered by a removable awning where Hathor was exposed to the sun's revivifying force. Also on the roof, but having nothing to do with the worship of Hathor, are the twin **chapels of Osiris** (one above the west stair, the other above the east). First there is an open court, decorated with a procession of priests; then a covered court, on its ceiling a zodiac, unique in Egypt (the original is in the Louvre), as well as two figures of Nut (the vagina of one well-worn by two millennia of fingers), with the boat of the sun shown at the different hours of night. Innermost is an entirely enclosed room, representing the tomb of Osiris and decorated with resurrection scenes.

On the outside rear (south) wall of the temple colossal reliefs show **Caesarion**, son of Julius Caesar, with his mother, the great **Cleopatra**, last of the Ptolemies, behind him, making offerings to a head of Hathor. The carvings are entirely conventional and in no way portraits. It is odd seeing Cleopatra in this anonymous form—for domestic consumption—when she is so much better known, or imagined, in flesh and blood, the centre-spread fold-out who bedded the two most powerful Romans of her day.

The **birth house** is a particular feature of Ptolemaic temples and served to legitimize the dynasty through its ritual association with the birth of Horus (*see* pp.304–5). At Dendera there are three birth houses. The Temple of Isis to the rear (south) of the Hathor temple was built by Augustus and is in ruins; a second monumental birth house, also built by Augustus, with reliefs completed under Trajan and Hadrian, is to the front of the Hathor temple court (an ancient Coptic church built of stones from this birth house is squeezed between them); a third, bisected by the west wall of the court, was begun during the reign of Nectanebos I (XXX Dynasty) and completed under the Ptolemies.

A scene from the second Dendera birth house, showing at the centre a figure of the child-god Ihy emerging from a lotus, observed on either side by Bes and Thoeris, both associated with childbirth (Description de l'Egypte, 1809–28).

Nag Hammadi

At Nag Hammadi (85km north of Dendera, 149km north of Luxor) on the west bank of the Nile, the river sweeps round in a great bend to the east and the main road and the railway both transfer to the opposite bank—the road passing over the Nag Hammadi barrage, the railway carried by a bridge. Ten kilometres south of the barrage 150 or so **ancient tombs**, later used by Christian hermits, are cut into the Gebel el Tarif on the east bank of the river; in one of these, in 1945, the now famous Nag Hammadi codices were discovered.

Gnostic Gospels

The Nag Hammadi codices are gnostic gospels in Coptic dating from the late 4th century but translated from Greek originals of the early 2nd century. One of them, the gospel of Thomas, might even date from AD 50–100 and therefore be as early as or even earlier than the gospels of Matthew, Mark, Luke and John.

Gnosis is Greek for knowledge, in this case the intuitive process of knowing oneself, and thereby knowing human nature and human destiny, and at the deepest level knowing God. In Judeo-Christian teaching the Creator and humanity are separate; in gnosticism the self and the divine are one. The Old and New Testaments discuss evil in terms of sin and repentance; the gnostics said the world was an illusion from which the escape was enlightenment. Jesus did not offer salvation by dying on the cross; he was a spiritual guide. 'If you bring forth what is within you,' said Jesus according to the gospel of Thomas, 'what you bring forth will save you. If you do not bring forth what is within you, what you do not bring forth will destroy you.'

Abydos: Shrine of Osiris

Let my name be called out, let it be found inscribed on the tablet which recordeth the names of those who are to receive offerings. Let meals from the sepulchral offerings be given to me in the presence of Osiris, as to those who are in the following of Horus. Let there be prepared for me a seat in the Boat of the Sun on the day whereon the god saileth. Let me be received in the presence of Osiris in the Land of Truth-speaking.

The Book of the Dead

One of the most sacred spots to an ancient Egyptian was the temple at Abydos, which is on the west bank of the Nile, about 200km north of Luxor. It is especially worth visiting for its finely carved and coloured reliefs which marked a renaissance in pharaonic art.

History

The local god of Abydos had been a patron of the dead, and the identification of **Osiris** with him towards the end of the Old Kingdom was both natural and rapid. The crucial role Osiris played in the Egyptian conception of the afterlife soon turned Abydos into a national shrine.

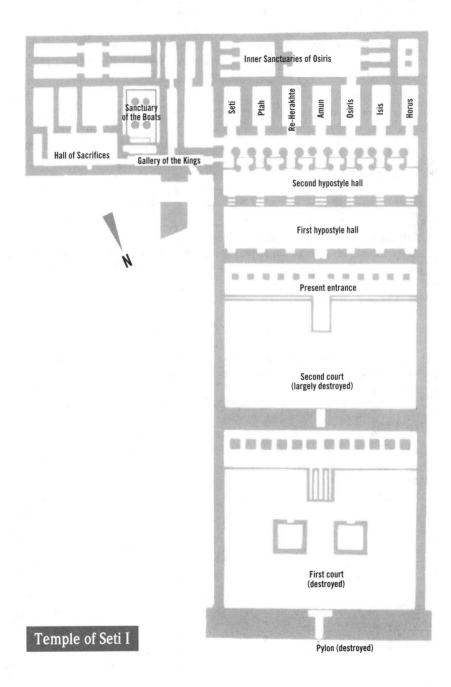

Inner Sanctuaries of Osiris

Sanctuary
of the Boats

Seti   Ptah   Re-Herakhte   Amun   Osiris   Isis   Horus

Hall of Sacrifices

Gallery of the Kings

N

Second hypostyle hall

First hypostyle hall

Present entrance

Second court
(largely destroyed)

First court
(destroyed)

Temple of Seti I

Pylon (destroyed)

Rather as Muslims regard Mecca today, it became the goal of all Egyptians to visit Abydos during their lifetimes or, failing that, between death and burial. Frequently on the tomb walls at the Theban necropolis you see the mummy of some notable making the voyage by river to Abydos. Some were even buried here as Old, Middle and New Kingdom tombs testify. The appeal was to lie for eternity at that very spot where the head of Osiris was buried after Seth had cut him to pieces and scattered his remains.

It is a measure of Akhenaton's assault on the established religion that not only did Aton supplant Amun but that the Judgement of Osiris did not appear on the tomb walls at Amarna. After Akhenaton and his successors were proscribed and Horemheb restored the old ways, the XVIII Dynasty was replaced by the XIX Dynasty from the northeastern Delta—by the brief reign of Ramses I and by Seti I who now had to consolidate. Ironically, **Seti** bore the name of Osiris' mortal enemy, Seth—his sensitivity on this point is demonstrated at Abydos where his cartouche reads Menmare Osiris-Merneptah rather than Menmare Seti-Merneptah—and both to remove any doubts about his loyalty to the past, and to identify his dynasty with the national god, Seti built a temple of fine limestone at Abydos. But Seti was more than a reactionary; he declared a renaissance, and in art he ignored both Akhenaton's expressionism and the overblown style of the XVIII Dynasty empire. His **bas-reliefs** at Abydos are finely formed and beautifully coloured Old Kingdom revivals, though perhaps a touch effete: it is these one comes to see.

The Abydos Site

Open daily 7–5; adm LE12.

The pylon of Seti's **mortuary temple** has collapsed and the walls of the first and second courts are reduced almost to foundation level. You enter the temple by the central door of seven (the three on either side were sealed by Ramses II) and pass through the first hypostyle hall, completed by Ramses and of inferior work, into the second hypostyle hall which was the last part of the temple decorated before Seti's death. The seven doors are explained by the unusual feature of seven sanctuaries lying beyond, dedicated, from right to left, to Horus, Isis, Osiris, Amun, Re-Herakhte, Ptah (with fine though bleak profiles of the god) and Seti himself. But it is in the second hypostyle hall that you should pause, for this contains the remarkable **reliefs**. Seti appears in distinctive profile, a stylized but close likeness to his mummy (at the Egyptian Museum in Cairo).

Also unusual is the wing built onto the temple to the left of the sanctuaries. The first passageway on the left is known as the **Gallery of the Kings** for its famous list of Seti's predecessors. Though the list is incomplete (in particular, Hatshepsut, Akhenaton, Smenkhkere and Tutankhamun are all missing, for political reasons) the 76 cartouches from Menes onwards have assisted archaeologists in determining the correct order of pharaonic succession. The list is on the right wall, upper two registers; represented as revering their ancestors are Seti himself and his son, the future Ramses II, with youthful side-lock and holding up two papyrus prayer rolls.

Immediately behind the temple is the **cenotaph of Seti I** or the Osireion. It stands on lower ground and was sunk within an artificial mound, an association, perhaps, with a creation myth (*see* p.253). Funerary texts decorate the interior, and across the ceiling of the fine transverse chamber is a beautiful relief of Nut, goddess of the sky. But the whole place is waterlogged now.

The **temple of Ramses II** is 300m to the right of Seti's but is almost wholly destroyed above foundation level. The fine-grained limestone, architectural details picked out in red and black granite, and the bas-reliefs (Ramses normally employed sunk relief) suggest a standard of execution higher than was to be bothered with later in Ramses' prodigal reign.

Abydos and Dendera   **Where to Stay and Eat**

The nearest accommodation is at **Qena**, the **★New Palace Hotel**, Midan Mahattat, ✆ (096) 322509, a bright blue edifice across from the railway station behind the Mobil garage. It should be carefully scrutinized first; it is dirt cheap but fairly clean. some rooms have bathrooms, though not necessarily hot water. There are several other hotels, all sleazy, around the square, and several simple places to eat along the main street.

At both sites there is a simple café.

The Nile South from Luxor to Aswan

The principal sites between Luxor and Aswan are the Ptolemaic temples at Esna, Edfu and Kom Ombo. Esna is also interesting for its local (and non-touristic) market street, which runs south from the front of the temple of Khnum. Edfu's gigantic temple is the best preserved in Egypt, and the temple at Kom Ombo is perhaps the most charmingly sited, with a grand vista over the Nile.

Getting Around

For additional travel information, see the Luxor and Aswan chapters. Bearing in mind the limitations that might be placed on your movements by the security forces, the following arrangements normally apply.

The temples at Esna, Edfu and Kom Ombo can be seen in a day if you **hire a car** with driver at either Luxor or Aswan, arriving in the evening at the other. If relying on **train**, **service taxi** or **local bus**, count on seeing only two temples en route, returning to the third from your new base—though you may be able to manage all three. The temple you would most kick yourself for not visiting is that at Edfu.

Reaching **El Kab** is more difficult and the effort will only repay the enthusiast; you either take the train or a service taxi to El Mahamid, from where it is a 2.5km walk to the site. Most cruises do not stop here.

Esna

A short walk up from the quayside through the constricting streets of Esna (54km from Luxor) and beside an awning-shaded market is the temple (*open 6am–5.30pm winter, 6am–6.30pm summer; adm LE8*), squatting in a pit. It had been covered over with houses;

now it is partly laid bare behind railings and you descend a staircase into the excavations. Ptolemy VI rebuilt this **Temple of Khnum**, the god who fashioned man on his potter's wheel, over the ruins of earlier structures, but almost all that remains to be seen is the later hypostyle hall begun by the Emperor Claudius in the 1st century AD. The carvings within are of a poor standard, but the roof is intact and supported by 24 columns with 16 different capitals, bearing their original colours well. It is these you come to see. It is best to stand, slowly revolving, looking upwards at the myriad palm and composite plant capitals, arranged without order or symmetry, but with the most pleasing effect, as though you were standing among trees, admiring the subtle and powerful architecture of a forest.

In the forecourt of the temple there are several blocks from an **early Christian church**, recalling a time when Esna was an important centre of Christian activity. Notice the lion-headed font carved from an ancient block bearing fine hieroglyphics on the reverse. The Emperor Decius (reigned AD 249–51) decreed that all Christians should sacrifice to the Roman gods or suffer death. His is the last cartouche carved on the temple walls, but he is commemorated too in a sense by Deir Manaos wa al-Shuhada 6km southwest of town, the **monastery of the Three Thousand Six Hundred Martyrs**, whose 10th-century church is one of the most beautiful in Upper Egypt.

Esna was once a terminus for caravans picking their way from oasis to oasis across the desert from the Sudan, but this trade virtually expired with the passing of the last century. It remains a merchant town and weaving centre, and can be interesting to wander about. It is worth walking south a bit through the covered **market street**, where lengths of fabric are sold or made up into clothing, and then back along it (north), passing the temple, into a quarter of old houses with fine brickwork and mashrabiyya screens. Where the street opens up into a little square, turn right towards the Nile and look in on the **Coptic church**. Along the corniche, north of the church, are more fine old houses. A barrage crosses the Nile here, built in 1906; it is busy with trucks and carts trundling from one side of the river to the other, and in the morning with barges and cruise boats waiting to pass through its locks. Back at the stone quay along that part of the corniche nearest the temple, notice the carved cartouches of the Emperor Marcus Aurelius.

It was perhaps here that Gustave Flaubert, future author of *Madame Bovary*, landed in 1850, though his interest was not antiquarian: by an edict of Mohammed Ali's in 1834 prohibiting prostitution and female dancing in Cairo, the *almehs* (literally 'learned women') of Egypt had concentrated in Qena, Esna and Aswan. Flaubert entertained a mystique about prostitution: 'A meeting place of so many elements—lust, bitterness, complete absence of human contact, muscular frenzy, the clink of gold—that to peer into it deeply makes one reel. One learns so many things in a brothel, and feels such sadness, and dreams so longingly of love!'

Flaubert Entertained in Esna

At Esna Flaubert was propositioned aboard his boat by an almeh followed by her pet sheep, its wool spotted with yellow henna. He went with her to the house of Kuchuk Hanem, 'a tall, splendid creature, lighter in colouring than an Arab; she comes from Damascus; her skin, particularly on her body, is slightly coffee-coloured. When she bends, her flesh ripples into bronze ridges. Her eyes are dark and enormous, her eyebrows thick, her nostrils open and wide; heavy shoulders, full, apple-shaped breasts.' She danced the Bee, which required that the musicians be blindfolded, and slowly removed her clothes. 'When it was time to leave I didn't leave. I sucked her furiously—her body was covered with sweat—she was tired after dancing—she was cold—I covered her with my pelisse, and she fell asleep with her fingers in mine. As for me, I scarcely shut my eyes. Watching that beautiful creature asleep (she snored), my night was one long, infinitely intense reverie—that was why I stayed. I thought of my nights in Paris brothels—a whole series of old memories came back—and I thought of her, of her dance, of her voice as she sang songs that for me were without meaning and even without distinguishable words. That continued all night. At three o'clock I got up to piss in the street—the stars were shining... As for the *coups*, they were good—the third especially was ferocious, and the last tender—we told each other many sweet things—towards the end there was something sad and loving in the way we embraced.' (*Flaubert in Egypt*).

Back in France, while he was writing *Madame Bovary*, he wrote to Louise Colet, his jealous mistress: 'You tell me that Kuchuk's bedbugs degrade her in your eyes; for me they were the most enchanting touch of all. Their nauseating odour mingled with the scent of her skin, which was dripping with sandalwood oil. I want a touch of bitterness in everything—always a jeer in the midst of our triumphs, desolation even in the midst of enthusiasm.' And he reminded Louise that 'you and I are thinking of her, but she is certainly not thinking of us. We are weaving an aesthetic around her, whereas this particular very interesting tourist who was vouchsafed the honours of her couch has vanished from her memory completely, like many others. Ah! Travelling makes one modest— you see what a tiny place you occupy in the world.'

Along the River to Edfu

Thirty kilometres south of Esna on the east bank of the Nile, right on the water's edge, is **El Kab** (*open daily 8–6; adm LE10*), the ancient Nekhab, important from Pre-Dynastic to Ptolemaic times. A massive mud brick enclosure wall surrounds the ruins, 11.5m thick and pierced by gates approached by ramps on the north, east and south. Of the two temples here, the finest is the small **Temple of Nekhbet**, the work of Amenophis II and later Ramses II, and next to it, also within an inner enclosure, a **Temple of Thoth** built by Tuthmosis III. Nekhbet was the white vulture goddess, the 'mistress of the valley' and cult goddess of Upper Egypt. The importance of the site as a national shrine is evidenced by the fact that the innermost mud-brick wall was rebuilt at least ten times.

Edfu

On the west bank of the Nile, equidistant from Luxor and Aswan (105km), Edfu is spread upon the mound of an ancient city. The **Temple of Horus** (*open 7–4 winter, 6–6 summer; adm LE20*) is on the western outskirts of the present town, at a spot where Horus and Seth met in titanic combat for the world (*see* pp.304–5). The temple, the second largest in Egypt, after Karnak, is suitably monumental and the best preserved in Egypt. Construction began under Ptolemy III Euergetes and it was completed, down to its decorations, by the mid-1st century BC. It is therefore hardly a century or two older than the many technically superior imperial ruins in Rome. But you forget this and applaud the Ptolemies' phoney archaic style, for this is pure theatre. Remembering Justinian's boast that with Hagia Sophia he had surpassed Solomon's temple, at Edfu despite a mouthful of popcorn you cry out, 'Cecil B. De Mille, they have outdone you!'

On the **pylon** Neos Dionysos, in New Kingdom gear, snicker-snacks among the Bandersnatch, while in the colonnaded **court**, against the elaborate floral columns of the pronaos, is the Jabberwock itself—one of a pair of granite falcon-Horuses which stood on either side of the entrance (the other, headless, has keeled over in the dust). You walk through a series of ever smaller, ever darker halls and chambers to the **sanctuary** of the god, weirdly illuminated through three small apertures in the ceiling by a dim green Nilotic light. The reliefs on the next-to-lowest row on the right-hand wall within correspond to those at Dendera, in this case showing Ptolemy IV Philopator entering the sanctuary and worshipping Horus, Hathor and his deified parents. His pendent arms indicate an attitude of reverence.

Leaving the sanctuary and walking back towards the pronaos, you enter an **antechamber**, off which, to the left (east), is a vestibule (a fair amount of red and blue paint on the capitals) giving onto (north) an elegant little New Year Chapel decorated on the ceiling with the goddess Nut, pale green with a blue skirt of stars. She is beautifully shaped, with unusually fine breasts and profile, as though here there is a Greek concern for beauty and not just conventional form. Returning to the antechamber you pass (south) to a second, outer antechamber with a staircase on either side leading to the roof. As at Dendera, the residing deity required at least an annual dose of sunshine, a reimpregnation of soul from the sun. This occasioned the New Year procession up to the roof, and the decorations along the staircase walls reproduce the ceremony in full detail.

The temple of Edfu before excavation, Description de l'Egypte, 1809–28

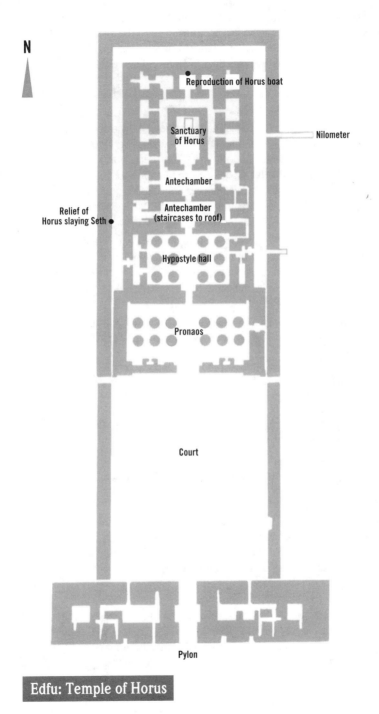

N

Reproduction of Horus boat

Nilometer

Sanctuary
of Horus

Antechamber

Relief of
Horus slaying Seth •

Antechamber
(staircases to roof)

Hypostyle hall

Pronaos

Court

Pylon

Edfu: Temple of Horus

Other **rites** celebrated annually were the conjugal visit of Hathor (*see* p.268); the triumph of Horus over Seth (note the inner face of the west enclosure wall); the coronation in the main court of a live falcon as the living symbol of Horus on earth; and the re-enactment of the divine birth of Horus and the pharaoh at the Birth House outside the pylon (with episodes of the ceremony carved on its walls).

Towards Kom Ombo

Southwards beyond Edfu the palms and cultivation on the east bank give way to the Eastern Desert and at **Silsileh** (145km from Luxor) the Nile passes through a defile, now with only hills on either side but thought once to mark a cataract. The rock bed of Egypt changes here from limestone to the harder sandstone used in almost all New Kingdom and Ptolemaic temple building. During the reign of Ramses II the Silsileh quarries were worked by no fewer than 3,000 men for the Ramesseum alone.

Above Silsileh the mountains again recede from the river and the desert is kept at bay by canals. Irrigation and the fellahin bring harvests of cane and corn to the fields. The reclaimed land on the east bank around **Kom Ombo** (164km from Luxor, 46km from Aswan) supports a large Nubian population displaced from their homeland by the rising waters of Lake Nasser. The village is on the Luxor–Aswan road; nearby is a sugar refinery supplied by barges landing near the temple 4km to the west.

Kom Ombo: the Temple of Sobek and Haroeris

Open daily 7–5; adm LE10.

The temple stands on a low promontory overlooking the Nile. Its elevation, its seclusion, the combination of sun and water flowing past as though in slow but determined search for the Mediterranean, at last suggests something of Greece. It has ruined well, and there is something in its stones of that Hellenic response to light, the uncompromising noonday glare, the soft farewell to the setting sun without fear of night.

The usual Ptolemaic (and Roman) appeasement of the fossilized Egyptian priesthood is apparent, however, as soon as you abandon mood for detail—even Marcus Aurelius must stoically appear on an outer corridor wall in pharaonic garb offering a pectoral to Sennuphis, divine wife of Haroeris. The naos was begun by Ptolemy VI Philometor; the hypostyle hall and pronaos were added by Neos Dionysos; and Augustus added the court, the outer enclosure wall and the now destroyed pylon. It is a symmetrically twin temple, the left side dedicated to falcon-headed Haroeris (the older Horus), the right to Sobek, the crocodile god. The two parts of the temple are physically divided, however, only at the two sanctuaries.

A Tour

The temple faces more or less west, towards the Nile. You approach from the south, past a massive ruined gateway built by Neos Dionysos. In front of you, between an ancient brick wall and the outer temple wall, is a small chapel of Hathor, the gift of a wealthy Roman woman. Through its gratings you can see sarcophagi and the piled-up mummies of crocodiles—they don't belong here, they were merely tossed in after being dug up in a nearby cemetery.

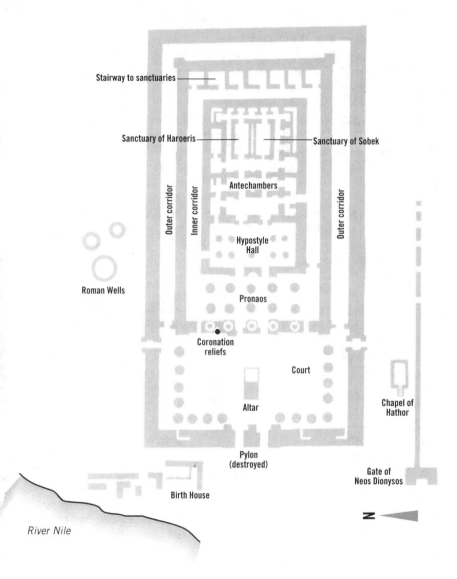

Stairway to sanctuaries

Sanctuary of Haroeris

Sanctuary of Sobek

Outer corridor

Inner corridor

Antechambers

Outer corridor

Hypostyle Hall

Roman Wells

Pronaos

Coronation reliefs

Court

Altar

Chapel of Hathor

Pylon (destroyed)

Gate of Neos Dionysos

Birth House

N

River Nile

Only a few courses of the temple **pylon** remain, and the stumps of the 16 columns once surrounding the court—at its centre is the stone altar used in sacrifices. Except for the three centre columns framing the dual passageways leading to the twin sanctuaries, the pronaos façade has lost the upper parts of its columns where they rise above the screen. But there is no loss of effect. The surviving columns burst in floral capitals, and above them, across the remaining section of the cavetto cornice, are two winged discs emphasizing again the duality of the divine presence here. Within the pronaos the ceiling is decorated with flying vultures and the supporting capitals proclaim the unity of Upper and Lower Egypt, some the lily, some papyrus—and one, eccentrically, a palm. On this side of the screen are coronation reliefs showing various Ptolemaic pharaohs receiving the blessings of Egypt's high gods and the double crown of the Delta and the valley.

In the hypostyle **hall** beyond, and in the three rising antechambers after that, are more reliefs. One, between the doors into the sanctuaries, shows Ptolemy Philometor and his sister-wife before Sobek, Haroeris and Khonsu, who inscribes the pharaoh's name on a palm stalk, the equivalent of St Peter confirming entry into Heaven. Philometor wears a full Macedonian cloak, a rare exception to the traditional guise. Little is left of the sanctuaries, but they are all the more revealing for that. Between them, at a lower level, is a **crypt** which communicates with one of the chapels to the east. The crypt is now exposed but was once covered with a sliding slab. It is not difficult to imagine someone creeping down there from the chapel to make spectral noises at appropriate moments—the priests to fool pharaoh, or one of pharaoh's men to fool the priests? Probably the priests fooling each other, the Ptolemies having the last laugh.

Beyond the rear wall of the naos are **seven chapels** leading off the inner corridor. A stairway in the centre chapel leads upwards for a view over the temple. The chapels are at various stages of decoration. An **outer corridor**, entered from either end of the court, is decorated with Roman reliefs. It is here, just to the left of dead centre along the north section of outer wall, that you will find Marcus Aurelius. To the left, in the northeast corner, is a display in relief of **medical instruments**: suction cups, scalpels, retractors, scales, lances, bone saws, chisels for surgery within the skull, dental tools—testimony to the remarkable degree of medical sophistication in Egypt nearly 2,000 years ago.

Along the north flank of the temple are a Roman well, cistern and basin, which perhaps had something to do with the worship of the sacred crocodiles. At the northwest corner of the temple is what is left of the birth house, much of which has fallen, along with its portion of the terrace, down to the Nile. It is Egypt reclaiming her own.

The Camel Market at Daraw

You sometimes get a surprise if your train stops at Daraw, 5km south of Kom Ombo. From railway wagons drawn up alongside, camels stare into your carriage window. For a month or so they have been plodding across the desert from northern Sudan, and at the Daraw camel market (*souk el gimaal*) they are sold, some for shipment all the way down to Cairo for resale at the Embaba camel market there. Service taxis between Kom Ombo and Aswan stop at Daraw (*market held every Tues morning*). The trade has been declining over the years, however, and with recent friction between Egypt and fundamentalist Sudan it may well be on its last legs.

Relief at Kom Ombo of Thoth and Horus pouring the water of life over the pharaoh.

Where to Stay and Eating Out

You should stay at **Luxor** or **Aswan**; what little accommodation there is in between is distinctly no-star. Esna has nothing speakable.

At **Edfu**, the best place to stay is the **Dar es-Salaam**, Sharia al-Maglis, ✆ 701727, near the temple entrance. Sharia al-Maglis runs east–west from the Nile to the temple; about two-thirds of the way towards the temple is the main town square; turn north here into Sharia Gumhuriya and in about 50m you reach the shabbier but friendly **El Medina**, ✆ 701326.

At **Kom Ombo**, by the service taxi depot just off Sharia 26 July, is **The Cleopatra**, ✆ 500325, with fairly clean rooms.

There are no restaurants worth a recommendation in this region; sometimes refreshments can be obtained near the temples.

Aswan

Aswan (210km from Luxor, 886km from Cairo) is where the valley closes upon the river: no more buffer of cultivation on either side, instead a universe of desert sundered by the pulsing Nile flowing out of Africa. At this point the Nile is only 87m above sea level, so low a height for so massive a river that you would think it would disdain the inducement to go further, but there is a continent of water behind, urging it on through the cataract above Aswan, and the current is strong. The layer of sandstone covering Upper Egypt from Edfu southwards is ruptured here by the thrust of underlying granite which the river has hewn into the rocks and islands of the First Cataract.

Even before construction of the British dam at the turn of the century and the giant High Dam in the 1960s, this was where traffic on the Nile stopped. Camels transported cargoes round the rocks while lightened boats took their chances through the granite passage. The more intrepid passenger might stay aboard:

> We see the whole boat slope down bodily under our feet. We feel the leap—the dead fall—the staggering rush forward. Instantly the waves are foaming and boiling up on all sides, flooding the lower deck, and covering the upper deck with spray. The men ship their oars, leaving all to helm and current; and, despite the hoarse tumult, we distinctly hear those oars scrape the rocks on either side.

Amelia Edwards, *A Thousand Miles Up the Nile*

Frontier Outpost

Aswan is where Egypt ends. Beyond lie Nubia and the Sudan, and the traditional routes of invasion and trade. The ancient Egyptians garrisoned the 500km stretch of river to the Third Cataract, and the fleet patrolled the Nile between the First Cataract and the Second at Wadi Halfa. An uprising or an attack on a caravan, and signal fires relayed the summons for help to Aswan. Two thousand years and more later, Aswan marked the southernmost margin of the Roman world, and when Juvenal fell into disfavour at Rome for writing satirical verses against the emperor's court, it was to Aswan that he was posted to guard the empire he had mocked. It is the High Dam that accounts for the modern military presence: its breach would send a tidal wave down the whole length of the Nile Valley and inundate half of Cairo. But that presence and the object of its protection lie out of sight some kilometres south of the town, which for all of its booming growth and the influx of workers in recent decades still clings to an atmosphere of remoteness and tranquillity.

Following the day's fierce sun and dry desert heat, there is the beauty at evening of sand, sky and water fading imperceptibly through deepening violet, a lift of breeze on the Nile, a movement of palms, a flight of hoopoes, and the graceful glide of swallow-tailed feluccas. The final pleasure is to know that when morning comes at Aswan there is so little to do. Those who insist on doing it can easily do it all in a couple of days. Those who want to do nothing will want to stay far longer.

Calculating the Earth's Circumference

Over the centuries the Tropic of Cancer has shifted slightly to the south, but in classical times it fell across Aswan, proved by a famous well into which the sun's rays plunged perpendicularly at midday during the summer solstice, leaving no shadow. Hearing of this, Eratosthenes (276–196 BC) of the Mouseion at Alexandria set out to measure the Earth. His method was as follows. He already knew that the Earth was round and that Aswan and Alexandria lay on the same longitude, but at that same moment in Alexandria the sun cast a shadow of seven and one-fifth degrees, that is one-fiftieth of a complete circle. Estimating the distance between Alexandria and Aswan as 805km, he concluded that the circumference of the Earth was 40,250km, an error of only 242km, and its diameter 12,819km, an error of only 77km. It was a triumph of constructive thought, inspired by a place whose genius lies in the inducement to idle contentment.

Long favoured as a winter resort with daytime temperatures around 23–30°C, the increase and changing style of tourism in Egypt has led greater numbers of travellers to challenge the summer heat which usually ranges from 38–42°C during the day, though it can climb much higher. Air conditioning and a siesta during early afternoon, and the low humidity, make even the hottest July and August days bearable.

Highlights

The chief purposeful activities are a visit to the **Nubia Museum** in Aswan and a trip by motor launch to the island of **Philae**. Mixing purpose with the pleasure of sailing about in a **felucca**, call at **Elephantine Island** and the **Botanical Island** and then land on the west bank to visit the **tombs of the Nobles** and **St Simeon's Monastery**. But for sheer pleasure, simply sail about aimlessly, or sit on the terrace of the **Old Cataract Hotel** and let the world float peacefully past. In the evening take a stroll along Sharia el Souk, Aswan's sinuous market street, the best **bazaar** outside Cairo.

Getting To and Around Aswan

At present there are certain **security** arrangements in place that restrict your freedom of movement between Aswan and Luxor to the north and Abu Simbel to the south. These particularly apply to road travel and feluccas; *see* below. For further information *see* p.321.

by air

Egyptair has direct flights between Aswan and Cairo, Luxor and Abu Simbel. The airport is 16km southwest of Aswan beyond the High Dam. Egyptair runs buses back and forth between the town and airport; its office is on the roundabout at the south end of the corniche. There are also taxis costing about LE20. For more information on flights, *see* p.7.

by train

Several trains a day link Aswan with Luxor and Cairo (*see* pp.7–8), with travel times and frequencies set to increase when a second track is completed between Luxor and Aswan. The train station is at the north end of the town, several blocks back from the corniche. A taxi or carriage from the station to, say, one of the Cataract hotels will cost about LE4.

by bus and taxi

The **bus depot** is in a square at the centre of town, behind the Abu Simbel Hotel, which is towards the north end of the corniche. The **service taxi** depot is just east of the railway station. At present foreigners are not permitted to travel in service taxis for security reasons, and you may experience some difficulty in travelling on the buses too. For up-to-date information, ask Shukri Saad at the Tourist Office near the railway station. In normal times, travelling by service taxi, it is quite practicable to visit Kom Ombo, Edfu and Esna in a day, ending up in Luxor, though a change of taxi is required at the end of each leg.

Travel by **private taxi** usually involves joining a police convoy. Before hiring a private taxi, try a bit of negotiating to get a feel for prices; you could also try making arrangements through one of the agents along the corniche, for example Misr Travel or Wagons-lits, thereby ensuring reliability and often obtaining a better price than you could manage yourself.

by boat

Numerous **cruise boats** ply between Aswan and Luxor, and some visit Dendera and Abydos too. At present cruises between Upper Egypt (Aswan and Luxor) and Cairo have been suspended for security reasons. Felucca trips between Aswan and Luxor have also been suspended. For more information, *see* pp.15 and 50–51.

to Abu Simbel

Abu Simbel can be reached by air (a 25-minute flight) and by cruise boat. For detailed information, *see* p.321.

Orientation

The railway station is at the north end of the town, some distance back from the river. The temperature, often 10°C higher at Aswan than in Cairo, hits you as you step off the train, and darker skins and lighter builds introduce you to the tropics. You may also notice Nubian spoken, if not here then when you are floating on a felucca and hear the boatmen calling to one another. A taxi, or better yet a carriage, will take you to your hotel and provide you with your first glimpse of the setting. As you emerge onto the corniche, you see a bare hill rising from the opposite bank and cut into its face the small dark openings of the ancient tombs of Aswan's governors and princes.

The façades along the corniche are mostly new and concrete, but the sweep of the Nile is impressive. The **older town** lies behind. A few streets back, running parallel with the corniche, is the best **bazaar** outside Cairo, alive with Egyptians, Nubians and Sudanese trading in gum, spices, ebony and other exotic prizes out of Africa, as well as local weaves

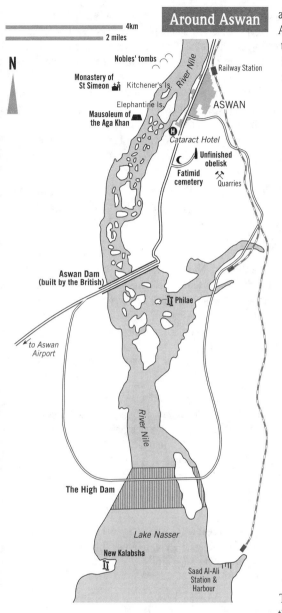

4km

2 miles

N

Nobles' tombs

Monastery of
St Simeon   Kitchener's Is.

Railway Station

River Nile

ASWAN

Elephantine Is.

**Mausoleum of
the Aga Khan**

Cataract Hotel

**Unfinished
obelisk**

**Fatimid
cemetery**

Quarries

**Aswan Dam
(built by the British)**

Philae

*to Aswan
Airport*

River Nile

The High Dam

Lake Nasser

New Kalabsha

Saad Al-Ali
Station &
Harbour

and manufactured goods. Although Aswan is not the crossroads of trade it once was, and the days of the caravans are gone, the flavour remains and the imagination recalls magnificently shawled and turbaned guards, huge scimitars dangling at their sides, accompanying a hundred camels laden with elephant tusks out of Ethiopia, driving the dust before them in clouds. The picturesque **inner town** deserves exploration, especially at evening.

In ancient times this area on the east bank, known as Syene, was famous for its nearby quarries of pink granite, but it was always secondary to the main commercial and administrative settlement of Yebu, which stood at the southern end of the long palm-covered island opposite the corniche. Yebu was Egyptian for elephant, and the island today bears the Greek translation, **Elephantine**. Perhaps in the earliest millennia of their history, before the desert had crept down to the Nile, the Egyptians first encountered elephants here, though it is more likely that Yebu owed its name and much of its importance to the ivory trade from the south. The most obvious feature towards the northern end of Elephantine is the unfortunate bulk of the Aswan Oberoi Hotel, like a control tower without an international airport; if that were not bad enough, an even larger hotel is under construction just north of it. On the far side of Elephantine, largely obscured by it, is the **Botanical Island**; Kitchener set out to conquer the Sudan in 1896–8 from Aswan and the island is a botanical garden begun by him.

Orientation   289

All along the corniche, cruise boats are tied up at the quayside, and towards the north end are many feluccas, while midway along it the Aswan Oberoi's ferry, designed to look like a pharaonic barge, makes frequent crossings to the hotel. At the south end of the corniche is a roundabout with the Egyptair office, behind which is a seldom-visited small Ptolemaic temple of Isis; it is here that the road from the airport enters town. Ferries leave from here to the southernmost Nubian village on Elephantine, and there are also launches to the Amun Island Hotel and the Isis Island Hotel in mid-river. Feluccas for hire concentrate here too. One arm of the Nile runs through the narrow channel between the massive embankments of ancient Yebu and the great dough-like outcrops of pink granite on the east bank, the road rising round the shaded **Ferial Gardens** that overlook the river here. Surmounting the outcrop is the **Old Cataract Hotel**.

Devotees of nostalgia must make a pilgrimage to this hotel, a russet pile atop a loaf of pink granite, surrounded by gardens, with beautiful views along the Nile in either direction and across the tip of Elephantine Island to the mausoleum of the Aga Khan and, against the distant desert horizon, the old monastery of St Simeon. John Fowles in *Daniel Martin* describes the interior as it was in the early 1970s: 'Pierced screens, huge fans, tatty old colonial furniture, stone floors, silence, barefooted Nubian servants in their red fezzes; so redolent of an obsolete middle class that it was museum-like'—in fact it was delightful, and though it has since been refurbished to the tastes of the nouvelle bourgeoisie, it has not been entirely spoilt. The exterior features in the film of Agatha Christie's *Death on the Nile*; the terrace, cocktail in hand, amid the calm, is the perfect place to plot an elegant murder.

Getting Around
by taxi

Unless you join a tour, you will need to hire a taxi for journeys to the granite quarry, the old Aswan Dam, the new High Dam, Philae and Kalabsha. All of these can be visited in one half-day's excursion (though including Kalabsha is pushing it). Expect to pay about LE60, including waiting at the granite quarry and the Philae landing stage, plus an additional LE20 if Kalabsha is included. It is best to arrange for a taxi the day before through your hotel or a travel agent. Sometimes an agent will know of other interested people with whom you can share, so reducing the cost per person.

by carriage

For journeys within town it is most agreeable to clop along in a carriage—perhaps taking one up to the terrace of the Old Cataract Hotel to enjoy the sunset, and then walking back, joining the promenaders along the corniche.

by ferry

You can cross to Elephantine Island and to the Tombs of the Nobles by ferry, the former from the southern end of the corniche, the latter from the northern end of the corniche.

by felucca

Getting to the **Botanical Island**, and also landing on the **west bank** of the Nile below the Aga Khan's mausoleum and at the closest point to the monastery of

St Simeon, means hiring a felucca along the corniche or below the Old Cataract Hotel. Whatever price you agree to after bargaining—you will do better in summer and if you do not hire at the Old Cataract—expect to be hit for baksheesh after-wards. You will be asked to pay anything from LE25 to LE40 an hour but can usually knock this down. So as not to rush things, arrange to have the felucca for four hours.

by camel

Once on the west bank of the Nile, you can hire a camel to save you the trudge up to St Simeon's Monastery (about LE20); you can also ride between there and the Tombs of the Nobles.

Tourist Information

Before doing anything, visit the **Tourist Office**, a small domed building just by the north corner of the railway station, ℭ 312811 (*open daily 8.30–2 and 6–8, Fri 10–2 and 6–8*). Its manager Shukri Saad is a helpful and friendly mine of information—in English, German and French. Here you can obtain in advance the official prices for taxis, carriages, feluccas and camels.

The **Tourist Police** have an office on the south side of the railway station, ℭ 233163, and another not far away at the north end of the corniche, ℭ 316436, just north of the Ramses Hotel; both branches are *open 24 hours.*

It can also be useful to make enquiries at the various travel agencies. Sometimes they can fix things up for you on an ad hoc basis, or they might have a tour which will suit your purposes. **American Express** is in the Old Cataract, ℭ 322909, and there are also various **travel agencies** along the southern end of the corniche, for example Misr, Eastmar, Wagons-lits and Thomas Cook (ℭ 304011, ℮ 306209), together with several **banks** where you can change money.

The **post office** is on Sharia Salah el Din, one block in from the centre of the corniche, nearly opposite the Aswan Oberoi Hotel. The **telephone office**, from where you can also send faxes, is at the southern end of the corniche just past the Egyptair office and provides both domestic and international services. **Emails** can be sent and received at the Governate, which is at the north end of the corniche just past the turning for the railway station. The Rosewan Hotel also has a cybercafé.

The Nubia Museum

Open daily 9–1 and 6–10; adm LE20.

The Nubia Museum, opened at the end of 1997, is a striking modern sandstone building on the slope of a granite outcrop at the southern end of town. Its entrance is opposite the Basma Hotel on a road running up from the Old Cataract Hotel.

In the museum garden is a reconstructed cave in which prehistoric rock carvings have been set; there is also a village house characteristic of those upriver from Aswan until the whole of Nubia was drowned beneath Lake Nasser in the 1960s. The entire span of time between cave and house—about 25,000 years—is represented within the museum.

You enter the museum on its upper level, where there are lecture rooms, a gift shop and a hall for temporary exhibitions. Steps descend to a vast lower hall illuminated by a dim sub-aqueous light so that like Nubia itself it seems under water. The exhibits, however, are picked out brightly. These are arranged chronologically, starting from the left and continuing round clockwise. All of the exhibits here have been salvaged from Nubia since the beginning of the twentieth century and have been brought together from Cairo's Egyptian, Coptic and Islamic museums and from the Aswan Museum on Elephantine Island. Everything is labelled in Arabic and English.

From the prehistoric period there are cosmetic palettes, delicate pots turned almost as thin as ostrich eggs (of which there are also several) and human and animal figures worked in ivory and other materials. These are the finest objects in the museum and repay close attention.

Throughout almost all subsequent periods, Nubia was dominated politically by Egypt, whose culture it crudely aped. Statues show that eminent Middle and New Kingdom Nubian personages felt honoured to dress up like their foreign masters; this was no less true, as his statue shows, of Taharka (XXV Dynasty), who as a pharoah of the 'Ethiopian' (i.e. Nubian) dynasty which ruled Egypt for nearly a hundred years built the last and largest of the pylons at Karnak. Also from the pharaonic period are a mummified ram with a golden mask, found at the temple of Khnum on Elephantine Island, and a colossal statue of Ramses II, rescued from his temple at Gerf Hussein, now submerged beneath the lake.

It was in its **folk art** that Nubian culture reasserted itself and is most interesting, stimulating and entertaining: in the tiny ceramic frogs used as playthings during the Graeco-Roman period, in the boldly painted murals of saints of the Christian period, and best of all in its domestic architecture. This last is found in the final ethnological section recreating village houses and community life during the twentieth century until all was lost with the construc-tion of the High Dam. In the burning heat of Nubia, everything was done to promote the cooling flow of air. The reconstructed houses are shown built round open courtyards, walls are pierced by a lattice-work of triangles, and reception rooms are wide open to the north to catch the prevailing breeze. But as in their prehistoric artefacts, nothing was ever simply functional: the Nubians would express their strong decorative sense by setting china plates into the façades of their houses and painting their exterior walls in brightly coloured geometric patterns.

Elephantine Island

Sites and museum open daily in winter 8–5, summer 8.30–6; adm LE10.

The purposeful reason for visiting Elephantine is to see the scant ruins of Yebu, the ramshackle museum and the ancient nilometer. For a few piastres, a small ferry will take you over to the island from the corniche, or you can hire a felucca; you cannot get to the rest of Elephantine from the Oberoi compound at the north end of the island.

The Nilometer

The nilometer is under a sycamore tree, a few boat-lengths north of embankments bearing inscriptions from the reigns of Tuthmosis III and Amenophis III (XVIII Dynasty) and Psammetichus II (XXVI Dynasty). Its square shaft can be entered directly from the river or

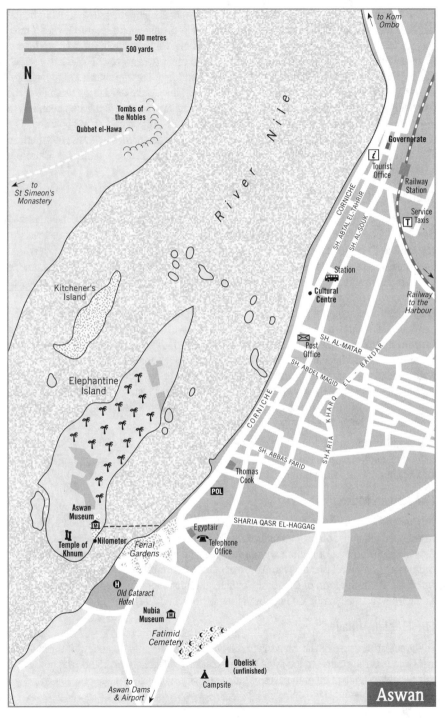

to Kom
Ombo

500 metres
500 yards

N

River Nile

Tombs of
the Nobles

Qubbet el-Hawa

to
St Simeon's
Monastery

Governorate

Tourist
Office

Railway
Station

Service
Taxis

CORNICHE

SH. ABTAL EL-TAHRIR

SH. AL-SOUK

Station

Cultural
Centre

Railway
to the
Harbour

Kitchener's
Island

Post
Office

SH. AL-MATAR

SH. ABDEL MAGID

EL-BANDAR

Elephantine
Island

CORNICHE

KHARQ

SHARIA

SH. ABBAS FARID

Thomas
Cook

POL

Aswan
Museum

Egyptair

SHARIA QASR EL-HAGGAG

Temple of
Khnum

Nilometer

Ferial
Gardens

Telephone
Office

Old Cataract
Hotel

Nubia
Museum

Fatimid
Cemetery

Obelisk
(unfinished)

to
Aswan Dams
& Airport

Campsite

Aswan

down steps from above. Though probably dating from an earlier period, it was rebuilt by the Romans, the scales marked in Greek. It was restored in the nineteenth century, when Arabic and French inscriptions were added. Strabo records that 'on the side of the well are marks, measuring the height sufficient for the irrigation and other water levels. These are observed and published for general information. This is of importance to the peasants for the management of the water, the embankments, the canals, etc., and to the officials on account of the taxes. For the higher the rise of water, the higher are the taxes.' The High Dam put an end to the annual inundation, and under Nasser this ancient basis of taxation was abolished. The more modest fluctuations in the level of the Nile are still measured, however. An American aid-sponsored satellite communications system now tells irrigation engineers in Cairo the level of every waterway in the country.

Yebu

The ancient town of Yebu stood at the southern end of the island. Its mound is being picked clean of debris by archaeologists, revealing mud brick structures of successive levels of occupation. Excavations began at the start of the twentieth century after the discovery that there had been a sizeable Jewish colony here in the 6th century BC with its own temple to Yahweh (Jehovah). From a military order of King Darius II in 419 BC permitting his Yebu garrison to celebrate the Passover, it is clear that the Jews here served in defence of the Persian Empire's southernmost border. The continuing excavations have revealed the existence of several temples, among them, to the west of the nilometer, a **Temple of Khnum** built during the XXX Dynasty and, to the north of the museum, a New Kingdom **Temple of Satet**, the female counterpart of Khnum. At the southern tip of the island by the water's edge the fragments of a small **Ptolemaic temple** have been reassembled with the aid of much yellow brick. Just to the west of this temple is a granite statue of an elephant with part of its head missing, recently excavated 250m northwest of the small **Ptolemaic temple of Isis** behind the Egyptair office.

The island was home to Khnum, a ram-headed god of the cataracts who was said to have fashioned man on a potter's wheel. Rams sacred to the god were mummified, and the sarcophagus of one, with mummy, is in the new Nubia Museum.

The Aswan Museum

Originally the villa of Sir William Willcocks, designer of the first Aswan dam, this is a verandahed old house on high ground overlooking the ruins and set in well-kept gardens. On view are a golden bust of Khnum with brown peaceful eyes, and an assortment of jewellery, pots, granite statues of island governors, weapons, bronze mirrors and beautiful slate palettes for cosmetics in the form of fish, birds, buffalo and hippopotamus—all of them local finds dating from the predynastic through Byzantine periods, and labelled in English and Arabic.

The Nubian Villages

The greatest pleasure of the island is to follow the pathways that wander off through the fields and luxuriant palms to the three Nubian-speaking villages on the island. The houses are pale yellow or brilliant blue, the eyes of the young girls alluringly black. Some doorways are carved with crocodiles at the foot, fish in the middle and a man on top, a woman's hand between fish and man, a statement of ideal proximities. The woman's hand is brass and serves as a door knocker, a ring on one finger. The Kaaba, the sacred black cube at Mecca, is painted on some housefronts to show that its owner has been on the hajj. Sometimes to show how he got there a boat will be added, or, fancifully, a single-engined propeller plane with open cockpit, or, more likely, a wide-bodied chartered jet.

At the north end of the island is that big hotel again, behind a 3m-high *cordon sanitaire*, erected not so much to keep the Nubians out as to keep the air-conditioned people in.

The Botanical Island (Kitchener's Island)

Open daily in winter 7–5, in summer 7–6; adm LE5.

The Botanical Island can be reached only by felucca, and you may wish to include it in a tour of west bank sites. On the way to the island, Aswan disappears behind Elephantine Island and you could be almost anywhere along the Nile, except that few stretches of the river are as lovely as this. Still widely known as Kitchener's Island, it was presented to General Kitchener when he became Consul-General in Egypt early in the twentieth century after retaking Khartoum in 1898, 13 years after Gordon had been overwhelmed there by the Mahdi and his dervishes. Here Kitchener indulged his passion for flowers, ordering plants from India and all over the Middle and Far East. The island attracts birds of remarkable pattern and colour. You should allow a guide to attach himself to you; he will skip about like one of Peter Pan's boys among the trees and plants in his sandals and galabiyya, picking leaves, flowers and fruits and crushing them in his fingers for you to smell, awakening all the pungency and variety of your surroundings.

The Noble Tombs

Open daily in winter 8–4, in summer 8–5; adm LE12.

Interred in the noble tombs on the **west bank** of the Nile opposite the north ends of Elephantine and the Botanical islands were the governors, princes and priests whose lives revolved around the control of the Nubian trade. The tombs date mostly from the end of the Old Kingdom through the First Intermediate Period and the Middle Kingdom. They can be reached by ferry from near the Tourist Office or as part of a felucca cruise. They can also be reached by camel or on foot from St Simeon's Monastery.

A slog up a sandy path from the landing stage brings you to the line of tombs cut into the cliff face. The tombs were originally approached by those steep **ramps** you see etched into the hillside, with steps on either side and a channel at the centre for dragging up the sarcophagi. Those ramps that are exposed are nevertheless sometimes partly sanded over; the more nimble visitor can afterwards pick and slalom his way back down to the Nile pretty quickly.

The tombs are numbered in ascending order from south to north. The path brings you up to the northern (high-numbered) tombs; after working your way south you can then zip down a ramp, or otherwise retrace your steps and return to the river by the path.

Tomb 36

This is the tomb of **Sirenput I**. It is about 60 years older than that of his namesake in Tomb 31, though both are XII Dynasty. These are the two finest tombs. Sirenput I was governor and overseer of the priests of Khnum and Satet. A limestone doorway leads to a six-columned courtyard decorated with the makings of a contented afterlife: a large figure of the deceased followed by his sandal-bearer and two dogs; another of his bow-bearer, dog and three sons; and other paintings of fishing, women bringing flowers and two men gambling.

Tomb 31

This tomb of **Sirenput II**, who was also a governor, is one of the largest and best preserved. It was constructed at the apogee of the Middle Kingdom, when Egypt extended its power beyond the Second Cataract. Beyond a six-pillared hall without decoration is a corridor with three niches on either side with Osiris statues of the deceased cut from the rock. The dead man appears with his son in a brightly coloured painting to the left of the first niche; he appears again on each of the four pillars in the small hall beyond, the artist's grid lines for setting out the pictures still visible on some. At the back of this hall is a recess with good paintings on stucco and very fine hieroglyphics. On the left wall Sirenput is shown with his wife and son; on the right wall his mother sits at a table while he stands to the right. On the centre wall Sirenput sits at a table and his son stands before him clutching flowers. Notice the wonderfully coloured and detailed hieroglyphics here, particularly of birds and animals, including (upper left) an elephant.

Tombs 25 and 26

These tombs of **Mekhu** and his son **Sabni** date from the VI Dynasty, a period of decline, and are crude both in construction and decoration. It is the entrance of Tomb 26 that is noteworthy: an inscription on it states that Sabni, governor of the south, mounted an expedition against the Nubians who had killed his father; that he recovered the body which was then mummified by embalmers sent by the pharaoh; and that Sabni went to Memphis to thank him and offer presents. Apart from instancing an occasion of Yebu's military role on Egypt's southern border, the inscription shows how much importance was attached to the outpost by Memphis.

The summit of the hill is crowned with the **Kubbet el Hawa**, the shrine of a local sheikh and holy man, and commands a magnificent view of the Nile valley, the cataract and the desert that more than compensates for the difficult climb. A path runs from here across the desert to **St Simeon's Monastery**, about 45 minutes by foot.

The Mausoleum of the Aga Khan and St Simeon's Monastery

Unless you cross the sands from the nobles' tombs, you must take a felucca to reach the west bank landing near the Aga Khan's Mausoleum. At a corral by the landing stage you can hire a camel for St Simeon's (about LE10, including waiting for an hour at the monastery); otherwise it is no more than a 20-minute walk.

The Mausoleum

Aga Khan is the title assumed by the dynastic spiritual leader of the Nizari branch of the Ismailis, a Shi'ite sect (as were the Fatimids) centred on India but with large communities in East Africa and elsewhere. Aga Khan III was an important figure in international affairs and in 1937 became president of the League of Nations. He was also a man of considerable bulk and was of such wealth that on his diamond jubilee in 1945 he was weighed in diamonds, which were then distributed to his followers. The succession passed over his playboy son Ali (who was briefly married to Rita Hayworth) and went to his more earnest grandson Karim, Aga Khan IV.

Closed to visitors since 1997, the mausoleum is built above the white villa where, until his death in 1957, Aga Khan III spent the winter months and where his French-born wife, the Begum, lived for three months each year until her death in 2000. Now she lies beside her husband in the mausoleum. Apart from its beauty, the Aga Khan associated himself with the spot after he found a cure there for his leg trouble by immersing himself up to the waist in the sand. The restrained proportions and the granite and sandstone of the domed mausoleum are entirely in keeping with the surroundings. The tomb within is of white Carrara marble, beautifully carved in Cairo with geometric patterns and Koranic inscriptions in high relief. Each morning in winter the Begum would lay a red rose on the tomb; the ritual was taken over in summer by the gardener. There is a story that one July not a single rose was to be found in Egypt and on six successive days a red rose was flown in by private plane from Paris.

St Simeon's Monastery

Open daily in winter 7–4, in summer 7–5; adm LE12.

The **monastery of St Simeon** (Deir Amba Samaan) with its towers and walls looms like a Byzantine fortress on a ridge at the head of a desert valley once cultivated with fields and gardens down to the Nile. Built in the 7th century and rebuilt in the 10th, it is the finest example of an original Christian monastery in Egypt, and is highly evocative. Little is known of St Simeon—he was not the Stylite—and in any case the monastery was first dedicated to Anba Hadra, a bishop of Aswan and saint of the late 4th century, who the day after his marriage encountered a funeral procession and decided to give up the world for a desert cave. The saint's tomb may have been here, a pilgrims' rest and monastery growing up afterwards. Fearful that the monastery might serve as a refuge for Christian Nubians during their forays into southern Egypt, Saladin destroyed it in 1173.

St Simeon's was built on a grand scale, with dressed stone walls 10m high. A small city lay within the walls, with cells for 300 resident monks and dormitories for several hundred pilgrims, as well as bakeries and workshops to support the community. The hills and desert around offered solitude and godly communion for probably thousands of monks and hermits. The lower storeys of the monastery are stone; the upper are mud brick and it is these that have mostly fallen into decay or vanished altogether.

You enter the portal, and before you, on a height, is the three-storey keep, open to the sky, cells on either side of the long corridors. Stucco seems to have been applied throughout the monastery, and on it, in the apses of the basilica to your left, are badly damaged paintings. There is a Christ Pantocrator in the central apse; on the sides, the faces of saints have been cut out. Names are carved right into the paintings by Arabs and tourists alike—it is not only time that has taken its toll. The monastery has never been systematically excavated, and repairs have been slight; it is largely a confusion of vaults, staircases, walls, workshops and quarters. From the tops of the walls there is a glimpse of Aswan, of green, but around 350 of the other degrees there is only the desert sea, luridly red at sundown. Yet there is an evening breeze, and amid the gardens and within the shadow of the towering walls it must have been cool. It is strange to wander round these arches, vaults and apses of familiar shape and significance; and even before the Arabs came it must have been like that, this comforting bastion against the fierce landscape.

Sailing on the Nile

By now you have become addicted to sailing in a felucca on the Nile, and the only cure is to have more of it. The longer journey upstream to the island of **Sehel** is recommended. The round trip takes about three hours and you will have to bargain over the price (expect to pay at least LE50, but first check for the official rate at the tourist office). The current is against you but the prevailing wind is in your favour and the gaff is extended upwards giving great height and grace to the sail. Sehel is just below the First Cataract, and even at the north end of the island the boat is shoved about by turbulent whirlpools. Hawks hovering above the cliffs wheel and dive for fish.

You land on the east side and walk southwards over the sands to a granite outcrop streaked with bird droppings and covered with inscriptions from the IV Dynasty to the Ptolemaic period. Up top and towards the south is one of the most interesting (no.81), Ptolemaic in date but depicting Zoser and the god Khnum. The inscription relates to a famine lasting seven years through Zoser's reign. Zoser asks the governor of Aswan why the Nile has not flooded and is told that it is in the power of Khnum to whom Zoser then erects a temple. From here there is a view of the rocks and swirling waters of the cataract, but the pounding Nile and foam passed into history with the construction of the British dam. It is cool as you sail upon the river, though the sun can be dangerous; on the island there is no mistaking its ferocity. You need to be well shod, for the sand and piles of rock are blisteringly hot. A **Nubian village** lies off to the west and here you may be asked into a house and invited to enjoy a refreshing cup of mint tea. The walls are thick and insulating, and the barrelled or domed roof reflects the heat at every angle; it is very cool inside.

The felucca tacks back down the Nile, taking advantage of the current. The boatmen drink directly from the Nile, pointing out that there is no bilharzia above Esna and certainly not in the middle of the river where the current flows swiftly. It is said that to drink from the Nile is to ensure your return; the water has a fresh and slightly organic taste. Nor, with bilharzia no nearer than Esna and the crocodiles held at bay by the High Dam, need you resist plunging into the river altogether and opening your eyes in the almost impenetrably green water. Afterwards, you smell like the Nile, but a shower admits you once again onto the terrace of the Old Cataract. Just as they are designed to catch the slightest breeze, so in the last faint blue of sunset the felucca sails catch that glimmer of light off the horizon, and like crescent moons glide among the rocks in the Nile below.

Getting Around

A visit to the granite quarry with its **unfinished obelisk**, to the old **Aswan Dam** and the new **High Dam**, as well as a trip out to **Philae** can be done in a morning, starting early. Taking an hour or two longer will allow you also to visit the **New Kalabsha** site.

There is a *son et lumière* programme at Philae. Shows are in various languages, including English, French, German, Italian, Spanish and Arabic, depending on the day of the week and the time of evening. There are three shows a night: *8, 9.30 and 11 in summer, usually two hours earlier in winter; adm LE33.*

The Fatimid Cemetery and Ancient Quarries

Open daily 7–5 in winter, 7–6 in summer. Adm to quarry LE10.

A road leading off the roundabout by the Ferial Gardens turns south towards the **Fatimid cemetery** with its domed mausolea of holy figures, some local, others—such as Sayyida Zeinab, Ali's daughter and granddaughter of the Prophet—more widely revered. A turning to the left brings you to an **ancient granite quarry**. From this and similar quarries around Aswan came the prized pink or red granite used for statues, columns and obelisks throughout Egypt and indeed throughout the ancient world. And here, still in place, is the **unfinished obelisk**. Roughly dressed and cut nearly free from the surrounding bedrock, in its finished state it would have weighed over 1 million kilos (2.3 million pounds) and would have been the largest piece of stone handled in history. But work stopped after a flaw was discovered in the stone; it may have been intended to complete the pair of which the lone Lateran obelisk, removed from the temple of Tuthmosis III near the east gateway of Karnak to Rome, was the other half.

The Aswan Dams

There is a LE5 fee if you get out of the car to look over the edge of the High Dam.

Back on the road south and 5km from town you come to the old **Aswan Dam**, built by the British between 1898 and 1902. The road passes over it and across the **First Cataract**; the water swirls round the jagged stones, plays white, but has lost its boil. The height of the dam was twice raised to increase irrigation and its hydroelectric capacity was multiplied, but Egypt's fast-growing population and the need both to increase her cultivable land area and to provide vast new supplies of power for Nasser's industrialization programme led to work beginning in the mid-1960s on the High Dam 6km upriver. The road linking the two runs through disturbed desert on the west bank, a giant disused sandpit it seems; you cannot imagine that this is the shore of an uncharted sand ocean stretching for hundreds of miles. Numerous electricity pylons add to the impression of it being a man-made litter ground. At the west approach to the dam there is a giant lotus-shaped monument originally commemorating Soviet–Egyptian co-operation.

The **High Dam** has commanded world attention. Its construction became a political issue between East and West. Its sheer size, its effect on the economic potential of the country and the sudden attention it forced on the Nubian antiquities threatened by the rising waters of Lake Nasser have all been extraordinary.

The dam was completed in 1971 and since then the water it contains has reached a height of 182m and has backed up 500km to the Second Cataract within the Sudan. Evaporation from the artificial lake amounts to 5,000 million cubic metres annually (about seven per cent of the lake's volume) and is causing unusual clouds and haze in the surrounding area, and even occasional rain. But the lake also retains the silt that once renewed Egypt's fields. Chemical fertilizer plants running off the dam's hydroelectric power are only partly succeeding in filling that gap—artificial fertilizers are no substitute for the nutrients in the silt on which a diversity of plant and insect life depended, so that there is now a marked decline in Egypt's birdlife. Also, where fields once received nourishing layers of silt, they are now sometimes suffering from mineral salts in the rising ground water. Against that, there are plans for a canal from the lake to draw water into the Western Desert, vastly increasing Egypt's cultivable land.

Though Egypt's population explosion and mistakes in economic policy have in some measure offset the dam's immediate benefits, it has already averted catastrophe. The droughts that have brought starvation to Ethiopia and the Sudan have recently seen the Nile fall to its lowest level in 350 years, and the same scenes of famine would be repeated in Egypt were it not for the High Dam. The British dam regulated the flow of the Nile during the course of the year; the High Dam can store surplus water over a number of years, balancing low floods against high and ensuring up to three harvests a year. The god Khnum has answered Zoser's prayer (*see* p.298).

The structure that achieves this contains the equivalent in material of 17 pyramids the size of the Great Pyramid of Cheops, and enough metal has been used in its gates, sluices and power plant to build 15 Eiffel Towers. The road runs across the top back to the east bank. In merely driving along, somehow the hugeness of the enterprise is lost upon you, and because it is not ancient, and because it is functional and it works, it is easy not to be impressed. It is even possible for some to complain that it was not worth the drowning of so many Nubian monuments. The same was said when the British built their dam, to which Churchill replied:

> *This offering of 1,500 millions of cubic feet of water to Hathor by the Wise Men of the West is the most cruel, the most wicked and the most senseless sacrifice ever offered on the altar of a false religion. The state must struggle and the people starve, in order that the professors may exult and the tourists find some place to scratch their names.*

Some feeling for the controlled energy of the place is realized at the **viewing platform** over to the eastern end of the dam. The green water rises in eddies, like large bursting bubbles from somewhere below the visible tops of the sluices. The generators hum as the river is put through its paces. Scores of lesser pylons flick currents of electricity towards the larger pylons striding across the desert, and bound by thick cables this energy is delivered into Egypt. Downstream, the Nile slips its harness and runs free beneath a glassy surface.

Open daily in winter 8–4, in summer 8–5; adm LE12.

Three principal monuments were moved to the archaeological site of New Kalabsha to save them from the rising waters of Lake Nasser. The site is on the west shore of the lake about a kilometre south of the High Dam. Access is by motor launch from the western end of the dam; also New Kalabsha is included in the sightseeing programme of the Lake Nasser cruise boats which moor at Sadd el Ali, the harbour at the eastern end of the dam. A launch from your boat will deliver you direct to the site.

The largest of the monuments at the site is the **Temple of Kalabsha**, which rises immediately beyond the landing stage. Its original site was 50km further south at ancient Talmis, now submerged, where it was the largest free-standing temple in Nubia and second in size only to the great rock-cut temple of Ramses II at Abu Simbel. Dedicated to Mandulis, a Nubian god associated with Isis, the temple was built during the reign of Augustus to the familiar blueprint of his Ptolemaic predecessors, though as it was being dismantled evidence was found of earlier structures dating from the times of Amenophis II and Ptolemy IX.

From the landing stage an imposing causeway of dressed stone leads westwards to the entrance pylon which admits to an open **court** and then to a **hypostyle hall** (the roof has fallen in), both with columns bearing elaborate floral capitals characteristic of the Graeco-Roman period. Only the columns on the north and south sides of the court stand at their full height, the style of their capitals mirroring one another, while the capitals of those in the hypostyle hall are so badly damaged that their style is difficult to make out at all. There is not much wall decoration in these parts of the temple, but there are crosses on the walls of the hypostyle hall, most noticeably to the left of the doorway, evidence that it later served as an early Christian church.

Three **chambers** lie beyond, the last being the sanctuary. All three are decorated with reliefs of Augustus making offerings to just about every god in the Egyptian and Nubian pantheons, which would have made him laugh had he ever come here to see for himself—after defeating Cleopatra and Antony, he was content to gaze at Alexander's preserved corpse in Alexandria but refused to visit any Egyptian temples, dismissing native beliefs and practices as bizarre.

Retracing your steps back to the hypostyle hall and passing round to the south side of the temple (that is, between the sanctuary and the outer enclosure wall), you come to a deep pit which is a **nilometer**. Returning to the open court, you notice openings at the north and south ends of the entrance pylon. These lead to interior **stairways** which ascend past chambers full of bats. The north stairway is the safest to climb; from the top of the pylon there is a good view over the whole of the temple and out across the waters of the lake.

Leaving the Temple of Kalabsha through its pylon doorway you see the **Kiosk of Qirtasi** a short distance to the south, a charming Ptolemaic edifice consisting of a single chamber formed by four columns with elaborate floral capitals. Two Hathor-headed capitals flank the north entrance: the kiosk originally stood by ancient sandstone quarries 40km to the south, and Hathor was the patron goddess of quarrymen and miners.

At the southwest corner of the Kalabsha temple is the small **Chapel of Dedwen**, a Nubian god, cut into the rock. Originally a mud brick wall enclosed this within the precincts of the main temple; it is thought to have served as a birth house.

A path leads northwest from here round to the small rock-cut **Temple of Beit al-Wali**, placed in the position relative to the Kalabsha temple it originally occupied before being removed to this site. Beit al-Wali in Arabic means House of the Governor, and it is thought to have been built by the viceroy of Cush (as Nubia was known in the New Kingdom) for Ramses II and dedicated to Amun-Re. Its walls are finely decorated with scenes of Ramses making offerings to the gods and of the youthful Pharoah in battle, carved in raised and sunk relief and once brightly painted; the colours have best survived in the interior of the temple.

Philae: Island of Isis

Open daily in winter 8–4, in summer 8–5; adm LE20, plus about LE20 per boat load. Launches depart on demand for the island site from the eastern end of the British dam.

Before the construction of the British dam, you could winter at Aswan and visit the **Temple of Isis** standing proud on its sacred island. But the dam all but submerged the temple for half the year during the winter, and Philae became a name only, hardly a place to visit. Yet there was romance in that visit, a romance, once established, far greater for some than any satisfaction gained from seeing the Temple of Isis raised again on new and profane ground. In *Daniel Martin*, John Fowles records the experience of many travellers from early in the twentieth century until the 1970s:

> *Then they drove to see the temple of Philae; a long row out into the lake, followed by the slow gondola-like tour round the submerged columns, shadowy shafts in the translucent green water. An exquisite light shimmered and danced on the parts that rose into the air. They and the guide were rowed by two old men, with scrawny wrists and mummified bare feet. Every so often, on the long haul, the pair would break into a strange question-and-answer boating-chant, half sung, half spoken. Work on transporting the temple to its new site, the guide proudly told them, would begin within the next few months; very soon sunken Philae would be abusimbelised. They didn't argue with him, but voted it a vulgarity, the whole project, over lunch.*

The annual rise and fall of the Nile, elevated behind the British dam, slowly wore on the inscriptions and reliefs of the temple and eventually, though perhaps after only hundreds of years, would have brought the whole thing down. But then the High Dam was built and the Temple of Isis, between the two, was permanently almost completely submerged; worse, where it rose just clear of the river it suffered swift daily tide-like movements that would have destroyed it (and Philae's other monuments) far sooner. With Hathor doubly gratified, it has now been the turn of professors and tourists to avenge Churchill's words.

Now Philae has been recreated. The nearby island of Agilqiyyah has been carved and sliced to replicate the original island, so that it is 450m long and 150m across, and the Temple of

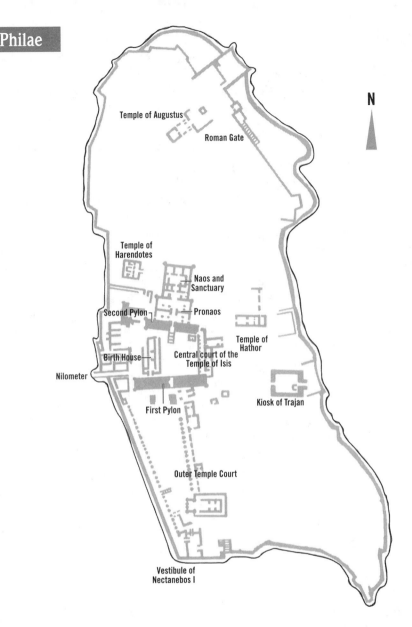

N

Temple of Augustus

Roman Gate

Temple of
Harendotes

Naos and
Sanctuary

Second Pylon

Pronaos

Temple of
Hathor

Birth House

Central court of the
Temple of Isis

Nilometer

First Pylon

Kiosk of Trajan

Outer Temple Court

Vestibule of
Nectanebos I

Isis as well as the Temple of Hathor and the Kiosk of Trajan have been placed in positions corresponding as nearly as possible to their previous relationship. (The plan shows the disposition of monuments on the original island of Philae, but those at the northern end of the island, in particular the Roman gate and the ruined Temple of Augustus, and also two Coptic churches and the remains of a monastery, were left where they stood.) The present site was opened to the public in 1980.

Approaching the Temple of Isis

The logical starting point for a tour of the Temple of Isis is the **Vestibule of Nectanebos I** (XXX Dynasty) at the southwest corner of the island (the landing stage is just below). The temple it once led to was washed away by the Nile, but this vestibule was rebuilt by Ptolemy II Philadelphos. Nearly every other monument on the island dates from the Ptolemaic and Roman periods, and Herodotus, who visited Elephantine *c.* 450 BC, seems to have found no reason to make any mention of Philae, though it is probable that older temples stood on the island then. Northwards extends the outer temple court, the first pylon of the Temple of Isis at its far end, **colonnades** on either side. The East Colonnade is unfinished, with many of the columns only rough-hewn; the West Colonnade follows the shoreline, its columns bearing reliefs of Tiberius offering gifts to the gods, the capitals of varying plant motifs, no two alike.

The **First Pylon**, 18m high and 45m wide, consists of two massive towers with a gateway between them. The towers were begun by Ptolemy II Philadelphos and completed by Ptolemy I Euergetes, though the decorations were carried out over a long period. On the front of the right or **eastern tower**, Ptolemy XII Neos Dionysos is shown in the traditional pharaonic pose of seizing his enemies by the hair, about to bash their brains out with a club; Isis, Hathor and the falcon-headed Horus of Edfu look on placidly. Above and to the right, Neos Dionysos offers the crowns of Upper and Lower Egypt to Horus the child. On the left or **western tower**, Neos Dionysos is again sacrificially braining his foes while above he appears before Unnefer (the name given to Osiris after his resurrection) and Isis, and before Isis and Harsiesis, a form of Horus. The reliefs have been severely damaged by the Copts. The vertical grooves on the towers were for holding flagstaffs. The main **gateway** was built earlier by Nectanebos and bears reliefs of his as well as Coptic crosses and, as you pass through, a French inscription on the right commemorating the victory of General Desaix over the Mamelukes in 1799 (*'L'an 6 de la Republique'*).

The gateway through the First Pylon admits to the forecourt of the temple, with the colonnaded quarters of the priests to the right, the **Birth House** to the left. The birth house became an essential feature of Ptolemaic temples, its purpose similar to Hatshepsut's depiction at Deir el Bahri of her divine birth. There, Hatshepsut justified her temporal rule by proclaiming her descent from Amun-Re: with the spread of the Osiris cult until under the Ptolemies it became the universal religion of Egypt, each pharaoh legitimized his accession by demonstrating his descent from Horus, first pharaoh and prime law-giver in the land.

The Cult of Osiris

There are many strands to the Osiris legend, and many accretions to the story and levels of meaning. Osiris, son of Re, was a king who ruled and was greatly loved in distant times. Isis was his sister and wife, Seth his brother. When Seth killed Osiris and dismembered his body, Isis searched out the pieces and put them together again, wondrously restoring Osiris to life in the underworld where he reigned as judge and king. Isis' son Horus was secretly raised to manhood in Lower Egypt and after a long and desperate struggle overcame Seth and established order over all Egypt. Historically, this may recall the subjection of the south by the north in pre-dynastic times. Mystically, Horus is the incarnation of his father, while Isis is the agent of both resurrection and reincarnation. Celebration of the rites relating to the legend, in particular to the birth of Horus, took place at birth houses such as this one at the Temple of Isis, the pharaoh proclaiming his legitimacy through his involvement in them.

The Birth House at Philae is surrounded on four sides by colonnades and round their walls and columns are reliefs and inscriptions dating from Euergetes II, Neos Dionysos, Augustus and Tiberius. In the last (northernmost) chamber within are reliefs of Horus as a falcon in the marshes, and Isis suckling Horus in the marshes of the Delta. On the west shore of the island, beyond the Birth House, is a nilometer.

The **Second Pylon** is at an angle to the first and not quite so large. Again, Neos Dionysos is shown before the deities, this time offering animal sacrifices and incense; the reliefs on the eastern tower are better preserved than those on the western. Shallow steps lead to the gateway between the two. Figures here of Euergetes II and deities are greatly defaced; on the right there is an inscription to Bishop Theodoros, in whose name, most likely, much of the defacement occurred. It is testimony to the sheer quantity of antiquities in Egypt that through 4,000 or more years, with one pharaoh defacing the work of another, Christians defacing the work of pagans, Muslims defacing the work of Christians and tourists defacing the work of everybody, there still remains so much to be defaced by those who can find the time and excuse for doing so.

Entering the Temple of the Goddess

It is through the Second Pylon that you enter the pronaos of the **Temple of Isis** proper. Pharaohs might have justified themselves at the Birth House, but this would have been the all-important goal of select pilgrims not only from Egypt but from all over the Mediterranean right through to the mid-6th century AD, for Isis was the hinge upon which the Osiris legend hung.

The walls of the pronaos are covered both outside and inside with **reliefs** of Ptolemies (Philadelphos, Euergetes II, etc.) and Roman emperors (Augustus, Tiberius, Antoninus) performing the customary ceremonies in the guise of pharaohs. Christian services, of which the numerous **Coptic crosses** chiselled in the walls are memorials, were celebrated in the court and pronaos. In the doorway of a room to the right is another Greek inscription to Bishop Theodoros, claiming credit for 'this good work'.

The three antechambers of the naos lead through to the **Sanctuary** with two small windows and a pedestal on which stood the sacred boat with the image of Isis. On the left wall is a relief of a pharaoh facing Isis whose wings protectively embrace Osiris; on the right wall (above) Isis enthroned suckles the infant Horus, and (below) Isis standing, her face gouged out by Christians, suckles a young pharaoh. Of course these pharaohs were Ptolemaic kings in pharaonic guise.

The Cult of Isis

Through her suffering and her joy the goddess offered an emotive identification so powerful and satisfying that she became identified too with all other goddesses of the Mediterranean, whom she finally absorbed. Isis was the Goddess of Ten Thousand Names, Shelter and Heaven to All Mankind, the House of Life, the Great Mother of All Gods and Nature, Victorious over Fate, the Promise of Immortality, Sexuality and Purity, the Glory of Women; when all else failed, she still could save. She was passionately worshipped by men and women alike. Cleopatra deliberately identified herself with Isis, and called herself the New Isis, casting Antony as Dionysos, the Greek equivalent of Osiris, so that on earth they affected the already existing cosmological bond.

Christianity, with its male-orientated antecedents in the Judaic and Greek religions, might never have given the prominence it did to the Virgin Mary had not a figure been needed to absorb the great popularity and success of the rival Isis cult. It was a rivalry that continued well into the Christian era. In spite of the edicts of the Roman Emperor Theodosius I, which succeeded in terminating the Olympic Games after a thousand years in the 4th century AD, pagan Philae continued as a centre of Isis worship till the reign of Justinian in the 6th century, while further into Nubia

Isis, from a relief at Dendera

the worship of Isis probably persisted until the Arab Islamic conquest.

West of the Temple of Isis

West of the second pylon is **Hadrian's Gateway** (which can be reached by leaving the naos of Isis' temple through a west doorway). It is preceded by a badly ruined vestibule which nevertheless preserves an interesting relief on the inside of its north wall (second register from the top), depicting the source of the Nile: the Nile god, entwined by a serpent, pours water from two jars.

The Source of the Nile

It is an ancient belief that the source of the Nile was at the First Cataract. The waters so swirled and seemed to flow in different directions that it was thought the river rose here from underground, flowing north to the Mediterranean and south into Africa. The belief hinged, as most beliefs do, on laziness and the desire not to spoil a good story: the most cursory examination of the river's flow at any point south of the First Cataract would have revealed, as no doubt it did reveal a thousand times, that the Nile always flows north. Herodotus, who enjoyed a good story himself, nevertheless dismissed the notion expressed in this relief. He traced the northerly flow of the Nile back deep into Africa, and even reported a theory, based almost certainly on lost knowledge, that the source of the Nile, and the cause of its floods, lay in distant snowfalls—a theory he rejected (though 2,000 or so years later it was proved right) because he could not imagine high snow mountains somewhere in the hot interior of Africa.

North of Hadrian's Gateway are the foundations of the **Temple of Harendotes**, built by the Emperor Claudius.

East of the Temple of Isis

East of the Second Pylon is the **Temple of Hathor**, a goddess comparable to the Greek Aphrodite despite the usual convention of cow's ears, built by Ptolemy VI Philometor and Euergetes II. The colonnade was decorated during the reign of Augustus with amusing **carvings** of music and drinking—apes dancing and one playing a lute, dwarfish Bes beating a tambourine, while Augustus offers a festal crown to Isis.

To the south stands the unfinished **Kiosk of Trajan**, a rectangular building of 14 columns with beautifully carved floral capitals. On the only two screen walls between the columns that have been completed are scenes of the Emperor Trajan offering incense and wine to Isis, Osiris and Horus. The elegance of the kiosk has made it the characteristic symbol of the island.

As you return to the landing stage, look south at the larger **island of Bigah**: this was the legendary burial place of Osiris. The original island of Philae, now submerged, lay alongside it to the east—in other words, the ancient priests and votaries of Isis would once have gazed westwards into the setting sun to see the resting place of the lord of the underworld.

Shopping

A couple of blocks back from the river is **Sharia el Souk**, Aswan's sinuous market street, the best bazaar outside Cairo, still with an atmosphere and an array of goods suggesting trade with Africa deeper south. Woven blankets and rugs are particularly good here and cheaper than elsewhere in Egypt; also there is silver, turquoise, ebony, spices, galabiyyas and much else besides. As you wander along, have a glass of pressed cane juice.

Like Luxor, Aswan's high season is from October to May when it is best to make reservations in advance. Summer can be slack and the heat should not deter you—it is a dry heat, and all but the cheapest places will have air conditioning.

very expensive

*****The New and Old Cataract Hotels**, Sharia Abtal el Tahrir, ✆ 316000 (New), ✆ 316002 (Old), 📧 316011, are beyond the Ferial Gardens south of the corniche. Like Luxor's Winter Palace, a new and characterless hotel has been given the name of a wonderful old hotel. **The Old Cataract** stands apart, on higher ground, with the most magnificent view in Aswan. Its outstanding amenity, happily open to everyone, is its terrace. Built in 1902, the Old Cataract has been well restored to the splendour of its early days and is the finest place to stay in Egypt. **The New Cataract** is a characterless modern place with shops, bank, and a hairdresser, and there is a swimming pool for both New and Old Cataract guests. Whether staying at the Old or the New, insist on a Nile-side room.

*****The Aswan Oberoi**, on Elephantine Island, ✆ 314667, 📧 313538, modern and slightly tacky, looks like an airport control tower rising absurdly from the north end of the island. It is owned by the same company as the Mena House at the Pyramids. It is reached by regular ferries designed like ancient Egyptian royal barges (free for guests and the curious alike). Deplorable though its concrete monumentality is, the Oberoi offers some fine views, particularly westwards at sundown from the rear terrace across to the Botanical Island. It has a bank, bookshop, hairdresser, café, nightclub, pool, boutiques and other trappings. Egyptair has a branch here.

*****Isis Island Aswan**, ✆ 317400, 📧 317405, is a 400-room resort hotel on a island in the Nile well to the south of Elephantine. That it was allowed to be built at all is most unfortunate, for apart from its being a scar on the landscape, and the noise of the launches which run like shuttle buses from the corniche by the Egyptair office, it encroaches upon a stretch of the river where several supposedly protected islands preserve the only original vegetation growing in Egypt. The greatest amenity of Aswan has been its tranquillity and sense of remoteness on the river which this vulgar hotel is helping to destroy. But if you find Aswan intolerable without a jogging track, mini-golf and temperature-controlled outdoor pool, this is the place for you.

expensive

****The Basma Swiss Inn**, ✆ 310901, 📧 310907, is on the hillside above the Old Cataract Hotel with fine views over the Nile. Rooms are stylish and fully equipped, and there is a large swimming pool. Distance is a bit of a problem, and so a free shuttle bus runs hourly to the Isis Hotel in town.

****The Isis**, Sharia Corniche el Nil, ✆ 315100, 📧 315500, a series of bungalows clinging step-like to the corniche embankment, offers views of the Aswan Oberoi blot opposite. It has all the usual facilities.

★★★★**Kalabsha**, Sharia Abtal el Tahrir, ✆ 302999, ✉ 305974, is a dull, misconceived block beyond the Cataract hotel, to be avoided unless you hanker after the atmosphere of 1960s public housing projects. It does have a nightclub, and guests can use the Cataract pool.

★★★**The Amun**, Amun Island, ✆ 313800, ✉ 317190, is arguably the hotel offering the most agreeable surroundings after the Old Cataract (and arguably before). The island is beautifully and peacefully situated just south of Elephantine and is reached by launches from the public gardens near the Egyptair office. The hotel, run by Club Med, is fairly small, which contributes to the atmosphere of peace and intimacy. There is a swimming pool, and the rooms, though not fancy, all have bathrooms and overlook the gardens and the Nile, alive with exotic birdlife. The restaurant perches above the rocks and the river, and you can watch the sails of feluccas gliding past your table, while enjoying an excellent meal.

★★★**The Cleopatra**, Sharia Saad Zaghloul, ✆ 324001, ✉ 314002, is a well-appointed place near the north end of the souk.

★★**The Ramses**, Sharia Abtal el Tahrir, ✆ 315702, at the north end of town near the train station, has comfortable rooms, most with balconies overlooking the Nile, all with air conditioning, private bathroom, fridge and TV. There is a bar, restaurant and disco.

★★**The Horus**, Corniche el Nil, ✆ 323323, ✉ 313313, is near the ferry landing for the Aswan Oberoi. Rooms are clean, air-conditioned, and have private bathroom, TV and Nile views.

★★**The Philae**, Corniche el Nil, ✆ 312089, is south towards the Thomas Cook office, and has small, clean rooms with showers, and either air conditioning or fans.

★★**The Happi**, Sharia Abtal el Tahrir, ✆ 314115, ✉ 314002, is just off the corniche and a bit north of the landing stage for the Aswan Oberoi. Its pleasant rooms are reasonably well appointed and have air conditioning and private bathrooms.

★★**The Oscar Hotel**, Sharia el Barka, ✆/✉ 326066, is between the bazaar street, Sharia el Souk, and the railway line, a situation that might not immediately recommend it, but it is well thought of by travellers. Some rooms have balconies and there is a rooftop terrace where beer is served.

★★**The Abu Simbel**, Corniche el Nil, ✆ 322888, is the best in this category, though improvements are moving it upwards into the *inexpensive* group. You come to it soon after reaching the corniche from the train station; it is surrounded by tree-shaded gardens. The rooms are air-conditioned, have private bathrooms, and many have fine views over the Nile. There is an outdoor café and a nightclub.

★**El Salaam**, Corniche el Nil, ✆ 322651, south of the Aswan Oberoi's ferry landing, offers clean rooms, all with bathrooms, some with air conditioning and balconies offering Nile views. Avoid the rooms at the back.

★The Hathor, Corniche el Nil, ✆ 314580, on the opposite corner to the El Salaam, has clean, bright rooms, many with Nile views, each with a tiny bathroom, and either fans or air conditioning. There is a pool and sundeck on the roof.

★The Mena, Sharia Atlas, ✆ 324388, is a trade-off of good value against inconvenient location, two blocks north of the train station and just back from the corniche. Clean rooms, most with air conditioning and all with bathrooms. There is a pleasant verandah and a roof garden.

★The Rosewan, Sharia Kamel Nour el Din, ✆ 304497 (turn right out of the train station, walk north one block, then left towards the corniche) is a clean and friendly place. The rooms are large and all have fans; private bathrooms cost extra.

Aswan's **youth hostel**, at the railway station end of Sharia Abtal el Tahrir, is a horrible place. The Aswan **campsite**, 2km south of town near the unfinished obelisk, is inconvenient unless you have your own wheels.

Eating Out and Entertainment

expensive

The **1902 Restaurant** at the Old Cataract Hotel is a sight in itself: a spacious chamber beneath a high dome supported by pillars and arches in ablaq style like a palace from the time of the Mamelukes—very impressive. Breakfast (included) is served here to guests; it is open to all for lunch and dinner.

inexpensive

Apart from dining at the hotels, there are several Egyptian restaurants along the corniche, sometimes with live Nubian music. Among these are the **Panorama** (near Egyptair), **El Shati** (just north of the police station), **Mona Lisa** and **Aswan Moon** (both opposite the Aswan Oberoi Hotel). All are inexpensive and some serve beer and wine.

Tucked away in the centre of town just east off the main market street, Sharia el Souk, is **El Masri**, a traditional place with excellent food. A bit to the south but also east of Sharia el Souk is **Al Saeda Nafesa**, a very friendly place and likewise inexpensive. Ask and you will be directed.

The Oberoi, New Cataract, Kalabsha and Abu Simbel hotels have nightclubs with Western and Nubian music, perhaps a belly dancer too, though the dancing is usually Nubian and worth seeing. In winter the **Aswan Cultural Centre** between the Abu Simbel and Philae hotels presents Nubian dancing.

Nubia: Lake Nasser and Abu Simbel

You feel you are now beyond the reach of history.

Dean Stanley in Nubia, 1852

South of the First Cataract at Aswan lay the ancient land of Nubia which extended along the valley of the Nile as far as the Fourth Cataract, a distance as the crow flies of about 700km. But much of Nubia now lies beneath the waters of Lake Nasser, 510km long. A third of southern Nubia, called Cush by the pharaohs and Ethiopia by the Greeks and Romans, which today lies in Sudan, has disappeared beneath the lake, while northern Nubia, which lies in Egypt, has been entirely submerged.

Both Nubians and ancient Egyptians were originally of the same Mediterranean stock, but their languages were distinct and the Nubians, as depicted in Egyptian art, had darker skins and curlier hair. Nubia tended to be dominated by Egyptian culture, and neither its resources nor its degree of centralized organization were as great as Egypt's, so that from the time of the Old Kingdom the Egyptians looked down on the Nubians as their poor provincial relations and regarded Nubia as theirs to exploit by right.

The pharaonic name for Nubia was *To-Kens*, meaning Land of the Bow, for the Nubians were famous as archers. The name *Nubia* itself came into usage only in Graeco-Roman times and seems to have been derived from the ancient Egyptian *nbw*, meaning 'gold'. Indeed, it was as a source of gold and of bowmen and other military recruits that Nubia was attractive to the Egyptians; also for its minerals, wood, incense and slaves, and because it was an avenue of African trade.

With the Middle Kingdom Nubia came under direct Egyptian military control as far south as the Second Cataract, near Egypt's present-day border with Sudan (that is, about 60km south of Abu Simbel), while during the New Kingdom the Egyptian presence was further asserted by the construction of numerous rock-cut temples, most of them during the reign of Ramses II. A thousand years later the Ptolemies, and the Romans who followed them, built in Nubia in their turn.

Therefore New Kingdom, Ptolemaic and Roman temples were the principal monuments that faced drowning beneath the waters of Lake Nasser as the High Dam at Aswan neared completion in the 1960s. Under the aegis of UNESCO, fifty countries contributed money and expertise, and, though some monuments were left to their fate, as many as possible were removed to other sites—some abroad, others on higher ground in Nubia itself; it is these latter you come to see.

The grandest of the monuments, Abu Simbel, can be visited by air, while New Kalabsha involves nothing more than a short trip in a motor launch

N

50km
30 miles

~~~~~ Original course of the Nile

○ *Dabod* Submerged ancient site

Lake Nasser

Nile

Kom Ombo

Elephantine **II** ○ Aswan

Aswan Dam (First Cataract)

II Philae
High Dam

New Kalabsha

Dabod

Qirtasi

(Beit el Wali)

Kalabsha

Dendur

Lake

Nasser

Gerf Hussein

Dakka

Maharraqa

W e s t e r n

E G Y P T

Wadi el Sebua

New Sebua **II**

New Amada
II Amada

Aniba

Derr

Canal to the New Valley

Qasr Ibrim

Toshka

Abu Simbel II

D e s e r t

Wadi Halfa

Second Cataract

S U D A N

from the Aswan High Dam. But several other monuments have been gathered at New Sebua and New Amada and can only be visited by joining a Lake Nasser cruise, calling in at New Kalabsha and Abu Simbel too, and mooring off the strange site of Qasr Ibrim.

What is almost entirely missing in Nubia, however, is Nubians. Their country began to be sacrificed to the larger needs of Egypt with the completion of the British dam at Aswan in 1902 when the drowning of Nubia began. At first the Nubians moved their villages to higher ground, and each time the height of the dam was increased, in 1912 and 1934, they moved their villages again. But with the construction of the High Dam in the 1960s, they had no choice but to accept relocation altogether. Their lives had always been bound up with the river, far more closely than the Egyptians were: 'We have lost our land, our way of life. We used to live entirely by the riverside, planting, fishing and hunting.' Apart from the few living on the islands of Elephantine and Shellal, most have been resettled in government housing well back from the Nile at Aswan, Kom Ombo, Daraw and towards the airport at Abu Simbel. 'We have lost nature', they will tell you. 'This is what we miss.'

Some of them return, as one man did after nearly thirty years in 1989, when the drought in the Sudan caused the level of the lake to drop by nearly half, exposing his village with its mosque, its houses—he recognized his own—and the cemetery where his grandparents lay. Now he works on a cruise boat plying Lake Nasser, and to the passengers who have come to see ancient temples salvaged from its depths, he speaks from his memory: 'Here we are moored above a date grove'. The monuments are set in a spectacular landscape, but a landscape even more beyond the feel of human life and history than a hundred and fifty years ago. Not even memories grow in Nubia now.

Cruising Lake Nasser

See pp.4–7 and p.321 for cruise operators

The cruise boats for Lake Nasser are at **Sadd al-Ali**, which is Arabic for the High Dam and is also the name of the railway station and of the small harbour facility, both to the east of the dam. The Sudan ferry also puts in here. The harbour is 12km south of Aswan; you will need to hire a taxi.

Even before you set sail you will be taken by motor launch from your boat across the south face of the High Dam to New Kalabsha on the far side of the lake (*see* p.301). The cruise boat now heads south on a long journey of 150km before reaching New Sebua. At 10km you sail over the original site of the Graeco-Roman temple of Isis at Dabod (it now stands in parkland in Madrid). At 35km you are over the original site of the Kiosk of Qirtasi and at 50km the original site of the temples of Kalabsha and Beit al-Wali—all three now removed to New Kalabsha. At 60km you cross the Tropic of Cancer, and at 70km you pass over the one-time home of the Roman Temple of Dendur, which has now been fostered out to the Metropolitan Museum of Art in New York. At 85km you are floating above the rock-cut temple of Gerf Hussein from which the colossal statue of Ramses II now in the Nubia Museum at Aswan was rescued. The temple itself, however, lies submerged in a realm of darkness; the average depth of the lake is 180m.

At one of the broadest expanses of the lake you sail over the original sites of the temples of Dakka and Maharraqa, 95km and 105km south of Sadd al-Ali, which have been removed to New Sebua. All along this stretch and nearly to New Sebua the lake is very broad, generally 20–35km across, and there is no sense at all of Nubia as it was when it hugged the Nile.

New Sebua

But that changes as you arrive at the west bank site of New Sebua, 150km south of Sadd al-Ali, where the lake narrows to the width of a broad river and the Nubian landscape in all its strangeness fills your eye. The launch brings you in over shallow marshes, where three temples are ranged on a ridge above you, rugged rock outcrops burst from the orange sand and low pyramidal peaks crouch darkly against the horizon.

The leftmost monument as you land at the site, standing apart from the other two, is the **Temple of Wadi el Sebua**. Moved here in the early 1960s from 4km further upstream, it was built for Ramses II in the middle years of his reign by his viceroy of Cush who also constructed the almost identical and now drowned temple at Gerf Hussein. *Wadi el Sebua* in Arabic means 'valley of the lions' and refers to the **avenue** of lion-bodied sphinxes that leads up through the two ruinous mud brick outer courts of the temple. The sphinxes in the first court bear the heads of Ramses II, while those in the second are falcon-headed. A stairway rises out of the second court and brings you before a sandstone pylon leading into the **hypostyle hall**, where Ramses appears in the form of Osiris on its ten crudely carved pillars, most of them headless—the hypostyle hall and the rock-cut part of the temple beyond it later served as a church, where the Christians hacked away or plastered over the pagan images. The sanctuary is at the most interior point and until the Christians got at them contained statues of Amun-Re, Re-Herakhte and the godly Ramses himself, the triad to whom the temple was dedicated. The temple was carved with dedicatory scenes throughout, and these have been laid bare again as most of the plaster has come away. But on the back wall of the sanctuary some of the plaster has survived, bringing the pharaonic and the Christian periods into surreal conjunction, for you see Ramses offering flowers not to a god but to St Peter.

Camels run a shuttle service for those who prefer not to walk between the Temple of Wadi el Sebua and the temples of Dakka and Maharraqa, about a kilometre to the north.

The rebuilt **Temple of Dakka**, dedicated to Thoth, has been faithfully aligned north–south, the pylon therefore facing downstream just as it was at its original site (*see* above), in contrast to the east–west alignment of most temples in Nubia. Though substantially of Ptolemaic construction, the temple was begun by a Nubian king based near the Fourth Cataract and received its sanctuary and its disproportionately large though elegant **pylon** during the reigns of the Roman emperors Augustus and Tiberius. Each tower of the pylon has an internal staircase leading up to the roof from where you gain a commanding view of the strange beauty of the landscape. Beyond the pylon is an open court, its side walls gone; then begins the temple proper, with a pronaos leading to a transverse chamber which in turn leads into the original Nubian-built sanctuary, offering reliefs of generally high quality throughout. The final chamber, the added-on Roman sanctuary, is crudely decorated.

The northernmost and smallest of the three temples at New Sebua, also moved here from the north (*see* above), is the Roman **Temple of Maharraqa**, which is believed to have been dedicated to Serapis. Its decorations were never completed, yet it is this that makes it interesting. Climb the spiral staircase (possibly a unique feature in ancient Egyptian building) at the northeast corner of the main hall so that you can look down on the unfinished floral capitals of the columns. They remind you of the story of the man who, presented with a solid block of stone, said that anyone could carve an elephant: 'You just cut away everything that doesn't look like an elephant'. Here a first attempt was made to cut away everything that did not look like a lotus, palm and papyrus bouquet, but the task was soon abandoned, leaving you full of admiration for the skill of those who elsewhere went beyond the preliminary outline phase seen here to produce capitals of astonishing delicacy.

From the top of the stairway at the Maharraqa temple you gain a wonderful view—including, if they are still at it, the work of the farming family who have raised a crop of tomatoes, courgettes and melons in a well-watered field just to the north, a gauze of green against the burning sand. This family here at New Segua and a few others near New Amada have recently come from the Delta to Nubia where they earn a premium price for producing crops two months earlier than their season in the rest of Egypt.

You might think that the shores of Lake Nasser would be brimming with enterprises such as these, for the sandy soil is ideal for crops of this type and water is unlimited. But the government makes it almost impossible for individuals to purchase land in Nubia, as that would involve investment in infrastructure—roads, electricity, markets, schools and security. Similarly, though Lake Nasser abounds in fish, next to nothing has been done to build up a local fishing-based economy. Instead the fishing rights have been leased to two large companies operating refrigerator boats to which local fishermen are obliged to sell their catch at a knockdown price, about one-tenth that paid in the Cairo market.

But the traveller gazing from the deck of his cruise boat can content himself with the vacancy of Nubia's austere and beautiful landscape. You watch the sun go down to the sudden cry of birds and then listen to the perfect silence. Moored out in the lake you look across to New Sebua, where after darkness falls the temples are illuminated, and this is magical. Then the switch is flicked and the shore goes black and the sky above goes thick with stars, bright ones, dim ones, some no more than dust and powder.

A Cruise Too Far?

When the sun goes down and the silence falls is the time to pick up a copy of Sir Arthur Conan Doyle's *The Tragedy of the Korosko*, published in 1898. The *Korosko* is a cruise boat not unlike your own, dear reader, and even in those days the landscape was bleak enough, deserts rising on either side, with Nubia writhing 'like a green sand-worm along the course of the river. Here and there it disappears altogether, and the Nile runs between black and sun-cracked hills, with the orange drift-sand lying like glaciers in their valleys. Everywhere one sees traces of vanished races and submerged civilizations. Grotesque graves dot the hills or stand up against the skyline: pyramidal graves, tumulus graves, rock graves—everywhere, graves... It is through this weird, dead country that the tourists smoke and gossip and flirt.'

Kitchener has not yet taken Khartoum and avenged the death of Gordon at the hands of the Mahdi and his fundamentalist Dervish followers, who threaten Egypt along its southern frontier. But the passengers of the *Korosko* form 'a merry party' as 'even Anglo-Saxon ice thaws rapidly upon the Nile', so that when the boat has tied up for the evening and from somewhere in the distant shadows there is 'a high shrill whimpering, rising and swelling, to end in a long weary wail', only the ladies give a start and are laughingly reassured that they have heard nothing more than the howl of a jackal. There are no Dervishes for miles about, one gentleman insists, as everyone goes to their cabins and shuts their doors to cheery calls of goodnight. The *Korosko* now lies tethered, silent and motionless against the bank, while 'beyond this one point of civilization and of comfort there lay the limitless, savage, unchangeable desert, straw-coloured and dream-like in the moonlight, mottled over with the black shadows of the hills'.

Of course what happens to the passengers is not what will happen to you. Even after the lights go out on the temples at New Sebua, you have always sunrise and croissants to look forward too—assuming nothing befalls you before the dawn.

New Amada

The sensation of voyaging along a broad river continues for nearly the whole 45km or so to New Amada. After New Sebua there is a bend in the lake towards the west, but soon you are sailing southwards again with high mountains closing in along the eastern shore. Then the lake sweeps away to the north at the place that was once Korosko, which until the beginning of the twentieth century was the starting point of the great caravan route that struck south across the desert, avoiding the Second, Third and Fourth Cataracts and further windings of the Nile, and in eight to ten days reaching Abu Hamed, 400km north of Khartoum.

New Amada, like New Sebua, lies off to starboard, but because the lake is now running north you land on its eastern shore. Crocodiles are an occasional hazard. Large numbers of them inhabit the lake, where they can grow to the length of a living room, and sometimes

Crocodile on a sandbank

they like to bask on shore, forcing tours to be postponed. Judging from sightings of their tracks, they are especially fond of New Amada.

At New Amada there are two temples and a tomb to see, all within a few minutes' walk of one another. The **Temple of Amada** was built during the reigns of Tuthmosis III, Amenophis II and Tuthmosis IV of the XVIII Dynasty and is the oldest surviving monument on Lake Nasser. Though its exterior is unprepossessing, the interior, partly restored under Seti I (XX Dynasty), is decorated with high quality raised reliefs which largely owe their preservation to having been plastered over when the temple served as a Christian church. For the sake of the reliefs the main body of the temple, instead of being dismantled like its forepart, was moved in a single piece—jacked up and placed on flatcars, then hauled along railtracks 2.5km away from its original location, now 60m below the lake. Many of the reliefs show the various pharaohs making offerings to Amun-Re and Re-Herakhte, to whom the temple, like most others in Nubia, was dedicated.

But most interesting historically is the hieroglyphic inscription on the rear wall of the sanctuary, where Amenophis II describes a victorious military campaign in Syria: 'His Majesty returned in joy to his father Amun after he had slain with his own mace the seven chiefs of the district of Takhesy, who were then hung upside down from the prow of the boat of His Majesty'. After battering out the brains of his enemies, Amenophis displayed six of their bodies from the walls of Thebes, while the body of the seventh was suspended upside down from the prow of a ship which sailed the entire length of Nubia as far as the Fourth Cataract to impress the inhabitants with his power. And indeed, if you count four registers up from the bottom and look about a third of the way from the left, there he is, the upside-down man, after three thousand four hundred years, suffering still an unwanted fame.

The rock-cut **Temple of Derr** was removed here from its original site 11km away to the southwest where it stood on the opposite bank of the Nile. Built during the second half of Ramses II's reign, it served the familiar purpose of associating his deified self with Amun-Re and Re-Herakhte, and also in this case Ptah. Their four statues, carved out of solid rock at the rear wall of the sanctuary, were hacked out by Christians when they made the temple into a church. In plan and decoration it resembles Ramses' great temple at Abu Simbel but on a smaller scale and without the colossal statues of himself set against the façade. The chief attractions are the painted carvings, in sunk relief, which though poorly executed are unusually bright and vivid.

From Aniba, which was 40km further along the Nile, comes the **Tomb of Pennut**, who was the chief administrator of northern Nubia under the viceroy of Cush during the reign of Ramses VI (XX Dynasty). He would seem to have been an Egyptianized Nubian, for he was buried at Aniba with other members of his family, whereas Egyptians usually made sure they were buried in their homeland. The tomb was already recorded as dilapidated in the 1920s, and half its painted reliefs had fallen or been hacked from the walls by the time it was moved to New Amada, but those that survive are delicately carved and often retain their colour, as for example on the rear right-hand wall of the tomb where his sons are shown bearing offerings to Re-Herakhte.

Qasr Ibrim

Soon the lake broadens and bends to the south, and 40km beyond New Amada, when you are hovering over what Baedeker described in 1929 as 'the pretty village of Aniba, shaded by palms' (and, long before that, Pennut's hometown), you see an island off to the east which was once a towering promontory overlooking the Nile. Your boat will slowly glide past the island, allowing you a leisurely look, but you will not be permitted to land: this is the only surviving original site in Nubia, and its rich and complex remains are reserved exclusively for archaeologists.

Where Baedeker could describe upon this 'lofty' pinnacle the 'extremely picturesque ruined fort of Qasr Ibrim, dating from Roman times', you now see only a jumble of stones and at the centre a collapsing cathedral. Founded in the seventh or eighth century, the basilica stands on the remains of a still earlier church, while off to the northwest stood a temple in the Egyptian style. These were the two most prominent buildings, standing among houses of the Ottoman period which completely filled the Roman fortress walls, which had replaced earlier Ptolemaic fortifications. But the history of the site goes back well beyond that, for incised in the steep west slope of the headland were several XVIII and XIX Dynasty stelae variously proclaiming the authority of Hatshepsut and Tuthmosis III, Amenophis II and Ramses II (these have been removed to New Sebua). Taharka (XXV Dynasty) also built a mud brick temple at what became the southwest corner of the fortress; converted to a Christian church, it remained a place of worship for two thousand years.

Indeed from pharaonic times through to the 19th century, Qasr Ibrim alternated between roles as a military bastion and a religious centre. Here, even later than at Philae, the worship of Isis persisted long after Egypt became a Christian country; this also became the last place in northern Nubia to fall to Islam when, following the Ottoman conquest of Egypt, a garrison of Bosnian mercenaries occupied Qasr Ibrim in 1528 and the cathedral became a mosque. During her return voyage from the Second Cataract in 1874, Amelia Edwards encountered their descendants who had intermarried with the local Nubians: 'At Ibrim, as at Derr, there are "fair" families [whose] light hair and blue eyes...date back to Bosnian forefathers of 360 years ago. These people give themselves airs, and are the *haute noblesse* of the place'.

Sailing on to Abu Simbel

From Qasr Ibrim to Abu Simbel the voyage is 60km, and here the lake becomes very broad again. At Toshka, halfway between the two, work has begun on a **canal** which will eventually be over 300km long and will link the lake with the oases of the Western Desert. The oases form a region known as the New Valley, so called in the expectation that its development will some day match the valley of the Nile for fertility. Until now the New Valley has relied entirely on local artesian water supplies, but the addition of canalized water from Lake Nasser could prove decisive in doubling Egypt's agricultural area. The canal is being financed by the sale of land along its projected path in lots of not less than 50,000 *feddans* to private companies of 'trusted' countries such as the United States and Saudi Arabia.

Finally the lake narrows again and the shore to the west runs flat against the sky—except for a pale mound into which you can just make out that something has been etched: the colossi of Ramses II set in the façade of his great rock-cut temple at Abu Simbel. The scene grows ever more imposing as you draw nearer, and you notice ant-like people scurrying about the site: these are the tourists who have arrived by air. By late afternoon the planes have taken them away, and with your boat tied up before the colossi, you have Abu Simbel to yourself. At night there is a *son et lumière* which is something like a drive-in movie: projected onto the façades of the temples, Ramses sighs for Nefertari, Nefertari sighs for Ramses, and chariots go galloping by. You are watching it all as you dine on deck by candlelight: it is wonderfully artful, thoroughly stupid and entirely delightful.

Abu Simbel

Originally the rock temples of Abu Simbel (280km south of Aswan, 40km north of Wadi Halfa on the Sudanese border) stared from the sandstone cliffs which rose like gigantic temple pylons over the narrow Nile. In 1812, John Lewis Burckhardt, the first European since classical times to visit Abu Simbel, was not immediately impressed; he had come upon the cliffs from above, and only as he gained the river and turned upstream was he struck by the four colossal statues of Ramses II. 'Could the sand be cleared away,' he said, 'a vast temple would be discovered.' The sand was repeatedly cleared away during the 19th century. Remarkable photographs were taken in the early 1850s by, among others, Maxime du Camp, Flaubert's travelling companion, of the sand rising over the faces of the two right-hand colossi. On Holy Thursday, Flaubert noted, 'We began clearing operations, to disengage the chin of one of the exterior colossi.' It was only later in the century, with the coming of the British, that Abu Simbel and so many other monuments were properly cleared. Then, usually by Cook's steamer, tourists came. Laid bare in all their glory, and enhanced by the unique and striking beauty of the setting, the temples of Abu Simbel excited the enthusiasm of early visitors. Baedeker allowed himself a large adjective: they 'are among the most

The Temple of Ramses in 1851

stupendous monuments of ancient Egyptian architecture'; and he went on to say: 'The temples produce a very grand effect by moonlight or at sunrise. The interior of the great temple is illuminated at night by electricity provided from the steamer.' Those were the days.

Getting There

by air

Abu Simbel can be reached by air direct from Cairo, Luxor or Aswan. Indeed, if the road is still closed (*see* below), this is the only way to get here apart from taking a cruise, and so, to make the temples more accessible to the indigent, the air fare has been temporarily halved. You should reserve a seat at the earliest opportunity, even from abroad if you can plan that far ahead, but it is always worthwhile trying at the last moment. If you want the sun shining full on the temple façades it is better to go in the morning, though that is also when the temples are most likely to be crawling with people. A two-hour stay at Abu Simbel is sufficient, and indeed you are usually issued with flight tickets timed to that assumption.

If you are flying from Aswan, the flight will take 25 minutes. Add to that the need to check in early and the likelihood that the flight will be delayed, and you can reckon that the expedition will take 5 hours in all. A bus will take you to the temples from the airport and back.

Thomas Cook, Misr Travel and others offer inclusive air tours from Aswan.

by cruise boat

Six cruise boats sail the waters of Lake Nasser between Sadd el-Ali (the port for Aswan) and Abu Simbel, calling at New Kalabsha, New Sebua, New Amada and Qasr Ibrim, the voyage taking three to four days. By far the two finest boats on the lake are the luxurious five-star MS *Eugénie* with *fin de siècle* décor, and the Art Deco MS *Kasr Ibrim*, each charging from $100 per person per day, all meals, site charges and the services of an excellent guide included. Both are operated by **Belle Époque Travel**, with offices in Cairo, ✆ 518 1857, ✉ 353 6114, and Aswan, ✆ 480391. Cruises are also included in packages by tour operators abroad, such as Cox and Kings. For more information *see* pp.4–7.

by road

A road from Aswan to Abu Simbel was opened in 1985, but it has been closed to foreigners since late 1997. Until then private taxis, luxury coaches and cheaper public buses used to ply the route from Aswan, taking three hours. Check at your hotel or the tourist office to see if the security situation has changed; meanwhile the only way to see the sites is to fly or take a cruise (*see* above).

Entrance to the Site

The site is *open daily from 6am to 5pm*, though if there are late-arriving flights it will stay open longer. Unless included in your air or coach tour, admission to both temples is LE30. The advantage of getting there early is that, as the temples face east, that is when the sun is shining on them. The disadvantage is that everyone else has the same idea. If the season seems busy and you want the place more to yourself, either stay overnight and see it at dawn, or consider coming later in the day.

Rescuing the Temples

As the waters of Lake Nasser rose during the mid-1960s, the original site of the temples was protected temporarily behind a coffer dam while the friable sandstone was injected with synthetic resin and then hand-sawn into 1,050 blocks. The first block was cut in spring 1965; by autumn 1967 block had been replaced upon block at the new site 210m from the old one and 61m higher up. The $42 million operation was organized and funded by UNESCO. The temples were saved, the dam was breached, and the sacred site, which had known human activity since prehistoric times, was swallowed by the lake.

If there is such a thing as spirit of place, it now lies behind and below you somewhere beneath the waters as you stand facing the colossi of Ramses. The reconstruction has been impeccable; you knock your knuckles against Ramses' foot and are assured it is stone, not plaster; you look for the filled-in joins in the torsos but cannot detect them; and if you are there at dawn you will see that the sun's rays fall flat upon the pharaonic faces and, if the temple door is open, penetrate to the innermost sanctuary. Everything is as it was before, except that it is here and not where it used to be, and that greatly weakens the force of the new Abu Simbel. The genius of the place lay in working with the living rock, the temple façades set into cliff faces seemingly prepared by nature for the purpose, the colossi of Ramses at the south temple and those of Nefertari at the north temple seeming to step out from the mountain, liberated from the imprisoning rock by the divine force of the rising sun. But when the cliffs are themselves reconstructions, that dramatic relationship between architecture and topography, and that mystical emergence of man from nature, suffers and perhaps is lost. To have left those ancient and powerful links intact would have meant surrendering the temples to the waters. Instead, it was decided to save the body and risk losing the soul. We now examine what remains.

Purpose of the Temples

The temples stand on the west bank of the lake, the more southerly **Temple of Re-Harakhte**, with its **colossi of Ramses II**, facing east, the smaller and more northerly **Temple of Hathor**, with its **colossi of Nefertari**, Ramses' wife, angled slightly towards the south. Before the lake, the temples overlooked a bend in the Nile and must have dominated the landscape. This in part explains their purpose. Travellers into Africa would first have seen the imposing colossi of Ramses, a proud spur to Egyptians, a warning of Egypt's might to any fractious Nubians. On the return, Hathor, in the guise of Nefertari, would welcome Egyptians and Nubians alike to the embrace of a great civilization. Also, the temples would have served as a convenient store for the gold and other riches exacted from Nubia as tribute, just as nearly a thousand years later the Parthenon served as the Athenian treasury. But the political and strongbox functions of Abu Simbel would have relied greatly on the religious character of the temples, and that the architects addressed themselves to religious symbolism of magnificent scale and quality there can be no doubt.

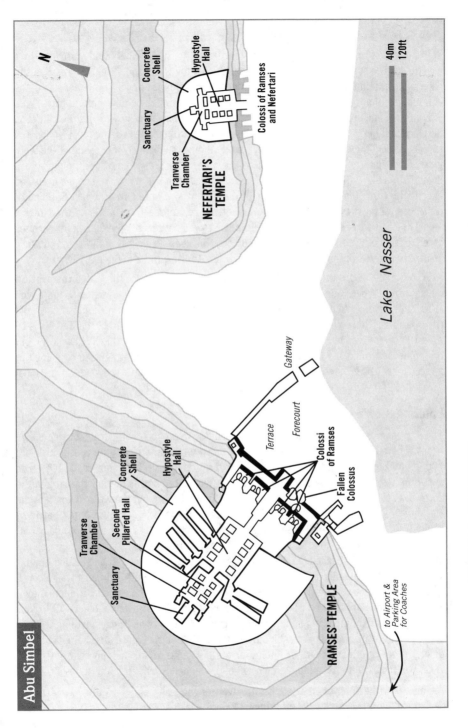

Abu Simbel

N

NEFERTARI'S TEMPLE

Concrete Shell

Sanctuary

Hypostyle Hall

Tranverse Chamber

Colossi of Ramses and Nefertari

40m
120ft

Lake Nasser

Tranverse Chamber

Sanctuary

Concrete Shell

Second Pillared Hall

Hypostyle Hall

Terrace

Gateway

Forecourt

Colossi of Ramses

Fallen Colossus

RAMSES' TEMPLE

to Airport & Parking Area for Coaches

You come first upon the **Temple of Re-Herakhte**, its trapezoidal façade crowned by a cavetto cornice surmounted by baboons worshipping the rising sun. The falcon-headed sun god stands within the niche above the entrance door. Arranged in pairs on either side of the entrance are the four enthroned **colossi of Ramses** wearing the double crown. Each figure is 20m high, taller than the colossi of Memnon at Thebes, and hewn from the cliff face. Between and beside the massive legs are smaller figures of members of the royal family. The feet and legs of the colossi are crudely carved, as though deliberately inchoate, but the work grows finer up through the torsos (the head and torso of the second colossus from the left fell in an earthquake during Ramses' own lifetime and has been left that way), and the heads are excellently executed. This is most true of the first head on the left, of which Burckhardt remarked, 'a most expressive, youthful countenance, approaching nearer to the Grecian model of beauty than that of any ancient Egyptian figure I have seen'. The sides of the **thrones** on either side of the entrance are decorated with Nile gods symbolically uniting Egypt, while below are fettered prisoners: those to the left black Africans; those to the right Syrians.

Also to the left of the entrance, on the nearest colossal leg, notice the Greek **inscription** which reads, 'When King Psammetichus came to Elephantine, this was written by those who sailed with Psammetichus the son of Theocles, and they came beyond Kerkis as far as the river permits. Those who spoke foreign tongues were led by Potasimto, the Egyptians by Amasis.' The reference is to the Nubian campaign of Psammetichus II (XXVI Dynasty), but the point is that already in the 6th century BC Greeks were operating in Egypt, albeit as mercenaries. At sea, however, they were in control of the Egyptian navy. With the arrival of Alexander 260 years later, they would be in control of Egypt itself.

Entering the Temple

The first room is the **Hypostyle Hall**, corresponding to an open court with covered colonnades. There are four pillars on either side, against which and facing the central aisle are 10m-high Osiris-type figures of Ramses, though this is Ramses alive, not dead, in athletic near-nudity showing a process of heroization at work. The best is the fourth figure in the north row. Heroic martial deeds are depicted in sunk relief around the walls. If you face the entrance you will see on the left (north) entrance wall a vigorous account of the **battle of Kadesh** in the fifth year of Ramses' reign. It was a battle Ramses endlessly boasted about, and boast he needed to do as it was no more than a Pyrrhic victory. Ramses cut himself out of a Hittite trap, but he failed to take Kadesh. Above Ramses is a vulture, and behind him his ka, who acted as guardian angel in the struggle. On the right (south) entrance wall a corresponding scene shows Ramses in the presence of Amun, to whom (as the inscription known as the **poem of Pentaur** tells it) the king appealed at his most desperate moment: 'What ails thee, my father Amun? Is it a father's part to ignore his son? Have I done anything without thee, do I not walk and halt at thy bidding? I have not disobeyed any course commanded by thee... What careth thy heart, O Amun, for these Asiatics so vile and ignorant of God?... What will men say if even a little thing befall him who bends himself to thy counsel?'

Facing again the interior, the left (south) wall of the hall bears an **epic masterpiece** depicting (below the top five reliefs showing Ramses making offerings to the gods) Ramses in his chariot storming a Syrian fortress, in the centre the pharaoh piercing a Libyan with his lance, and to the right his triumphal return from battle with black captives. On the opposite (north) wall are further scenes from the Hittite campaign while on the rear wall Ramses is shown leading Hittite and black captives. Lateral chambers leading off from this top end of the Hypostyle Hall were probably used for storing the Nubian tribute.

In the next hall of four pillars, reliefs on the left (south) wall show Ramses and Nefertari before the sacred boat of Amun, and on the opposite (north) wall a similar scene before the boat of Re-Herakhte. Three doors lead from here into a transverse chamber from which in turn three doors lead off, the central one into the **Sanctuary**. Four seated mutilated figures are carved out of the rear wall: Ptah, god of Memphis, Amun, god of Thebes, the divinized Ramses, and Re-Harakhte, god of Heliopolis. Before them is a stone block on which would have rested the sacred boat. The symbolism is one of unity, the pharaoh and gods of Egypt's three greatest cities as one; but there is also Ramses as the living and visible god, perhaps again to awe the Nubians. The entire temple leads to this central message: Ramses as conqueror, hero and then god, the awesome progression enhanced by the heightened perspective of ever-smaller chambers, ever-smaller doorways, and at dawn when the sun rose exactly opposite the temple, a brilliant shaft of light pointing to the sacred boat and Ramses with his fellow gods in the sanctuary. Leaving the temple you should stand before the façade again, before the entrance with its falcon-headed sun god, and imagine that effect.

You now walk on to the Temple of Hathor. Nearby there is a refreshment stand with trees and welcome shade. A while ago, and perhaps now too, there was a low mud rectangle beneath these trees, hardly more than an outline on the ground with a gap at one end, a niche at the other. It was a mosque, just broad enough for two prostrate figures, so great a contrast to the massive temples, so great a witness to the immanence and power of Allah.

The Temple of Hathor

The **Temple of Hathor** is secondary and complementary to the larger Temple of Re-Harakhte, and in some ways more symbolically satisfying. Hathor was wife to the sun god during his day's passage and mother to his rebirth. As Ramses is identified with the god of the first temple, so his wife Nefertari is identified with the goddess of this, and so god, goddess, pharaoh and wife are each mated with one another. The façade is again a pylon, though the cavetto cornice has fallen. A series of buttresses rise into the cliff, and between them six **colossal statues of Ramses and Nefertari**. You should get up close to them. There is the uncanny impression that they are emerging from the rock, that they are forming and will at any moment stride out towards the sunrise. The royal children stand knee-high in the shadows. Ramses framed these figures with a bold hieroglyphic inscription cut into the façade: 'Ramses II, he has made a temple, excavated in the mountain, of eternal workmanship, for the chief queen Nefertari beloved of Mut, in Nubia, forever and ever, Nefertari for whose sake the very sun does shine' (*see* p.250).

Inside the **Hypostyle Hall** with its crudely carved heads of Hathor on the six pillars, turn to examine the entrance wall. Ramses is smiting his enemies; Nefertari's hands are raised, perhaps as part of the ritual, though she seems to be seeking to moderate her husband's fury.

In any case, she cuts a delightful figure, a slender form in flowing dress, appealing, graceful, dignified. The side walls show Ramses before various gods, while the rear wall shows Nefertari before Hathor (left) and before Mut (right), consort of Amun and the pre-eminent goddess of Thebes. Three doors lead to a transverse chamber. On either side is a further chamber above the entrance to which is Hathor's cow in her boat. In the **Sanctuary** there is the startling sight of the divine cow emerging from the rear rock wall, a suggestion of the world beyond where her milk brings life to the souls of the dead.

The Bubble of Reality

If you enter the small door leading into the rock face to the right of Re-Harakhte's temple, the atmosphere is suddenly air-conditioned. You climb some stairs at the back and with even more surprise than at seeing a cow coming at you from a stone wall you enter a vast echoic dome. It is the bubble that surmounts the major temple and over which fill has been dumped and shaped to recreate the contour of the original bluff. A walkway runs right round the inside where there are abandoned displays and sheets of data explaining how it was all done. There is much to be said for this bubble. It is the one thing at Abu Simbel that is real.

Where to Stay

expensive

★★★★**The Nefertari**, ✆ 400508, overlooks Lake Nasser and is about 500m from the temples. Though often nearly empty during summer, it fills up during winter, when you should book ahead as far as possible. Rooms are of course air-conditioned, and there are tennis courts, a swimming pool and a restaurant.

moderate

★★★**The Nobaleh Ramses**, ✆/📠 400380, is in Abu Simbel town, about 1.5km from the temples. Its rooms are air-conditioned, large, clean and pleasant. You are usually required to take half board.

cheap

You can no longer spend a windy night sleeping out at the temples themselves to catch the magnificent dawn, but there is a **campsite** at the Nefertari Hotel.

Eating Out

You can have lunch at the **Nefertari** or **Nobaleh** hotels; there is little that is appealing in town.

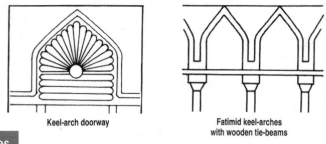

Keel-arch doorway

Fatimid keel-arches with wooden tie-beams

Arches

Ablaq: In Arab architecture, the alternating use of red and white or black and white stone.

Abu: Arabic for holy man or saint, whether Muslim or Christian.

Archimedes' screw: An irrigation device introduced during the Ptolemaic period for raising water by means of an inclined screw.

Amun: God of Thebes; as Amun-Re he was associated with the sun god and became the national god during the New Kingdom. His sacred animal was the ram. Amun was one of the Theban triad along with his wife Mut and their son Khonsu.

Ankh: The hieroglyphic sign for life, resembling a cross with a loop in place of the upper arm.

Anubis: God of the dead, associated with interment. His sacred animal was the dog or jackal.

Apis: The sacred bull of Memphis, buried in the Serapeum at Saqqara (*see* Ptah).

Apse: A semi-circular domed recess, most frequently at the east end of a church (*see* heikal).

Aton: The sun's disc; the life force. Worshipped by Akhenaton (see pp.53–5), who attacked the priesthood of Amun.

Atum: A sun god of Heliopolis, creator of the universe, often combined with Re and represented as a man.

Azan: The Muslim call to prayer (*see* muezzin).

Ba: A spirit that inhabits the body during life but is not attached to it; at death it leaves the body and joins the divine spirit (*see* ka).

Bab: A gate, as Bab Zuwayla.

Basilica: A building, for example a church, in the form of a long colonnaded hall, usually with one or more apses at the east end, and a narthex at the west end.

Bastet: The goddess of Bubastis, a goddess of joy. Her sacred animal was the lioness or cat.

Glossary

Bayt: A house, or the self-contained apartments into which Ummayad mansions and Abbasid palaces were divided.

Birth house: A temple annexe where the annual rites associated with the birth of the god-king were performed. On its interior walls are scenes of the divine marriage and the king's birth.

Benben: The primeval hill which first arose from the waters.

Bes: A protective dwarf-god, averter of evil, helper in childbirth.

Book of the Dead: The generic name given to a variable collection of spells (including for example the Amduat and the Book of the Gates) which from New Kingdom to Ptolemaic times were written on papyrus and buried with the mummy. They continue the tradition of the Pyramid Texts such as at the Pyramid of Unas and the funerary texts on tomb walls in the Valley of the Kings.

Cadi: A judge knowledgeable in Islamic law.

Caliph: Literally 'successor' to Mohammed, the title taken by those claiming the spiritual and temporal leadership of Islam.

Canopic jars: Containers placed within ancient tombs to preserve those organs and viscera thought essential for the dead man's continued existence in the afterlife.

Capitals: Pharaonic and Ptolemaic temples employed capitals decorated either with plant forms (palmiform, papyriform, lotiform) or other motifs (Hathoric, with the human face and cow's ears of Hathor; forms deriving from timber construction such as tent poles).

Cartouche: In hieroglyphics, the oval band enclosing the god's or pharaoh's name and symbolizing unchanging continuity.

Cataract: Rapids along the course of the Nile, caused by granite outcrops. The First Cataract is at Aswan and there are five more upriver to Khartoum, the Second Cataract near Wadi Halfa being the most formidable. Historically, all have been hazards to navigation.

Cavetto cornice: One of the most characteristic decorative features in ancient Egyptian architecture, a concave moulding decorated with palmettes. It was used along the tops of walls and pylons, projecting at front and sides. Below it would be a torus moulding.

Cenotaph: A symbolic rather than actual tomb.

Colossus: A greater than life-size statue, usually of a king.

Colours: Primary colours usually had particular applications and significance in ancient Egyptian painting. Black represented death: mummies, also Osiris as king of the dead, were commonly depicted in black. Blue was for sky and water, the sky gods were painted this colour. Green was the colour of rebirth: Osiris, who overcame death and was reborn, often had his face and limbs painted green; the solar disc was commonly painted light green on sarcophagi, instead of its usual red. Red was for blood and fire: men's bodies were depicted as reddish-brown or brown. It also had a maleficent connotation: Seth was painted reddish-brown. White represented silver and was the colour of the moon; it was also the colour of the garments of the gods and the crown of Upper Egypt. Yellow represented gold and was also used as the colour for women's bodies until the mid-XVIII Dynasty; thereafter the only women painted this colour were goddesses.

Columns: Like capitals, ancient columns followed certain decorative motifs, for example papyrus columns modelled either after a single stem and therefore smooth, or after a bundle of stems and therefore ribbed.

Crowns: The red crown of Lower Egypt was joined with the white crown of Upper Egypt to represent unification of the country. The blue crown or headdress was worn when riding a chariot; it appears after the introduction of the horse into Egypt by the Hyksos *c*. 1600 BC. No matter what headdress the pharaoh wore, he was always shown with the uraeus on his forehead.

Electrum: An alloy of gold and silver. The tips of obelisks were covered with electrum. In ancient Egypt, where gold was mined in abundance, both silver and electrum were more precious metals than gold alone.

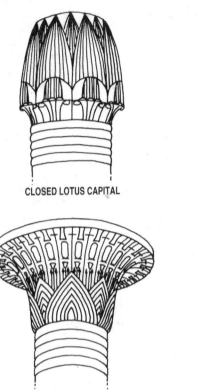

CLOSED LOTUS CAPITAL

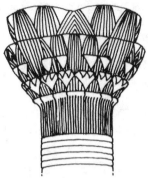

OPEN LOTUS CAPITAL

OPEN PAPYRUS CAPITAL

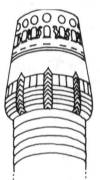

CLOSED PAPYRUS CAPITAL

Capitals

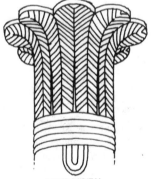

PALM CAPITAL

Ennead: A group of nine deities associated with a cult centre such as Heliopolis, where it consisted of the creator sun god Re-Atum and his descendants Shu (god of sunlight and air), Tefnut (goddess of moisture), Geb (earth god), Nut (sky goddess), Osiris (god of the underworld), Isis (goddess of magical powers), Seth (god of chaotic forces) and Nephthys (a funerary goddess).

Evil eye: The superstition that the envious glance of any passer-by, attracted by an immodest show of wealth, achievement or beauty, can harm or bewitch. Reciting certain verses of the Koran is one way of warding it off. Uzait Horun, the Eye of Horus, is meant to ensure safety and happiness and wards off the evil eye; it may be painted on cars, trucks and fishing boats, or worn as an amulet, particularly by children, who are especially vulnerable. Children also leave their handprints on walls to avert the evil eye. The probable value of the belief is as a social control, minimizing at least the appearance of disparity in people's fortunes and so promoting solidarity.

Exonarthex: The outer vestibule of a church.

Faïence: Glazed earthenware, often decorated, formed as pottery or in blocks or tiles as a wall facing.

Fellahin: Egyptian peasants. The singular is fellah.

Flagellum: A flail or rattle to drive away evil spirits, it could be used only by a pharaoh and so represented the royal authority in carvings and statues. The crook was held in the other hand, another royal symbol.

Geb: Personification of the earth.

Hajj: The pilgrimage to Mecca that all Muslims should make at least once in their lifetime. When they have done so, they will often paint a scene of the event on their houses.

Hamam: A bath, public or private.

Hapy: God of the abundant Nile, represented as a man with pendulous breasts.

Harem: The private family (or specifically the women's) quarter in a house.

Haroeris: The elder Horus.

Harpocrates: Horus as child.

Hathor: The goddess of heaven, joy and love; the Greeks identified her with Aphrodite. She was the deity of Dendera and protector of the Theban necropolis. Her sacred animal was the cow.

Heb-Sed: The jubilee marking the thirtieth year of a pharoah's reign (*see* p.178).

Hegira: Mohammed's flight, or more properly his 'withdrawal of affection' from Mecca in AD 622. The Muslim calender starts from this date.

Heikal: The sanctuary of a Coptic church; usually there are three.

Herakhte: A form of Horus, 'Horus of the horizon', often combined with the sun god as Re-Herakhte and so worshipped at Heliopolis. The falcon was sacred to him.

Horus: The son of Isis and Osiris, and revered as the sun god. He was represented as the sun disc or a falcon, his sacred animal.

Hyksos: A foreign people who ruled Egypt from Avaris in the Delta during the Second Intermediate Period. Probably Semites and possibly a displaced ruling caste from Palestine, they did not introduce a new culture but rather respected and encouraged Egyptian civilization and its institutions. Nevertheless, the propaganda of the Theban princes who ejected the Hyksos from the country, initiating the New Kingdom, made the period of Hyksos rule synonymous with anarchy and destruction.

Hypostyle: A hypostyle hall is any chamber whose ceiling is supported by columns or pillars.

Iconostasis: The screen carrying icons between the main part of a church and the sanctuary or choir.

Isis: Sister and wife to Osiris, mother of Horus, the patron goddess of Philae. She was most highly revered at a late period. She is often shown with a throne on her head.

Ithyphallic: Denoting the erect phallus of a depicted god or pharaoh, most commonly the god Min. It was a sign of fertility.

Ka: A spirit that inhabits the body during life and may leave it in death, but requires the continued existence of the body (hence mummification or, by substitution, ka statues) for its survival. The ka was personal and individual, in a sense the ideal image of a man's own life (*see* ba).

Khan: *See* wikala.

Khedive: Viceroy. Mohammed Ali was recognized in 1805 as viceroy of the Ottoman sultan in Istanbul, and his successors retained the title until the outbreak of the First World War in 1914. Egypt's nominal allegiance to the sultan thereupon ceased and its rulers assumed the title of king.

Khnum: The patron god of Elephantine Island and the Cataracts. He fashioned man on his potter's wheel. His sacred animal was the ram.

Khonsu: Son of Amun and Mut; god of the moon. The falcon was sacred to him.

Kom: The particularly Egyptian word for a tell, those great mounds of debris marking the site of ancient settlements.

Kufic: An early style of Arabic calligraphy with angular letters.

Lily: The plant identified with Upper Egypt.

Liwan: A vaulted hall (*see* mosque).

Maat: The goddess of truth, whose symbol was the ostrich feather. Maat is actually the deification of a concept for which Egyptians strove, both personally and for the state. As well as truth, one can attempt to define it as justice, correctness, balance. The best definition is the now rare English word 'meet'.

Madrasa: *See* mosque.

Maristan: A hospital.

Mashrabiyya: Interlaced wooden screenwork, used for example to cover street-facing windows in a house.

Mausoleum: A domed chamber with one or more tombs inside; though simple in form, these structures, characteristic of the City of the Dead, are sometimes of considerable beauty.

Mihrab: The niche in the qibla wall of a mosque, indicating the direction of Mecca.

Min: The god of the harvest, frequently amalgamated with Amun. He was ithyphallically represented. The Greeks identified him with Pan.

Minbar: The pulpit in a mosque from which the Friday prayer is spoken.

Monophysitism: Strictly, the Christian doctrine that the two natures of Christ (human and divine) are absorbed into one nature (the divine). Though this has often been said to be Coptic belief, that is not true: the Copts do not deny the continued existence of the two natures but stress their unity after the Incarnation. The Latin and Greek Churches emphasize the two natures of Christ, holding that they are unmixed and unchangeable even though indistinguishable and inseparable (Council of Chalcedon, 451); they are diophysite.

Mont: A Theban god of war, represented with a falcon's head.

Mosque: The first mosque was the courtyard of Mohammed's house at Medina, with no architectural refinements except a shaded area at one end. Indeed, the only requirement for a mosque is that it should demarcate a space in which people may gather for saying prayers, such as an open quadrangle marked off by a ditch. From this notion developed the congregational mosque, of

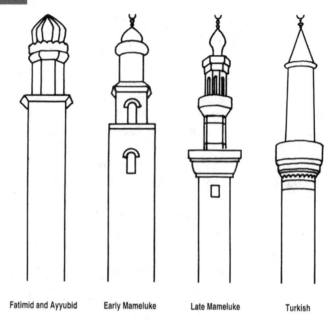

Fatimid and Ayyubid   Early Mameluke   Late Mameluke   Turkish

which the Ibn Tulun is the most outstanding example. Among non-congregational mosques are two special types which are of Cairene inspiration and development, the **cruciform madrasa** and the **sabil kuttab**. The madrasa served as a theological college, introduced by Saladin to combat Fatimid Shi'ism. Later it became more complex, a tomb appended and the madrasa formed of four liwans, each opening into a central court, hence cruciform. The outstanding example of this type is the Hassan. This pattern was subsequently modified: the court covered over, the east and west liwans reduced to vestigial proportions, and a Koranic school for boys (kuttab) added as a floor above, a public fountain (sabil) below.

Moulid: The birthday of a saint or holy man, Coptic or Muslim. This will often be celebrated at the level of folk religion, a pharaonic deity transformed into a Christian saint who in turn resurfaces as a Muslim sheikh.

Muezzin: A crier who, as from a minaret, calls the faithful to prayer (*see* azan).

Mut: The wife of Amun and mother of Khonsu. Her sacred animal was the vulture.

Naos: The enclosed inner 'house of the god' (also *cella*), the central room of a temple, though sometimes referring to the entire temple. The sanctuary.

Narthex: The entrance vestibule at the west end of a church.

Nashki: A cursive form of Arabic writing, subsequent to Kufic.

Necropolis: Greek for cemetery, literally city (*polis*) of the dead (*necros*).

Neith: Goddess of Sais, shown wearing the red crown of Lower Egypt. She was one of the goddesses who protected the dead and the Canopic jars.

Nephthys: Sister of Isis and Osiris, married to Seth. Shown with outstretched wings, one of the protector goddesses of the dead, guardian of the Canopic jars.

Nome: An administrative province of ancient Egypt. The chief official of a nome was the nomarch.

Nut: Goddess of the sky, often shown supported by Shu.

Opening of the Mouth: Funerary ceremony by which the mouth of the mummy was symbolically opened to ensure it could partake of nourishment in the afterlife.

Osiris: Originally a vegetation god, later the god of the underworld. Murdered and dismembered by Seth, he was the husband and brother of Isis and father of Horus.

Ostracon (plural **ostraca**): Potsherds bearing inscriptions.

Papyrus: A plant identified with Lower Egypt; it served as a writing material from I Dynasty to Islamic times.

Osirid Pillar

Pronaos: A columned porch, leading to the naos.

Ptah: The patron god of Memphis and father of the gods. His sacred animal was the Apis bull.

Pylon: Arranged in pairs, forming a monumental gateway to a temple. Where there are several sets of pylons, each preceding a court, they descend in size as the sanctuary of the god is approached, while the floor level rises, creating a focussing or tunnelling effect.

Pyramidion: The capstone of a pyramid.

Qibla wall: The wall of a mosque facing Mecca.

Re: The sun god, usually combined with another god, such as Atum-Re, Amun-Re or Re-Herakhte. His priesthood was at Heliopolis.

Riwaq: The arcade around a sahn, or a student apartment within the arcade.

Sabil kuttab: *See* mosque.

Sahn: An interior court, usually in a mosque.

Sakiya: An irrigation device introduced during the Ptolemaic period, consisting of buckets attached to a wheel which is driven by circling oxen and thus lifts water to the fields.

Sebakh, sebakhin: Koms, those mounds of debris that cover ancient sites, contain sebakh, an earth made up of as much as 12% potassium nitrate, sodium carbonate and ammonium chloride, which is used as fertilizer. Those who work the mounds are sebakhin.

Sekhmet: The lion goddess of war.

Selket: Scorpion goddess, often shown with a scorpion on her head; she was a guardian of the dead.

Serapis: A god invented by the Ptolemies, looking like Zeus but identified with Osiris-Apis.

Seth: God of chaos, brother and slayer of Osiris, adversary of Horus, he became a god of war, though after the XXII Dynasty he was reduced to the god of the impure. His sacred animal was possibly the aardvark.

Shaduf: A simple lever device for lifting water to irrigate the fields. It is operated by hand.

Shia or Shi'ites: Literally partisans, that is those who believe Ali, son in law of the Mohammed, should by divine right have succeeded to the caliphate, and that certain of his descendants have inherited that right. In their view, therefore, the first three caliphs were usurpers. Few Egyptians are Shi'a; nevertheless, the head of Hussein, son of Ali, is supposedly at the Mosque of Sayyidna al-Hussein in Cairo (*see* pp.104–5 for an account of the Shi'a–Sunni split). *See* Sunni.

Shu: The god of the air. He is often shown supporting Nut.

Sobek: God of the waters, patron of the Fayyum, the crocodile was sacred to him.

Squinch: Small arch or support across the corners of a square, enabling the carriage of a dome.

Stele: An upright stone slab or pillar with an inscription or design, which is used as a monument or grave marker.

Sunni: Orthodox Muslims, who attribute no special religious or political function to the descendants of Mohammed's son-in-law Ali. Virtually all Egyptian Muslims and close to 90 per cent of Muslims worldwide are Sunni. *See* Shia.

Tell: *See* kom.

Theban triad: Amun, his wife Mut and their son Khonsu.

Thoth: A moon deity and the god of science. The ibis and baboon were sacred to him.

Torus: A convex moulding (*see* cavetto cornice).

Uraeus: The cobra worn on the forehead of a pharoah as both an emblem and an instrument of protection, breathing flames and destroying enemies.

Ushabti: A mummiform figurine, serving in the tomb as deputy for the dead man, carrying out his labour obligations.

Wikala: An inn for travelling merchants built around a courtyard, with stables and warehouses at ground level and living accommodation above. Other names are khan and okel.

Pharaonic architectural features

Waqf: An endowment for the upkeep of a mosque, for example a nearby apartment house, or shops built into the street level of the mosque, earning rents.

Ziyadah: The outer court of a mosque.

The language of the country is Arabic, but English is taught to every schoolchild and is the foreign language most spoken by Egyptians, with French a close second. In particular, most staff at hotels, restaurants and travel companies catering to foreigners will speak English, probably French, and perhaps also German and Italian. So along the well-beaten tourist paths, language is unlikely to prove a problem. Even so, the purchase of a **traveller's phrasebook** at home or in Egypt can prove useful, and knowledge of a few words and phrases is always appreciated. Here are some courtesies and simple questions and remarks to set you off on the right track. Note that the ' (ain) is a gutteral vowel sound, achieved by constricting the throat as far back as possible.

Hello	*ahlan*
Hello/goodbye	*Salaam aleikum* ('peace be upon you', to which the reply is *wa aleikum el salaam*, 'and peace be upon you').
Please	*minfadlak* (if addressing a man) *minfadlik* (if addressing a woman)
Thank you	*shukran*
No thank you	*la shukran*
Yes	*aywa* or sometimes *nam*
No	*la*
I want	*'aayiz* (if addressing a man) *'ayza* (if addressing a woman)
How much?	*bekaam?*
Good	*kuwayyis*
Bad	*mish kuwayyis*

Used throughout this guide are the words *sharia* (street), and *midan* (square).

As well as learning to speak a few words in Arabic, it's useful to be able to recognize the Arabic numerals. As in the West, units are at the right, preceded by tens, hundreds, etc, as you move left. Recognition will prove a great help when shopping, examining bills, catching numbered buses, boarding numbered train carriages and looking for your numbered seat.

Note that there are several methods of transliterating Arabic into the Latin alphabet. For example, Giza can also be written as Gizeh, Dendera as Dandara, Edfu as Idfu, while Sultan

Language

Qaytbay can be written as Kait Bay, Qaitbai, Qait Bey, and so on. So in consulting the index or looking for places on maps, bear in mind possible variant spellings.

The literature on Egypt is vast, and apart from pursuing your interest in libraries and book-shops at home there are several bookshops in Cairo worth visiting. The American University in Cairo Press publishes a growing list of books on many aspects of Egypt past and present, including fiction, non-fiction and guides; their titles are widely available in Egypt and they have their own bookshop in Cairo.

A number of authors are quoted throughout the text of this guide, and you might like to pursue their books according to your interest. However, the following titles will provide introductions to various periods or aspects of Egyptian history.

Baines, John and Malek, Jaromir, *Atlas of Ancient Egypt* (Oxford, 1980). As well as an atlas, a description of sites and a history, this also covers social and cultural aspects.

Bowman, Alan K., *Egypt After the Pharaohs* (London, 1986). The Graeco-Roman period.

Carter, Howard, *The Tomb of Tutankhamen* (London, in three volumes, 1923, 1927, 1933). Subsequently reprinted in various forms, e.g. abridged, or the first volume only (the most immediate and exciting) as *The Discovery of the Tomb of Tutankhamen*, this is the first-hand account of the greatest Egyptological find of all.

Edwards, I.E.S., *The Pyramids of Egypt* (Harmondsworth, 1980). An expert and orthodox study by the late Keeper of Egyptian Antiquities at the British Museum.

Hart, George, *A Dictionary of Egyptian Gods and Goddesses* (London, 1986). A useful travelling companion, though short on help with visual identification.

Kamil, Jill, *Coptic Egypt* (Cairo, 1990). A history, guide and cultural summary.

Kitchen, K.A., *Pharaoh Triumphant* (Warminster, 1982). The life and times of Ramses II by the leading expert on the XIX Dynasty.

Lane, E.W., *Manners and Customs of the Modern Egyptians* (London, 1836, reprinted). The classic survey of early 19th-century Cairo.

Manley, Deborah, *The Nile: A Traveller's Anthology* (London, 1991). A varied, fascinating and hugely entertaining selection of travellers' responses to Egypt.

Mansfield, Peter, *The Arabs* (London, 1985). A review of Arab history and the present situation.

Moorhead, Alan, *The Blue Nile* (London, 1962). The splendidly readable account of the Ottomans, Napoleon and the British imperium in Egypt and up the Nile.

Rodenbeck, Max, *Cairo, the City Victorious* (London, 1998). An interweaving of history and anecdote from Pyramids to traffic jams.

Further Reading

Main page references are in **bold**. Page references to maps are in *italics*.

Index

DISCOVER EGYPT WITH COX & KINGS

Escorted Brochure Tours
Tailor-made Itineraries
Expert Service

Cox & Kings, the longest established travel company in the world, specialises in high quality cultural and natural history tours for both groups and individual travellers.

Cox & Kings is delighted to offer a comprehensive choice of holidays to Egypt, featuring some of the most prestigious boats and hotels including the M.S.Oberoi Philae, the Mena House in Cairo and the Old Winter Palace in Luxor.

- **Deluxe Nile cruises**
- **Lake Nasser cruises**
- **Cairo city breaks**

For further information on our Egyptian programme featured in the COX & KINGS' MIDDLE EAST & CENTRAL ASIA brochure please call **020 7873 5000** or visit our website: **www.coxandkings.co.uk** alternatively, return this coupon.

Cox & Kings, Gordon House, 10 Greencoat Place, London SW1P 1PH
Please mail me the Cox & Kings' Middle East & Central Asia brochure.
Mr/Mrs/Ms...
Address..
Postcode.. CADEGYPT

Specialists in Tailor-made Travel and Group Tours